# The Cambridge Companion to Bach

# Cambridge Companions to Music

## Composers

**The Cambridge Companion to Bach**
Edited by John Butt

**The Cambridge Companion to Bartók**
Edited by Amanda Bayley

**The Cambridge Companion to Berg**
Edited by Anthony Pople

**The Cambridge Companion to Beethoven**
Edited by Glenn Stanley

**The Cambridge Companion to Berlioz**
Edited by Peter Bloom

**The Cambridge Companion to Benjamin Britten**
Edited by Mervyn Cooke

**The Cambridge Companion to Brahms**
Edited by Michael Musgrave

**The Cambridge Companion to John Cage**
Edited by David Nicholls

**The Cambridge Companion to Chopin**
Edited by Jim Samson

**The Cambridge Companion to Handel**
Edited by Donald Burrows

**The Cambridge Companion to Schubert**
Edited by Christopher Gibbs

**The Cambridge Companion to Ravel**
Edited by Deborah Mawer

## Instruments

**The Cambridge Companion to Brass Instruments**
Edited by Trevor Herbert and John Wallace

**The Cambridge Companion to the Cello**
Edited by Robin Stowell

**The Cambridge Companion to the Clarinet**
Edited by Colin Lawson

**The Cambridge Companion to the Organ**
Edited by Nicholas Thistlethwaite and Geoffrey Webber

**The Cambridge Companion to the Piano**
Edited by David Rowland

**The Cambridge Companion to the Recorder**
Edited by John Mansfield Thomson

**The Cambridge Companion to the Saxophone**
Edited by Richard Ingham

**The Cambridge Companion to the Violin**
Edited by Robin Stowell

## Topics

**The Cambridge Companion to Pop and Rock**
Edited by Simon Frith, Will Straw, and John Street

The Cambridge Companion to

# BACH

Edited by John Butt

CAMBRIDGE
UNIVERSITY PRESS

PUBLISHED BY THE PRESS SYNDICATE OF THE UNIVERSITY OF CAMBRIDGE
The Pitt Building, Trumpington Street, Cambridge, United Kingdom

CAMBRIDGE UNIVERSITY PRESS
The Edinburgh Building, Cambridge CB2 2RU, UK
40 West 20th Street, New York, NY 10011–4211, USA
10 Stamford Road, Oakleigh, VIC 3166, Australia
Ruiz de Alarcón 13, 28014 Madrid, Spain
Dock House, The Waterfront, Cape Town 8001, South Africa

http://www.cambridge.org

First published 1997

Reprinted 1998, 1999, 2000, 2001

Printed in the United Kingdom at the University Press, Cambridge

Typeset in Minion 10.75/14pt, in QuarkXPress™ [SE]

*A catalogue record for this book is available from the British Library*

*Library of Congress Cataloguing in Publication data*
The Cambridge Companion to Bach / edited by John Butt.
    p.   cm.
    ISBN 0 521 45350 X (hardback). – ISBN 0 521 58780 8 (paperback)
    1. Bach, Johann Sebastian, 1685–1750.   I. Butt, John.
    ML410.B13C36   1997
    780′.92–dc20   96–22581 CIP
    [B]

ISBN 0 521 45350 X hardback
ISBN 0 521 58780 8 paperback

# Contents

# Plates

# Contributors

**Malcolm Boyd** has recently retired as senior lecturer at the University of Wales, Cardiff. His major study of Bach (Dent, 1983) has become perhaps the most important general book on the composer's life and works in the English language. He has also written a seminal study of D. Scarlatti (1986) and contributed to the *New Grove* dictionaries. His latest study – of the Bach Brandenburg concertos – has recently been published by Cambridge University Press.

**Werner Breig** is professor of musicology at the Ruhr-Universität Bochum. He has been responsible for much of the new edition of Heinrich Schütz and his Bach research has centred mainly on the organ music and concertos. His articles (largely in German publications) present some of the most important research on the chronology of Bach's concertos in recent years.

**John Butt** has held positions at Aberdeen University and Magdalene College, Cambridge, and is now associate professor of music at the University of California, Berkeley. His career centres on both performance and musicological research; three books on Bach have already been published by Cambridge University Press, the latest being a survey of the educational background to practical music during the German Baroque. He has made seven solo recordings on organ and harpsichord for Harmonia Mundi.

**Stephen A. Crist** is associate professor at Emory University. His articles have appeared in *Early Music, Bach Studies* (Cambridge University Press), *Bach Perspectives, College Music Symposium* and other publications. He has also published a facsimile edition of a rare Low German hymnal dating from Luther's lifetime and is working on a book on the Bach arias.

**Stephen Daw** is a principal lecturer at the Birmingham Conservatoire, the music faculty of the University of Central England. He has pursued a research career in the field of Bach for nearly thirty years. His publications include a book on the vocal works and a seminal article on the Walther/Krebs manuscripts of organ music. He has also written articles on Bach reception in England and an introduction to a facsimile edition of Bach's autograph of the *Well-tempered Clavier* Book II.

**Laurence Dreyfus**, Thurston Dart professor of performance studies in music and head of department at King's College London, began his career in Bach studies with a ground-breaking examination of Bach's continuo practice (Harvard University Press); his latest book, for the same publisher, surveys the entire field of Bachian invention. He has also written extensively on the aesthetics of performance practice, new directions in musical analysis and on linguistic and hermeneutic approaches to music history. He concurrently pursues an international career as a gambist.

**Richard D. P. Jones** is a graduate of Oxford University and has subsequently taught at University College, Cardiff; in 1982 he was awarded the D. F. Tovey Memorial Prize for research. His publications include a volume for the *Neue Bach-Ausgabe*, a new edition of the complete works for violin and obbligato harpsichord and numerous editions for the Associated Board. His writings have been published in *Music and Letters, The Musical Times* and in a book on the work of Howard Ferguson. His edition of *The Well-tempered Clavier* was published in 1994 as a replacement to Tovey's edition for the Associated Board.

**Robin Leaver** is well known in both musicological and theological circles; his particular interests have been J. S. Bach and the areas of liturgy and hymnology. Having held appointments at Latimer House and Wycliffe Hall, Oxford, he is currently professor of sacred music at Westminster Choir College of Rider University, Princeton, New Jersey and Visiting Professor of Liturgy, Drew University, Madison, New Jersey. Of his 25 published books and over 200 other publications, his Bach research includes a book on Bach's Passions from the perspective of music as preaching, another on Bach's theological library and a major book on Bach's faith and theology.

**Ulrich Siegele** studied musicology, classical philology and history at the University of Tübingen, where, from 1965 until his retirement in 1995, he has been lecturer and subsequently professor of musicology. His contributions to Bach scholarship began with a seminal study of Bach's activity as transcriber and revisor of his own music and have continued with a remarkably wide range of books and articles presenting detailed and provocative musical analyses and penetrating political and social studies of Bach's age and career.

**George B. Stauffer** is professor of music history at Hunter College, the Graduate Center of the City University of New York, and Organist and Director of Chapel Music at Columbia University. He has written a chronological survey of the organ preludes of Bach, is editor of *The Forkel–Hoffmeister & Kühnel correspondence* and *Bach Perspectives* II, and contributor to numerous American and European journals. He has recently completed a volume on Bach's B minor Mass for the *Monuments of Western Music* series of Macmillan.

**Martin Zenck** has established himself as the major authority on Bach reception. His main work has been on the reception of Bach by Beethoven (one book and several articles) but he has also written essays on the position of Bach within the Second Viennese school (*Bach Studies*, Cambridge University Press).

# Abbreviations

| | |
|---|---|
| *AfMw* | *Archiv für Musikwissenschaft* |
| *BACH* | *BACH – The Journal of the Riemenschneider Bach Institute* |
| *BC* | *Bach Compendium: Analytisch-bibliographisches Repertorium der Werke Johann Sebastian Bachs*, ed. H.-J. Schulze and C. Wolff (Leipzig, 1985–) |
| *BG* | *J. S. Bach: Werke*, ed. Bach-Gesellschaft, vols. 1–47 (Leipzig 1851–99) |
| *BJb* | *Bach-Jahrbuch* |
| *BR* | *The Bach reader* (revised edition), ed. H. T. David and A. Mendel (New York and London, 1966) |
| *BWV* | W. Schmieder, ed., *Thematisch-systematisches Verzeichnis der musikalischen Werke von Johann Sebastian Bach: Bach-Werke-Verzeichnis (BWV)*, 2nd edn (Wiesbaden, 1990) |
| *BzAfMw* | *Beihefte zum Archiv für Musikwissenschaft* |
| *BzBF* | *Beiträge zur Bach-Forschung* |
| *CM* | *Current Musicology* |
| *CMS* | *College Music Symposium* |
| *Dok* | *Bach-Dokumente*, ed. W. Neumann and H.-J. Schulze, 3 vols. (Leipzig and Kassel, 1963, 1969, 1972) |
| *EM* | *Early Music* |
| *JAMS* | *Journal of the American Musicological Society* |
| *JM* | *Journal of Musicology* |
| *LW* | *Luther's works: American edition*, ed. J. Pelikan and H. T. Lehmann (St Louis and Philadelphia, 1955–86) |
| *Mf* | *Die Musikforschung* |
| *MGG* | *Die Musik in Geschichte und Gegenwart* |
| *ML* | *Music and Letters* |
| *MMg* | *Monatshefte für Musikgeschichte* |
| *MQ* | *The Musical Quarterly* |
| *MT* | *The Musical Times* |
| *MuK* | *Musik und Kirche* |

NBA      *Neue Bach-Ausgabe*, ed. Johann-Sebastian-Bach-Institut, Göttingen,
         and Bach-Archiv, Leipzig (Kassel and Basle, 1954–)

      *KB  Kritischer Bericht*

NG       *The new Grove dictionary of music and musicians*, 20 vols.,
         ed. S. Sadie (London, 1980)

Notes    *Notes: Quarterly Journal of the Music Library Association*

NZM      *Neue Zeitschrift für Musik*

OY       *The Organ Yearbook*

PRMA     *Proceedings of the Royal Musical Association*

WA       *D. Martin Luthers Werke: kritische Gesamtausgabe* [*Weimarer
         Ausgabe*] (Weimar, 1883–1983)

      *Br  Weimarer Ausgabe: Briefe*

      *Tr  Weimarer Ausgabe: Tischreden*

# Chronology of Bach's life and career

1685 21 March – Johann Sebastian Bach born in Eisenach.

1693 Registered at the Lateinschule, Eisenach (fifth class).

1695 After the recent death of both parents, Sebastian moves to Ohrdruf under guardianship of his brother, Johann Christoph. Enters the Ohrdruf Lyceum.

1700 Leaves Lyceum owing to lack of free place ('ob defectum hospitiorum'), transferred to the Michaelisschule, Lüneburg.

1703 March–September – Court musician at Weimar (*Laquey*).
9 August – Appointed organist at the Neue Kirche, Arnstadt. Möller Manuscript begun (finished c. 1707).

1705 August – Bach's brawl with the bassoonist Geyserbach; departure for Lübeck and encounter with Buxtehude (returning early 1706).

1706 February – Consistory's complaints about Bach's prolonged absence, various other complaints concerning accompaniment and refusal to undertake concerted music.

1707 14–15 June – appointed organist at the Blasiuskirche, Mühlhausen (released from Arnstadt post, 29 June).
17 October – marries Maria Barbara Bach at Dornheim (near Arnstadt). Begins Mühlhausen cantatas, e.g. BWV 4, 106, 131.

1708 4 February – Cantata 71 performed for changing of town council, Bach's first published work.
25 June – Bach requests dismissal from Mühlhausen (dismissal granted following day), on his appointment as organist and chamber musician at Weimar (to Duke Wilhelm Ernst).
29 December – baptism of Catharina Dorothea Bach (first child of Johann Sebastian and Maria Barbara Bach). Andreas Bach Book begun (finished c. 1713). *Orgelbüchlein* may have been begun as early as 1708 (most of it finished by 1717).

1709 7 February – payment for a further printed Mühlhausen cantata for changing of town council, with expenses for Bach's travel from Weimar (work lost).

1710 22 November – Wilhelm Friedemann Bach born (composer, first son of Johann Sebastian and Maria Barbara; baptised 24 November).

1712 27 September – Bach is godfather for baptism of son of Weimar town organist, J. G. Walther.

1713  c. 23 February – visit to Weissenfels on occasion of Duke Christian of
      Saxe-Weissenfels' birthday – probable first performance of 'Hunt'
      Cantata, BWV 208.
      July – Prince Johann Ernst of Saxe-Weimar returns from his study-trip
      to the Netherlands, bringing with him many modern Italian concertos,
      including Vivaldi's Op. 3.
      December – Bach is a candidate for the post of organist at the
      Marktkirche in Halle.

1714  Halle position declined.
      2 March – Bach promoted to *Konzertmeister* at Weimar, with increased
      salary and commission to compose monthly cantatas.
      8 March – birth of Carl Philipp Emanuel Bach (baptised 10 March with
      Georg Philipp Telemann as godfather).
      25 March (Palm Sunday) – performance of first Weimar church cantata,
      BWV 182.

1717  Earliest printed reference to Bach, in Mattheson's *Das beschützte
      Orchestre.*
      5 August – appointed *Kapellmeister* for Prince Leopold of Anhalt-Köthen.
      Visit to Dresden for competition with Marchand (from which the latter
      fled).
      6 November – 2 December – Bach under arrest for too forcibly
      demanding dismissal. Set free with unfavourable discharge.

1719  1 March – Bach receives payment for travel and purchase of harpsichord
      in Berlin.

1720  22 January – begins *Clavier-Büchlein* for Wilhelm Friedemann Bach.
      May–July – Bach travels with Leopold to Karlsbad.
      Maria Barbara dies, buried 28 September.
      November – Bach applies for post of organist at the Jacobikirche,
      Hamburg.
      December – Bach declines post, owing to simony associated with
      appointment (incident recorded in Mattheson's *Der musicalische Patriot*,
      1728).

1721  24 March – Brandenburg Concertos dedicated to Margrave Christian
      Ludwig.
      3 December – Bach marries Anna Magdalena Wilcke (daughter of court
      trumpeter at Weissenfels), in Köthen.
      Begins first *Clavier-Büchlein* for Anna Magdalena.
      Writes title page for first book of *The Well-tempered Clavier*.

1722  21 December – Bach becomes a candidate for the post of Cantor and
      *Director Musices* at the Thomasschule, Leipzig.

1723  February – Bach auditions in Leipzig.
      April – Bach appointed at Leipzig, receiving dismissal from Köthen.
      5 May – Bach signs contract for cantorship.

22 May – Bach and family arrive in Leipzig.

30 May – first performance at Leipzig (Cantata 75), received 'mit guten *applausu*' – opens first Leipzig cycle of cantatas.

14 June – Wilhelm Friedemann and Carl Philipp Emanuel Bach accepted into Thomasschule.

25 December – first (?) performance of Magnificat, BWV 243a.

1724 7 April – first performance of St John Passion, Nikolaikirche.

11 June – opening of second Leipzig cycle of cantatas (Cantata 20).

1725 September – Bach gives an organ recital in the Sophienkirche, Dresden.

September–December – Bach petitions Friedrich August I, Elector of Saxony and King of Poland, for the restitution of his right to the 'old service' and salary, at the university church (King grants Bach's right to 'old service' and salary, 21 January 1726).

Third Leipzig cycle of cantatas begins (lasting into 1727).

Mattheson complains of Bach's text underlay (in Cantata 21) in his *Critica Musica*, 8.

1726 Publication of Partita 1, of Bach's *Clavier-Übung* (remaining five partitas published over subsequent years).

1727 11 April – probable first performance of St Matthew Passion.

17 Oct – *Trauer-Ode*, Cantata 198, performed at memorial service for Electress Christiane Eberhardine (commissioned by a university student, with words by J. C. Gottsched).

1728 September – dispute with sub-deacon of Nikolaikirche over who should choose hymns for Vespers (customarily the prerogative of the cantor).

19 November – Prince Leopold of Anhalt-Köthen dies.

1729 23–4 March – Bach visits Köthen for performance of funeral cantata for Leopold (BWV 244a).

April – Bach becomes sales agent for Heinichen's *Generalbaßlehre* and Walther's *Lexicon*.

Bach takes over direction of the *Collegium musicum.*

1730 August – dispute with the town council, over Bach's disinclination to teach Latin.

23 August – Bach's 'Short but most necessary draft for a well-appointed church music' sent to town council, outlining severe problems in maintaining the musical establishment at the Thomasschule.

28 October – Bach sends letter to school friend, Georg Erdmann, expressing dissatisfaction with Leipzig and seeking employment in Danzig (Gdansk).

1731 All six Partitas published together as *Clavier-Übung* I.

14 September – Bach gives an organ recital in Sophienkirche, Dresden, and other performances at court during following week.

1732 21 June – Johann Christoph Friedrich Bach born.
Short biography of Bach appears in Walther's *Lexicon* – here Bach has
title of 'Sachsen-Weißenfelsischer Capell-Meister', which he presumably
received some time after death of Leopold of Anhalt-Köthen.

1733 Bach composes and performs several cantatas in honour of the new
Elector, Friedrich August II, and his family (BWV 213, 214, Anh. 12).
23 June – Wilhelm Friedemann Bach appointed organist of
Sophienkirche, Dresden.
July – Bach presents *Missa* (Kyrie and Gloria, of what later became Mass
in B Minor) to Friedrich August II, with request for a court title.

1734 Bach composes and performs more cantatas in honour of Friedrich
August II, including BWV 215, performed in his presence for the
Michaelmas Fair, 5 October.
25–7 December – Christmas Oratorio, parts I-III performed.

1735 1–6 January – Christmas Oratorio, parts IV-VI performed.
Bach is sales agent for harpsichord works by C. F. Hurlebusch.
*Clavier-Übung* II published.
June – Johann Gottfried Bernhard Bach appointed organist at the
Marienkirche, Mühlhausen.
5 September – Johann Christian Bach born.

1736 Easter – Publication of G. C. Schemelli's *Musicalisches Gesangbuch*,
advertised as containing some new melodies and bass-lines by Bach.
July – dispute begins with Rector Ernesti over the right to appoint
prefects in the school (continues until early 1738).
7 October – Bach performs birthday cantata in honour of Friedrich
August II.
19 November – Bach given title of *Hofcompositeur* to the Elector of
Saxony, Friedrich August II.
1 December – Bach gives an organ recital in the Dresden Frauenkirche,
in the presence of the Russian ambassador.

1737 April – Johann Gottfried Bernhard Bach appointed organist of the
Jakobikirche, Sangerhausen (he is soon to fall into debt and abscond).
14 May – J. A. Scheibe criticises Bach and his music in *Der critische
Musicus*, sparking pamphlet war over Bach's merits as a composer.
17 December – Friedrich August II intervenes in prefects' dispute, on
Bach's behalf.

1738 27 April – Bach performs cantata in presence of Friedrich August II at
Leipzig Easter Fair.
Carl Philipp Emanuel appointed harpsichordist to Frederick of Prussia
(later Frederick II ('the Great')).

1739 March – Bach cancels Passion performance owing to dispute with town
council.
27 May – Johann Gottfried Bernhard Bach dies.

October – Bach takes over *Collegium musicum* after a two-year break.
7 October – Bach performs birthday cantata for Friedrich August II
*Clavier-Übung* III published.
Bach gives organ recital in the Schlosskirche, Altenburg. Bach probably began work on compiling/copying *The Well-tempered Clavier* Book II (finished c. 1742).

1740   3 August – Bach performs cantata for name-day of Friedrich August II.

1741   Anna Magdalena very ill during Bach's visit to Carl Philipp Emanuel in Berlin.
*Clavier-Übung* IV ('Goldberg Variations') published.

1742   Bach drafted early version of *The Art of Fugue* around this time.

1745   Bach is sales agent for Wilhelm Friedemann's harpsichord sonata in D.

1746   April – Wilhelm Friedemann Bach becomes organist of the Marktkirche (Liebfrauenkirche), Halle.
After 1746 (1748?) – 'Schübler' chorales published.

1747   May – Bach visits Potsdam court of Frederick II of Prussia; plays at court and the Heiligegeistkirche; probably also visits Berlin and its new opera house at this time.
June – Bach joins Mizler's Corresponding Society of the Musical Sciences.
Canonic Variations on 'Vom Himmel hoch' presented to society and published.
September – *Musical Offering* published.

1748   Bach is sales agent for Wilhelm Friedemann Bach's harpsichord sonata in E♭.

1749   20 January – Bach's daughter Elisabeth Juliana Friederica marries Johann Christoph Altnikol.
8 June – Gottlob Harrer auditions for Bach's post in Leipzig.
Bach's work on the Mass in B Minor probably completed.

1750   Bach directing work on *Art of Fugue* engraving.
March – Bach has eye operation.
28 July – Bach dies.

1751   *Art of Fugue* published.

1754   Bach's Obituary (by Carl Philipp Emanuel Bach and Johann Friedrich Agricola) published by Mizler.

# Introduction

*John Butt*

## The context and aims of the project

Twenty years ago it would have been relatively easy to predict the contents of a *Cambridge companion to Bach*: a basic introduction to the composer's life and works, fundamental information to enhance analysis and appreciation, perhaps also a summary of recent research and performance. While the present volume hardly represents a radical departure from this brief, the situation is now considerably more complex than it was in the 1970s. First, with the publication of the *New Grove dictionary of music and musicians* and several important monographs on the life and works of J. S. Bach, there is already a sizeable and reliable literature for readers of every level. Secondly, there is the mushrooming of published material throughout all fields of music scholarship: now it is virtually impossible to do justice to every slant, every area of study, even to every field of Bach's compositional output. Finally, there are the interesting issues concerning musicology that have come to the fore during the last decade or so: what actually is music scholarship? what are its aims? how much should we be catering for 'music appreciation'? what is the significance today of a 'great' composer?

Bach studies have, in fact, set the tone for much music scholarship during the last thirty years. With the spectacular revisions to the chronology of Bach's cantatas in the late 1950s by Alfred Dürr and Georg von Dadelsen, overthrowing many fundamental assumptions about Bach's creative life and ever-increasing piety,[1] the next two decades were dominated by a style of research that valued certifiable fact above critical judgement or informed opinion. Much has changed during the last decade or so: 'positivism' – as the activity of fact-gathering has, somewhat grandly, been named – has often been branded the occupation only of the dull and bibliographically-minded, while 'criticism' and – most importantly – interdisciplinary work are, to some, the direction for the elect.[2]

Of course, this attitude may not always take it into account that not all 'new musicology' achieves Olympian heights of insight and inspiration and that 'positivism', at its best, often produces information that is of enduring value, providing the basis for a wide range of interpretative approaches. Furthermore, the vast majority of 'newer musicology' is concerned with music of the nineteenth century and beyond, the era in which musical culture becomes self-reflective and concerned with its own hermeneutic richness; in other words, only composers later than Bach have so far proved suitable objects for the (post)modern approaches. I suspect that many people who are attracted to Bach, as listeners, musicians or scholars, find it difficult to question what they see as the innate quality of his music. To the 'Bach believer' this music may seem to exist on its own terms, to a degree enjoyed by virtually no other repertory; only the plethora of attitudes towards Bach tend to be open for discussion and evaluation.

On the other hand, given that there is much new critical work on the Renaissance and early Baroque, it might not be too long before Bach is drawn into the 'new musicological' fold. There is a small but growing body of writing linking Bach's career and compositional achievements to a specific cultural and social commentary,[3] and Adorno's occasional use of Bach and the concept of counterpoint in his more abstract cultural theory has been emulated and developed in recent years by the work of Edward Said.[4] Bach has also made a tentative entrance into the field of gender studies.[5]

Of course, many readers will find these more radical approaches irrelevant – at best – to Bach studies and appreciation. Yet few could maintain that Bach is entirely unaffected by the turn against the factual and the certain. Indeed, it is almost ironic that a general concern with criticism and hermeneutics has engendered a return to something of the style of scholarship that was prevalent before the positivist revolution of the late 1950s. Eric Chafe's recent book on allegory in Bach's music can almost be seen as an update of the theological-hermeneutic approach of earlier scholars, such as Friedrich Smend.[6] At the very least, studies of this kind provide material for a type and level of debate that was all but impossible during the 1960s and 70s. Bibliographic, factual scholarship still provides the mainstay of Bach studies; indeed, the sources are still by no means comprehensively examined, and, if they were, each new generation would continue to bring new approaches and outlooks that might ask new questions and, indeed, find new 'facts'. But the most productive sign of a newer approach to Bach scholarship is the widening of the field by scholars who have already proved their qualifications in studies of the sources and historical context.

One of the primary aims of this *Companion* is to show both the achievements of Bach research and the possibilities for further directions. It is designed to provide much of the background information for Bach's career and social context together with proposals for the analysis and understanding of the music. The foremost purpose might be to offer a companion to 'thinking about Bach', the angles from which he and his music might be viewed. There is, after all, no extant study that attempts to summarise much of the current thinking on Bach and his oeuvre. We need an introduction to this great composer from perspective of the late twentieth century, something which will appeal to a wide readership, going beyond a basic biographical 'life and works' study.

   *The Cambridge companion to Bach* draws on a remarkably rich consortium of Bach scholars – German, American and British – all commissioned to present material which summarises the current state of Bach research while pointing towards possible directions for further enquiry. The book is designed in three major sections: 1. the historical context of Bach, the society, beliefs and world-view of his age; 2. profiles of the music, and Bach's compositional stance; 3. finally, influence and reception, a field that is central to cultural history today and one that is relatively new in Bach research. The bibliography provides an up-to-date, but critically selective list of the most important writings to appear since the *New Grove* publication; it also lists some of the more enduring writings from earlier years.

## Summary of chapters

The *Companion* begins with Malcolm Boyd's examination of the phenomenon of the musical family, considering the extent to which this reflects the conception of music as a craft to be passed from one generation to another. This chapter provides a useful background to the Bach family as a whole and to the shape of Bach's career with regard to the family tradition. In Chapter 2 Ulrich Siegele examines the shape of Bach's Leipzig career within the political context of his age, showing how most of his conflicts with the school and town council stemmed from his attempts to fulfil an absolutist commission within a municipal city. It is impossible that Bach could have stood apart from the local and state political conficts of his age. This angle, virtually ignored in the past, illuminates many aspects of his creative personality which are usually seen as belonging exclusively to the religious or 'purely musical' realms.

   In recent years, the religious context of Bach's career has regained something of its former status as a primary focus of Bach studies. However, there is not much reliable general information on the actual quality and shape of religious practice in Bach's age; much previous writing is overly conditioned by the authors' own confessional beliefs and thus often fails to recognise the diversity of Reformation traditions, even within Lutheranism itself. In Chapter 3 Robin Leaver provides an overview of the Lutheran Reformation, a summary of the reformer's theological understanding of music and an investigation of the various musical implications of the liturgical reforms. The chapter concludes with an outline of the musical content and scope of the Lutheran liturgies.

In Chapter 4 John Butt considers Bach's attitude to music, his conception of both its manner of existence and its function. This approach not only complements the more usual religious explanations of Bach's creative stance but actually suggests that there may have been a conflict between his beliefs in the metaphysics of music and his religious orthodoxy. The following chapter examines some of the same attitudes in the light of three of the major rationalist philosophers of the seventeenth and eighteenth centuries. While it would be fallacious to posit a direct, influential link between Bach's musical thought and that of contemporary philosophers, the juxtaposition may show how Bach's conception of music may run parallel to certain attitudes to metaphysics and the nature of reality and, from the historical angle, that the beliefs and conceptions of a particular age can pervade more than one mode of creative thought.

Stephen Crist opens the second part of the study with a summary of the current state of research on Bach's early works (pre-Weimar), with special emphasis on their relationship to the musical traditions of seventeenth-century Germany. No field of Bach research has changed more over the past fifteen years or so, and the general picture of the early years that is emerging will greatly influence our picture of Bach as a musical personality. In all, this study does much to compensate for the bias towards 'late works' that is prevalent in so many studies of the greater composers.

In Chapter 7 Robin Leaver, building on the background of Chapter 3, provides a thorough survey of liturgical practice in Leipzig. After discussing the 'problem' of Bach's frequent reuse of music written for secular purposes within a sacred context (the issue of *parody*), he examines some of the major church music with special attention to how the various categories of church composition fulfil differing roles within the liturgy. Although there is hardly space to do justice to all fields (such as the vast majority of church cantatas), the information is presented in such a way that it can illuminate virtually any church composition by Bach. Werner Breig's study of the instrumental music in Chapter 8 shows the various biases in the stylistic categorisation and examination of Bach's instrumental music and proposes using Bach's own stylistic and generic distinctions as a starting point. He examines the varying functions and forms of the instrumental music throughout Bach's career, giving particular attention to his reworking of established genres.

Richard Jones's examination of the keyboard music shows that the 'Clavier' is the medium through which Bach united his own study of music, composition, performance and instruction. The initial interest in keyboard performance and composition evidences the two contrasting pillars supporting so much of his compositional career, namely his facility in virtuoso improvisation, on the one hand, and his desire to create order in sound, on the other. This concise survey shows that Bach's development as a keyboard composer reflects much of his entire career as a composer.

In Chapter 10 Werner Breig looks at Bach's habit of arranging and transcribing music by himself and others. The insights we gain into Bach's work as editor and arranger give us a clue as to how he may initially have learned and developed as a composer. Moreover, given that he was still reusing earlier music in the very last years of his life, it seems that the impulses to arrange, transcribe, transfer and improve are all fundamental to his character as a composer *per se.*

Part II closes with an appropriately 'close reading' of Bach's music. Laurence Dreyfus, in Chapter 11, adopts an analytical stance that values the composer's intentions and mechanisms of composition above any purely abstract and formal results. Using some techniques and terminology from linguistics, he shows how Bach chooses to emulate the rigours of a highly intelligent machine which researches musical material for both its possibilities and its limitations. He shows that Bach's activity at the level of *invention* (as opposed to the formal layout and ultimate *disposition* of the material) is central to Bach's work as a composer and represents the area in which the supreme quality of his music resides. Far from being the anonymous transmitter of pure abstracted form, Bach emerges as a profoundly human figure.

Opening Part III, on Bach's influence and reception, Stephen Daw's study (Chapter 12) straddles the divide between those figures who were influenced by Bach during his lifetime, through his direct teaching, and the 'grandpupils' and collectors of his music in the latter part of the eighteenth century. The diversity and flexibility of his approach to teaching pupils of various abilities and backgrounds throughout his career provides an interesting window into his priorities and conceptions as a composer.

One aspect of Bach reception that is especially relevant to the present age is the variety of ways in which his music has been interpreted in performance. In Chapter 13 George B. Stauffer surveys the history of Bach performance, showing how each generation has performed Bach's music in its own way – a way that usually reflects the cultural ideology of the time. Stauffer gives particular attention to the development of the 'historical performance movement', the attitude that seeks to restore the styles and methods of performance advocated by the composer. In the case of Bach, this can be traced back to the editions and writings of the mid-nineteenth century and to the rebellion against Romantic style in the first decades of the twentieth century. The chapter concludes with a look at the most recent trends in historical performance, which include the turn towards a more subjective approach to interpretation.

In Chapter 14 Martin Zenck summarises the parameters within which the history of Bach reception can be written, drawing particular attention to the problems involved: the ubiquity of Bach's influence, the mythologising of Bach and the question of the historical and ontological difference between Bach's perspective and our own. In fact, the history of Bach reception has been characterised by a constant reinterpretation of Bach's music: it has continually been brought into the present. In Chapter 15, rather than giving a sequential account of the entire history of Bach reception, Zenck offers several case studies of composers who have drawn on Bach's influence, showing – above all – that the most interesting composers are those who show their debt to Bach by changing and adapting his music rather than slavishly following his model.

PART I

# The historical context: society, beliefs and world-view

# 1 The Bach family

*Malcolm Boyd*

The musical family is by no means an unfamiliar phenomenon, and nearly everyone must be acquainted with at least one household in which practically every member delights not only in listening to music but also in singing or playing musical instruments. Even with the weakening of family ties and the proliferation of ready-made forms of home entertainment in western society today, it is still possible for many a *paterfamilias* to echo the words that J. S. Bach wrote in 1730 in a famous letter to his former schoolmate Georg Erdmann:

> From my first marriage three sons and a daughter are still living ... [and] from my second marriage one son and two daughters ... The children from my second marriage are still small, the boy (as firstborn) being six years old. But they are all born musicians, and I assure you that I can form both a vocal and an instrumental *Concert* within my family, especially since my present wife sings with a pure soprano voice, and my eldest daughter, too, can join in quite well.[1]

Moreover, musical talent of an unusual kind has manifested itself in modern times in families such as the Menuhins and the Torteliers. One could discuss at length the relative importance of heredity and environment in the formation of musical families at whatever level of attainment, but it seems quite clear that the role played by environment is more important in fostering a talent for music than it is in influencing other forms of artistic and intellectual endeavour. By its nature, musical activity impinges on everyone within earshot (and, some would say, even on the child in the womb) and therefore invites at least some degree of communal engagement. Literature, painting and mathematics (to mention three branches of cultural activity closely connected to music) are, on the other hand, solitary pursuits, and – the Brontës, the Breughels and the Bernoullis notwithstanding – the musical family is a phenomenon rarely paralleled in the other arts.

We have so far mentioned musicians only as performers (as did Bach in his letter to Erdmann); when we turn to composition the picture appears somewhat different. The popular view of the 'great composer' as a solitary creative artist struggling for self-expression in an indifferent and uncomprehending world is largely a legacy of the nineteenth and early twentieth centuries, when many of the foremost composers found themselves in conflict both with their parents and with society at large. The Strauss family in Vienna was perhaps the only one to produce several composers of note in the nineteenth century, and it is probably no accident that they excelled in genres in which elegance and craftsmanship counted for more than self-expression. The nineteenth century was also a period which saw an increasing separation between composer and performer, the two activities usually being combined in the case of instrumental virtuosos such as Liszt and Paganini or (at a relatively humble level) in the church organ loft.

Such a dichotomy hardly existed in earlier centuries, when practically every notable performer, whether church organist, court *maestro* or opera singer was expected in some measure to be a composer. Like other branches of musical activity, including instrument-making, composition was a craft which could be handed down from one generation to the next; indeed the seventeenth and eighteenth centuries produced a number of particularly prominent and prolific musical families, among them the Couperins in France (who flourished from the early seventeenth century to the mid-nineteenth), the Scarlattis in Italy (from the mid-seventeenth to the late eighteenth) and the Bendas in Bohemia and Germany (from the early eighteenth century to the early nineteenth). A feature of all three families, one which distinguishes them from the Bachs, is that the most important representatives of each dynasty came near the beginning of the line (Louis, c. 1626–61, and François *le grand*, 1668–1733, among the Couperins; Franz, 1709–86, and Georg, 1722–95, among the Bendas; the lives of its two most gifted members, Alessandro, 1660–1725, and his son Domenico, 1685–1757, almost define the chronological boundaries of the Scarlatti family).

The Bach family, by contrast, reached prominence only after several generations of musicians – with Johann Sebastian (1685–1750) and his two most important and influential sons, Carl Philipp Emanuel (1714–88) and Johann Christian (1735–82) – and then declined rapidly. It is almost inevitable, given the standard dictionary meaning of the German word 'Bach', that the history of the Bach family from about 1550 to 1750 and its impact on European music should be likened to a stream which gradually widens into a river and gains strength until it overflows into the surrounding territory. According to another etymology, however, the word 'Bach' (and variants such as 'Bachen', 'Pach' and 'Pachen') was used from at least the fourteenth century in certain countries of eastern Europe (including Hungary and Moravia) to mean 'musician'.[2] Günter Kraft has suggested that, as in so many other cases, the word for an occupation was gradually adopted as a surname.

**Plate 1**  Bachhaus Wechmar; home of Veit Bach and his son, Hans Bach, c. 1590–1626

It was in fact from Hungary (or, more accurately, from what was known in the eighteenth century as 'Ungarn' – a region which included the Habsburg territories of Moravia and Slovakia) that the first of the Bach musicians (if that is not a tautology) came, when

> Vitus Bach, a *Weißbecker* [baker of white bread] in *Ungern*, was forced to flee the country in the sixteenth century because of his Lutheran religion. After selling his belongings for as much as he could get, he left for Germany and, finding adequate protection for his Lutheran religion in Thuringia, settled in Wechmar, near Gotha, where he continued in his baker's trade. His greatest delight was a small cittern [*Cytheringen*] which he took with him to the mill and played while the grinding took place [see Plate 1].[3]

Such, at any rate, is the account given in the Genealogy that J. S. Bach compiled in 1735, to which I shall refer later in this chapter.[4]

From these humble beginnings can be traced the seven generations of the Wechmar line that produced over seventy sons who earned their living as musicians. But it is not only the unprecedentedly large number and long lineage of its members that distinguish the Bach family from the

Couperins, the Scarlattis and the Bendas. The Bachs seem to have shown a particularly keen self-awareness, a consciousness of their place in society, and even (at least by J. S. Bach's time) of their place in history. This sense of family, and more particularly of a musical family, is manifest in the annual reunions that J. S. Bach's first biographer, J. N. Forkel, describes:

> the different members of this family had a very great attachment to each other. As it was impossible for them all to live in one place, they resolved at least to see each other once a year, and fixed a certain day, upon which they all had to appear at an appointed place. Even after the family had become much more numerous, and many of the members had been obliged to settle out of Thuringia, in different places of Upper and Lower Saxony, and Franconia, they continued their annual meetings, which generally took place at Erfurt, Eisenach, or Arnstadt. Their amusements, during the time of their meeting, were entirely musical.[5]

J. S. Bach himself must have been present at family reunions such as these, but his own awareness of the tradition to which he was heir – his sense of destiny, in a word – showed itself with particular clarity during the last two decades of his life. The 1730s, in particular, were of special significance for Bach. After completing an incomparable repertory of music – cantatas, Passions and other works – for the Leipzig churches during the 1720s, he appears almost to have given up composing new works during the 1730s. The 'ordinary' weekly meetings of the *Collegium musicum*, which he directed from 1729, seem not to have spurred him to write much new instrumental music, and most of the large-scale homage cantatas he performed with the *Collegium* on 'extraordinary' ceremonial occasions may be seen as a bid for court employment in Dresden. He was, on the other hand, much concerned with arranging, perfecting and publishing his music, and with bringing his musical legacy to a final form.

It is in this context that we may view Bach's involvement with two documents, or sets of documents, which are concerned with his forebears in the Bach clan. One of these is the *Alt-Bachisches Archiv*, a collection of works by older members of the family which his father Ambrosius is reputed to have assembled. Bach cared for and added to the archive, which on his death went to his son Carl Philipp Emanuel. By the time it became part of the library of the Singakademie, Berlin, it included twenty sacred vocal works by at least four of the Bachs (Johann, 1604–73; Georg Christoph, 1642–97; Johann Christoph, 1642–1703; and Johann Michael, 1648–94).[6] From this anthology, and from works preserved in other sources, Johann Christoph is seen to be the most gifted of the early Bachs, but there is considerable merit, too, in some of the music by Johann Michael, father of J. S. Bach's first wife, Maria Barbara.

One cannot be certain about the date of Bach's contributions to the *Alt-Bachisches Archiv* (the manuscripts were destroyed in World War II),[7] but 1735 was the year in which he compiled a Genealogy, the *Ursprung der musikalisch-Bachischen Familie*, which has remained of fundamental importance to Bach studies ever since. In it he listed fifty-three members of the family (including himself) with brief biographical notes on each. Bach's original manuscript has not survived, but a copy made in 1774–5 by Carl Philipp Emanuel's daughter Anna Carolina Philippina (1747–1804), with additions by Emanuel himself, was sent to Forkel, and has often been quoted and reproduced. Modern scholarship has added other musicians to the list and extended it beyond Bach's own time, resulting in a total of over seventy Bachs who earned their living wholly or partly from music between the early sixteenth century and the mid-nineteenth.

A study of J. S. Bach's forebears throws interesting light on the composer's origins and background. For old Veit (or Vitus) Bach, the founder of the Wechmar line, music was no more than an accompaniment to his work as a *Weißbecker*. Veit's son Hans/Johannes (?1575/80–1626) also started out in his father's trade, but, the Genealogy informs us, 'as he showed a particular gift for music the *Stadtpfeifer* of Gotha took him as an apprentice' and Johannes 'remained with him for some time after his apprenticeship was complete'. Several of the early Bachs, and even some of Johann Sebastian's generation, are named in the Genealogy as *Stadtpfeifer, Stadtmusicus, Ratsmusikant* etc. – town musicians whose duties included playing on civic occasions, at weddings, in church services and so on. Although well organised, jealous of their training and privileges, and a cut above the common *Bier-Fiedler* (beer-fiddlers), these musicians were on the lowest rungs of the professional ladder. A court appointment might elevate their social status, as was the case with some of the Bachs, but most *Stadtpfeifer* and court *musici* earned less than a church organist or cantor.

Johannes's eldest son, also called Johannes (or Johann, 1604–73), was the first Bach mentioned in the Genealogy to combine the calling of *Stadtpfeifer* with that of organist, first at Schweinfurt and then at the Predigerkirche, Erfurt, where he was appointed in 1636. The next generation brought the first of the Bachs to achieve the status of cantor, a position which usually combined overall responsibility for the music of a church with a senior post at the local school. In 1668 Johann's son Georg Christoph (1642–97) was appointed cantor at Themar and later (probably in 1688) at Schweinfurt; his distant cousin Johann (1621–86), not included in the Genealogy, had been appointed cantor at Ilmenau in 1659.[8] The posts of organist and cantor were those most frequently occupied by members of the Bach dynasty in subsequent generations.

For the court *musicus*, especially if he were a string player, the first promotion to aim for was that of *Konzertmeister*. The Genealogy records only one such appointment (apart from that of J. S. Bach himself), when Bach's son Johann Christoph Friedrich (1732–95) was made *Konzertmeister* to Count Wilhelm at Bückeburg in 1756 (this is, of course, mentioned in one of C. P. E. Bach's additions to the Genealogy). The ultimate goal for an aspiring instrumentalist was the post of Kapellmeister, the person charged with directing the music, both sacred and secular, of an entire court, and usually expected to compose as well. The first Kapellmeister in the Bach family, and the only one before Johann Sebastian himself, appears to have been Johann Ludwig (1677–1731), who belonged to what is usually referred to as the Meiningen branch of the family and was appointed Kapellmeister to the court there in 1711. The only other Bach to achieve a similar position was apparently Sebastian's pupil Johann Ernst (1722–77), who was appointed Kapellmeister at Weimar in 1756.

A survey of the earlier Bach generations illuminates certain features of Johann Sebastian's life and career. We find, for instance, that there was a tendency among the Bachs to produce twins,[9] and that Sebastian's son Gottfried Heinrich (1724–63) was not the first in the wider family to be mentally retarded.[10] It might be wrong to suggest that these characteristics necessarily resulted from intermarriage, but one is struck by the number of times that the same few family names – the Lämmerhirts, the Wedemanns, the Schmidts – become entangled with the Bachs. This is well illustrated by the case of J. S. Bach's father, Johann Ambrosius, who was first married in 1668 to Maria Elisabetha Lämmerhirt (1644–94), half-sister of Hedwig Lämmerhirt (c. 1617–75), who had married Ambrosius's uncle Johann in 1637. After his first wife's death in 1694 Ambrosius was briefly married to the widow Barbara Margaretha Bartholomaei, *née* Keul, whose first husband had been Ambrosius's cousin Johann Günther Bach (1653–83). Johann Sebastian's first marriage was to his second cousin Maria Barbara Bach (1684–1720); their paternal grandfathers were brothers.[11]

It is interesting, too, to see how closely J. S. Bach's own career mirrored the development of the Bach family as a whole. In the Genealogy he describes his first post at Weimar in 1703 as that of 'HoffMusicus' (court musician); he is then employed as an organist at Arnstadt (1703),[12] Mühlhausen (1707) and Weimar (1708); he does not omit to mention his promotion to *Konzertmeister* at Weimar in 1714; his post at Köthen (1717) he lists as 'Capellmeister u[nd] *Director* derer Cammer Musiquen' and at Leipzig as '*Director Chori Musici* u[nd] *Cantor* an der *Thomas Schule*'. The actual wording here is significant. Although the post at

Leipzig was one of considerably greater importance than those occupied by earlier Bach cantors, at Ilmenau and Schweinfurt for example, the title itself carried less prestige than that of Kapellmeister, and Bach's move from Köthen to Leipzig would not have been regarded by most of his contemporaries as an advancement. That Bach himself was fully aware of this is shown in the above-mentioned letter to Georg Erdmann, in which he commented that 'it seemed to me at first not at all the right thing to become a cantor after being a Kapellmeister, and I postponed my *resolution* for three months'.[13] In letters, title-pages and other documents he usually avoided referring to himself as cantor, preferring the title of *Director* [or *Directore*] *Musices*, and he was always ready to avail himself of his honorary titles as *Kapellmeister von Haus aus* at Weissenfels, Köthen or Dresden.

A fortune-teller with any knowledge of the Bach family would have risked little by predicting a musical career for the newly-born Johann Sebastian in 1685, but it would have required remarkable prescience to prophesy his eventual standing as a composer. Only two of the Bachs in the Genealogy are mentioned as composers – Johann Christoph, the 'profound composer', and Johann Michael, 'like his brother, an able composer' – and one must go back three generations, to Veit's son Johannes, to find a common ancestor between Johann Sebastian and these two distant cousins. The other composers of note among the Bachs were all sons of Johann Sebastian and, while some geneticists might be impressed by the fact that Bach's first marriage brought together the two most creative lines of the family to produce Wilhelm Friedemann (1710–84) and Carl Philipp Emanuel (1714–88), his second marriage, to Anna Magdalena Wilcke (1701–60), was no less fruitful: Johann Christoph Friedrich (the 'Bückeburg Bach') was no mean composer and Johann Christian was arguably the most individual and influential of the younger Bachs.

Once again it seems that environment, rather than heredity, was the determining factor. Sebastian, like most of his kinsmen, had found employment in Thuringia and its immediately neighbouring territories, rarely venturing further afield. With him the stream had broadened into a river which nourished the whole land. But the institutions that had supported the Bachs (and which the Bachs had supported) – the Kantorei and the minor courts – were in decline, while municipal and public music-making, to which J. S. Bach and his sons (especially Johann Christian) made important contributions, was in the ascendancy. Bach's eldest son, Friedemann, was by all accounts at least as well endowed with talent as were his younger brothers. His failure to develop that talent to the full may have resulted from weaknesses of character, as is often suggested, but it must also have had something to do with the fact that, as an organist in Dresden and then in Halle, his orbit and aspirations remained those of his father (his post at the Marktkirche in Halle was actually one which his father had declined some thirty-two years earlier). The success of Emanuel and Johann Christian, on the other hand, may be attributed to their having sought new areas (both geographically and artistically) in which to develop their gifts. Emanuel's appointment as harpsichordist at the court of Frederick the Great in Berlin brought him into contact with a variety of musicians and musical styles limited only by the tastes of Frederick himself. His pupil and half-brother Johann Christian departed still further from family traditions, visiting Italy, converting to Roman Catholicism, becoming a freemason and spending the last and most fruitful period of his life in England.

J. C. Bach's nephew and pupil Wilhelm Friedrich Ernst (1759–1845) lived long enough to witness the revival of his grandfather's music and to be present at Mendelssohn's unveiling of the Bach memorial at Leipzig in 1843. The Bach genealogy has been traced, through two further generations, well into the twentieth century. But as proud guardians of the finest musical tradition in central Germany, the dynasty had come to an end with J. S. Bach's sons, and Carl Philipp Emanuel may have realised this when, in his copy of the Genealogy, he penned against the name of his half-brother Johann Christian the remark: '*inter nos*, machte es anders als der erliche Veit' ('between ourselves, he did things differently from honest Veit').

# 2  Bach and the domestic politics of Electoral Saxony

*Ulrich Siegele*

This essay places Johann Sebastian Bach within the context of the domestic policy of his time.[1] That is unquestionably an unusual viewpoint, since Bach is known as 'Germany's greatest church composer', the embodiment of the Lutheran cantor. Nonetheless, we must become accustomed to seeing this man in a political function, because Bach lived in a time of fundamental domestic conflict. Everyone who held a public office had to take a position in this conflict. I have concentrated on the Electorate of Saxony and the city of Leipzig, because Bach reached his ultimate and lasting professional position there; he worked for twenty-seven years, 1723–50, as cantor of the Thomasschule and music director of the city.

## Absolutism in the Electorate of Saxony

The fundamental domestic conflict of the era was that between the ruler, who strove for absolute unlimited power, and the Estates, who limited this power. The Estates system or absolutism? – this was the question which even Bach had to face. In the Electorate of Saxony, the Estates essentially comprised two bodies, the nobility and the cities, with spiritual foundations and universities playing a minor role. The Landschaft, the parliament of the Estates, had an extraordinarily complex protocol, proceedings between the various groups usually being conducted in writing. Responsibility for secretarial duties was assumed by the body of cities, with Leipzig presiding over its select committee. The deputies from Leipzig drafted the papers and therefore had a key role in the politics of the Estates.

Friedrich August I, known as August the Strong, ruled as Elector of Saxony from 1694 to 1733, followed by his son Friedrich August II who ruled until 1763 (their reigns together being known as the 'Augustan Age'). Like other German electors, August the Strong sought to improve his status by venturing beyond the borders of the German empire. He achieved his goal in Poland, whose crown he acquired in 1697 by paying huge sums of money and through military intervention. Until 1763, both electors ruled there under the names August II and III. The union of the monarchies of Saxony and Poland in one and the same person was terminated by Frederick II of Prussia and the Seven Years War.

In the Saxon Electorate, the relationship of ruler to the Estates developed along specific lines. Absolutism developed only belatedly and never succeeded completely in dominating the Estates. In his will of 1652, Johann Georg I not only left the title of elector to his eldest son but also granted his three other sons secondary rights of inheritance. After his death in 1656 it became important for the bearer of the title of elector, Johann Georg II, to bind these secondary heirs as closely as possible to the Electorate and to limit as much as possible their independence, thereby mitigating the consequences of land division. In this he was effectively supported by the Estates at their session of 1657. Consequently, at this time and again in 1661, their position improved and remained strong until the end of the reign of Johann Georg II (1680). With this, the height of their influence had been reached and subsequently began to decline. Johann Georg III (1680–91) strengthened his power by creating a standing army which was first employed internally by Johann Georg IV (1680–91) as a threat against the Estates near the end of his short reign.

Friedrich August I came rather abruptly to power following the premature death of his brother Johann Georg IV. The first three years of his reign reveal the first tendencies toward the expansion of absolutist power. However, only the acquisition of the Polish crown in 1697 brought about the first trial of strength with the Estates. For the precondition of his election as Polish king was conversion to the Roman Catholic Church, and it was inevitably necessary for him to go to Poland. He thus appointed a governor of Saxony in his absence. Both these acts would have necessitated the consent of the Estates. The Elector, however, proceeded upon his own authority, and thereby committed a double violation of the constitution. But he went even further. He invested the governor with full authority and allowed him to investigate the administration, particularly the tax system, with the assistance of a general Review Commission. Given that the Estates took part in the administration of taxes, which they themselves had approved, they would also have had to participate in this examination. That they did not was a further breach of the constitution. The investigation by the Review Commission certainly brought to light a deplorable state of affairs but unearthed little money. But since August was in need of money and support for the Northern War, the Estates were successful in buying him off, with a special allowance at their session of 1700–1 amounting to one million guilders, in return for the suspension of the review. The Estates had won a victory which had cost them dearly.

The governor realised he had been abandoned and changed sides, now siding not with the sovereign but with the Estates.

August, too, felt humiliated. In any case, he did not give up, but instead changed his strategy. The work of the Review Commission amounted to a reform of the existing administration. But in this particular goal, August was thwarted. He therefore built up parallel structures which could render him independent of the Estates. From 1701 to 1707 he introduced a general consumption excise tax, i.e. a city excise duty, industry and land tax, which was independent of the Estates' consent. In 1706 he established a Private Cabinet, the ruler's personal governing body, which was superior in status and rank to the Privy Council, which until that point had been the highest body governed by the Estates. Against the opposition of the Estates, whose committee session was terminated without decree in 1704, August's position was strengthened to such a level that in 1709 he was able to suspend the standing representation of the Estates and, in 1711, he limited their rights to the approval of taxes and the lodging of grievances.

It was during this period that Count Jakob Heinrich von Flemming became the Electorate's leading politician. In 1694 he entered the service of the Electorate and rose in 1712 to the position of directing cabinet minister; he counselled the Elector-King, and had, in effect, the position of a prime minister. In 1715 he began an absolutist reorganisation of the Privy Council, which was dominated by the Estates. With the 'Silent Parliament' of 1717, all Saxon government officials were required to leave Poland and the Saxon administration was once again concentrated in Dresden. By 1719 the reorganisation was complete and August's government was independent of the Estates.

Nevertheless, August had to overcome a serious quarrel with the Estates. The heir to the throne, travelling since 1711, had converted to Catholicism in Bologna in 1712. His conversion was announced in 1717 after years of secrecy. August succeeded in calming the Estates by repeating a guarantee of the Lutheran confession of faith, one which had been repeatedly articulated since 1697. As a result, in 1719 he was able to bring about the famous festivities celebrating the marriage of the heir to the Austrian Archduchess Maria Josepha, the eldest daughter of Emperor Joseph I.

In this way the domestic political development towards absolutism was achieved in constitution and administration. Nevertheless, in 1727, August considered abolishing the Estates' right to tax consent. But Flemming persuaded him against it. In Flemming's view, a ruler and his country were dependent upon one another, the national interest requiring a balance between the two. Furthermore, the Estates were the guarantors of Lutheranism as the state's religion. Although the effective end of the Northern War and Sweden's recognition of August as the King of Poland were achieved by 1719, foreign and economic political interests were still moving into the foreground.

Flemming died in 1728. Shortly thereafter, still during the reign of August the Strong, Count Heinrich von Brühl began his rise to power as the leading politician of Saxony. His political advancement continued under August's son and successor. From 1740 Brühl was de facto prime minister, being named to the post in 1746. From 1740 he was solely responsible for leading politics in Saxony, at a time when changes of power were occurring in Brandenburg-Prussia, Austria and Russia. It was the beginning of a new era.

It has often been remarked that Brühl assumed absolute political power. We must take into consideration that August the Strong had also accorded his minister Flemming great authority, although he was certainly more involved politically than his son. It must be noted that Friedrich August II put himself so completely at the mercy of Brühl's council that no one but his closest family members was allowed to speak to him without Brühl's being present. Friedrich August II, born in 1696, had lived almost completely behind closed doors until the age of twenty-three because of the religious-political situation of the Electorate. At first, he was in the care of his Lutheran mother and grandmother and then later in the Catholic custody of his Jesuit retinue. A consequence of this is that, as Elector and King, he was incarcerated in a world of illusion, to which belonged painting, music and especially opera.

## The consequences of absolutism for Leipzig

In 1701 August the Strong intervened in the administration of the city of Leipzig for the first time, when he forcibly imposed the appointment of thirty-year-old Franz Conrad Romanus as mayor (Bürgermeister). Leipzig was, on account of its thrice-yearly fairs, the city with the greatest economic potential in the state. Owing to its elevated position, it was excluded from the general review. Romanus managed to persuade the Leipzig Council to make huge sums of money available to the Elector-King. However, he was arrested in January of 1705 and was never released before his death in 1746.

The reason for his arrest was not so much his rather dubious financial dealings as his proposal to the Elector-King in the presence of the governor that the cities should be stripped of their autonomy and transformed into state entities. Had this suggestion been carried out, it would have led to the immediate impotence of the city curia, the corporation of cities, and thus the destruction of the parliament of the Estates and the Estates themselves. It is obvious that either it had not been clear to Romanus that the governor had aligned himself with the Estates, or he believed that August could protect him. August was able, in fact, to prevent him from being sentenced; but the Estates prevented his release.

And Romanus had an additional handicap. He stood quite alone, a single voice representing the ruler's interests in the Leipzig Council. This problem must also have been apparent to August. Therefore, he made certain from then on that men whom he could trust received appointments to the Leipzig Council (just as he did in other areas of administration). One of these men was Gottfried Lange, a man slightly younger than August and Romanus. Born to a church pastor in Upper Lusatia, he first studied theology, then turned his efforts to the study of jurisprudence. In this discipline he completed a university career of almost twenty years, most of which he spent in Leipzig (including the Romanus era); a professorship at the University of Leipzig in 1707 brought the finishing touch to his career.

He had barely reached this goal when he turned his attention from scholarship to politics and joined the court of August the Strong. There he became subordinate to Count Flemming in the Private Cabinet. He formulated the important constitutional manifesto for the reclamation of the Polish throne, which August the Strong published under his own name on 8 August 1709. Lange gained a position of confidence with the absolutist reorganisation of the Privy Council in 1716. By 1710 he had already been accepted into the Leipzig Council (obviously as a result of pressure from August the Strong) without actually performing his duties on any regular basis. Therefore, in 1714, the Council denied a demand to promote Lange to proconsul, thereby refusing to grant him the promise of an eventual appointment as mayor. After this, the sovereign nominated him to two electoral boards sitting in Leipzig, the higher court and the consistory (the administration of church and school affairs) and drew up a secret mandate which granted Lange the very next available position of mayor.

The mandate was carried out in 1719. Until his death in 1748, Lange was one of the three mayors (Bürgermeister) in Leipzig, who took turns serving in year-long terms of office but in no particular order. In Lange, the sovereign once again had a man he could trust, a representative of his interests at the apex of Leipzig's administration. Lange was not alone and was able to draw support from a faction. He arrived just as the quarrel between the Estates and the sovereign had been settled to the sovereign's advantage. Romanus during his time ought to have created a situation which Lange could immediately exploit. From the time of Gottfried

Lange's appointment as mayor at the latest, there were two parties in Leipzig, the absolutist court party and the Estates' city party. The head of the absolutist court party was Gottfried Lange; that of the Estates' city party was Abraham Christoph Platz, who, as Romanus's successor, became mayor in 1705. After his death in 1728, Platz was succeeded by Jakob Born.

## Bach's appointment to office in Leipzig

This political constellation made the selection of Johann Kuhnau's successor as cantor of the Thomasschule in 1722–3. The divergent cultural and musical goals of the two groups were determined by their differing political aims. The Estates' city party sought to fill the vacancy in accord with the traditional office of cantor. The incumbent should certainly have as good an understanding of music as possible, but should be able to teach school subjects equally well. The absolutist court party, on the other hand, had a more modern music directorship in mind. The appointee should be a highly qualified musician in terms of compositional, practical and organisational capabilities, but should be freed from the obligation to teach, so that he might concentrate solely on music. In short, the Estates' city party wanted a cantor in the traditional sense; the absolutist court party, by contrast, wanted a Kapellmeister.

Discussions centred specifically on whether the occupant of the office would give the customary five hours' weekly instruction of Latin to the Tertia and Quarta (i.e. the middle years). This was, in fact, the question which was to determine the relative dependence or independence of the individual appointee and the office itself; if the instruction were made compulsory, it would reflect the subordination of both personnel and subject matter to the school's purposes. The cantor would be subject to the hierarchy of the school, within which music, as part of the regular instruction, was ranked. If the occupant of this post were to be released from instruction, music would thereby be recognised as a separate, independent sphere under his direction. In this case, he would be considered a Kapellmeister.

Because of the split between the two groups, the appointment proceedings were protracted for months. Their differing goals were made concrete in the candidates each party presented. In the course of the proceedings twelve names were introduced, five by the Estates' city party and seven by the absolutist court party.

The list provided by the Estates' city party revealed no particular subdivisions: every candidate was a cantor. The list provided by the absolutist court party, in contrast, reveals two distinct groups of three and one additional candidate who belonged to neither group. The candidates in the first group were academics and came from an operatic background; those of the second group were organists and non-academics. In presenting these two groups, the absolutists assembled two counter-images of cantors. With the candidates from an operatic background, they promoted a new aesthetic, giving precedence to international rank at the expense of the traditional music theory of the central German cantor. With the organists, they gave precedence to competent specialists who were exclusively musicians instead of being also school teachers.

The three candidates from the field of opera were Georg Philipp Telemann, music director for the Free Hanseatic City of Hamburg; Johann Friedrich Fasch, a Kapellmeister in the employ of Count Morzin of Bohemia; and Christoph Graupner, court Kapellmeister for the Count of Hesse-Darmstadt. The three organists were Christian Petzold, court organist in Dresden, Georg Friedrich Kauffmann, court Kapellmeister in Merseburg, and Johann Sebastian Bach, court Kapellmeister in Köthen. The remaining candidate was Georg Balthasar Schott, organist and music director of the Neue Kirche in Leipzig.

The opera candidates were the absolutists' first choice. All three enjoyed an international reputation, having worked outside the lands of their birth. Each had studied in Leipzig and therefore already had a relationship with the city. Two of them, Telemann and Fasch, were associated with local institutions, having founded respectively the first and the second *Collegium musicum* of the city. This secured them the first and second places on the list. Graupner, who could not boast any such contribution to the city's musical life, therefore came in third place.

The organists were the absolutists' second choice. None of them had lived in Leipzig for any extended period, so they were evaluated from a national perspective. Petzold, who was employed at the electoral court in Dresden, had an advantage over Kauffmann, who worked at the subsidiary court of Merseburg; Bach, who had never been employed in the Electorate and who at the time was employed outside Saxon territories in the court of Anhalt-Köthen, was the youngest of the group and lay in third place. Finally, Schott, who stood at the very end of the list, was nominated on account of his position as organist and music director of the Neue Kirche and because he had succeeded Telemann there and as director of the first *Collegium musicum* of the city.

The sequence seems quite odd to us today, particularly with Bach in sixth place on the absolutists' list. However, if we consider the viewpoint of the absolutists, we, too, would have to put them into this sequence. Bach, the organist, has since gained a reputation far superior to that of the three opera candidates; more than anything else, it is this discrepancy in the impact of the candidates' respective achievements in music history that makes the proceedings regarding the appointment of a new cantor at the Thomasschule seem so difficult to understand.

The absolutist court party was ultimately unable to engage any of the three opera candidates. Telemann was offered an increase in his salary in Hamburg to the amount which he might have expected in Leipzig and he thus declined the position. Fasch took over as Kapellmeister at the court of Anhalt-Zerbst during the course of the appointment proceedings, probably in the belief that the vacancy in Leipzig had been taken by Telemann. He withdrew his application for the position when his name came up for consideration. Graupner was unable to obtain a release from his current position, despite a request from the city of Leipzig addressed to the Count of Hesse-Darmstadt. Of the organists, the first, Petzold, was never taken into formal consideration. The Estates' city party ultimately found none of their candidates available. So, in the end, the competition came down to the three remaining candidates initially proposed by the absolutist court party. Bach had managed to move from the next to last place on the list to one place higher by virtue of his accomplishment during the trial. This was the entire room for manoeuvre that a man of Bach's unique capacity had at his disposal. Bach, now in a position ahead of Kauffmann and Schott, was eventually selected.

The unanimous vote involved the agreement of the Estates' city party. A compromise had been necessary, though, since the Estates' city party sought to preserve the traditional definition of the office while the absolutist court party sought a new one. During the final session, just as Bach was about to be chosen from among the remaining three candidates sponsored by the absolutist court party, the speaker for the absolutists introduced a motion to redefine the position as a musical directorship. In a counter-move, the speaker of the Estates' party made a motion to consider a new candidate – of course, one who fitted his party's idea of a qualified applicant. Resolution stood against resolution. As a formal compromise, each side withdrew its respective motion. In practice, this meant that the city party accepted the candidate presented by the court party, while the court party accepted the definition of the office supported by the city party.

However, since the candidate put forward by the absolutist court party could not be employed under the definition of the office supported by the Estates' city party, the latter made a concession. The absolutist party candidate could transfer the five weekly hours of Latin instruction to one of his subordinate colleagues, thus releasing himself from the duty by making a private agreement and paying the expenses out of his own pocket. The absolutist party had indeed won its choice of candidate but had been unable to carry out the public and legal act of redefining the office. It was unsuccessful in establishing a music directorship as the new norm. The post remained very much the traditional, conventional one of cantor, which was filled just this once by a Kapellmeister. Bach's tenure in office was defined as an exception.

Bach, as a candidate of the absolutist court party, was not required to become a cantor and could remain a Kapellmeister. Both employer and appointee were in agreement on this. The man who – according to one historical conception – became the arch-cantor of Protestantism was in his own view, as well as that of his employer, never a cantor; from the very beginning he administered his office completely as a Kapellmeister. Indeed, the administration of such an office, connected with both school and church, by such a highly qualified professional musician is a principal reason for this historical conception, the condition for its possibility, so to speak.

Bach's candidacy was opposed by Abraham Christoph Platz, speaker of the Estates' city party, and supported by Gottfried Lange, speaker of the absolutist court party. Gottfried Lange, who emerged politically from the Private Cabinet of Count Flemming, had probably heard Bach play in 1717 at Flemming's Dresden palace. It was on the occasion of the planned competition between Bach and the French virtuoso Marchand in which Bach triumphed, his rival having disappeared. Recollecting their first meeting, Lange recommended Bach to the Leipzig Council with the words 'he excels at the keyboard'. While this remark had little to do with the office in question, it emphasises the absolutist court party's interest in engaging a musician who was outstanding, well known, and possessing generally recognised qualifications.

Lange was also a writer. Perhaps he was one of Bach's librettists and remained anonymous out of concern for his social and political status? Bach himself revealed the identity of his patron, whom he had to thank for his position in Leipzig. He asked Gottfried Lange to be the first god-father to his first child born in Leipzig, his son Gottfried Heinrich (to whom Lange gave the first name).

## Bach's professional circumstances

Bach was chosen as a candidate of the absolutist court party and, as such, had the informal duty of realising absolutist cultural politics in Leipzig within the sphere of music. Like Gottfried Lange, he came to act as an external agent of the Dresden court. As a cultural-political representative of the absolutist party, he was subject to repeated attacks and criticism from the Estates' party, the main problem of his entire Leipzig career.

Until now, the opposition between Kapellmeister and cantor has been seen as Bach's subjective problem. In reality, this opposition was an objective problem resulting from the divergent cultural-political views of two competing political parties. Subjectively, Bach had made a decisive choice in favour of absolutism and of being a Kapellmeister. He identified with his absolutist task. In the two cities where he worked, Mühlhausen and Leipzig, Bach argued using the analogy of an absolutist instrument of power, the standing army. His goal of a regular church music is consonant with the purpose set forth in his 'Entwurff einer wohlbestallten Kirchen Music' (Draft for a well-appointed church music). Bach seeks to establish a permanent 'standing' performance apparatus, made up of professional musicians who would be appropriately compensated. His petition of 25 June 1708 for release from the position in Mühlhausen documents the discrepancy between the conditions set by the Estates and absolutist convictions. It reveals how Bach made the effort to get away from cities, which were influenced by the system of the Estates and to escape to the absolutist courts – in spite of the uncertainties which inevitably accompanied court service – just as he had sought to leave the artisan-milieu of his father for a middle-class existence. The position in Leipzig was acceptable to him because it was linked to an absolutist mandate. Later, though, he was burdened by Estates' party opposition and countered it with his 'Entwurff einer wohlbestallten Kirchen Music' of 23 August 1730.

In this document, Bach takes up a topical economic argument. He proposes that ideally a musician need be competent on only one instrument (and emphasises correspondingly the apparently less-than-obvious notion that a singer need be competent in only one register). This is the competence of a factory worker, who is no longer required to be responsible for all phases of the production process like the craftsman, but rather for 'his' phase alone and this single phase he must execute perfectly. This is a departure from the concept of the *Stadtmusikant*, who could play all instruments, and a defence of the specialised virtuoso who had mastered his chosen instrument.

Bach had to fulfil his absolutist mission in Leipzig within the traditional context of the Estates. The Thomasschule and the *Stadtmusikanten* in particular were institutions entirely dominated by the Estates. His salary was also paid according to an old-fashioned custom favoured by the Estates, consisting of both payment in kind and a considerable number of small sums paid on an irregular basis. This method contrasted with the manner of the absolutist court, which simply paid a cash stipend, and whose payments were scheduled at fixed intervals (if not always actually forthcoming).

The fundamental domestic conflict of the era between the Estates and absolutism never died down and was still going on when Bach's first and second successors were appointed. Bach had taken a position in this conflict. Now he had to answer for it, drawing on support from the absolutist court party. The Estates' city party did, however, observe some limits in their persecution of Bach. Even they acknowledged that he was a great musician and that he fulfilled the compositional, practical and organisational tasks of a music director professionally and perfectly. In this regard, there were no complaints from any quarter. But Bach was precisely that, a competent professional musician in a directorial position; he remained a Kapellmeister and never transformed himself into a school teacher.

The position in Leipzig gave Bach the opportunity to resolve satisfactorily a problem of his professional life. His specific, renowned talent lay in his mastery of keyboard instruments, particularly the organ. On account of his extraordinary qualifications, Bach was doubtless entitled to a directorship. How should he, as an organist, attain such a position? In most positions he would be forced either to give up the practice of his specific talent or to forgo a directorship. But Leipzig offered him both opportunities, though under specific conditions. In accordance with absolutist policies, Bach had obtained permission to buy his way free of the portion of his job which entailed school instruction, by transferring it to a colleague. The resulting free time could be filled with secondary activities related to keyboard instruments. He travelled widely as a virtuoso and authority on organs; he composed and published keyboard music; he gave private lessons primarily as a keyboard teacher. Not only were there no complaints about his performance as music director, but equally little was heard in relation to the entire area of his related activities. They must have been generally endorsed. The city party's proposal, in summer 1730, to introduce express ratification of Bach's trips is evidence in itself of the general approval of his travel and other related activities.

Officially, Bach served as the city's music director; privately, his interest was keyboard instruments. He held a Kapellmeister's position but the organ was his hobby; he enjoyed the social status of a directorship and the freedom to develop his own talents. The solution to his professional dilemma also determines the respective categories of his work. These areas comprise the ensemble music for a Kapellmeister and the solo music for an organist – in other words, music requiring the participation of other musicians and music he could perform alone.

## Specific controversies

The Estates' city party accepted this arrangement only reluctantly, since Bach's field of interest and activity lay mostly outside the school. He was employed in the school; he lived in school quarters, but he did almost nothing for specifically school-related purposes. This was the point which caused the city party to take offence. Such an arrangement was against all tradition. In two instances they felt compelled to intervene rather forcefully.

The first of these relates to the directorship of the city's first *Collegium musicum*, founded by Telemann. This had always been linked with the position of organist and music director at the Neue Kirche. At the time of Bach's arrival in Leipzig, these posts were held by Georg Balthasar Schott, the candidate in last place on the absolutist party's list. When Schott left in 1729, this scheme was altered. Schott and his successor, Carl Gotthelf Gerlach, usually directed the cantatas of the first Kantorei in Bach's absence, thus acting as substitute music directors at the Nikolaikirche and the Thomaskirche. Gerlach was chosen on Bach's recommendation, something which reflected Bach's position as the city's principal musician, someone with the right to recommend his substitute during absences. But Bach himself took over the direction of the *Collegium musicum*.

Although the *Collegium musicum* was not a municipal institution, when the cantor of the Thomasschule took over the directorship of the *Collegium musicum* (which had been linked to the Neue Kirche for over twenty-five years), it was perceived as a serious change in the structure of Leipzig's musical life. We can hardly presume that this change could have been undertaken as a result of a purely private agreement between Schott and Bach or between Bach and Gerlach; at the very least, the absolutist party's agreement would have been required. It is in fact much more likely that the reorganisation had been authorised and set into motion by the party itself and by its speaker, Gottfried Lange, who was by now senior among the mayors and in charge of the government. For the new structure was entirely in line with the aims of the absolutist party, who had wanted to transform the cantor's post into a music directorship and its occupant into a central figure not only in church music but also in concert matters of the city generally. Perhaps an arrangement was made at the time of Bach's appointment to enact the change as soon as the incumbent at the Neue Kirche resigned.

Now that he was involved in concert matters, the city's music director put on one concert each week, and two per week during the three annual fairs. That amounts to about fifty regularly scheduled concerts each year, (not including special unscheduled concerts), given that during Advent and Lent there was neither church nor concert music. If we assume that five to six works were included in each concert programme, Bach performed 250–300 pieces a year. Composing his own works and procuring those of others required tremendous organisational and artistic skills and was an impressive accomplishment. Perhaps even more important was the influence Bach exercised over what musical repertoire became known in Leipzig.

As director of the *Collegium musicum* Bach had a core group of qualified instrumentalists at his disposal to whom he could turn when he required assistance with church music. Now he took up the question of vocalists. The admission of students to the Thomasschule and the award of scholarships followed the rule that the rector was allowed precisely the same number of candidates as the cantor: that is, one academically gifted student for each musically gifted student. Now the quota of students chosen by the cantor was to be raised to the detriment of the rector's quota, preferably with the 1:1 relationship altered to 0:1. But it appears that the influence of the absolutist court party was not sufficient to alter the existing regulations. Their efforts presumably failed owing to the opposition of the Estates' city party, to whom belonged the Councillor responsible for the Thomasschule. Such a threat to the structure of the school had to be resisted by both the Councillor and the city party, because this intrusion would have transformed the school into an institution subordinated to the cantor (who was actually a Kapellmeister) and deprived the rector of his power. Music would have been valued at the expense of the other subjects.

In the city party's view, the reorganisation already proved irritating enough. For they had granted Bach directorship in city concert matters and, in doing so, presented him with the opportunity for the lavish development of church music. The court party had given him a lasting organisational basis for his effectiveness as a Kapellmeister. The city party saw this as disruptive to the delicate balance of power and in August 1730, with Jakob Born as their new speaker, in charge of government for the first time, prepared a counter-attack. What they had in mind had its own logic. Bach had managed to establish a firm basis of influence outside the school. If the balance of power was to be preserved, Bach would have to become more involved in school matters. This was to be achieved by revoking his exemption from teaching. In the event that this did not succeed, the intention was to dismiss him. As speaker of the court party, Gottfried Lange artfully deflected this counter-attack and thus cemented the new position and the expanded sphere of influence enjoyed by the city's music director.

The city party's threats provide the background for Bach's letter to his childhood friend, Georg Erdmann, on 28 October 1730 and in particular for his 'Entwurff einer wohlbestallten Kirchen Music' of 23 August that same year. This statement documents the controversy between the absolutist court and the Estates' city parties within the Council, not one between Bach as an individual and the Council of the city of Leipzig. Bach's 'Entwurff' is addressed to the city party and represents the position of the court party (who perhaps requested him to write it). He argues that the vocal and instrumental resources available to him by virtue of his position are insufficient to allow him to fulfil the task of his office. This, therefore, justifies his demand to change the regulation regarding the admission of boarding students to the cantor's benefit and additionally justifies his assumption of the directorship of the *Collegium musicum*.

The so-called 'prefects' dispute' which broke out in the summer of 1736 and continued until the spring of 1738 can be understood within the framework of the controversy between the city party and the court party. The dispute over the appointment and dismissal of prefects (assistant musical directors) was merely a continuation of the discussion regarding the definition of the office in a more concrete form: specifically, whether the Thomasschule cantor was bound by the advice of the rector in carrying out his task (a cantor) or whether he enjoyed unrestricted authority in directing music matters (a Kapellmeister). Once again, Bach's level of involvement in the school was at issue. And once again it was Gottfried Lange, speaker of the absolutist court party, who brought about a solution satisfactory for Bach.

There was another aspect to the dispute which explains Bach's agitation. The primary prefect also served as the cantor's assistant and therefore held a position of confidence. The rector, Johann August Ernesti, was an eminent scholar and, as the Councillor responsible for the Thomasschule, he was aligned with the city party too. Ernesti appointed a student in his confidence to the position of primary prefect during this dispute. In this way he managed to plant an agent of the opposition in Bach's own house.

## Questions relating to music

A musician of Bach's calibre could only have had the opportunity to serve as cantor at the Thomasschule within this unique historical situation, where absolutism held domestic power in the Electorate of Saxony and a trusted confidant of the sovereign stood at the apex of Leipzig's administration. The absolutist court party had made the selection and the appointment proceedings were a part of the cultural politics of August the Strong's representational system. It was for this reason that the issue of renown played such a considerable role in the appointment proceedings.

Bach was commissioned by the sovereign, although the city of Leipzig was his employer. Therefore it was unnecessary for him to hold a position at court, although he naturally had excellent connections there. In view of this, we might ponder the relationship between Bach's compositional development since 1717 and the Dresden court and its musicians. To what extent did political developments influence Bach's musical development? This question relates not only to the year 1733, the year in which a new sovereign came to power, but also to 1728, the year Jakob Heinrich von Flemming died, and 1740, the beginning of Heinrich von Brühl's rule. Of these last two, 1728 is also a date of historical significance for the city, since Abraham Christoph Platz died leaving Gottfried Lange as the highest-ranking mayor. In view of this, what is the significance of Bach's court titles and their chronology? What was the meaning of his appeals to the sovereign?

Is there a relationship between the representative artistry of his compositions and the absolutist mandate? Was the St Matthew Passion – whose librettist, Picander, was also a partisan of the absolutists – meant as an extraordinary accomplishment of this mandate? Was it, in addition, supposed to prove the musical superiority of the Lutheran state confession, which offered the Protestant hymns and the diverse methods of elaborating their tunes in counterpoint – an option out of reach of the church music at the Roman Catholic court of Dresden? How can we evaluate the parodic relationships between works of homage for the court and church music, when presumably both the secular and religious works originate from an absolutist mandate? Does the Christmas Oratorio originate in a suggestion from Gottfried Lange, who became Privy War Councillor to Friedrich August II in 1734 and who governed in Leipzig during the same period?

In 1740 Heinrich von Brühl published anonymously the German version of a French devotional book entitled 'Die wahre und gründliche Gottseligkeit aller Christen insgemein'. The title itself ('The true and thorough piety of all Christians in general') reveals an urge to embrace all confessions of faith. Are perhaps the Mass in B Minor and the D major version of the Magnificat reflective of such tendencies to stress the common characteristics of the different confessions? That was natural for a politics which sought to transform the personal union of the sovereigns of Lutheran Saxony and Catholic Poland into a real union, into a lasting constitutional union between both the states.

Was composition or selection of music for each of the two main churches affected by the councillors responsible for each of the churches? The councillors responsible for the Nikolaikirche were Abraham Christoph Platz followed by Jakob Born, while Gottfried Lange was responsible for the Thomaskirche. There, immediately following his appointment as mayor in Leipzig, Lange had a new high altar built with components finished in Dresden; the marble was a gift from August the Strong. He chose to be buried in front of the altar (just about at the place where Bach's memorial stone stands today). Thus the tone of the Nikolaikirche was set by the Estates' city party and that of the Thomaskirche by the absolutist court party; following Lange's death in 1748 the Thomaskirche, too, fell under the influence of the city party.

There is evidence that Bach was subject to certain restrictions in the Nikolaikirche. There he performed passions by other composers twice between 1724 and 1731: in 1726 the St Mark Passion by Reinhard Keiser and, probably in 1730, the St Luke Passion; the performance of passions by other composers in the Thomaskirche is not documented. When he took over the direction of the *Collegium musicum* in 1729, Bach soon demonstrated the instrumental power he now commanded. He introduced Cantata 174 with a richly scored version of the first movement of the third Brandenburg Concerto. However, he did not present this piece in the Nikolaikirche on Whit Sunday, but waited until Whit Monday, when it was the turn of the Thomaskirche.

How and to what extent, then, did Bach's music relate to the political conditions to which he was subject?

## From Kuhnau to Bach

The selection of Johann Kuhnau, Bach's predecessor, took place in 1701, after the Estates had triumphed over the sovereign on 17 March and before mayor Romanus took over his office on 29 August. Kuhnau was entirely the choice of the Estates. They could hardly have been successful in doing this after Romanus's assumption of office: as early as 19 September a decree from the sovereign demanded, among other things, that the standard of church music be improved, on account of foreign visitors who came to Leipzig, particularly during the fairs.

Romanus, unable to dismiss Kuhnau, solved the dilemma in a characteristic manner. Georg Philipp Telemann had been a student at Leipzig University since the winter semester of 1701. Romanus heard about his musical accomplishment and commissioned him to compose – and probably perform – a cantata for the Thomaskirche every fourteen days, that is, probably whenever Kuhnau was busy at the Nicolaikirche. In return, he granted Telemann a considerable reward. Telemann, who shortly there-after took over the direction of the Leipzig opera, also founded the *Collegium musicum* and thereby initiated a regular schedule of concert performances. When the organ of the Neue Kirche was completed in 1704, Telemann was engaged as organist. He also functioned as music director and presented his own cantatas on feast days and during the fairs. His *Collegium musicum* took part in these performances, as also did the 'band' of musicians led by the watchman Christoph Stephan Scheinhardt. Over decades, Scheinhardt had improved the untrained and unlicensed musicians to such an extent, that on 27 October 1701 (thus following Romanus's assumption of office) the privileged *Stadtpfeifer* and *Kunstgeiger* finally signed a contract acknowledging him.

Romanus proceeded in this matter completely in accord with the maxims of his sovereign, who sought absolute rule. He created a parallel structure which left the traditional system completely intact but at the same time competed with it. This parallel structure comprised dilet-tantes, which is not to deny their musical qualifications, but acknowl-edges that they were persons without a traditional training and without conventional positions. He honoured their private initiative, in that he, so to speak, accorded them privileges as court craftsmen. In this way they remained outside the guild system, and thus outside the organisation of the Estates. Romanus was himself a musical dilettante, who had a 'clavier' smuggled in to him during his incarceration. His daughter, Christiane Mariane von Ziegler, one of Bach's librettists, also played the 'clavier', lute and transverse flute. A taste for music may have been widespread among people in the vicinity of an absolutist court.

After this parallel musical structure had been created, it remained in place even after Romanus had been arrested and after Telemann left Leipzig some six months later. At the time of Bach's arrival in Leipzig, the situation had changed. While Telemann and Bach belonged to the same generation, Telemann had been in his early twenties when he lived in Leipzig and Bach was now in his late thirties. Youth had moved into adult-hood. Absolutism had established itself in the domestic sphere. Therefore Bach could be introduced to the traditional post as a musician who had already 'arrived'.

Like absolutism, Leipzig's new musical establishment had become institutionalised. Though the city began to provide financial support for music at the Neue Kirche, the *Collegium musicum* established by Telemann and the one founded somewhat later by Fasch remained private entities. In private enterprises such as these (which undoubtedly served public interests) Bach was free of the chains of the Estates. Private enterprises seem generally to have been a recognised means – in the face of the ponderous, even immutable, Estates' administration – of setting projects into motion which had public interest at their centre. From this point of view Bach's unfolding private initiatives, going beyond the boundaries of his office, were well received.

Bach came to Leipzig in a consolidated political situation. The institute from which he was to operate, however – the Thomasschule – was in a state of upheaval. The inspection in 1717 (which had been impending since almost the beginning of the century), and the resulting school ordinance of 1723, caused the school to falter economically. Only the fixing of burial fees by the city in 1740 re-established economic stability. From this year on the general political conditions began to change with the shift in cultural-political power within Leipzig itself. Aside from the ongoing tension between his absolutist mandate and the school, dominated by the Estates, for one reason or another Bach was unable to enjoy any period of complete peace.

From the viewpoint of his position in Leipzig, Bach's professional path can be understood. He was born the son of the leading musician of the city of Eisenach. His own professional life began in Arnstadt, which, like Eisenach, was also the seat of a court. After a brief stay in the free imperial city of Mühlhausen, Bach pursued his aims first in the court of Weimar and then in the court of Köthen. In Weimar he was the organist but was unable to obtain a directorship; in Köthen he had a directorship but had no opportunity to be the organist. In contrast, Leipzig offered the optimal professional compromise which Bach could possibly achieve in light of his specific qualifications and under the concrete conditions of the time and place. He was elected to office as a candidate of the absolutist court party and was certain of their support. However, as a result, Bach had always to expect opposition from the Estates' city party and often enough had to struggle with it. The discord which characterised Bach's professional position was the historical discord of the Electorate of Saxony at that time.

*Translated from the German by Kay LaRae Henschel, revised by the editor and the author*

# 3  Music and Lutheranism

*Robin A. Leaver*

Some understanding of the theological content and the liturgical practices of Lutheranism is essential for the historical appreciation of Bach's music. Bach's theological thinking was formed by the distinctively Lutheran responses to the Reformation debate of the sixteenth century, and he composed a great deal of his music for the Lutheran liturgies of his day. For example, the church cantatas usually relate in some way to the biblical readings, liturgical provisions, congregational hymnody, and ecclesiastical monody of the particular day, season or celebration. This chapter therefore outlines some of the distinctive features of the Lutheran Reformation in general, and Luther's musical and liturgical reforms in particular, as they relate both to later Lutheranism and to Bach's life and works.

## The Reformation

Although it is customary to employ the term 'Reformation' as the ecclesiastical analogue of the 'Renaissance' of sixteenth-century Europe, it might be more accurate to speak of the 'Reformations' of the period. Although there were certainly a number of common concerns – such as the authority of the Bible in contradistinction to the authority of the church of Rome, or the concept of the general priesthood of all believers set against the particular priesthood of Catholicism – the Reformation in each European area developed its own characteristics, both theological and practical. Thus the Reformation in Switzerland, centred on such cities as Geneva, Basle and Zurich, was strongly influenced by the theology of such Reformers as Zwingli, Calvin and Bullinger. This Calvinist or Reformed tradition was essentially antithetical to Catholic doctrine, especially the Roman Mass, and therefore more simple structures of worship were developed in which music, if used at all, was accorded a somewhat limited function.[1] In Alsace – southwest Germany, bordering on France and centred on Strasbourg – a churchly evangelicalism flourished under the leadership of the primary Reformer of the area, Martin Bucer. Here a more pronounced liturgical order was followed within which music was given a fairly prominent place. However, as the

Reformation developed in this region, liturgical music became primarily limited to congregational song. The influence of the European reformations was also felt in England, but here – under the guidance and direction of the Archbishop of Canterbury, Thomas Cranmer – a specific liturgical agenda was created, the *Book of Common Prayer*. This was substantially based on Catholic rites, suitably modified to reflect the essential biblicism of the reforming movement as a whole. But the English Reformers were in the main somewhat ambivalent regarding the role of music in the liturgy and ultimately two traditions of church music developed: the parish church tradition, which was almost exclusively restricted to the congregational metrical psalm, and the cathedral, choral tradition which was virtually unrelated to the parish church tradition.

In Germany, the catalytic centre of the sixteenth-century Reformation, the emphases and practices of emerging Lutheranism were different again. But even within Lutheranism there was no rigid uniformity of practice. For example, the Lutheran Reformation in such Nordic countries as Denmark, Sweden, Iceland and elsewhere developed characteristics distinct from those of Lutheran Saxony. Moreover, there were regional differences within Lutheran Germany itself: the Reformation in north Germany, in such cities as Hamburg, Lübeck and Rostock (where Low German was generally spoken), was not a mirror image of that in Wittenberg, and similarly the Reformation in such south German cities as Nuremberg and Augsburg had its own characteristics.[2]

This diversity of Reformation tradition has not always been recognised in the Bach literature, especially contributions published in English, which often reflect more of their authors' confessional background than Bach's essential Lutheranism. Charles Sanford Terry's anthology of English translations of Bach's cantatas arranged according to their liturgical usage frequently betrays an Anglican perspective, and Alec Robertson's study of the church cantatas similarly reveals the author's Catholicism.[3] But, if a reliable representation of the man and the context of his music is to be made, the Lutheran perspectives of Bach's environment must be borne in mind, perspectives that were shaped by the debates of the sixteenth century.

## The Lutheran Reformation

Although specific practices differed across Lutheran Germany, the various territorial churches nevertheless shared a basic theological unity. In the decades following Luther's death in 1546 a number of internal theological controversies disturbed the Lutheran churches. After much

debate a unity was achieved with the publication of *Concordia . . .*
*Christliches widerholtes einmütiges Bekenntnis nachbenannter Kurfürsten,*
*Fürsten und Stände Augsburgischer Konfession und derselben zu Ende des*
*Buchs unterschriebener Theologen Lehre und Glaubens* (Dresden, 1580),
usually referred to in English as *The Book of Concord*.[4] It contained such
documents as the unaltered Augsburg Confession of 1530 – the primary
confessional document of Lutheranism[5] – Melanchthon's 'Apology' of the
Augsburg Confession, Luther's Schmalkald articles, his small and large
catechisms, and the Formula of Concord, in which points of Lutheran
theology were stated both positively and negatively. Some years later, in
1593, Saxon Visitation Articles were issued in order to purge the Lutheran
church of crypto-Calvinism. Thereafter these Visitation Articles, which,
like the Formula of Concord, outline the positives of the Lutheran position and the negatives of the Calvinist errors in relation to specific points
of doctrine, were appended to the *Book of Concord*.[6] Thus the *Book of*
*Concord* is an anthology of confessional documents embracing fundamental Lutheran theology, which is defined both in its own terms and in
contradistinction to the doctrines of Catholicism, Calvinism and the
doctrinal deviations within its own ranks.

Before being appointed to any position in the church all pastors, teachers and musicians had to give formal and written assent to the *Book of*
*Concord*. Thus, as part of the preliminaries to Bach's appointment as
Thomaskantor, Johann Schmid, professor of theology at Leipzig, examined Bach on or before 8 May 1723, and reported that the cantor-elect had
satisfactorily responded to his questions.[7] The substance of those questions related to biblical theology in general and to Lutheran theology as
delineated in the *Book of Concord* in particular. Salomon Deyling, professor of theology, pastor of the Nikolaikirche, and Superintendent in
Leipzig, endorsed Schmid's document of examination and also examined
Bach himself a few days later, on 13 May 1723. In a letter to the
Consistory, written the same day, Deyling states that Bach had subscribed
to the Formula of Concord,[8] which means that he formally accepted the
theological position of the *Book of Concord* as a whole. The actual document that Bach signed on 13 May 1723 reveals that he subscribed to the
Formula of Concord twice: once positively, endorsing Lutheran doctrines, and once negatively, denying non-Lutheran beliefs.[9]

This is not the place for a detailed discussion of Lutheran theology, but
it is necessary at least to outline some of the more important emphases.
The watchwords of the Lutheran Reformation were *sola scriptura, sola*
*gratia* and *sola fide*: that is, one's standing before God rests not with
the authority of the church but on the authority of scripture; that one's
salvation – or justification, to use Reformation vocabulary – depends

upon the grace of God in Christ, rather than on any human endeavour; and that this salvation can only be appropriated by faith. The fourth article of the Augsburg Confession expresses it thus:

> It is also taught among us that we cannot obtain forgiveness of sin and righteousness before God by our own merits, works, or satisfactions, but that we receive forgiveness of sin and become righteous before God by grace, for Christ's sake, through faith, when we believe that Christ suffered for us and that for his sake our sin is forgiven and righteousness and eternal life are given to us.[10]

This is clearly a theme that is frequently enunciated in the libretti of Bach's cantatas. Much of this theological position was, of course, shared by other Protestants of the Reformation era. Where Lutheran theology is particularly distinctive is in its approach to the sacraments and the relationship between Law and Gospel. Sacramental theology will be referred to later. The Formula of Concord (Epitome V) deals with Law and Gospel as follows:

> We believe, teach, and confess that the distinction between the Law and Gospel ... is to be maintained with great diligence in the church ... We believe, teach, and confess that, strictly speaking, the Law is a divine doctrine which teaches what is right and God-pleasing and which condemns everything that is sinful and contrary to God's will ... But the Gospel, strictly speaking, is the kind of doctrine that teaches what a man who has not kept the Law and is condemned by it should believe, namely, that Christ has satisfied and paid for all guilt and without man's merit has obtained and won for him forgiveness of sins, 'the righteousness that avails before God' [Rom. 1:7; 2 Cor. 5:21] and eternal life.[11]

As the doctrine of original sin declares that 'since the fall of Adam all men ... are born in sin ... which even now damns and brings eternal death',[12] the Law condemns, in contrast to the Gospel, which converts. Of course there is much more to the distinction between Law and Gospel than this, but this is sufficient to understand the conceptual structure that underlies many of Bach's cantatas. In the opening chorus the problem is stated, often in biblical words, that we humans are afflicted in some particular way by the dilemma of sin and stand under the condemnation of the Law. Succeeding recitatives and arias explore some of the implications of the impasse. Then a movement, often an aria, presents the Gospel answer to the Law question. Thereafter the mood of both libretto and music take on the optimism of the Gospel, the final chorale being an emphatic endorsement of the Gospel answer.[13]

But was Bach a Lutheran by conviction or convenience? In the latter part of the nineteenth century Bach's Lutheran convictions were taken for granted. Indeed, an exaggerated image of Bach was constructed: Bach the pious Christian, the supreme Lutheran cantor. He was even elevated to the level of a primary author of the New Testament and was commonly accorded the title of 'The Fifth Evangelist'! The first part of the twentieth century therefore inherited a view of Bach that was created by nineteenth-century Romanticism, filtered through the perspectives of Christian piety, a view that was seriously questioned by the scholarly research of the 1950s and early 1960s. The new chronology of Bach's works, as established primarily by von Dadelsen and Dürr,[14] suggested that Bach gave up writing religious music sometime around the early 1730s. In a celebrated lecture given at the Mainz Bachfest in 1962, Friedrich Blume questioned Bach's specific Christian commitment: 'Did Bach have a special liking for church work? Was it a spiritual necessity for him? Hardly. There is at any rate no evidence that it was. Bach the supreme Cantor, the creative servant of the Word of God, the staunch Lutheran, is a legend.'[15] Blume's lead was followed by others, notably scholars working in what was East Germany, who argued that Bach was not specifically religious but worked for the church as the most convenient arena to exercise his gifts and abilities.

But Blume delivered his lecture some years before the significance of the marginalia found in a three-volume Bible commentary once owned by Bach was made known. This was Abraham Calov's annotated version of the Bible, *Die deutsche Bibel* (Wittenberg, 1681–2), with Bach's monogram on each of the title pages, now in the Ludwig Fuerbringer Library of Concordia Seminary, St Louis, Missouri, USA, and exhibited publicly for the first time at the Heidelberg Bachfest of 1969. These volumes provide the kind of documentary evidence that Blume thought was lacking in 1962.[16] The marginalia and underlining, written for no one but the Thomaskantor himself, reveal that he was a careful student of the Bible. Some scholars, such as Denis Arnold, remained unconvinced. Referring to these underlinings and marginalia of Bach, Arnold wrote: 'They have been used to show Bach's continuing faith in and deep knowledge of the Bible; but coming from the hand of such a seasoned campaigner, they look all too clearly like the texts to be used in a coming battle against the unmusical members of the Town Council.'[17] On their own these handwritten additions could be interpreted in this light, but, taking into consideration these marginalia as a whole, the content of Bach's personal theological library (which many of his contemporary pastors would have been proud to have owned), and recent research into the significance of these theological books for Bach's life and music, it seems unequivocal that the Thomaskantor's attachment to Lutheranism was more than just convenient.[18] Bach owned two different editions of Luther's collected works and, indeed, the Calov Bible was virtually another, in the sense that the editor arranged Luther's writings in biblical order and only supplied a comment on a text when Luther had not already done so. In addition Bach owned a single volume from another edition of Luther's collected works, the *Tischreden* (Table Talk), and two different editions of the Reformer's *Hauß Postilla*, sermons on the Sundays and festivals of the church year.[19]

Although the prodigious output of church music did indeed moderate after 1730, Bach certainly did not give up composing religious music; indeed, at the end of his life he was working on the B minor Mass, a musical statement of faith.[20] To be sure the hagiographic image of Bach inherited from the late nineteenth century is no longer tenable, but neither is the twentieth-century creation of the agnostic Bach who simply tolerated Lutheran theology and practice so that he could compose and perform. Both icons are constructs reflecting the spirit of ages later than Bach's. He was in many respects a typical middle-class Lutheran of the first half of the eighteenth century who had a particular attachment to the writings of Martin Luther.

## Luther and music

Unlike other Reformers of the sixteenth century, who were rather cautious and circumspect with regard to music, Luther understood music as a *donum Dei*, a gift from God, rather than a human invention, and made frequent references to the interconnections between music and theology.[21] In his preface to Georg Rhau's *Symphoniae iucundae* (Wittenberg, 1538), he wrote:

> I would certainly like to praise music with all my heart as the excellent gift of God which it is and to commend it to everyone . . . Here it must suffice to discuss the benefit [*usus*] of this great thing [music]. But even that transcends the greatest eloquence of the most eloquent, because of the infinite variety of its forms and benefits. We can mention only one point (which experience confirms), namely, that next to the Word of God, music deserves the highest praise.[22]

He wrote a letter to the composer Ludwig Senfl, dated 4 October 1530, in which he stated:

> I plainly judge, and do not hesitate to affirm, that except for theology there is no art that could be put on the same level with music, since except for theology [music] alone produces what otherwise only theology can do, namely, a calm and joyful disposition.[23]

In the *Tischreden* there are numerous references to music, such as: 'I place music next to theology and give it the highest praise.'[24] This collection of verbatim reports of Luther's conversations at table and elsewhere, as recorded by various scribes, and edited by Johann Aurifaber, was first issued twenty years after Luther's death (Eisleben, 1566).[25] It was structured according to the basic *loci* of Lutheran theology. What is significant is not so much that chapter 69 is headed 'Von der Musica', but that discussions of fundamental theology are frequently dealt with in musical terms. Thus Luther's statements about the relationship between music and theology are borne out by his theological method. For example, in dealing with the distinction between Law and Gospel, something fundamental to Lutheran theology, he likens the Gospel to music in performance and the Law to musical notation on the page:

> The Gospel is the same as the *bfa bmi* as it is performed [that is, *musica ficta*, the unwritten adjustments in pitch made by singers in performance], the other pitches [*Claves*, that is, written pitches] are the Law. And the same as the Law obeys the Gospel so must the written pitches submit to the *bfa bmi*.[26]
> What is Law does not make progress, but what is Gospel does. God preached the Gospel through music, too, as may be seen in Josquin, all of whose compositions flow freely, gently, and cheerfully, are not forced or cramped by rules, and are like the song of the finch.[27]

The connection between music and theology for Luther also included the function of proclamation. In the preface to *Geystliche Lieder*, published by Valentin Bapst (Leipzig, 1545), Luther wrote:

> God has cheered our hearts and minds through his dear Son, whom he gave for us to redeem us from sin, death, and the devil. He who believes this earnestly cannot be quiet about it. But he must gladly and willingly sing and speak about it so others also may come to hear it. And whoever does not want to sing and speak of it shows that he does not believe and that he does not belong under the new joyful testament.[28]

In the *Tischreden* Luther acknowledged that 'Music is the greatest gift of God which has often induced and inspired me to preach.'[29] Lutheran liturgies, therefore, as they were developed from Luther's liturgical reforms, included both preaching and music as essential and complementary elements.[30]

Set against this background, the marginalia Bach entered into his copy of the Calov Bible can be seen in sharper focus. 1 Chronicles 29:21 reads: 'Here are the divisions of the priests and the Levites for all the service of the house of God . . .' Alongside Calov's commentary on the verse Bach wrote: 'NB. Splendid proof that, besides other arrangements of the service of worship [Gottesdienst], music too was instituted by the Spirit of God through David.'[31] The heading in the Calov Bible for the section 2 Chronicles 5:11–15 is 'How the Glory of the Lord appeared After Beautiful Music [in the Temple]'. In the margin by verse 13, Bach added: 'NB. Where there is devotional music, God with his grace is always present.'[32]

Bach's approach to his art was clearly in the theological tradition of Luther, but there were also practical implications of Luther's theology that had a material effect on his profession as a musician and teacher in the service of the Lutheran church.[33] The following comment of Luther is recorded in the *Tischreden*:

> Music I have always loved. He who knows music has a good nature.
> Necessity demands that music be kept in the schools. A schoolmaster must
> be able to sing; otherwise I will not look at him. And before a young man is
> ordained into the ministry, he should practice music in school.[34]

Luther did not destroy the choral tradition of the medieval school system but modified it and insisted that the teaching of music in these schools should have a primary importance, since they nourished and promoted the music of the church.[35] For example, the Thomasschule in Leipzig issued regulations in 1634, 1723 and 1733 in which the teaching and practice of music was carefully prescribed.[36] Thus Luther's association of theology and music was both theoretically and practically maintained in the Lutheran church. Until the latter part of the eighteenth century, when the combined influences of the Enlightenment and Pietism effectively destroyed the tradition, it was customary for students of theology to study music and, conversely, for musicians to study theology. On the one hand, this accounts for the fact that Henry Melchior Muhlenberg, 'the Father of American Lutheranism' (ordained in Leipzig in 1739), not only taught children in Pennsylvania in the early 1740s the substance of the catechism but also how to sing.[37] On the other hand, it also explains why the Thomaskantor in Leipzig was required to teach Luther's small catechism in Latin on Saturday mornings.[38]

## Luther's liturgical reforms

Luther's liturgical reforms, not always well understood in recent scholarship, were simultaneously conservative and radical: they were conservative in terms of liturgical change but radical with regard to theologically content.[39] The structure of the Latin Mass remained virtually intact in Luther's liturgical reforms, but the heart of the Roman rite, the Canon of the Mass, was severely abbreviated and theologically reinterpreted. In the medieval Mass the Canon was long, largely inaudible, and interpreted as a propitiatory sacrifice. Luther essentially replaced it with just the Words of Institution, or *Verba testamenti institutionis,* which were not simply to be audible but also to be sung by the celebrant. For Luther these words of Jesus Christ were not of propitiatory prayer addressed to God but words of open proclamation from God. Since these words proclaim the Gospel of Christ, Luther insisted that they should be sung.

Luther's two primary liturgical documents are the *Formula missae et communionis pro Ecclesia Vuittembergensi* (1523) and the *Deutsche Messe und Ordnung Gottesdienstes* (1526).[40] The *Formula missae* preserves the traditional structure of the Latin Mass, together with the associated chant. The Ordinary (Kyrie, Gloria, Credo, Sanctus and Agnus Dei) was also substantially retained,[41] as were most of the Propers (Introit, Collect, Epistle, Gospel, Gradual etc.), although there was a tendency towards simplification and the elimination of references to the sacrifice of the Mass. Most sequences were removed; those retained were related to the primary festivals, such as *Grates nunc omnes* for Christmas, and *Victimae paschali laudes* for Easter. In contrast to the Roman Mass, in which the congregation was essentially mute, Luther actively promoted the regular singing of vernacular hymns by the congregation within the evangelical mass. Thus from the beginning, Lutheran hymnody was closely related to the Eucharist,[42] which was defined thus in the Augsburg Confession (Art. 10):

> It is taught among us that the true body and blood of Christ are really present in the Supper of the Lord under the form of bread and wine and are there distributed and received.[43]

Although hymnody was employed elsewhere, the primary locations for vernacular hymns were after the Gradual and during communion. Sometimes *Graduallieder,* as they came to be known, effectively replaced sequences, but at festivals both a sequence and a hymn were sung, such as *Gelobet seist du, Jesu Christ* with *Grates nunc omnes* at Christmas, and *Christ ist erstanden,* or later Luther's reworking of it, *Christ lag in Todesbanden,* with *Victimae paschali laudes* at Easter. In the course of time, as congregational hymnals appeared, a distinctive corpus of *Graduallieder* developed so that eventually every Sunday, festival and special celebration had its own particular hymnody. By the eighteenth century these 'hymns of the day' had grown into a rich corpus of hymnody for the church year,[44] and the primary hymns of this sequence occur again and again in Bach's organ works and cantatas.[45]

In the *Deutsche Messe* of 1526 Luther provided for a vernacular mass.

But, as he explained in the preface, it was intended for villages and small towns where Latin was not understood and was therefore not a replacement for the *Formula missae*. The main differences, apart from language, are the expanded role of congregational hymnody and the musical implications of the *Formula missae*, which are fully worked out with specific notation in the *Deutsche Messe* of 1526. Here Luther develops the principle of the congregational hymnic versions of the Ordinary. In the course of time particular chorales came into almost universal use throughout Lutheran Germany:

| | |
|---|---|
| Kyrie | *Kyrie, Gott Vater in Ewigkeit* |
| Gloria | *Allein Gott in der Höh sei Ehr* |
| Credo | *Wir glauben all an einen Gott* |
| Sanctus | *Jesaja dem Propheten das geschah* |
| Agnus Dei | *Christe, du Lamm Gottes,* or |
| | *O Lamm Gottes, unschuldig* |

The Gloria hymn, *Allein Gott in der Höh sei Ehr*, was used almost every Sunday, which accounts for the large number of extant chorale preludes on the melody by Bach and other Lutheran composers.[46] Bach also included extensive organ settings of the Kyrie and Gloria melodies in the first part of his *Clavier-Übung* III,[47] composed various chorale preludes and at least one vocal setting of *Wir glauben*,[48] and included both German versions of the Agnus Dei in his choral music: for example, *Christe, du Lamm Gottes* in the final movement of Cantata 23 and *O Lamm Gottes, unschuldig* in the opening chorus of the St Matthew Passion. In the course of time the German Sanctus, *Jesaja dem Propheten*, was not sung as frequently as the others and it is therefore not surprising to find that it does not feature in any of Bach's compositions.

In addition to the eucharistic Hauptgottesdienst on Sundays and primary festivals, Luther also had a concern for corporate daily prayer. Luther and his colleagues developed a pattern for daily congregational worship in the morning and afternoon from the pre-Reformation monastic offices. These were essentially revised forms of the old offices of Matins and Vespers, with the addition of congregational hymnody and preaching. On the eves of special days, and on the afternoons of Sundays and major feasts, the vesper services were expanded to include additional material, such as extended prayer, and special music. These various vesper services came to be known by such differing names as *Betstunde*, *Vesperpredigt* and *Vespergottesdienst* (Prayer Hour, Vesper Sermon, Vesper Worship). Another name was *Katechismusexamen*, derived from the fact that it was customary to teach the substance of Luther's catechisms at Sunday Vespers, as well as on some weekdays. Luther provided hymns for each of the six parts of the Catechism:[49]

| Ten Commandments | *Dies sind die heilgen zehn Gebot* |
| Creed | *Wir glauben all an einen Gott* |
| Lord's Prayer | *Vater unser im Himmelreich* |
| Baptism | *Christ unser Herr zum Jordan kam* |
| Repentance | *Aus tiefer Not schrei ich zu dir* |
| Eucharist | *Jesus Christus unser Heiland, der von uns* |

As with hymnic versions of the Ordinary, the melodies associated with these hymns formed the basis for many congregational, choral and organ settings by Lutheran composers. The second part of Bach's *Clavier-Übung* III comprises two complete cycles of organ chorale preludes on these catechism chorales: one of settings for manuals alone and the other for manuals and pedal, corresponding to Luther's 'small' and 'large' catechisms.[50]

Following Luther's example, other prominent towns, cities and areas drew up their own church orders which incorporated most of the provisions of Luther's two liturgical forms; indeed, in the thirty years following the publication of the *Formula missae* in 1523, approaching 150 different Lutheran church orders were issued. Although the liturgical forms of these church orders had their distinctive features, the common use of Luther's liturgical writings nevertheless created a substantial unanimity of content. Saxony was divided into two territories: Ernestine Saxony, in which Wittenberg was situated, espoused the Reformation; but Albertine Saxony, which included Leipzig, was ruled by the pro-Catholic Duke Georg. However, Duke Georg died in 1539 and was succeeded by his brother Heinrich, who immediately made moves to introduce the Lutheran Reformation into Albertine Saxony. Luther preached in the Thomaskirche in Leipzig at Pentecost, 25 May 1539.[51] Later in the year a new hymn book was issued,[52] and a provisional church order, prepared by Wittenberg theologians, appeared on 19 September 1539. The following year it was revised, expanded and issued as *Agenda das ist kirchenordnung für die diener der kirchen in herzog Heinrich zu Sachsen fürstenthum gestellet* (Leipzig, 1540).[53] This church order was reprinted numerous times and remained authoritative throughout Bach's years in Leipzig. In practice throughout Lutheran Germany, such liturgical provisions combined much from the two liturgies of Luther, which, in such important towns as Leipzig, meant a liturgical practice which combined both Latin and German.

With an openness to traditional plainsong, the introduction of congregational singing, and Luther's positive endorsement of the role of music in worship, Lutheran liturgical forms led to the development of specific congregational, organ and choral music in the generations following on from the sixteenth century.[54] Lutheran liturgical music is a rich and distinctive tradition, which in many respects is both exemplified and extended in much of the music of Bach.

# 4 Bach's metaphysics of music

*John Butt*

NB. Where there is devotional music, God with his grace is always present
*(J. S. Bach, annotation to Calov's Bible commentary)*[1]

Pious men of strict observance can hardly see in art an obedient
maidservant ... rivalry begins, first, in rivalry between the religious spirit
and the aesthetically ... oriented man ... Religion is always imperialistic ...
but science, art, and ethics are also imperialistic ... and yet, the paths of
religion, art, ethics, and science not only cross, they also join.
*(Gerardus van der Leeuw)*[2]

Studies of theology, religious symbolism, allegory and rhetoric tell us
much about the historical context and function of Bach's music, but
alone they do not adequately reveal how Bach conceived of his music. In
other words, the purely theological viewpoint often illuminates the
message of Bach's music without giving any explanation of his conception of the medium. It is the very basis of my approach here to contend
that there may indeed be contradictions between the historical religious
context and, specifically, the metaphysical basis of his creative work.
Throughout, I negotiate a delicate and speculative tightrope: on the one
hand in conjecturing about Bach's own view of the task of composition
(and performance) from a sparse array of verbal documents, and on the
other in surmising what his music and certain tendencies in his compositional output may tell us.

While I offer a general study of some of the conceptions of music and
its relation to religion in Bach's age, I give particular attention to one particular hypothesis: that Bach saw the very substance of music as constituting a religious reality, that the more perfectly the task of composition
(and, indeed, performance) is realised, the more God is immanent in
music. Traditionally, something of this conception has been inferred
from the intertwining of the sacred and secular in Orthodox Lutheran
thought,[3] and indeed in Luther's own attitude towards music as a vital
aspect of the Christian life (see Chapter 3). Furthermore, the
Pythagorean tradition of viewing music as the sounding evidence of
God's creation was still evident in the writings of music theorists who
embraced natural theology. But an outright avowal of the immanence of
God and the sacred in music would have been unthinkable within
Orthodox Lutheranism.[4] As in most of the monotheistic religions, God is

essentially a figure transcending the imperfect earthly realm, accessible only through specific avenues (e.g. Revelation and the discipline of *faith*). To affirm – unequivocally – an immanent sacrality in music is to be open to the charge of pantheism, something which undercuts the distinction between God and this world, and something which could be seen to undermine the very transcendent basis of Christian morality.

In this light, the position of developed music *per se* is ambiguous, even within Orthodoxy and, specifically, in the case of Bach and his music. God who was central to Bach's life as an active and devout Lutheran is not always the same as the God of his compositional mind. And, as I hope to show in the next chapter, Bach's compositional mind can be illuminated – if it cannot directly be explained – by analogy with the metaphysics of rationalist philosophers of the seventeenth and eighteenth centuries, such as Leibniz and Wolff, and particularly by one of the most talented, yet marginalised, figures of the time, Benedict de Spinoza.

## Theological prescriptions for music

As a prelude to an examination of Bach's own attitude to the essence of music, the general context of theological opinion about music needs to be surveyed. In what ways was the nature of music associated with the religious? Here I consider prescriptions relating to sounding music as part of Lutheran worship, since these often reveal general presuppositions concerning its inherent value and sacred content. While this is only one side of the religious conception of music – the other being the music theorists' view of music as sounding number that was still held within the surviving scholastic field of *musica theorica* – the attitudes to music as practice are particularly telling, especially when music and Scripture are effectively placed in competition with one another. Which, according to the Orthodox Lutheran, should have priority? Much here helps to explain the environment for Bach and his creative career, yet it also uncovers new problems and inconsistencies and leaves Bach's untexted music virtually unexplained.

First, as Friedrich Kalb has shown, Orthodox Lutheran theologians of the seventeenth century never really accounted for the type of music that could loosely be defined as 'Baroque', i.e. that music which adopted the latest expressive devices from Italian opera and concertos.[5] In Kalb's words,

> The attitude of the Orthodox theologians toward music was throughout determined by the Netherland school, just as in the case of Luther . . . [who] often praises the beauty and the value of music with glowing words by referring to very specific examples. Orthodoxy follows him; but one looks in vain for a reference to contemporary music.[6]

Kalb stresses that music in worship is part of the by no means indispensable category of *adiaphora* (things that were neither commanded nor forbidden by Scripture) which includes such elements as Communion vessels, vestments, lamps and candles. But within this limitation, Lutheran Orthodoxy offers some of the most enthusiastic justifications of music in the history of church music: it 'is a spontaneous activity of life, inherent in God's creation'.[7] Joyce Irwin offers a modification of this view by showing that music was often elevated beyond the level of adiaphora, such as when the threat from Calvinism was great at the outset of the seventeenth century, and, of course, in the writing of some of the music theorists close to Bach's own age.[8]

Many seventeenth-century writers stress the parallels between the harmony of music and that of creation, often paraphrasing a popular line from the apocryphal Book of Wisdom (11:21) to the effect that God has ordered everything by mass, number and weight. This aphorism provided a useful synthesis of medieval theocentric thinking with the new mechanistic universe of the seventeenth century.[9] Some writings suggest that music is indeed a 'foretaste' of eternal life since there are Scriptural references to heavenly singing in praise of God. In terms of earthly function, music serves order, beauty and edification, and has a direct influence on the emotional disposition of human beings.[10]

While many theologians give enthusiastic justifications for the use of music, the stress they lay on the importance of the verbal text is crucial: both composer and performer should pay assiduous attention to what is being sung if the music is to have its correct affective result. For Frick, writing one of the most extreme defences of music in 1631,[11] good music with a bad text can be saved by applying a good text,[12] something which suggests that music has inherent worth, but that its 'magic' is dependent on text and the pious intentions of composer and performer.[13] Instrumental music is sometimes encouraged (in the light of many Old Testament references) but generally as an activity secondary to vocal music, and always as a support for singers and the all-important text.[14]

In short then, there is a tension between an appreciation of the intrinsic, God-given properties of music itself and the vital necessity that the music be put only to good use, always serving a suitable text. At the very least, one could infer that music could serve both God and the Devil with equal indifference. When it comes to text-setting, music is what one might term a 'promiscuous signifier'; it can – seemingly miraculously – be adaped to a variety of contexts.

A new respect for music for its own sake is evident with Erdmann Neumeister, the cleric who was largely responsible for introducing new

operatic forms into cantata texts around the turn of the eighteenth
century. He implies that his work as a poet is an extension of his vocation
as a preacher; his cantata texts are conceived as poetic elaborations and
compact summaries of sermon texts appropriate for each Sunday of the
church year. Beyond this, all his comments on the text relate to its structure and poetic style; elaborate music is to be seen in the same light as the
sermon, something which is obviously instructive and reliant on
Scripture, but also unashamedly poetic and, most importantly, rhetorical. While the concept of rhetoric strictly relates to the persuasive and
ordered presentation of a specific argument, it also carries with it the
sense of elaboration and, ultimately, openness of meaning. The emphasis
on ornament and style allows – knowingly or not – for a semantic ambi-
guity in both poetry and music. These two arts can both serve the interests of persuasive delivery and interpretation of Holy Writ, but they may
also serve to render its meaning so elaborate and multi-layered that a
closed interpretation is effectively postponed. Thus there inevitably arose
the considerable opposition to elaborate church music during the first
decades of the eighteenth century, Christian Gerber and Joachim Meyer
being the most avid Pietist protesters.[15]

## Religious music in music theory

It perhaps should also come as no surprise that many musicians from
within Lutheran Orthodoxy were also forceful objectors to the newest
operatic elements in church music. Bach's predecessor at Leipzig, Johann
Kuhnau, was suspicious of arias and recitatives as being connotative of
theatrical music.[16] Ironically, the surviving corpus of his cantatas shows a
plethora of arias (including da capo arias) and recitatives, revealing a tendency to absorb secular forms and styles that was not unlike Bach's.
According to the introduction to his *Biblische Historien* (1700) Kuhnau
still believed in a relationship between music and its affects on the listener
that was ultimately mathematically verifiable, but, at the same time, he
insisted that a textual programme was necessary to clarify the meaning of
any particular piece. For Kuhnau, then, several conceptions of music
seem to lie side by side: the 'old' view of music as sounding number, the
'newer' view that accounted for the connotative significance of certain
musical styles for particular audiences, and the traditional theological
view of music as unable to express anything unequivocally without a suitable text. Similar conflicts are evident in virtually all writings dealing with
the influx of newer, secular styles into church music during the first
decades of the eighteenth century, suggesting that music theorists were

unable to reconcile the Pythagorean priority of musical substance with the implications and decorum of stylistic categories.

Few writers, even those comparatively close to Bach, seem adequately to account for his creative personality. Buttstett, for instance, takes an approach that is altogether too conservative to account for Bach's attitude to composition. He wrote his *Ut, mi, sol, re, fa, la, tota musica et harmonia aeterna* (1716) as a rebuff to Mattheson's first treatise, *Das neu-eröffnete Orchestre* (1713). He accused Mattheson of a tendency to mix up and confuse the three traditional styles of music, 'Ecclesiae, Theatri, & Camerae':[17]

> What difference is there today between church, theatre, and chamber music?
> One is pretty much the same as the other. Nearly every kind of songful
> stuff is presently brought into the church along with the *stylus recitativus*
> *theatralis*, and the more merrily and dancingly it goes, the better it pleases
> most people.[18]

Thus, to an Orthodox theorist such as Buttstett, tradition was of foremost importance in defining church music and justifying its place within the liturgy; there was no sense of music, in all its manifold styles, as being essentially sacred. He could hardly have approved of Bach's blatant mixing of various musical styles and forms.

Mattheson's categorisation of style underwent considerable revision between the time of *Das neu-eröffnete Orchestre* (1713) and his largest and most developed treatise, *Der vollkommene Capellmeister* (1739). First, in 1717, he adopted Kircher's categories, as advocated by Buttstett (in the modernised form of the French lexicographer Sébastien de Brossard); in the 1730s he adopted (via the music critic Johann Adolph Scheibe) the categories advocated by Johann Christoph Gottsched in his groundbreaking study of German poetry: high, middle and low. By the time of the 1739 treatise, all these approaches were blended together. As Palisca has aptly put it,

> we have something that grew plantlike into a creeping, climbing organism
> that clings to the earliest triple trunk, while branching off into Kircher's
> nine-stemmed system, pruned by Brossard's sharp lexicographical shears,
> and finally domesticated to thrive in Gottsched's triple-tiered garden.[19]

By now church and private devotions are, to Mattheson, 'music's noblest mission', in which all styles can ultimately serve.

Here then, we have something which, superficially, looks tailor-made for Bach's creative activity: all styles can, and should, serve all levels of public and private devotion. As Irwin notes, Mattheson was the first theorist to suggest that music can serve as well as the sermon in proclaiming the Gospel, that preacher and cantor are to be placed on the same level;

indeed, she is prepared to admit that Bach's religious conception of music might owe more to Mattheson than to Luther himself.[20] Yet, as Arno Forchert shows, Mattheson's interest in church music seems to have been spurred on by the collapse of the Hamburg opera and, in particular, by current polemics about theatrical church music. For him, the stylistic advances of opera could now be defended only within the institutional framework of the church.[21] This is not to doubt the sincerity of his growing interest in the vitality and spiritual necessity of church music as the end to which all music should aim, but it is clear that his point of departure – in the operatic world – and his early Enlightenment musical tastes, do not immediately conjure up the figure of J. S. Bach. Indeed, he seems never to have shown particular concern for the latter's music. And, in any case, Bach's compositional style and attitude were formed well before the relevant writings of Mattheson appeared, in the mid to late 1720s.

Another author who seemingly offers an appropriate intellectual context for a composer such as Bach is M. H. Fuhrmann (1669–1745); he was, after all, one of the first writers to acknowledge the extraordinary art of Bach, especially as an organist.[22] He was brought up and worked in the Orthodox Lutheran tradition, and, like figures such as Kuhnau, Ahle and Werckmeister, was extremely learned. In one treatise in particular, *Die an der Kirchen Gottes gebauete Satans-Capelle* (1729), he treads a delicate course between allowing certain dramatic elements in church music and decrying 'those that are rich and fat in the spirit of opera' (p. 45).

There are, though, several ways in which Fuhrmann does not seem so appropriate a model for Bach. While much of his opening justification for music – that earthly music is a foretaste of that in heaven, and that musicians who perform the 'monophony' of earth will soon be performing the eternal 'polyphony' of heaven (pp. 19–20) – is typical of Orthodox Lutheran writings, he shows an unusually close allegiance with the Lutheran Pietists. At several junctures he evokes the authority of the leading Pietist, Spener, although he tries to present the latter's negative attitude towards elaborate music in a positive light (p. 48).[23] Given that he opposes cantatas with long recitatives, which are children of the fantastic theatrical style, from which hangs 'a large Italian afterbirth' (p. 41), it would be difficult to predict how he might have reacted to the extremely extensive and dramatic recitatives of a Bach Passion. Moreover, his comments on how negligent composers chop up texts (p. 43) are not dissimilar to Mattheson's own criticisms of Bach's text-setting.[24]

There is certainly no consensus concerning the sacred nature of music *per se*, and the general emphasis on the stylistic conservatism of church music hardly accords with Bach's Lutheran music. Furthermore, the status of secular music is left unclear (though writers such as Kuhnau, Buttstett and Fuhrmann imply that it is of lower status than texted sacred music). Bach's very considerable secular oeuvre thus appears problematic if viewed solely from within the context of Orthodox Lutheranism.[25] And herein perhaps lies the central question: did Bach really consider the value and meaning of music to be purely contingent on the use to which it is put and the appropriateness of its style for any particular context (as would be suggested by the writings of traditional theologians, theorists and the new breed of Enlightenment aestheticians), or is it to some degree independent of such considerations, something to be valued on account of its craftsmanship and specifically musical qualities? I will contend that his musical personality inclines more towards the latter.

## Bach's conception of music

Bach's own comments (and those from his closest circle) concerning the nature and function of music are few and far between. If we turn first to the ultimate purposes of music, the handful of dedications on title pages from Bach's oeuvre present a rather mixed picture. While the title page to the *Orgelbüchlein* presents the 'Praise of God' as the foremost aim, none of the others makes this explicit. The standard initials 'J. J.' ('Jesu juva' – 'Jesus help!') and 'S. D. G.' ('Soli deo gloria' – 'To God alone be glory!') are found at the beginning and end of church compositions, and of some, but by no means all, of the secular pieces.[26] Most dedications – unless explicitly made to an aristocratic patron, as in the case of the Brandenburg Concertos sent to Berlin and the *Missa* parts (BWV 232, Kyrie and Gloria) sent to Dresden – refer to the didactic purpose of the music or to the delight of the heart. In the case of the *Orgelbüchlein*, the didactic purpose ('for my neighbour's instruction') comes second to praise of God, but Bach dedicated works such as *The Well-tempered Clavier* Book I and Inventions solely to the instruction of youth (although he closed both with 'S. D. G.' or 'Soli Deo Sit Gloria'). The introductions to all parts of the *Clavier-Übung* (including the individually published Partitas of part I) affirm that the aim of the publication is the refreshment of the music lover's spirit.[27] Such dedications – central to the teleology of early aesthetic thought – were becoming standard practice in keyboard publications, and, indeed, Bach probably gave little attention to such conventional matters.

A rather different picture is suggested by the title-page to the short manuscript thorough-bass primer of 1738 attributed, relatively securely, to Bach:[28]

The thorough-bass is the most perfect foundation of music. It is played with both hands in such a way that the left hand plays the prescribed notes while the right adds consonances and dissonances so that a well-sounding harmony results for the glory of God and the permissible delight of the soul. And so the ultimate end or final purpose of all music and therefore also of the thorough-bass is nothing other than the praise of God and the recreation of the soul. Where this is not taken into account, then there is no true music, only a devilish bawling and droning.[29]

In fact, this is a direct paraphrase of the opening definition of F. E. Niedt's figured bass treatise of 1700,[30] and the basic dedication to the glory of God is a commonplace in German music theory up to the early eighteenth century. Furthermore the tone of the passage is entirely consonant with contemporary theory, showing the late flowering of the Pythagorean view of well-composed music as natural harmony.[31] It should also be noted that this is the opening of a treatise for keyboard and is only indirectly connected with texted church music. Thus Bach presumably held the view of traditional music theory that music *per se* is of sacred value.

However, the end of the quoted passage implies that the correct *intention* of the composer and performer is more important than the actual musical result, thus tempering the notion of music's intrinsic value. In contrasting this with the patently secularist title-pages of such publications as the *Clavier-Übung* cycle, we might perhaps conclude that Bach retained the glory of God as the ultimate purpose of all his compositional activity, but did not necessarily prescribe this for the public reception of his music. It may almost be that he assumed that his (the composer's) 'glory of God' would result in the 'permissible delight of the soul' on the part of the player and listener, as if there were a mechanical connection between a sacred compositional intention and a secular, earthly effect.

We might compare Bach's conception of the composer with his attitude towards his employment, specifically that within the Lutheran church. Much has been written on Bach's supposed 'Endzweck', as originally stated in his resignation letter as organist of St Blasius, Mühlhausen in 1708, namely his ultimate aim to establish a 'well-regulated Church Music'.[32] This term has been accepted to refer to the composition and performance of church music for every Sunday and feast day of the liturgical year, a patently Orthodox aim and one that was continually frustrated by Pietists (as was the case for Bach in Mühlhausen). Something of Bach's sentiment can also be sensed in the famous 'Entwurff' he sent to the Leipzig town council over twenty years later in 1730; this document is entirely preoccupied with the pragmatics of maintaining a 'well-appointed Church Music'.[33] Nowhere does he countenance that some may believe such music not to be necessary, and he clearly does not construe the document as a justification of established church music *per se*. He draws attention to the fact that many boys have been admitted to the Thomasschule who have no talent for music, suggesting that this violates the policy that all resident boys should be admitted primarily for their musical – rather than academic – talents (the policy is, incidentally, implied in the statutes for the school). It was this stipulation that lay at the heart of so many disputes between cantors and school rectors, from the closing decades of the seventeenth century to the end of the eighteenth.[34]

As William Scheide has argued, there is no doubt that Bach's 'Endzweck' played a large part in the development of his career: e.g. the organ preludes following the church year in the *Orgelbüchlein*, the Weimar cantatas and the three (or more) cycles of Leipzig cantatas. But, by 1730, it seems that he had largely fulfilled this aim, and indeed was sometimes quite nonchalant concerning the actual performance of his music in church.[35] It may well be that his concerns had changed somewhat by this time, his 'Endzweck' now being the preservation of a particular conception of music that was under increasing threat from early Enlightenment principles. This conception which I attribute to Bach I will term 'musico-centric', the view that the very substance of music both reflects and embodies the ultimate reality of God and the Universe.[36] In this view, music can be an important, and rhetorical, purveyor of text and semantic material, but it is not subservient to these functions. Clearly, such an attitude may derive from natural theology, and is obviously latent within Luther's own conception of music (see Chapter 3). However, as I have demonstrated above, by Bach's time there were evident tensions between a traditional respect for the innate goodness of music (something disputed even among the Orthodox Lutherans) and a general awareness of the subversive potentials of the art. In short, it was becoming ever more difficult to argue for the innate goodness of music in an age when reason was virtually the only arbiter and verbal text the only clear and 'natural' purveyor of human concerns, both sacred and secular.

Evidence for Bach's 'musico-centric' viewpoint can be found in his copy of the Calov Bible Commentary; here he emphasises both the godly origins of music and the sacredness of its practice. With the outline of 1 Chron. 26 he writes: 'This chapter is the true foundation for all church music that is pleasing to God etc.'[37] At 1 Chron. 29:21 he adds, 'NB. Splendid proof that, besides other arrangements of the service of worship, music too was instituted by the Spirit of God through David'.[38] Finally, and most tellingly, for 2 Chron. 5:13 he remarks that 'When there is a devotional music, God with his grace is always present',[39] something which suggests that the very act of music conjures up the presence of God.

Here we have the closest reference to music as a medium through which God becomes immanent, something which would have been heretical to the Pietists and perhaps also somewhat disturbing to many Orthodox thinkers, since it implies that music was on an equal footing with Scripture, officially the only true revelation of the transcendent godhead.

In all, it is obvious that Bach saw music as a fundamental tool of religion and essential to his religious life. It can further be argued that he believed music to be an essential component of the religion itself, indeed one of its defining characteristics. In the last year of his life he was accused of embellishing a pamphlet he had commissioned from the organist and theorist Christoph Gottlieb Schröter, a rebuttal to a notorious pamphlet criticising music in education by Johann Gottlieb Biedermann, school rector of Freiberg. Particularly significant is the addition (Bach's?) of the title 'Christliche Beurtheilung' (Christian judgement), which Schröter considered inappropriate for the content of his text. But for Bach – if he was indeed the editor – the cultivation of music clearly *was* a fundamental element of Christian dogma; it was part of the definition of being a Christian.[40]

While the comparatively small number of writings directly attributable to Bach himself has already given us a view of his conception of music, the most productive source from his circle is the defence written by the Leipzig lawyer and man of letters[41] Johann Abraham Birnbaum, in response to a famous criticism of Bach by Johann Adolph Scheibe (*Der critische Musicus* VI, 14 May 1737, pp. 46f.). This dispute has been widely covered in the literature,[42] but it is worth considering here the place of Scheibe's criticism within the context of the early Enlightenment attitude to music: as Scheibe affirms, Bach's music is indeed filled with 'an excess of art', his pieces are extremely difficult to perform, virtually every ornament that could be conceived is present in the notation, and indeed 'all the voices must work with each other and be of equal difficulty and none of them can be recognised as the principal voice'.[43]

Günther Wagner has stressed the fact that Scheibe is primarily concerned with Bach's vocal music, and observes that he is indeed quite complimentary towards Bach's music in other contexts.[44] Scheibe was certainly no advocate of simple, banal music, any more than his mentor, Gottsched, was necessarily an advocate of simplicity with regard to literature; nevertheless, Wagner perhaps underestimates the magnitude of Scheibe's criticism (after all, the texted music he addresses accounts for a large proportion of Bach's output, and the clear presentation of text was central to early aesthetic conceptions of music).[45] Scheibe's use of the term 'Schwulst' (turgidity) comes directly out of Gottsched's critical theories, where it was applied to the outmoded 'second Silesian School';[46] the specific Silesian poet with whom Scheibe compares Bach, Lohenstein, is also central to Gottsched's stylistic categories. Both keywords – 'Schwulst' and 'Lohenstein' – point to the inappropriateness of the poem and its ornamentation for the occasion it was written for, and to its over-rich expression and over-artistic construction; in short, this is a direct application of Gottsched's critique of the previous century's courtly bombast to Bach.

Underlying Scheibe's critique is the notion that Bach has no awareness of the differentiations of style and the proprieties of taste (this is made clearer in his second, and longer, article of 1738), and that he is so entirely preoccupied with music and so unfamiliar with the intellectual currents of the time, that he has had to employ the services of Birnbaum to make the defence for him (see also his satire of 1739[47]). There is probably a grain of truth in all these points, and indeed his use of the somewhat demeaning term 'Musikant' to describe Bach, was in some sense appropriate: a more honourable and traditional term such as 'Musicus' would apply rather to a university-educated scholar, someone with a keen interest in wider intellectual issues and the speculative theory of music (and indeed there is much evidence that these traits do not apply to Bach).[48] Scheibe clearly admired much about Bach's music *as music,* but he had strong reservations about the composer's aesthetic attitude, his whole concept of what music should be and how it should function in society. Indeed, given that Scheibe was a former pupil of Bach, it may well be that his criticism derives as much from his experience of the composer's personality as from the music itself.

We cannot be certain that Birnbaum wrote his first defence under the direct supervision of Bach,[49] but, as Christoph Wolff has observed, his detailed musical references (in particular to de Grigny, du Mage, Lotti and Palestrina) imply that he may have been working with material – and probably opinions – supplied by the cantor himself.[50] Furthermore his line 'The true amenity of music consists in the connection and alternation of consonances and dissonances without hurt to the harmony' is strongly reminiscent of the opening definition in the thoroughbass treatise that Bach adapted from Niedt (see above). In any case, portions of Bach's Obituary (prepared by C. P. E. Bach and Agricola, published 1754) and comments by other close pupils such as Marpurg and Kirnberger provide remarkably consistent substantiation of Birnbaum's points.

First there is a sense that the rules of music are an eternal and determined part of nature. As much as we today might see Bach's musical language and styles as historically contingent, there is a definite essentialist bias here: 'Where the rules of composition are most strictly observed, there without fail order must reign.' Birnbaum is also the first source for the well-known comment attributed to Bach:

that which I have achieved by industry and practice, anyone else with
tolerable natural gift and ability can also achieve . . . One can do anything
if only one really wishes to, and if one industriously strives to convert
natural abilities, by untiring zeal, into perfected skills.[51]

Here, then, we have a conception of the composer as somewhat akin to a
craftsman (ironically, this must have struck Scheibe as a telling justification for his use of the term 'Musikant'). The priestly model might also
come to mind: it is incumbent on the composer to do nothing more than
accurately expound the eternal mysteries of his particular faith. This attitude is also evident in much of Kirnberger's writings on his teacher. As he
said in a letter to the publisher of a new edition of Bach's chorales (J. G. I.
Breitkopf of Leipzig): 'The great J. Seb. Bach used to say: "It must be possible to do anything" and he would never stand to hear of anything not
being feasible. This has always inspired me, with my slight abilities, to
accomplish many otherwise difficult things in music, with effort and
patience.'[52] According to an anecdote, Bach did not ask for gratitude from
Kirnberger, but stressed that it depended only on the pupil to learn for
himself what had 'become known' to Bach, and that he should pass that
on, in turn, to the minds of 'other good students who are not satisfied
with the ordinary lirum-larum, etc.'[53] Again there is a clear sense here of
music as a timeless art which Bach saw as his responsibility to pass on to
all those who were not merely concerned with the contingencies of
fashion and taste.

As a corollary to the sense of Bach following – even discovering – the
'eternal rules of music' ('like no other in his time'), Birnbaum also considers the depth of Bach's ideas, all of which are followed through to the
smallest ornamental detail. We get the impression of a composer who
believed that every theme and formal strategy brings with it a host of
implications that can be realised sequentially or in combination and that
the completeness or perfection of any particular piece of music lies in the
satisfaction of the entire potential of a musical idea. Indeed the German
word 'Vollkommenheiten' (perfections/completeness) virtually becomes
a motto in Birnbaum's essay, a term which effectively unites the concept
of honest craftsmanship with a rather more metaphysical sense of 'perfection', as if the music acted as an immanent realisation of cosmic necessity. The Obituary notes that the deceased needed only to hear a theme in
order to be instantaneously aware of every artistic intricacy it implied and
C. P. E. Bach's letter to Forkel of 1774 contains a vivid anecdote about the
way his father listened to fugues, anticipating which contrapuntal devices
it would be possible to apply and joyfully nudging his son when his expec-
tations were fulfilled.[54] In the same letter, Emanuel also gives a sense of his
father's tendencies towards perfection/completeness, his ability to

convert a trio into a quartet in the spontaneous act of accompaniment. Indeed, one Leipzig intellectual from the Gottsched circle, T. L. Pitschel, noted in 1741 that Bach liked to take some notated music 'inferior to his own ideas' as the source for his inspiration, in order to set in motion his own superior ideas.[55] This is a particularly useful observation since it implies that Bach did not have the modern conception of individual genius, of copyright masterworks; all music could be the object of his own artistry, it was merely his business – perhaps, even, moral necessity – to improve and perfect the art.

It is interesting that Birnbaum joins the Enlightenment bandwagon of regarding art as the imitation of nature. However his modification of this fledgling aesthetic principle entirely unhinges his allegiance to the 'enlightened':

> The essential aims of true art are to imitate Nature, and, where necessary,
> to aid it . . . If art aids Nature, then its aim is only to preserve it, and to
> improve its condition; certainly not to destroy it. Many things are
> delivered to us by Nature in the most misshapen states, which, however,
> acquire the most beautiful appearance when they have been formed by
> art. Thus art lends Nature a beauty it lacks, and increases the beauty it
> possesses.[56]

Nature is thus conceived as something flawed, a haphazard allusion to a more perfect nature, which art can recover.

Most significant is the total lack of any reference to God within Scheibe's or Birnbaum's writings. Perhaps it would have been unseemly to invoke God in an 'enlightened' intellectual debate, where sacred and secular issues were to be strictly separated. On the other hand, it is not difficult to conjecture that a particular conception of God lies behind virtually every line by Birnbaum/Bach: God as the source of the language of music, God as the pattern of all perfection and God as the model of (misshapen) nature. In other words, God is so immanent that he virtually no longer needs to be mentioned.

These writers also see Bach's art as a matter for connoisseurs (a point that Bach himself made particularly clear on the title page of his *Clavier-Übung* III of 1739). A similar view is suggested by Agricola, in his defence of Bach against the criticism of Finazzi in 1750:

> Granted, the harmonies of this great man were so difficult that they did not
> always have the desired effect; for that reason, however, they serve as true
> refreshment for connoisseurs of music. Not all learned people have the
> ability to understand a new sound, but those who have gone so far into the
> profound sciences that they can understand him find, however, all the more
> pleasure and true use, if they read his [compositional] writings.[57]

Thus, the very difficulty of Bach's music in practice – indeed its failure to serve its immediate purposes – is testimony to its greater significance, requiring almost as much diligence from the connoisseur as the composer himself expended.

This point is taken up by Marpurg in his preface to the 1752 edition of the *Art of Fugue*:

> One would have to lack confidence in the insight of musical connoisseurs if one were to tell them that in this work are contained the most hidden beauties possible in the art of music . . . one could also draw the conclusion, taking into consideration everything that has ever come to pass in music past or present, that no one has surpassed him in thorough knowledge of the theory and practice of harmony, or, I may say, in the deep and thoughtful execution of unusual, ingenious ideas, far removed from the ordinary run, and yet spontaneous and natural; I say natural, meaning those ideas which must, by their profundity, their connection, and their organisation, meet with the acclaim of any taste, no matter of what country.[58]

Here, again, we encounter the 'natural', this time in the sense of the universal and timeless.[59]

Christoph Wolff, in his excellent study of these issues, suggests that Bach can only incompletely be appreciated according to the aesthetic preconditions of his own day. As many other scholars have affirmed, the aesthetic and critical apparatus of later ages helps us to appreciate the extent of Bach's genius. It is, after all, easy to see that he was largely unappreciated in his own age and that, in an historical sense, the intense concerns of his music leapfrog past the priorities of the Enlightenment and become more valid in the early years of the nineteenth century, when music was appreciated as an 'absolute', autonomous art. Thus concepts such as genius, the individuated autonomous art work, and the separability of the aesthetic from other aspects of life, culture and experience may legitimately be used from the standpoint of the *reception* of Bach's music. Nevertheless, the historical context is not necessarily exhausted or unproductive, particularly when it can reveal such inconsistencies and tensions between the various systems of belief. Bach's unique character and quality as a composer can thus be seen as partly generated by the frictions within his environment and career, frictions which help to render his music dynamic and challenging to later ages.

## 5 'A mind unconscious that it is calculating'? Bach and the rationalist philosophy of Wolff, Leibniz and Spinoza

*John Butt*

I shall attempt in this chapter to open up another mode of understanding Bach within his historical context. This involves comparing his attitude to music with the metaphysical theories of certain rationalist philosophers of the Baroque era. Much of what I propose here is certainly conjectural: there is no question of a direct line of influence, or even that Bach was necessarily conscious of these parallels. I intend rather to show that Bach's musical thinking and that of the metaphysicians might depend on a similar historical world-view and, more importantly, that Bach's musical mind is equal to the greatest intellects of the age, even though he had no academic pretensions himself.

Gottfried Leibniz (1646–1716) and particularly his pupil Christian Wolff (1679–1754) are certainly very close to Bach historically; indeed Leibniz's name has occurred intermittently in Bach criticism and research, particularly in the decades leading up to 1950.[1] Bach was closely associated with a follower of Leibniz and Wolff, Lorenz Mizler, who published Leibniz's famous dictum concerning music in the second issue of his *Musikalische Bibliothek*: 'Music is the hidden arithmetical exercise of a mind unconscious that it is calculating.'[2] But the metaphysics and personality of an older, consistently shunned figure, Benedict de (or Baruch) Spinoza (1632–77), may be even closer to Bach's creative personality, although – for religious reasons – this was something that Bach could not possibly have acknowledged consciously.[3]

It can be argued that the natural theology that emerges from the work of Leibniz and Wolff does not necessarily conflict with Orthodox Lutheranism,[4] since it offers an explanation of God's creation based on the observation and rationalisation of nature, which can stand next to – rather than against – Scriptural revelation. Nevertheless, there was always a potential tension between the two systems, especially when the rationalist philosophy was followed to its logical limits. Leibniz perhaps never satisfactorily explained away the determinist elements in his system, while Spinoza freely accepted the unpopular consequences of his.

Given that Bach was apparently not keenly interested in the 'drier' aspects of music theory,[5] there is no certainty that he necessarily read or even knew much of the rich tradition of rationalist philosophy in the seventeenth and early eighteenth centuries; indeed he would probably consciously have regarded it of little relevance either to his religious standpoint or to the activity of making music. However, Leibniz's pronouncements about music and mathematics share much with the basic stance of German music theory up to Mizler; together they embody the last flourishing of the Pythagorean approach to speculative music. The traditional elements of *musica theorica* are barely concerned with the actual practice of composition, other than providing the ultimate basis for the rules of harmony. Thus I shall largely ignore the significant mathematical element of rationalist philosophy. What I suggest, rather, is that Bach's attitude to music, his way of musical thinking,[6] closely paralleled the way in which Spinoza and Leibniz saw the world and its constitutive substance cohere. Indeed, his oeuvre might be viewed as the articulation of a metaphysical theory, not only of music but also of matter in general.

If Bach *were* to have possessed any philosophical writings in his library during the Leipzig years, they would almost certainly have been primarily those of Wolff, since his writings were those most widely published and used. Wolff was the primary philosopher of the early German Enlightenment, providing the philosophic basis for Gottsched's and later Baumgarten's poetics and aesthetics. Indeed, he is the only one of the three philosophers discussed here to develop a fledgeling aesthetic theory, and this perhaps makes him a figure more suited to illuminating the early *reception* of Bach's music than to portraying his attitude as a creative agent.

Advocating the complete synthesis of human knowledge and thought, Wolff's system is archetypally rationalistic and deductive, drawing much from Leibniz's famous contention that the solution of any human argument or conflict should commence with the words: 'Let us calculate.' On the other hand, his system was sufficiently flexible to be of influence on two figures, Lorenz Mizler and Johann Scheibe, who held essentially opposing positions, for and against the aesthetic legitimacy of Bach.[7] Moreover, it may well be that Birnbaum drew something of his terminology from Wolff in his defence of Bach.

An obvious similarity between Wolff and Bach is the uncompromising thoroughness of their respective methods. Indeed when Kant affirmed in the preface to the second edition of his *Critique of pure reason* in 1787 that Wolff was the 'author of the by no means vanquished spirit of thoroughness in Germany',[8] his comment could equally well have applied to Bach in the field of German composition. Furthermore, Wolff's definition of the art work, which is a part of his definition of the 'thing' in general, might well have resonated with Bach's conception of the musical work: an *opus* is a thing that has fulfilled its possibilities; in each there is something necessary by which it is determined in its own particular fashion. Such analysis could easily be applied to Bach's ability to construct a composition out of no more – and no less – than the possibilities of its themes and stylistic premises. The art of the composer resides in understanding both the possibilities of any particular situation and those factors which are 'determined'.

This is all basically a tame version of Leibniz's theory of substance, a fundamentally metaphysical outlook which does not account for the 'provincial' issue of practical art, but which might be even more illuminating of Bach's creative personality. Central to Leibniz's later thought is the concept of the world consisting of an infinite plurality of simple indivisible substances called 'monads', organised in a hierarchy with God as the keystone. Not only has each monad its own determined character and course, but, theoretically, the entire world can be inferred from a single monad. On the other hand, monads are not causally connected – while each is a mirror of (or 'expresses') creation, it is also 'windowless' – connections are the result of God's pre-conceived order.

Another means Leibniz uses to understand substance is his definition of propositions. He affirms that the concept of the subject also contains the concept of its predicates, or that everything that is true concerning a substance is also part of the concept of its substance:

> we should think of God as choosing, not just any Adam vaguely, but a
> particular Adam, of whom there exists among the possible beings in the
> ideas of God a perfect representation, accompanied by certain individual
> circumstances ... we must think of God, I say, as choosing him with an eye
> to his posterity, and so as equally at the same time choosing the one and the
> other.[9]                                                    (Letter to Arnauld, 12 April 1686)

Leibniz makes a distinction between logically necessary truths (where the inclusion of the predicate in the subject can be demonstrated in a finite number of steps) and the contingent truth (where an infinite number of steps are required); the latter is determined by the free decrees of God, while the former is derived from logically necessary laws that he has already set in place.

Although there are obvious problems with this system for someone – such as Bach (or indeed Leibniz himself) – who believes that human beings enjoy a measure of freedom, there is perhaps comfort in the fact that we as humans cannot possibly calculate the infinite steps required to determine a contingent truth. Moreover, Bach may well have thought in this manner when composing, determining which strategies followed by necessity from a particular theme or process (as determined, quasi-mathematically, by the rules of harmony and counterpoint) and those which followed contingently, where composition involved discerning something of the predicates pertaining to the idea.

Wolff applies some of this thinking to the intertwining elements of an art work. He sees the force which binds together compound things as order, which he defines as the similarity of manifold things in their presence beside one another, in other words, the element that allows us to see a compound thing as 'one'.[10] He subtly mixes the creative activity with the receptive facility by suggesting that each particular order works by its own set of general rules, rules which a creative agent must somehow recognise in advance. Furthermore, the more complex a thing, the greater the number of orders that must work together. By suggesting that every art work has a pre-ordained order, Wolff implies that each has an eternal and unchanging being, however this may be realised in practice.[11] While this view resonates with the concept of the autonomous art work in Romantic aesthetics, Wolff retains a strong teleological element: the work should be judged successful according to whether it fulfils the function for which it is designed; it is not an end in itself.

Wolff's theory comes closest to Birnbaum's defence of Bach when he deals with the concept of perfection, the qualitative purpose of a thing; Wolff demonstrates this with the typically Leibnizian example of a clock, the sum of whose parts work towards a single end. Perfections thus relate to the common ground to which everything is connected, the number of correspondences determining the number of perfections. Furthermore, from the standpoint of the beholder, true pleasure resides in contemplating perfection, something presupposing receptive ability and a knowledge of the rules of perfection; if one enjoys an art work without the requisite abilities, then one experiences only 'apparent pleasure'.[12] Indeed many deceive themselves when they judge a complex network of perfections, such as nature, and they are often not much better in judging a complex work of art.

With his belief in the certain power of mathematics to explain everything in every dimension, Wolff shared the view of many eighteenth-century post-Newtonians, that everything would ultimately be explained once humankind had enough time to perform the necessary calculations. We may surmise here that Birnbaum and Scheibe drew on two different aspects of Wolff's theory to arrive at their contradictory judgements of Bach: Birnbaum viewed Bach's music as a complex fabric of correspondences or perfections, the significance of which is not immediately evident to the untutored critic; Scheibe, on the other hand perhaps drew on Wolff's functional definition of perfection, the end to which a work is constructed. To Scheibe, such ends would include the decorum of style, particularly vocal, and the satisfactory communication of verbal text.

The concept of perfection is central to Leibniz's view of God and the world, since he believes that God has chosen what is ultimately the most perfect world from an infinite number of possibilities. Although many aspects of existence might seem imperfect to us, this is because we are unaware of the totality of things. Thus, while Wolff tends to view perfection as the fulfilment of certain worldly things (a rather more 'modern', Enlightenment view), Leibniz still leaves God and his eternal intentions as the central subject. Furthermore, God, as the most perfect being, is obviously a model for all other perfections. The formula he offers in *Monadology* (1714) for God's creative strategy may well work as an ideal summary of Bach's approach to composition: '[the differing] perspectives of a single universe in accordance with the different points of view of each monad . . . is the means of obtaining as much variety as possible, but with the greatest order possible; that is to say, it is the means of obtaining as much perfection as possible' (*Monadology*, paragraphs 57–8).[13] This statement sums up a dynamic specific to Bach's music, where the tendency towards variety is constantly challenging, and being challenged by, the tendency towards order and unity. Ulrich Leisinger has applied this line of Leibnizian thought to Bach's St Matthew Passion, linking it, on the one hand, to the variety of musical forms and genres and the double-chorus disposition of forces, and, on the other, to the supreme unity and cohesion of the whole.[14]

Rather than employing metaphysics to develop an aesthetic of the art work, Leibniz conversely often uses the specific example of music to demonstrate his metaphysics. For instance, the mixture of dissonance with consonance in music often creates more ultimate pleasure, since the restoration of order is that much more striking than a banal adherence to consonance (*On the ultimate origination of things*).[15] This is a useful way of demonstrating the reason for apparent imperfection in the universe; it all works towards an ultimate level of perfection. In this issue Leibniz perhaps comes closest to Orthodox Lutheran theology, where the trials of this world render the ultimate happiness of eternity that much more striking.

Furthermore, Leibniz's reference to consonance and dissonance relates directly to many statements in German compositional theory, not least that of Niedt/Bach (see Chapter 4, p. 53 above), to the effect that consonances and dissonances create a 'well-sounding harmony . . . for the glory of God and the permissible delight of the soul'. The emotive value of dissonance is also acknowledged in the standard contrapuntal treatises of the mid-seventeenth century, by Christoph Bernhard and W. C. Printz; their writing is the immediate source for the comment by J. G. Walther, Bach's Weimar associate and cousin by marriage, that 'Dissonances are the night, consonances are the day; the light would never again be as pleasant, if it was always day and never night. Dissonances are the winter, consonances the summer. The one is bitter, the other sweet. The one is black, the other white' (*Praecepta*, MS 1708, book 2, chapter 4).[16]

Thus the metaphysics of the Leibniz school provides an important key to Bach's creative mind, even – as Eggebrecht[17] suggested – the most directly appropriate and apt context for the principal forces in Bach's creative world. However, in some ways, the two are very different beings. For Leibniz, God is clearly still the ultimate origin of all things, but he plays a somewhat passive role, that of a supreme mathematician who seemingly waits until Creation has fulfilled its eternal purpose; and, given Leibniz's view of time and space as local illusions, God may never actually play an active role in creation. For an entirely immanent conception of God, we need to turn to Leibniz's elder contemporary Spinoza, someone whose obvious influence Leibniz was seldom willing to admit, since Spinoza's uncompromising positions exiled him from the mainstream of seventeenth-century thought and, indeed, society.

In some ways the association of Bach with Spinoza is curiously apt: like Bach, Spinoza could not have written as he did without the historical context of his particular age (in his case, the rationalist revolution of Descartes); yet he was largely misunderstood and ignored during his own lifetime. His radical theories resonate with the needs and perceptions of an astonishingly wide range of historically distinct ages and cultures. Like Bach, Spinoza seems to sit both in and yet somehow slightly outside the cultural mainstream of his age. Furthermore, virtually none of the individual components of their respective systems was, in itself, new; it was the way in which they were connected that was radically original.[18] For both, the process might be even more important than the remarkable conclusions.

Of course, there are many ways in which Spinoza seems an inappropriate figure to associate with Bach: he was the son of a Jewish family that had fled to Amsterdam from the Inquisition in Portugal, and his beliefs were such that he was excommunicated from the synagogue. His attitude to God would have clashed violently with Bach's Orthodox Lutheran beliefs: he advocated absolute determinism (at least for what he terms *true substance*), believed that the concepts of intellect and will (in the usual human sense, at least) do not apply to God and that reliance on the will of God means taking refuge in 'the sanctuary of ignorance' (*Ethics*, Part I, appendix).[19] But the very rigour and assumed certainty of his method closely parallels Bach's attitude to composition: Spinoza asserts that the entire propositional content of his *Ethics* follows by necessity from its first definitions and axioms, that the whole unfolds deductively as a necessity that any wise person could realise. In other words, the process is as important as the individual propositions. Spinoza concludes – just as Birnbaum or Marpurg might have done for Bach – that:

> If the way I have shown to lead to these things now seems very hard, still, it can be found. And of course, what is found so rarely must be hard. For if salvation were at hand, and could be found without great effort, how could nearly everyone neglect it? But all things excellent are as difficult as they are rare. (*Ethics*, Part V, Scholium to proposition 42)

For Spinoza, God is not only entirely immanent, he is – as a necessary and omnipotent being – the totality of all substance and thus the indwelling cause of all things (Part I, proposition 18). For Spinoza, as perhaps for Bach the composer, God might be conceived as a 'verb' rather than as a fixed, transcendent subject; the act of creation is a continuous process. This contrasts with Leibniz's conception of God as more the infinite subject in the grammar of the universe. Moreover, the infinite essence of Spinoza's God implies his very existence (Part I, proposition 11); this is the so-called *ontological* argument for God, which originated with St Anselm and – although rejected by the mainstream of philosophers and theologians – has been periodically affirmed by several figures since Spinoza, most notably Hegel.[20] One particular formulation of the ontological argument underlies much of Spinoza's thinking on God – and thus on reality – and this is the definition of God as the most perfect being that can be conceived; in other words, were God not to exist, he would be less than perfect. Although many subsequent writers have drawn attention to the wanton mixing of the categories of quality and existence, it is clear that Spinoza subscribes to the notion that not only does perfection necessitate existence but the more perfection anything has, the more 'reality' it possesses (Part I, proposition 11, Scholium; Part II, definition 6; Part V, proposition 40, demonstration).[21] There is also an important sense in which the perfection required by the ontological argument is of a very different order from the teleological perfection implied by Wolff (see p. 63 above), where an object is made perfect for a particular *purpose*. This is a sense of inherent, purposeless perfection, perhaps something suggesting a transcendence of common human inadequacies.[22]

We can sense a parallel between Spinoza's uncompromising attitude to reality and Bach's to music. The greater the perfection, the greater the reality and the more properties a thing possesses. This tendency can be traced not only in Bach's successive versions of certain pieces but also in his attempts to assemble comprehensive collections of particular genres (e.g. cantata cycles, Brandenburg Concertos) or compositional techniques (the late essays in variation, fugue and canon). Furthermore, perfections for Spinoza are not to be judged 'because they please or offend men's senses, or because they are of use to, or are incompatible with, human nature' (Part I, appendix); they point directly to – and indeed are part of – the true nature and perfection of God. Much of this could well have appealed to Birnbaum, Marpurg and Kirnberger, in their 'connoisseur's' view of Bach: perfection/reality exists and operates in a certain manner 'without any consideration of time', and the perfection of a piece of work is evident only to someone who 'knows the mind and purpose of the author of the work' (Part IV, preface); indeed, as Agricola suggested, the immediate effect of some of Bach's pieces on the listener might not have been the desired one.

The question of perfection also leads directly into the concept of the good: the good pertains to our attaining 'the model of human nature we set before ourselves' (Part IV, preface), in other words, the inescapable reality of being that particular modification of the godly substance that is human. Later on, Spinoza affirms that 'if joy, then, consists in the passage to a greater perfection, blessedness must surely consist in the fact that the mind is endowed with perfection itself' (Part V, Scholia to proposition 33) and, finally, that 'blessedness is not the reward of virtue, but virtue itself' (Part V, proposition 42). Thus blessedness is a particular state, associated with virtue, as it were a by-product of the process towards perfection. This is also the source of true *pleasure*, something akin to the 'permissible delight of the soul' which Bach allowed as the corollary of creating music to the glory of God (see p. 53, above).

There is certainly a sense in which Bach saw the act of perfecting compositions and completing compositional tasks as a vital, almost ethical, necessity. It is perhaps not surprising that Bach never completely 'finished' works in the sense that would have been understood in the era of Beethoven, a period with which so much of his compositional thinking struck a particular resonance. His obsessive 'tinkering', even with works that were to all intents and purposes 'finished',[23] suggests that the process towards perfection was continuous, one that would essentially last until the end of his life. In this sense then, the reworking and compilation of earlier compositions was just as vital an activity as 'original' composition. Bach shared much with his age in the sense that he saw the product of composition as 'music' rather than 'musical works';[24] it was common practice to transfer music from one functional context to another, thus conveniently satisfying the demands of a specific occasion rather than the ethical pursuit of 'the original'. However, when, in the latter part of his lifetime, time was not so pressing as to necessitate recycled composition, he nonetheless still drew together pieces of earlier origins.[25]

Spinoza's act-oriented approach to perfection and blessedness, his emphasis on immanence, is also a useful means of understanding Bach's attitude to *sounding* music. In other words, the act of performance is the archetypical way of 'completing' a piece, of rendering music as a living process. Today, when the notated bulk of Bach's oeuvre is all that remains, it is easy to forget his stature as a performer, and the importance he accorded to music as an active process. Bach certainly held something of a Spinozian view of music when he affirmed that 'Where there is devotional music, God with his grace is always present' (see p. 46, above).

In accordance with Spinoza's particular conception of God, his view of substance is inevitably monist; all substance is essentially one. In Leibniz's terms then, Spinoza's infinite substance is somewhat akin to a single monad. Thus those things which appear to us as separate things are not strictly *substances* but *modifications* (modes) of substance, modifications of attributes of God (Part I, corollary to proposition 25). Bach's attitude to the musical substance of his day is equally monist: all styles and idioms seem subjugated to the one concept of music; styles and instrumentations can be combined in entirely unorthodox ways which often run in the face of the functional categories of music. To him, the conventional categories and stylistic prescriptions were doubtless ephemeral 'modes' rather than essential characteristics of the one substance of music. While he omitted to compose in a few particular genres (opera, in particular), not one style that was available to him seems to be absent from his oeuvre; he treated the lightest *galant* and the strictest *stile antico* idioms with equal intensity. Furthermore, he did not have a concept of individual, strictly differentiated musical works; those pieces which he seems to have preserved with particular pride (such as the Mass in B Minor and the St Matthew Passion) are, rather, more-or-less perfected exempla of his larger work. In some ways, it may well be productive to consider his entire oeuvre as a single musical work, of which the individual instances are – literally – *pieces* ('Stücke').

The other side to Spinoza's metaphysics is the concept of the *idea*, which is a direct corollary of the single, infinite substance. Here he differed from Descartes, who had advocated that thinking and extended substance were entirely different entities. Indeed, as Spinoza affirms, 'the order and connection of ideas is the same as the order and connection of things' (Part II, proposition 7). And, just as human substance is part of the infinite substance of God, so is the human mind 'part of the infinite intellect of God' (Part II, corollary to proposition 11). The human mind usually has only 'a confused and mutilated knowledge of itself', its body and external bodies (Part II, corollary to proposition 29); yet since all *individual* things are contingent and corruptible, 'every idea which in us is absolute, or adequate and perfect, is true' (proposition 34). There are many ways in which Bach's music can be seen as blurring the distinction between 'idea' and 'extended substance'. Bach's famous title page to the second autograph of his Inventions and Sinfonias states that the pieces are designed not alone to show the student how to have 'good inventions', but also how to develop and extend these ideas and at the same time to develop a specifically *cantabile* style of playing.[26] To Bach, any particular idea immediately implied its own extension in notated musical substance, which in turn promoted further ideas in realised musical performance.

True ideas (which can be manifest in extended substance) are directly bound into Spinoza's theory of knowledge: knowledge of the first and lowest kind is *opinion* or *imagination*, the second kind is the knowledge gained purely through *reason*, while the third and highest kind is *intuition*, that which 'proceeds from an adequate idea of the formal essence of certain attributes of God to the adequate knowledge of the essence of things' (Part II, Scholium 2 to proposition 40). Spinoza demonstrates this with a simple mathematical problem, the answer of which leaps out intuitively when the numbers are small (i.e. we use the third kind of knowledge),[27] but has to be calculated with larger integers (i.e. we have to resort to the second kind of knowledge). The third type of knowledge thus transcends mere technique and calculation, just as Bach could apparently conceive of a musical idea and its extension in a single instant. Such knowledge, which is 'necessarily true', is, to Spinoza, clearly akin to the creative act of God, something free from any of the anthropomorphic trappings of reason, emotion and will. As he later concludes, 'knowledge of God is the mind's greatest good; its greatest virtue is to know God' (Part IV, proposition 28). The direct consequence of the third type of knowledge is 'the intellectual love of God', which is 'joy, accompanied by the idea of God as its cause', the only love (and emotion) that is eternal (Part V, propositions 32–4).

Another consequence of this third type of knowledge is that the closer one comes to an adequate idea, the less personal it becomes, individuality persisting only in error, as it were. This seems very close to Bach's personality, for whom basic talent and industry are the only secrets of his art; according to him, anyone who had achieved the same intuitive level of knowledge would compose in much the same manner. The activity of invention is thus close to realising the spirit of discovery.

Spinoza does not resort to a callous, passive form of determinism: we should derive infinite satisfaction from the *active* pursuit of the necessary: 'we can want nothing except what is necessary, nor absolutely be satisfied with anything except what is true. Hence, in so far as we understand these things rightly, the striving of the better part of us agrees with the order of the whole of Nature' (Part IV, appendix 32). Freedom entails the acceptance of absolute determinism and the fullest possible awareness of it; at the same time, it means that we should not be subject only to the influence of external, merely contingent objects and emotion. This delight in the necessary accords closely with Bach's intense concern for the possibilities and ramifications of any particular musical idea; in a sense, his pieces, as notated musical substance, end when these have been fulfilled. He would surely have agreed with Spinoza's statement that 'the more we understand singular things, the more we understand God' (Part V, proposition 24).

Bach and Spinoza share a similar distrust for the contingencies of fashion and the concept of historical progress: 'all particular things are contingent and corruptible . . . we can have no adequate knowledge of their duration' (Part II, corollary to proposition 31). Furthermore, reason dictates that we perceive things 'under a certain species of eternity' (Part II, corollary 2 to proposition 44). Both the Birnbaum defence and the Obituary of Bach suggest that he saw music 'under a certain species of eternity', and that, while he was aware of the changing tastes and styles of his age, he thought of music as a timeless art that transcended nation and time. While Scheibe might have considered him to be ignorant of the decorum for the styles and genres of the age, Bach quite simply had no interest in the issue of appropriateness. On the other hand, he was intensely interested in all the styles of his age with his tendency towards the comprehensive assimilation of each dialect and his continual search for new possibilities of adaptation and combination.

Spinoza dedicates a large part of his *Ethics* to the understanding and control of the emotions ('affects'); these he sees as 'modifications of the body' rather than aspects of the one true substance; they are 'inadequate ideas' with which we are passively, rather than actively, involved. While he could hardly advocate a complete negation of the passions, their inadequacy can be mitigated through understanding them and by directing them in such a way that they become part of the mind's endeavour 'to persevere in its being'. This attitude to the emotions is a useful way of interpreting Bach's treatment of the *affects* in his own music. The emotional content of both his texted and untexted music is certainly as intense as that in any music of the time. However, Bach is never satisfied merely with representing or even *imitating* the various affects; there is a real sense in which they become part of the very substance of the music, in one way objectified and controlled, but in another entirely immanent in the notes. The 'normal' effect of the emotions is somehow transcended to give the ultimate catharsis in which the music does for us our weeping, consolation and transcendence of the passion in a single piece. This is particularly evident in Bach's very Lutheran tendency to provide cheerful, dance-like music for the believer's acceptance of death; quite often he employs the most patently secular music at this juncture as if to suggest that the impulse for worldly joy can be redirected towards heavenly joy. In a real sense, then, both the rhetorical texted works and the most abstract polyphony of the late works demonstrate a distillation of the one eternal emotion, 'the intellectual love of God'.

In all, Bach's creative activity needs to be seen from several angles: the functional context for music lies largely in the long tradition of Orthodox Lutheranism, with all its tensions and internal inconsistencies. Bach doubtlessly saw the value of music in this field as indispensable, as indeed he probably also saw its role in royal courts. Such functional motives need to be matched – and in some ways, contrasted – with the metaphysical conceptions Bach held of music. Something of this can be gleaned from the long traditions of music theory which stress, in varying degrees, the mathematical certainty and the emotive value of music. However, a study of the rational metaphysics of the seventeenth and early eighteenth centuries is even more productive, since it can show that the intensity and sophistication of Bach's musical thought matches that of the most outstanding philosophers of the age. It may be, moreover, this intellectual weight – the Spinozian fusion of active thought and notated musical substance – that rendered the reception of Bach so significant during the nineteenth century.[28] A high point in musical metaphysics retroactively becomes the foundation of an aesthetically based approach to music history. I do not contend that there is a causal relation between the philosophy of Spinoza and Leibniz and the musical thought of Bach; rather – to use a favourite analogy of Leibniz – the two coincide like two perfectly-crafted clocks, pre-ordained to give the same readings by the relentless will of God – or is it culture?[29]

PART II

# Profiles of the music

# 6 The early works and the heritage of the seventeenth century

*Stephen A. Crist*

Johann Sebastian Bach's earliest compositions have long occupied an ambiguous position within his oeuvre. On the one hand, many musicians and scholars have compared them unfavourably with the masterpieces of his later years. As early as 1802 Johann Nicolaus Forkel wrote that, despite 'undeniable evidences of a distinguished genius', at the same time Bach's early works contain 'so much that is useless, so much that is one-sided, extravagant, and tasteless that they are not worth preserving (at least, for the public in general)'.[1] Nearly 200 years later, Malcolm Boyd has stated his opinion that 'few, if any, of the works [Bach] wrote before leaving Mühlhausen at the age of twenty-three would be remembered to-day if they had been composed by anyone else'.[2] On the other hand, even if Bach's earliest efforts do sometimes disappoint, they nonetheless possess a certain inherent interest because of what he subsequently accomplished, and they have therefore spawned a large body of research. As Peter Williams has eloquently put it, 'the stages by which the world's most gifted step beyond the confines of local art must always be of great interest and importance'.[3]

The early works have not yielded their secrets willingly, however. On the contrary, although several discoveries have greatly increased what is known about them, many fundamental questions remain unresolved. For this reason, the present chapter must be regarded as a report of an on-going discussion. There has not even been general agreement about what constitutes Bach's 'early' period. Although Alfred Dürr included the Weimar works (1714–16) in his monograph on Bach's 'early' cantatas,[4] Christoph Wolff subsequently advocated limiting this classification to the instrumental and vocal works composed up to c. 1708, when Bach began his tenure as court organist in Weimar and simultaneously 'left behind the truly formative stages [of composition] and established his own stylistic personality'.[5]

## Obstacles to research

The list of unanswered questions about Bach's early years is already lengthy and continues to grow. This is largely a consequence of the regrettably small amount of documentary evidence surviving from this period. For instance, there is no direct testimony about when Bach began to compose, although one assumes that it was between the ages of twelve and fourteen (1697–9), when he was living with his eldest brother, Johann Christoph, who was organist at the Michaeliskirche in Ohrdruf and had been a student of Johann Pachelbel.[6] To illustrate the uncertainties that attend the investigation of this music, one must look no farther than to some of the best-known pieces among the three performance media that dominate the early period. Take, for instance, the famous Toccata in D minor for organ (BWV 565), which was popularised in Walt Disney's animated film *Fantasia* (in Stokowski's orchestral transcription) and remains the quintessential example of Bach's music in popular culture. Is it not ironic that serious questions have been raised about whether this supposed paragon of Bach's style (and of Baroque music in general) actually has anything at all to do with Bach?[7] Or consider, among the harpsichord works, the 'Capriccio on the absence of his most beloved brother' (BWV 992), traditionally associated with the departure of Bach's brother, Johann Jacob, to join the Swedish army. It has now been pointed out that the word 'fratro' in the earliest manuscript sources refers not to a blood brother but rather to any close fraternal relationship, and that there is actually no evidence whatsoever connecting the piece with Johann Jacob or any other specific individual.[8] Even a seemingly rudimentary matter, such as determining which cantata is the earliest, bristles with questions. The discovery that *Denn du wirst meine Seele nicht in der Hölle lassen* (BWV 15) was composed by Bach's cousin Johann Ludwig[9] served as the point of departure for Gerhard Herz's essay on *Aus der Tiefe rufe ich, Herr, zu dir* (BWV 131), the next candidate as Bach's earliest cantata.[10] Subsequently, this work's privileged position was called into question by stylistic evidence suggesting that *Nach dir, Herr, verlanget mich* (BWV 150) predates all the other early cantatas (BWV 4, 71, 106, 131 and 196).[11]

The reason for such uncertainty is not difficult to discern. Only a handful of autograph manuscripts of Bach's early works has survived.[12] The other compositions are preserved in a motley assortment of manuscript copies with varying degrees of proximity to the composer. While some were notated by Bach's relatives, friends, and students during his lifetime, others were copied out by anonymous scribes in the second half of the eighteenth century or even later.[13] The wide variety in both the quality and the number of manuscripts for a given work has meant that each composition must be evaluated on its own merits.

Another vexing problem is the stylistic gulf between Bach's early compositions and his later, more familiar, works. Earlier in this century, the unfamiliar traits of many youthful pieces engendered an attitude of extreme scepticism and led to the rejection of some as inauthentic.[14] Later, scholars became more generous in their opinions, recognising that extreme stylistic differences between works composed during Bach's adolescence and those written later in life are to be expected. It remains to be seen, however, whether it is possible to formulate reliable criteria for distinguishing authentic early Bach compositions from those by other composers.

## Delimitation of the repertory

Two important discoveries of the 1980s have already put studies of Bach's youthful output on a more solid footing and may eventually provide keys to resolving some of the uncertainties concerning authenticity and dating. The first is the identification of the compiler and main scribe of the Möller Manuscript and the Andreas Bach Book (the two most important sources containing keyboard music by the young Bach) as the composer's eldest brother, Johann Christoph.[15] Not only does this solve a mystery that had eluded several generations of scholars, but it strengthens immeasurably the case for the authenticity of the twenty-seven pieces attributed to J. S. Bach in the two books.[16] For it stands to reason that the brother who was Sebastian's surrogate parent for five years and gave him his first keyboard lessons would be an exceptionally reliable witness concerning the authorship of these pieces.

The Möller Manuscript, the older of the two, was compiled between the end of 1703 and c. 1707.[17] In addition to works by approximately twenty other German, French and Italian composers, it contains a dozen pieces by J. S. Bach (out of fifty-four), more than any other individual:

> Prelude and Fugue in C major BWV 531
> Prelude and Fugue in G minor (early version) BWV 535a
> Prelude and Fugue in D minor BWV 549a
> Canzona in D minor BWV 588
> 'Wie schön leuchtet der Morgenstern' (organ chorale) BWV 739
> Suite in A major BWV 832
> Suite in F major BWV 833
> Prelude and Fugue in A major BWV 896
> Toccata in D major (early version) BWV 912a
> Fantasia in G minor BWV 917
> Sonata in A minor BWV 967
> 'Capriccio on the absence of his most beloved brother' BWV 992

The compilation of the Andreas Bach Book began around 1708, shortly after the Möller Manuscript was finished, and was completed c. 1713 or later.[18] It too contains over fifty keyboard works, including fifteen by Bach:

Fantasia in B minor BWV 563
Fantasia in C major BWV 570
Fantasia in C minor BWV deest
Fugue in C minor on a Theme of Legrenzi BWV 574b[19]
Fugue in G minor BWV 578
Passacaglia in C minor (early version) BWV 582
'Gott durch deine Güthe' (organ chorale) BWV 724
Overture Suite in F major BWV 820
Toccata in F♯ minor BWV 910
Toccata in C minor BWV 911
Toccata in G major BWV 916
Prelude in C minor BWV 921
Fantasia and Fugue in A minor BWV 944
Fugue in A major BWV 949
*Aria Variata* BWV 989

Now that the authenticity of these pieces is secure, they can be used as a base line against which to judge many others in manuscripts whose connections with Bach are less certain. Among the free organ works, this includes five additional preludes and fugues (BWV 533/533a, in E minor; BWV 536, in A major; BWV 543a, in A minor; BWV 545a, in C major; and BWV 550, in G major), three individual preludes (BWV 551 and 569, both in A minor; and BWV 568, in G major), the toccatas in D minor (BWV 565) and E major (BWV 566), the Fugue in B minor on a Theme of Corelli (BWV 579), and the Pastorale in F major (BWV 590). A lively discussion about several of these pieces is already under way. As was mentioned earlier, there are good reasons for doubting the authenticity of the Toccata in D minor (BWV 565). Similarly, on the strength of a detailed reexamination of the sources and style of BWV 536, David Humphreys has argued that only the prelude is by Bach, and that the anonymous fugue is 'a wooden, pedestrian piece of work composed in a faceless idiom which could on internal evidence be attributed to any one of a dozen minor organist-composers active during or slightly after Bach's lifetime'.[20] The case for the authenticity of the Pastorale (BWV 590), on the other hand, has received strong, new support, and its date of origin has been shifted from the early period to the Leipzig years.[21]

An even larger number of harpsichord works attributed to the young Bach are transmitted in sources other than the Möller Manuscript and the Andreas Bach Book. These include three suites (BWV 821, in Bb major; BWV 823, in F minor; and the *Ouverture* in G minor BWV 822), three toccatas (BWV 913–15, in D minor, E minor and G minor, respectively), the Prelude and Fugue in A minor (BWV 895), an isolated prelude (the Praeludium in A minor BWV 922), six fugues (BWV 946, 950 and 951a, in C major, A major and B minor, all on themes by Albinoni; BWV 947, in A minor; and BWV 954 and 955, both in Bb major on themes by Reincken and Erselius, respectively), three sonatas (BWV 963, in D major; and BWV 965 and 966, in A minor and C major, both of which borrow from sonatas by Reincken) and the Capriccio in E major (BWV 993). Although they are covered briefly in an excellent book on Bach's keyboard music published in 1992,[22] these pieces have not yet received the intensive scrutiny they deserve.[23] Again, the repertory of the Möller Manuscript and the Andreas Bach Book is sure to play a key role in resolving the remaining questions about their authenticity and dating.

The other major recent contribution, which has already begun to cast new light on the early works, is the discovery of thirty-three Bach organ chorales in a manuscript at Yale University.[24] Although it was penned in the last decade of the eighteenth century,[25] the Bach pieces it contains apparently were written about 100 years earlier, when the composer was a teenager. The so-called Neumeister chorales are an uneven mixture, containing embarrassing errors of musical grammar (e.g., numerous parallel fifths and octaves) alongside glimmers of the greatness that was to come.

Thirty-one of the thirty-eight organ chorales attributed to J. S. Bach in the Neumeister manuscript were hitherto completely unknown (they have been assigned the numbers 1090–1120 in the revised edition of the BWV).[26] Two others (BWV 714 and 957) were known from other manuscripts, but in different forms from those in the Neumeister Collection. The authenticity of two of the other five Neumeister chorales with concordances in other manuscripts (BWV 719 and 742) was previously considered so doubtful that they were excluded from the new critical edition of Bach's works (however, a third, BWV 737, was included).[27] The two remaining pieces (BWV 601 and 639) were the last J. S. Bach works to be copied into the Yale manuscript. They were also the first entries in the autograph of the *Orgelbüchlein*. As such, they constitute an important link between the two collections. It is now clear that the Neumeister chorales preceded the *Orgelbüchlein* and paved the way for it.[28]

Although the pieces in the Neumeister Collection match other early Bach organ chorales in their level of technical mastery and expressivity, their authenticity has not been universally accepted.[29] It has been noted, however, that despite occasional lapses, the highly original compositional approaches in the chorales attributed to Bach constitute strong stylistic evidence that they were indeed composed by him.[30] Werner Breig has shown that Bach attempted to give each work its own individual profile (the principle of *Werkindividualisierung*).[31] Moreover, Russell Stinson has strengthened the case for the authenticity of the Neumeister chorales by pointing out several stylistic features that are present both in the Neumeister pieces and in indisputably authentic Bach compositions but are not otherwise characteristic of organ chorales from this period.[32]

The Neumeister Collection provides a much clearer picture of Bach's early chorale style than was previously attainable. It also reveals valuable new insights about his models. In particular, the dozen chorale settings by Bach's father-in-law, Johann Michael Bach, substantially increase our knowledge of his output.[33] It is now clear that J. M. Bach was 'one of the major seminal figures who established the style and typology of the late-seventeenth-century Middle German chorale prelude', and from whom J. S. Bach derived the basic idea and structure of compositions in this genre. Bach was apparently acquainted with J. M. Bach's organ chorales as much as a decade before 1707, when he married the latter's daughter, Maria Barbara.[34]

As with the free organ and harpsichord works discussed earlier, a large number of organ chorales in other manuscripts are thought to date from Bach's early period. These include BWV 700, 723 and 741 ('very early', according to Ernest May); BWV 696–9, 701–5, 707, 712, 716, 718, 720, 724, 733 ('pre-Weimar', i.e., before 1708); and BWV 694–5, 710, 715, 722, 726, 729, 732, 734, 738 (possibly pre-Weimar).[35] To this group should be added the sets of variations on chorale tunes, the partitas (BWV 766–8 and 770).[36] While May has provided a useful overview of Bach's chorale-based compositions, much work remains to be done in establishing a definitive roster of early works and especially in assimilating the stylistic evidence from the Neumeister Collection.

## The changing face of Bach's early works; influences and their assimilation

It should be clear by now that many of the remaining questions about Bach's youthful compositions concern fundamental matters of chronology and authenticity. While the willingness to reconsider these factors is a welcome change (especially after decades of extreme, and often unwarranted, scepticism), too generous an attitude can lead to distortions in the opposite direction. For instance, it has been suggested that a Fantasia in B minor in a mid-eighteenth-century miscellany in Durham (Durham

Cathedral, Ms. Mus. E 24) might be an authentic Bach work that originated 'in the first decade of the 18th century'.[37] But David Schulenberg is surely justified in noting that it 'is in the style of a late seventeenth-century violin piece, resembling Bach's early style only superficially'.[38] Similarly, the sources and style of the 'Dobenecker' Toccata (BWV Anh. II 85) require particular circumspection. Although a plea to re-evaluate its authenticity has recently been made, the jury is still out concerning this piece.[39]

Another vital area of enquiry is the relationship between Bach's early works and the music of his predecessors and contemporaries. While the task of evaluating his output in its music-historical context dates back to Spitta in the last third of the nineteenth century, in the intervening years Bach's greatness has too often been extolled at the expense of the seventeenth-century masters whose music he took as models for his own.[40] In addition, since Bach rarely appropriated the elements of his models wholesale, it is often difficult to pinpoint influences precisely. Nonetheless, a good deal of progress has been made.

Bach possessed highly developed powers of discrimination as well as an uncanny ability to assimilate diverse ideas and techniques. He strove at all times to develop, improve and even perfect the traditions to which he was heir.[41] Bach's earliest music was most strongly indebted to the Central German (especially Thuringian) musical culture in which he grew up. But early on he assimilated into his style elements of the North German tradition, and a number of studies have sought to define the exact nature of this influence.

The chorale fantasy and the monodic organ chorale are both North German forms that made a decisive impact on Bach's music.[42] Specific characteristics of Bach's organ chorales that reveal his absorption of North German traditions include idiomatic writing for the organ, heightened expressivity, increased length, and the thematic individuality of each piece.[43] In the realm of the free organ works, the influence of the North German *stylus phantasticus*, with its improvisatory qualities (especially the sectional approach to form and extreme contrasts in tempo and dynamics), is found occasionally in works such as the Toccata in E major (BWV 566). It is more readily observable in the keyboard toccatas (BWV 910–16), however, despite their lack of obbligato pedal.[44] Bach inherited from the multipartite toccata (the chief form of the *stylus phantasticus*) the tendency towards formal expansiveness, the virtuoso treatment of the pedal in organ works, and the propensity to write at a professional level (in contrast to the focus on the amateur in the Central German tradition).[45]

Among specific individuals, the great organist in Lübeck Dietrich Buxtehude has long been recognised as a seminal influence on the young

Bach. Perhaps the most important aspect of Buxtehude's legacy was his preference for 'diversity and individuality', which was to become a hallmark of Bach's approach to composition as well.[46] It used to be thought that Bach's journey on foot from Arnstadt to Lübeck during the winter of 1705–6 marked the beginning of his acquaintance with Buxtehude's music. It has become increasingly clear, however, that Bach knew at least a few of Buxtehude's compositions long before they met in person. Not only are pieces by Buxtehude found in both the Möller Manuscript and the Andreas Bach Book, but it has been determined that a manuscript of Buxtehude's Praeludium in G minor (BuxWV 148) at the Carnegie Library in Pittsburgh was copied out by Bach's eldest brother, Johann Christoph, between 1695 and 1700. A portion of it may even have been written by Sebastian, then between ten and fifteen years of age, who was living there at the time.[47]

A second major figure in Bach's early musical life was Georg Böhm, organist at the Johanniskirche in Lüneburg for many years. Böhm's influence on Bach (who was a boarding student at the Michaelisschule, 1700–3) has long been evident in the chorale partitas (BWV 766–8 and 770), which belong to a genre that was cultivated especially intensively by Böhm. Recently, however, it has been shown that Böhm's influence was not limited to the first two or three years of the eighteenth century, but that elements of his style can be traced in Bach's compositions from the period c. 1704–8, especially in the cantatas of 1707–8.[48]

It is more difficult to assess the influence of Johann Adam Reincken, the third member of the great triumvirate of North German organist-composers. Despite the Obituary's claim that, while Bach was a student in Lüneburg, he 'journeyed now and again to Hamburg, to hear the then famous Organist of the Catharinen-Kirche, Johann Adam Reincken', and the fact that Reincken is listed as one of the composers whose works Bach took as models for his own compositions,[49] Reincken's role has been underestimated. The problem is largely a consequence of the fact that so few of Reincken's compositions have been preserved.[50] But even these have not yet received the attention they deserve.[51] Christoph Wolff has proposed a radical revision of the date for Bach's arrangements of sonata movements by Reincken (BWV 954, 965 and 966) from 1720 (Spitta) to 1710 or earlier, based on the provenance of the sources and by analogy with other arrangements of Italian trio-sonata models (BWV 574/574a/574b, 579, 946, 950 and 951/951a).[52]

It has been possible, though, to trace the role of North German musical culture in the development of one particular type of movement: the so-called permutation fugue, a device that formerly was thought to have been invented by Bach.[53] Research has since shown that it originated with a group of North German musicians in the second half of the seventeenth century (including Buxtehude, Reincken, Matthias Weckmann, Christoph Bernhard, and Johann Theile), whose studies of Sweelinck's translation of Zarlino's famous compositional treatise, *Le istitutioni harmoniche* (1558), stimulated their interest in invertible counterpoint. The idea of merging this strict procedure with the fugue led them to begin composing vocal and instrumental fugues with two or more subjects. Rather than creating a new musical genre, then, Bach's contribution was to infuse this abstract theoretical model with musical vitality.[54]

Some important studies of selected repertories have helped to clarify our view of Bach's early compositional output. In addition to those that have already been cited,[55] it is worth mentioning George Stauffer's monograph on the free organ preludes, which he later followed up with an essay on the fugues.[56] The former, in particular, opens new perspectives of the early works, including a proposed chronology and observations about possible influences on the young Bach. Also noteworthy is Karl Heller's article about the free Allegro movements in Bach's early keyboard music, which points to the concertos of Italian composers before Vivaldi (e.g., Torelli and Albinoni) as models.[57] Surely the most significant contribution, however, is Friedhelm Krummacher's paper on Bach's early cantatas, which considers these works within the context of late seventeenth-century German vocal music.[58] Bach's early vocal compositions basically follow Central German norms with respect to text types and musical forms. At the same time, however, they are highly individual works of art that bear Bach's own unmistakable stamp of originality and reveal his intimate acquaintance with the expressive music of the North German organists.

The decade 1985–95 has witnessed the publication of several valuable essays that shed new light on Bach's relationship to the other musicians and musical institutions in the towns where he grew up, studied and began his professional career. For Eisenach, where Bach was born in 1685 and spent the first ten years of his life, we have an important study by Claus Oefner, which is largely based on information from the municipal archives.[59] Oefner's investigations suggest that Bach probably sang in the *Chorus musicus*, the student choir that was led by the cantor and *Quartus* of the Lateinschule (Johann Andreas Schmidt, until his death in 1690, and Andreas Christian Dedekind thereafter) and that provided music for the Georgenkirche, the Nikolaikirche and the Annenkirche. If so, the young Bach probably had his first instrumental lessons here as well, for boys in the *Chorus musicus* were given the opportunity to learn to play musical instruments. For Arnstadt, where Bach began his career as organist (1703–7), we are indebted to the research of Markus Schiffner for several new insights. Most significantly, it is now known that the church library contained a large amount of music by earlier and more recent masters.[60] It also seems likely that Bach participated in music at the court, as well as in the church, since there was a precedent for including town musicians from Arnstadt and neighbouring communities.[61] It is not known to what extent Bach was allowed to use the considerable resources of the music library at the Michaeliskirche in Lüneburg – from which he might have absorbed many musical ideas and techniques – while he was a student there in 1700–3.[62]

Two additional lines of research that have helped to reshape our view of the young Bach will round out our discussion. The first is investigation of the theological context of Bach's early life and music. In an important and broad-ranging essay, Martin Petzoldt has considered Bach's theological education as a student in Eisenach, Ohrdruf and Lüneburg (i.e., through to his eighteenth year).[63] In addition to updating Gustav Fock's older account of the Lüneburg years,[64] Petzoldt has unearthed valuable new information about Bach's theological instructors at the schools in Eisenach (Andreas Christian Dedekind) and Ohrdruf (Martin Georg Hülsemann) and the content of their curricula. He also stresses the significance of one of Bach's first schoolbooks, the Eisenach hymnal of 1673, which exerted its influence throughout his entire life. In the interpretative realm, the chapter on the *Actus tragicus* (Cantata 106) in Eric Chafe's book on tonal allegory shows how Bach 'reached out to touch the central issues of Lutheran Christianity' in this early work.[65] Despite its adherence to the conventions of the seventeenth-century German cantata, the *Actus tragicus* is a forward-looking composition that 'contains hints not only of the depth of the interaction between music and theology throughout Bach's mature work but of many of the specific means by which Bach eventually achieved his goal'.[66]

In the other area of enquiry, performance practice, surely the most provocative hypothesis concerns the question of the instrumental designation of a number of works whose manuscripts bear the heading 'manualiter'. Based on studies of terminology in the original sources, coupled with other kinds of evidence, Robert Marshall has concluded that the 'Clavier' toccatas (BWV 910–16), which traditionally have been considered harpsichord works, 'must have been intended by Bach for the organ'.[67] So far, the most serious challenge to this theory has come from Christoph Wolff, who has presented stylistic evidence regarding idiomatic keyboard writing that appears to contradict Marshall's findings. Although Wolff argues persuasively that 'the young Bach aims at a deliberately idiomatic differentiation of musical textures that are not interchangeable but exclusively designed either for execution on the organ or for performance on the harpsichord',[68] much additional work will be necessary in order to reconcile these two opposing points of view.

## Conclusion

While our knowledge of the early works has increased dramatically, we are merely in the beginning stages of formulating an increasingly precise and detailed portrait of the young Bach. The task of uncovering the hidden secrets of this repertory does not require new critical perspectives or radical methodologies so much as a renewed commitment to becoming thoroughly familiar with this music. We must continue our attempts to formulate a profile of Bach's earliest style on the basis of careful examination of the indisputably authentic works. Discussion about the authenticity and dating of other works must also go forward, drawing on both source-critical and style-critical evidence.

The most pressing task, however, remains the evaluation of Bach's earliest music in relation to the heritage of the seventeenth century. Not until we gain a more comprehensive view of the rich tapestry of seventeenth-century music itself will it be possible to determine the specific ways in which Bach made use of conventional techniques, and to identify the features that are unique to his early compositional output and paved the way for the masterworks of the future.[69]

# 7 The mature vocal works and their theological and liturgical context

*Robin A. Leaver*

Many superlatives have been lavished on Bach's mature vocal works, such as Georg Nägeli's acclamation of the B minor Mass as one of the 'greatest musical works of art of all times and of all peoples',[1] or Mendelssohn's veneration of the Matthew Passion as 'the greatest of Christian works'.[2] But such evaluations have usually been based on the concept that these incomparable works of Bach are self-standing musical monuments. Following Mendelssohn's revival of the Matthew Passion in 1829, Bach's cantatas, oratorios, passions, Magnificat and the B minor Mass have generally been performed as autonomous works in a concert setting. But this later usage was not what the composer envisaged. What Robert Marshall writes with regard to the cantatas applies equally to most of Bach's other vocal works: 'such compositions were not intended primarily for the "delectation" of a concert *public*, but rather for the "edification" of a church *congregation* . . . Bach's cantatas, in fact, were conceived and should be regarded not as concert pieces at all but as musical sermons; and they were incorporated as such in the regular Sunday church services.'[3] This chapter therefore discusses these works against the background of the liturgical imperatives that brought them into being.

## Liturgy and music in Leipzig

The specific liturgical practices of Leipzig provide the immediate context for the creation of Bach's mature vocal works.[4] Liturgical usage in Leipzig during the eighteenth century was somewhat conservative. Compared with other areas of Germany, where traditional Lutheran liturgical forms, based on Luther's two liturgies, were already beginning to be eroded,[5] Leipzig retained a highly developed and rich liturgical and musical tradition. The details of this tradition can be reconstructed from a number of sources, such as the Saxon *Agenda* (1539/40), the manuscript notes of the Thomaskirche Custos (Sacristan) Johann Christoph Rost, the *Neu Leipziger Gesangbuch* (1682) edited by Gottfried Vopelius, and a number

86

of lay devotional books, such as the *Leipziger Kirchen-Andachten* (1694) and the *Leipziger Kirchen-Staat* (1710).

But an important source is Bach himself. According to the *Nekrolog*, the obituary written primarily by C. P. E. Bach, Johann Sebastian Bach composed 'Five annual cycles of church pieces, for all Sundays and Festivals [of the church year]'.[6] The compositional chronology of the first three annual cycles of cantatas has been fairly completely identified, largely by the researches of Dadelsen and Dürr;[7] the evidence for the fourth and fifth cycles remains fragmentary. The creation and compilation of these 'Jahrgänge' began with the First Sunday after Trinity each year, because it was on this Sunday that Bach assumed his duties in Leipzig in 1723. This 'Jahrgang' division is appropriate for establishing the sequence of Bach's composition and performance of his cantatas but this is not how he would have assembled them in his library of scores and parts.

The *Nekrolog* states that the annual cycles were 'for all Sundays and Festivals', which implies that Bach would have collected each 'Jahrgang' according to the sequence of the church year. The first Sunday of the church year is the First Sunday in Advent (hereafter Advent 1). For his first 'Jahrgang' (1723–4) Cantata 61 was performed on this day, and for the second (1724–5) Cantata 62 was specifically composed and performed. It is highly significant that both these cantatas for Advent 1 should have on their covers a listing of the basic eucharistic liturgy in Leipzig.[8] There have been many hypotheses as to when Bach might have penned these, but the editors of *Bach-Dokumente* suggest that the list on Cantata 61 – originally composed in Weimar in 1714 – was probably written in November 1723 when the cantata was first performed in Leipzig; and the list on Cantata 62 – composed in 1724 – was probably written in 1736, around the time of its second performance in Leipzig. But since the two lists are virtually identical, they may well have been written around the same time. Whatever the dating, they suggest that Bach was organising his scores and parts into complete (or near complete) cycles of cantatas according to the church year, thus underlining the liturgical purpose not only of these cantatas for Advent 1 but also for all the cantatas in the respective 'Jahrgänge'.

The eucharistic order of worship for Advent 1 is given in Bach's hand on the cover of Cantata 61 thus:

1   [Organ] Preluding
2   [Latin] *Motetta*
3   Preluding on the *Kyrie*, which is wholly concerted
4   [Collect] intoned before the altar

5   Epistle read

6   The Litany is sung [only in Advent and Lent]

7   Preluding on the chorale [which is then sung]

8   Gospel read

9   Preluding on the principal music [i.e., the cantata, which follows]

10   The Faith [Der Glaube] is sung [i.e., the credal hymn *Wir glauben all an einen Gott*]

11   The sermon [which concludes with confession and absolution, intercessions and notices]

12   After the sermon, the usual various verses from a hymn are sung

13   *Verba Institutionis*

14   Preluding on the music. And after which alternating preluding and the singing of chorales until communion is ended *& sic porrò.*

The reference to the Kyrie (3) designates a Lutheran *Missa*, that is, a concerted Kyrie and Gloria. Although the Gloria was traditionally omitted during the season of Advent, Advent Sunday itself was considered a major feast of the church year and therefore a complete *Missa*, both Kyrie and Gloria, was necessary, as the Leipzig liturgical sources indicate. That Bach should refer only to the Kyrie is not surprising, since both Kyrie and Gloria usually appeared under a single number in contemporary hymnals; for example, in the Vopelius *Neu Leipziger Gesangbuch* the heading is: 'MISSA, oder, das Kyrie Eleison'.

The congregational chorale (7) before the Gospel refers to the traditional Lutheran *Graduallied* (Gradual hymn) that underscored the primary teaching of the day or celebration, found in the Gospel that follows. In Bach's time a core repertory of such *Graduallieder* had been established,[9] and its principal chorales are frequently found in his cantatas, such as the use of Luther's *Nun komm der Heiden Heiland* in the Advent 1 cantatas BWV 61, 62 and 36.

On Advent 1 and other major festivals, the cantata (9) immediately followed the reading of the Gospel of the day (8) and was, in a sense, its musical counterpart. On other Sundays the Latin Nicene Creed was sung between the Gospel and the cantata – usually in chant, although it could, from time to time, be a more expansive setting. Thus the cantata was closely associated with the *Graduallied*, the Gospel of the day, the exposition of the Gospel in the sermon and the confession of faith in Luther's credal hymn, *Wir glauben all* (which was sung congregationally, though from time to time the Latin Credo was also sung).

At principal celebrations such as Christmas, Epiphany, Easter,

Ascension, Pentecost and Trinity (but not Advent 1), the 'Sursum corda' and a Latin Preface were intoned, leading into the Latin Sanctus, before the *Verba Institutionis*. The Sanctus could either be sung in simple monody, a six-part setting in Vopelius's *Neu Leipziger Gesangbuch*, or a concerted setting.[10]

Following the *Verba Institutionis* there was *musica sub communione* (14) – that is, the second part of a two-part cantata, another cantata, or some other appropriate music – performed at the beginning of the distribution of communion. Thus, as part of his candidature for the vacant position of Thomaskantor, Bach presented two cantatas on 7 February 1723, on *Estomihi*, the Sunday before Lent. The first, *Jesu nahm zu sich die Zwölfe* (the opening words of the Gospel of the day) (BWV 22), was performed during the earlier part of the eucharistic Hauptgottesdienst, in close proximity to the reading of the Gospel and the sermon. The second, *Du wahrer Gott und Davids Sohn* (BWV 23), was performed as *musica sub communione*, three of its four movements being appropriately based on the German Agnus Dei, *Christe, du Lamm Gottes*, which in Lutheran usage was associated with the distribution of communion.

After the cantata, or other concerted music, Bach notes that there should follow 'alternating preluding and the singing of chorales until communion is ended' (14). Various liturgical sources list the appropriate eucharistic hymns that could be sung at this juncture. The Saxon *Agenda* gives the further information that the Latin Agnus Dei could also be sung during the distribution, but that the German version, *Christe, du Lamm Gottes*, should customarily conclude the *musica sub communione*.

The cantata which had been sung in the morning at the Thomaskirche was repeated in the afternoon Vespers at the Nikolaikirche (or vice versa). The liturgical structure of Vespers was simpler and more straightforward than the morning eucharistic Hauptgottesdienst:

1   Organ Prelude
2   Latin motet
3   Cantata
4   Hymn, appropriate to the day or season
5   Sermon, preceded by the reading of the Epistle in German; concludes with confession and absolution, intercessions and notices.
6   Second part of the Cantata (if necessary)
7   Magnificat
10  Verse and Collect
11  Benediction
12  Hymn

As with the morning Eucharist, the cantata was primarily associated with the controlling biblical lection, the Gospel in the morning and the Epistle in the afternoon. The function of the cantata, however, remained the same: a musical homily, which, if in two parts, effectively framed the sermon. On most Sundays the congregation sang the Vespers canticle (the German Magnificat), to the *tonus peregrinus* chant, but on major festivals and special days the choir sang this in Latin, either to a psalm tone or in a concerted setting.

## Parodied creativity or creative parody?

There are two problems that have created an uneasiness in students of Bach for more than a century. One has to do with the nature of creative genius, the other with the tension between sacred and secular. Both problems are to a large degree the product of the nineteenth century, and both arise from Bach's propensity to parody his own music. The nineteenth-century understanding of creative genius was that it is essentially original, conceiving new artistic works that are both novel and unique. But the problem with many of Bach's mature vocal works is that they frequently draw from music written for other purposes. The notion that the spheres of sacred and secular were distinct implied that secular music adapted for sacred purposes lacked integrity, and, worse, religious music adapted for secular use was akin to sacrilege. Yet this is apparently what Bach did: passion music was reused as funeral music, funeral music was adapted to become passion music, and music composed to honour the birth of the son of a king was later reused to celebrate the nativity of the Son of God.

Various arguments have been employed from time to time in attempts to resolve the apparent contradictions.[11] Thus the short Lutheran *Missae* (BWV 233–6) have been regarded as of no great significance because they are essentially reworkings of earlier cantata movements. It was argued that this parody procedure demonstrates that Bach was not particularly interested in their composition. But the problem with this line of reasoning is that the B minor Mass, which has been universally praised as a work of superlative quality, also incorporates much parodied music. Others have argued that Bach's intention was always to write 'sacred' music, even for a 'secular' context, so that it could later be incorporated into a 'sacred' work. Thus Spitta opined: 'His secular occasional compositions were not genuinely secular; as such they scarcely fulfilled their aim, and the composer only restored them to their native home when he applied them to church uses.'[12] Similarly, Leo Schrade, in a classic essay, characterised the basic problem with regard to Bach as the 'conflict between the sacred and the secular'.[13] But much of the conflict has been created by nineteenth- and twentieth-century interpreters of the composer.

Writers such as Oskar Söhngen, Günther Stiller and others have shown that within Lutheranism a synthetic – rather than an antithetic – stance towards sacred and secular music developed from the Reformation era onwards.[14] While such writers are on sure ground when they stress what had long been implicit in the practice of Lutheran church music, they overstate the case when they claim that the synthesis effectively meant that there was no distinction between the sacred and secular. Lutheran clergy were somewhat conservative with regard to the introduction of new musical styles and frequently spoke about the 'abuses' of new music in the sanctuary. A frequent criticism, which grew in intensity throughout the eighteenth century, was of music that was overly 'theatrical', that is, music for effect rather than for edification. But such criticism did not imply a sharp distinction between sacred and secular music, at least on the part of Orthodox Lutherans. Certainly the Pietists increasingly moved towards a clear-cut distinction between 'secular' and 'religious' music, but this was not fully articulated until a later generation. Indeed, the distinction between 'sacred' and 'secular' cantatas was not Bach's own but a later classification. That the composer viewed his own music as a unity is implicit in his use of the letters 'S. D. G.' – 'Soli deo gloria' – which are inscribed not only at the end of many of the manuscript scores of his 'sacred' cantatas but also at the conclusion of 'secular' cantatas, such as one written for the installation of a professor of jurisprudence (BWV 207), another for the birthday of a prince (BWV 213) and yet another for the birthday of a queen (BWV 214).

Within his synthesis of sacred and secular Bach appears to have adopted a primary controlling principle: parody allows music written for a specific occasion to be heard in a more general and recurring context. Typical of the eighteenth century, the age of the encyclopedia, is Bach's comprehensive concern to cover a wide variety of musical forms, genres and national styles. Reusing music allowed Bach to compile such system- atic collections as the various parts of the *Clavier-Übung*, the two parts of the *Well-tempered Clavier*, the English and French Suites and the 'Schübler' chorale preludes. A similar process was followed with regard to the vocal music: a composition specifically written for an unrepeatable occasion, such as a royal funeral, or for performance within a limited context, such as a birthday at court, could be performed more frequently and more universally if the music was adapted for one of the Sundays or celebrations of the church year.

## Music as *proprium*

As outlined above, cantatas in Leipzig were performed at both the morning eucharistic Hauptgottesdienst and the afternoon Vespers. The cantata was closely associated with the primary Propers of the day, the Gospel at the Hauptgottesdienst and the Epistle at Vespers. Each explores in some way the general content and specific themes of the respective readings.[15] The Christmas Oratorio, essentially a cycle of cantatas, can be taken as representative of the cantatas as a whole, even though it contains one or two unique features.

### The Christmas Oratorio

The Christmas season in Leipzig was celebrated with a rich tapestry of special music. Between the thirteen days that span Christmas and Epiphany, 25 December to 6 January, no less than six different cantatas were performed, some of them in both of the two principal churches of the city. But other concerted music was performed in addition to these cantatas during this active period of celebration. For example, Bach's first Christmas in Leipzig was preceded by an extraordinary period of creativity. During the four weeks of Advent in 1723 (when, apart from the First Sunday in Advent, there was no concerted music), Bach composed or revised for the forthcoming Christmas–Epiphany celebration the first version of the Magnificat (BWV 243a), a Sanctus (BWV 238), and six cantatas (BWV 63, 40, 64, 190, 153 and 65). Eleven years later he again composed and adapted a sequence of cantatas for this season, this time devising a series of interrelated pieces.

Bach's Christmas Oratorio, *Oratorium Tempore Nativitatis Christi,*[16] although conceived with an overall unity, is a cycle of six cantatas.[17] It was originally designed to be performed in its individual parts, beginning on Christmas Day 1734 and ending on the Feast of the Epiphany 1735. The printed booklet containing the libretti for use by the Leipzig congregations, and issued towards the end of 1734, reveals the following sequence of performances:[18]

> *25 December 1734 – Christmas Day*
> Part I was performed in the principal worship service of the day – the morning Eucharist in the Nikolaikirche – and repeated in the afternoon Vespers at the Thomaskirche.

> *26 December 1734 – St Stephen's Day*
> Part II was performed in the morning Eucharist in the Thomaskirche and repeated in the afternoon Vespers at the Nikolaikirche.

*27 December 1734 – St John's Day*
Part III was performed in the morning Eucharist in the Nikolaikirche, but not repeated in the Thomaskirche.

*1 January 1735 – Feast of the Circumcision*
Part IV performed in the morning Eucharist in the Thomaskirche and repeated in the afternoon Vespers at the Nikolaikirche.

*2 January 1735 – Sunday after New Year*
Part V performed in the morning Eucharist in the Nikolaikirche, but not repeated in the Thomaskirche.

*6 January 1735 – Feast of the Epiphany*
Part VI performed in the morning Eucharist in the Thomaskirche and repeated in the afternoon Vespers at the Nikolaikirche.

Parts III and V were not given second performances because it was not the custom to have concerted music at Vespers on the third day of Christmas and on the day following New Year.

The Christmas Oratorio is a skilful parody of movements from a number of 'secular' cantatas Bach had composed in 1733 and 1734. *Laßt uns sorgen, laßt uns wachen* (BWV 213), a classical 'Dramma per Musica' featuring Hercules and Mercury,[19] was originally composed for the eleventh birthday of Prince Friedrich Christian of Saxony on 5 September 1733, and first performed by the 'Bachische[s] Collegium Musicum' in Zimmermann's garden outside the Grimma Gate.[20] Six movements, that is all the choruses and arias except the final chorus, were parodied in the Christmas Oratorio: one in each of Parts I–III and three in Part IV. *Tönet, ihr Pauken! Erschallet, Trompeten!* (BWV 214) was originally written for the birthday of Maria Josepha, Electress of Saxony and Queen of Poland (and mother of Friedrich Christian), on 7 December 1733, and performed by the *Collegium musicum*, probably in Zimmermann's coffee house in the Katharinenstrasse. Bach incorporated four movements into the Christmas Oratorio, one in each of Parts II and III, and two in Part I, including the spectacular first movement with its opening solo for timpani, an extremely rare occurrence in concerted church music. *Preise dein Glücke, gesegnetes Sachsen* (BWV 215), a congratulatory cantata written to celebrate the first anniversary of the accession of August II/III, Elector of Saxony and King of Poland, was first performed on 5 October 1734 in the market place in Leipzig, in front of the Apel house, where August III, Maria Josepha and Prince Friedrich Christian were staying during the Leipzig fair. An unfinished sketch originally intended as movement 7 of Cantata 215 was re-worked for Part III (No. 31), and the movement that replaced it was taken over in Part V (No. 47). The fourth cantata parodied in the Christmas Oratorio is a

**Table 7.1** *Sources of the Christmas Oratorio*

| BWV 248 | BWV 213 | BWV 214 | BWV 215 | BWV 248a | Recits. | Chorales | Other |
|---|---|---|---|---|---|---|---|
| Part I | | | | | | | |
| 1 | | 1 | | | | | |
| 2–3 | | | | | 2–3 | | |
| 4 | 9 | | | | | | |
| 5 | | | | | | 5 | |
| 6–7 | | | | | 6–7 | 7 | |
| 8 | | 7 | | | | | |
| 9 | | | | | | 9 | |
| Part II | | | | | | | |
| 10 | | | | | | | 10 |
| 11 | | | | | 11 | | |
| 12 | | | | | | 12 | |
| 13–14 | | | | | 13–14 | | |
| 15 | | 5 | | | | | |
| 16 | | | | | 16 | | |
| 17 | | | | | | 17 | |
| 18 | | | | | 18 | | |
| 19 | 3 | | | | | | |
| 20 | | | | | 20 | | |
| 21 | | | | | 21 | | |
| 22 | | | | | 22 | | |
| 23 | | | | | | 23 | |
| Part III | | | | | | | |
| 24 | | 9 | | | | | |
| 25 | | | | | 25 | | |
| 26 | | | | | | | 26 |
| 27 | | | | | 27 | | |
| 28 | | | | | | 28 | |
| 29 | 11 | | | | | | |
| 30 | | | | | 30 | | |
| 31 | | | [7] | | | | |
| 32 | | | | | 32 | | |
| 33 | | | | | | 33 | |
| 34 | | | | | 34 | | |
| 35 | | | | | | 35 | |
| Part IV | | | | | | | |
| 36 | 1 | | | | | | |
| 37 | | | | | 37 | | |
| 38 | | | | | 38 | 38 | |
| 39 | 5 | | | | | | |
| 40 | | | | | 40 | 40 | |
| 41 | 7 | | | | | | |
| 42 | | | | | | 42 | |

**Table 7.1** *Contd.*

| BWV 248 | BWV 213 | BWV 214 | BWV 215 | BWV 248a | Recits. | Chorales | Other |
|---------|---------|---------|---------|----------|---------|----------|-------|
| **Part V** | | | | | | | |
| 43 | | | | | | | 43 |
| 44 | | | | | 44 | | |
| 45 | | | | | | | 45 |
| 46 | | | | | 46 | | |
| 47 | | | 7 | | | | |
| 48–50 | | | | | 48–50 | | |
| 51 | | | | | | | 51 |
| 52 | | | | | 52 | | |
| 53 | | | | | 53 | | |
| **Part VI** | | | | | | | |
| 54 | | | | 1 | | | |
| 55 | | | | | 55 | | |
| 56 | | | | 2 | | | |
| 57 | | | | 3 | | | |
| 58 | | | | | 58 | | |
| 59 | | | | | | 59 | |
| 60 | | | | | 60 | | |
| 61 | | | | 4 | | | |
| 62 | | | | 5 | | | |
| 63 | | | | 6 | | | |
| 64 | | | | 7 | | | |

fragment known only from the incomplete original parts (BWV 248a).
The occasion for which it was originally written is unknown. All seven
movements became the substance of Part VI of the Christmas Oratorio,
to which were added just three recitatives and a chorale. (Details of all
the parodied movements are summarised in the first five columns of
Table 7.1; numbers in the columns refer to the movements of the respective works.)

The Oratorio as a whole is given a cohesive unity by the narrative of the
nativity as found in Luke 2:1–21 and Matthew 2:1–12, and by the chorales
that function as reflective commentary at specific points in the narrative.
In both these respects the Christmas Oratorio is related to the Passions,
except that it was performed over several days rather than at one time.
The recitatives and chorales were presumably specifically composed for
the Oratorio, though it is possible that some of the chorales were taken
over from earlier works. The five remaining movements, for which no
earlier form has been discovered, may have been written for the Oratorio
towards the end of 1734, but it is more than likely that they too were

Table 7.2 *Symmetrical structure of the first three parts of the Christmas Oratorio*

---

I

1. Chorus: 'Jauchzet, frohlocket! auf, preiset die Tage' – tutti, with trumpets and timpani
9. Chorale: 'Ach mein herzliebes Jesulein' – tutti, with trumpets and timpani

II

10. Sinfonia – woodwinds and strings
16. Evangelist: 'Und das habt zum Zeichen'
17. Chorale: 'Schaut hin, dort liegt im finstren Stall' – with woodwinds and strings
23. Chorale: 'Wir singen dir in deinem Heer' – with woodwinds and strings

III

24. Chorus: 'Herrscher des Himmels' – tutti, with trumpets and timpani
36. 24 repeated.

---

parodied from now lost works. (These 'new' movements are summarised in the three right-hand columns of Table 7.1.)

Later generations have had problems with the concept of Bach adapting royal birthday cantatas to celebrate the birthday of Christ. But in the period prior to the French and American Revolutions royalty was understood in theological terms. When Bach and his contemporaries celebrated the earthly majesty of their ruler they did so with the understanding that such dignity is God-given, and that, however imperfectly the ruler may exercise his office, it is the office as embodied by the person, rather than the person alone, that is being celebrated. From Bach's point of view, the celebration of the birthday of a prince is also a celebration of the majesty of God, and therefore the music composed for such an occasion can be reused for the overt praise of the 'royal' birth of the Son of God.

The first three parts of the Christmas Oratorio performed on consecutive days are also linked by Bach's use of a symmetrical structure (see Table 7.2). The first and third parts begin and end with suitable music celebrating the birth of Christ, 'of David's *royal* line', with full orchestral and choral resources, including trumpets and timpani, the instruments particularly associated with festive, royal occasions. Part II, the centre of the first three of the cycle, dealing primarily with the Lukan narrative of the Bethlehem shepherds, begins and ends with an evocation of the pastoral scene with the lighter orchestration of woodwind and strings. At the centre of this middle cantata is the heart of the Christmas story: 'And this shall be the sign for you . . . a Child lying in a manger.'

**Table 7.3** *Symmetrical structure of Parts IV and VI of the Christmas Oratorio*

IV

36. Chorus: 'Fallt mir Danken'
37. Evangelist: 'Und da acht Tage'
38. Recit. & Chorale: 'Immanuel, o süßes Wort'
39. Echo Aria: 'Flößt, mein Heiland'
40. Recit. & Chorale: 'Wohlan, dein Name soll allein'
41. Aria: 'Ich will nur dir zu Ehren'
42. Chorale: 'Jesus richte mein Beginnen'

VI

54. Chorus: 'Herr, wenn die stolzen Feinde schnauben'
55. Evangelist: 'Da berief Herodes'
56. Recit.: 'Du Falscher, suche nur den Herrn'
57. Aria: 'Nur ein Wink von seinen Händen'
58. Evangelist: 'Als sie nun den König gehörig'
59. Chorale: 'Ich steh an deiner Krippe hier'
60. Evangelist: 'Und Gott befahl ihnen im Traum'
61. Recit.: 'So geht!'
62. Aria: 'Nun mögt ihr stolzen Feinde'
63. Recit.: 'Was will der Hölle Schrecken nun'
64. Chorale: 'Nun seid ihr wohl gerochen'

The remaining parts, IV–VI, were not performed on consecutive days, as were Parts I–III, and do not have such a close-knit overall structure as the first half of the Oratorio, although Parts IV and VI are proportionally arranged (see Table 7.3).

Part IV was performed on New Year's Day 1735, the Feast of the Circumcision of Jesus, also known as the Feast of the Naming of Jesus. This latter association explains the many references to 'name' and the frequent occurrence of 'Jesus' in the libretto. The soprano aria, 'Flößt, mein Heiland', the centre-point of the cantata, is an adaptation from the birthday cantata of 1733 (BWV 213) in which it was a simple echo aria. Here it is transformed – by the new libretto – into a dialogue in which the Saviour confirms the prayers of the believing soul.[21] The resulting intimate dialogue belongs to a long tradition, beginning in sixteenth-century Christ–Soul hymns and continuing in the church music of Andreas Hammerschmidt and others, as well as in a number of other cantatas of Bach, especially those he titled 'Dialogus' (for example BWV 32, 49, 57, 58, 60, etc.; see also 140/6). The bass recitatives (movements 38 and 40, framing the central soprano aria) are meditations on the name of Jesus and are combined with the chorale *Jesu, du mein liebstes*

*Leben*. The stanza refers to the crucifixion, which might be thought to be out of place in an oratorio celebrating the Incarnation. But the Feast of the Circumcision, the first shedding of the blood of Christ, was traditionally regarded as prefiguring the crucifixion. Further, the explanation of the name Jesus, 'he will save his people from their sins', also points to the crucifixion. Thus on this Feast of the Circumcision, or Name-day of Jesus, the connection between Incarnation and Atonement is clearly made. Part V was written for the Sunday after New Year, which in 1735 was 2 January. The music of the opening chorus (43), a sectional fugue in *da capo* form, may well have been adapted from a now-lost cantata. In the following two movements of Biblical narrative (44–5) the Evangelist tells of the arrival of the wise men and leads into their question – 'Where is he that is born King of the Jews?' – which is sung by the chorus in a motet style. The interchange of recitative and chorus is reminiscent of the *turba* choruses in Bach's passions, a fact that has led some to speculate that it may have been parodied from the now lost Mark Passion (BWV 247).[22]

Part VI, the final cantata of the cycle, is for the Feast of the Epiphany. It mostly comprises music drawn from a cantata known only from a few surviving orchestral parts (BWV 248a). Just three recitatives of Biblical narrative (55, 58, 60) and the central chorale (59), 'Ich steh an deiner Krippe hier', are newly composed. In the final recitative all four soloists enter with a theme that is closely related to the fanfare motive that breaks out at bar 19 in the alto aria 'Es ist vollbracht' of the John Passion (see Example 7.1, p. 103, below). Here again is another link between Incarnation and Atonement, a connection reinforced in the finale chorale, a celebratory setting of the melody *Herzlich tut mich verlangen*, the 'Passion Chorale'. That Bach deliberately intended a passion reference here has been called into question, since the melody was used with other hymn texts. But, at least in Leipzig hymnals in use during Bach's time, the other hymn texts sung to this melody all had passion connections.[23] The chorale text itself celebrates Christ's victory over death, Satan, sin and hell – the common theme of crucifixion/resurrection hymns. Furthermore, this 'Passion Chorale' melody of the final movement of the Christmas Oratorio was heard earlier, in the central movement of the first cantata (movement 5) performed on Christmas Day. The familiar melody is both the first and the last chorale heard in the complete cycle of cantatas comprising the Christmas Oratorio, thus underlining again the connection between Incarnation and Atonement,[24] a theme commonly found in the many theological and devotional writings by Lutheran theologians and preachers during the period between Luther and Bach. Here the connection is particularly appropriate since all the six parts of the Christmas

Oratorio were first heard in the Eucharist, the Atonement meal in Western Christianity.

## The Passions

In the same way that a cantata was effectively part of the Propers for a given Sunday or celebration, a setting of the passion at Good Friday Vespers was in a more direct sense music as *proprium* for this very important day in the church's calendar. At both the eucharistic Hauptgottesdienst and afternoon Vespers it was customary for Biblical pericopes to be read, usually the Epistle and Gospel in the morning and the Epistle in the afternoon. But on Good Friday the musical setting of the passion included the Biblical narrative itself, as well as being a musical meditation on its unfolding detail. The Good Friday Vespers performance of the passion is analogous to the singing of the old responsorial passions (attributed to Johann Walter) as the Gospel at the eucharistic celebrations on Palm Sunday and Good Friday mornings: the Matthew Passion as the Gospel for Palm Sunday and the John Passion as the Gospel for Good Friday.[25] These somewhat austere passions continued to be sung liturgically throughout Bach's time in Leipzig. The large-scale concerted passion came late to Leipzig, the first being Johann Kuhnau's Mark Passion, performed in the Neue Kirche on 26 March 1717. Such performances at Good Friday Vespers were intended to complement the liturgical passions of Walter, which, like the passions of Schütz, included only the Biblical narrative with a suitable brief chorus at the beginning and end. In contrast, Bach's passions – in common with eighteenth-century practice – included recitatives, arias and choruses, as well as chorales, which added a meditative dimension to the progress of the passion narrative.

The liturgy for Good Friday's Vespers was a simplified form of Sunday Vespers. The Latin motet was deferred to later in the service and the worship began with a hymn. Effectively the passion replaced both the cantata before the sermon and the Magnificat after it to give the following form:

1   Hymn
2   Passion, part I
3   Sermon
4   Passion, part II
5   Motet: *Ecce quomodo moritur* (Gallus)
6   Verse and Collect
7   Benediction
8   Hymn

The passion was therefore closely associated with the sermon, which it effectively framed by each of its two parts.

Bach was actively involved in composing and performing various passion settings for practically the whole of his time in Leipzig. According to the *Nekrolog,* he composed 'five passions, of which one is for double chorus'. The reference to a double-chorus passion is almost certainly the Matthew Passion; of the other four, two must be the John and Mark Passions, and two are uncertain. These could be the anonymous Luke Passion and possibly a fragment of a Weimar passion. The following outline records only those passions composed by Bach, or that included some of his music, and performed during his time in Leipzig:

1724    John Passion (BWV 245), first version
1725    John Passion, second version
1726    Keiser's Mark Passion, including movements composed by Bach, first performed in Weimar in 1713 or earlier; additional chorales included for this Leipzig performance[26]
1727    Matthew Passion (BWV 244), earlier version
1729    Matthew Passion, earlier version (?)
1730    Anonymous Luke Passion (BWV 246), including at least one movement by Bach[27]
1731    Mark Passion (BWV 247)
1732?    John Passion, third version
1735?    Anonymous Luke Passion
1736    Matthew Passion, later version
[1739 Revision of John Passion begun]
1742?    Matthew Passion, later version
1747/8?  *Passionspasticcio,* incorporating the music of Handel and Keiser[28]
1749    John Passion, fourth version

Bach's John Passion was presumably written between the end of 1723 and the beginning of 1724, his first year in Leipzig, since it was first performed on Good Friday, 7 April 1724. But it is possible that the period of gestation was somewhat longer.[29] What is clear is that over the years, with each new performance in Leipzig, Bach made significant alterations and changes to the John Passion. It was performed again at the Good Friday Vespers in 1725, but in a revised form. During his second year in Leipzig Bach was composing chorale cantatas and two of the significant changes made for the second version of the John Passion involved the introduction of two chorale movements: the opening chorus, 'Herr, unser Herrscher', was replaced by the chorale fantasia 'O Mensch, bewein' dein Sünde groß', and the final four-part chorale 'Ach Herr, laß dein lieb Engelein' was displaced by the extended chorale 'Christe, du Lamm

Gottes', the concluding chorale of the 1723 version of Cantata 23. Both movements may have originated in a passion that Bach had composed – or partially composed – in Weimar. This second version of the John Passion Bach also includes three arias that may come from the conjectural Weimar passion.[30] For another performance that took place around 1732 a third version of the John Passion was created. Now that the substitute opening chorus of the second version of 1725 had been incorporated into the Matthew Passion (see further below), the original 1724 opening chorus was restored; other changes included the deletion of the interpolations from St Matthew's gospel, and the addition of a new aria in Part I and a sinfonia in Part II, neither of which has survived. In 1739 the composer began work on a fair copy revision of the John Passion which, however, he apparently abandoned after the tenth movement, so the proposed performance apparently never took place. For the fourth and final version of the passion in 1749, Bach restored the movements deleted in the third version and enriched the instrumentation.

Friedrich Smend's image as a leading Bach scholar is somewhat tarnished by his unfortunate edition of the B minor Mass, but this should not be allowed to overshadow his earlier substantial work in other areas of Bach research, notably on the passions. Although with the wisdom of hindsight some of his detailed theories have proven to be invalid, much of his methodology and insight opened up new avenues of investigation that have not yet been fully explored. In the *Bach-Jahrbuch* of 1926 he published a brilliant essay on the structure of the John Passion in which he detected various symmetrical groupings of movements within the two halves of the passion.[31] That Bach should use such symmetrical patterns in the structure of the passion is understandable, given that the term for such symmetry is *chiasmus*, derived from the Greek letter *chi*, X, the 'sign of the cross'. Thus in the manuscript score of Cantata 56, *Ich will dem Kreuzstab gerne tragen* (I will gladly carry the cross-staff) Bach actually wrote 'X-stab'. But since *chi* is also the first letter of *Christos* it is also used to signify Christ, so in the heading of Cantata 61 Bach wrote: 'Domin: 1 Advent Xti'. The use of chiastic structures is a marked feature of Bach's mature vocal works, such as the passions, which portray the death of Christ, the Christmas Oratorio, which celebrates the birth of Christ, and the B minor Mass, which expresses both – especially in the Gloria and *Symbolum Nicenum* (see further below).

In his analysis of the John Passion, Smend found that there were several chiastic structures that focused on important details of the passion narrative,[32] especially the pivotal 'Herzstück' (see Table 7.4).[33] This central chiasmus is clearly audible, since the music of No. 21$^d$ is repeated at No. 23$^d$, and that of No. 21$^f$ repeated at No. 23$^b$, with only

**Table 7.4.** *Symmetrical structure of the 'Herzstück' of the John Passion*

18[b]. Chorus: 'Nicht diesen, sondern Barrabam!'
18[c]. Recit.: 'Barrabas aber war ein Mörder ...'
19. Arioso: 'Betrachte, meine Seel ...'
20. Aria: 'Erwäge, wie sein blutgefärbter Rücken ...'
21[a]. Recit.: 'Und die Kriegsknechte ...'
21[b]. Chorus: 'Sei gegrüßet, lieber Jüdenkönig!'

21[c]. Recit.: 'Und gaben ihm Backenstreiche ...'
21[d]. Chorus: 'Kreuzige, kreuzige!'
21[e]. Recit.: 'Pilatus sprach zu ihnen ...'
21[f]. Chorus: 'Wir haben ein Gesetz ...'
21[g]. Recit.: 'Da Pilatus das Wort hörete ...'
22. 'Durch dein Gefängnis, Gottes Sohn ...'
23[a]. Recit.: 'Die Jüden aber schrieen ...'
23[b]. Chorus: 'Lässest du diesen los ...'
23[c]. Recit.: 'Da Pilatus das Wort hörete ...'
23[d]. Chorus: 'Weg, weg mit dem, kreuzige ihn!'
23[e]. Recit.: 'Spricht Pilatus zu ihnen ...'

23[f]. Chorus: 'Wir haben keinen König ...'
23[g]. Recit.: 'Da überantwortete er ihn ...'
24. Aria + Chorus: '... nach Golgatha!'
25[a]. Recit.: 'Allda kreuzigten sie ihn ...'
25[b]. Chorus: 'Schreibe nicht: der Jüden König ...'

changes in key and the rhythmical adjustment necessitated by the different text. At the centre is the quasi-chorale, No. 22, 'Durch dein Gefängnis, Gottes Sohn', which is not only the centrepiece of the second part of the John Passion but also the heart and focus of the entire work. The melody Bach chose, *Machs mit mir*, was associated with hymns on death and eternal life, but the text he assigned to it is not a stanza from a congregational hymn. It is rather the text of an aria found in a John Passion libretto, c. 1700, by C. H. Postel, that had been set in other passion music, such as Mattheson's *Das Lied des Lammes* (1723), and a passion once attributed to Handel:[34]

| | |
|---|---|
| Durch dein Gefängnis, Gottes Sohn, | Through thy captivity, Son of God, |
| muß die Freiheit kommen; | Freedom to us has come, |
| Dein Kerker ist der Gnadenthron[35] | Thy prison is the throne of grace, |
| die Freistatt aller Frommen | The refuge of all the faithful, |
| denn gingst du nicht die Knechtschaft ein | For if thou hadst not been enslaved |
| müßt unsre Knechtschaft ewig sein. | Our slavery would last forever. |

If this quasi-chorale lies at the heart of the John Passion then its climax is to be found in the words from John 19:30: 'It is fulfilled/finished' (30).

**Example 7.1**  Christmas Oratorio BWV 248/63
St John Passion BWV 245/30

Again Bach stresses the importance of these words by placing them at the centre of another chiastic structure:

28.  Chorale: 'Er nahm alles wohl in acht'
29.  Recit.: 'Und von Stund an nahm'
    30.  Aria: 'Es ist vollbracht'
31.  Recit.: 'Und neiget das Haupt'
32. Chorale: 'Jesu, der du warest tot', with Aria: 'Mein teurer Heiland'

The chiasmus is emphasised by the framing of the meditative aria (No. 30) within the recitatives of Biblical narrative and two stanzas of Paul Stockmann's passiontide hymn, *Jesu Kreuz, Leiden und Pein*, set to its associated melody by Melchior Vulpius. Chorale No. 28 anticipates the impending death of Christ with some remarkably intense harmonies for the last two lines, and Chorale No. 32 meditates on the continuing significance of the death of Christ. Intertwined with and between the lines of this chorale is the calm and confident bass aria which takes comfort in the security of the finished work of Christ, expressed in the three words 'Es ist vollbracht'. At the centre of the chiasmus is the devastatingly beautiful meditation on these three last words (No. 30). But the grief-laden atmosphere is broken in the middle of the aria by the sudden fanfare motive 'Der Held aus Juda…', 'The Hero of Judah triumphs with might and has finished the fight' (see Example 7.1). Here is Bach the preacher in sound, whose purpose is not simply to relate in musical terms the great dramatic story, as if he had written a religious opera, but rather to draw the worshipper at Good Friday Vespers into the story itself and to find within it a contemporary significance.[36]

The Matthew Passion, the most complex – and for many the most sublime – of all Bach's vocal music, was for a long time thought to have been first performed in 1729, but recent research suggests that this event occurred some two years earlier.[37] Evidence for performances in 1727 and 1729 is incomplete, as the earliest surviving sources date from the year 1736. Nevertheless, at least something of the origins of this masterpiece can be pieced together.

**Example 7.2** Cantata BWV 127/4

St Matthew Passion BWV 244/27b

Cantata BWV 127/4

ich  bre - che  mit  star - ker  und  hel - fen - der  Hand . . .

Matthew Passion BWV 244/27b

Sind  Blit - ze,  sind  Don - ner  in  Wol - ken  ver - schwunden . . .

It now seems likely that Bach may have been planning this ambitious work at least as early as 1725. First there is the musical and textual connections between the fourth movement of Cantata 127 and the chorus 'Sind Blitze, sind Donner' (BWV 244/27[b]; see Example 7.2). Cantata 127 was first performed on *Estomihi*, the Sunday before Lent, 11 February 1725. While 'we have no means of proving which movement was written first', Eric Chafe nevertheless concludes that 'in every detail, the matching of text and music gives the impression that the version of the Passion was the first'.[38] This fact, taken with others, led Chafe to suggest the possibility that Bach had already begun not only to plan but also to compose the Matthew Passion by the beginning of 1725. 'If the connection between Cantata 127 and "Sind Blitze" constituted a deliberate reference, then Bach must have intended to point ahead across the musically silent Lenten season to the coming Passiontide.'[39] It is therefore possible that Bach planned the Matthew Passion as the 'chorale' passion to be performed in connection with the 'Jahrgang' of chorale cantatas. Presuming that the Matthew Passion was incomplete at the beginning of 1725, Chafe suggests that the second version of the John Passion, with its two chorale movements borrowed from the conjectural Weimar passion, was 'a temporary solution, modified to fill the place of its successor for one year only'.[40] Such a scenario would help to explain why essentially the same passion setting was performed in consecutive years, 1724 and 1725, why the second version of the John Passion was performed only once, with its substitute opening movement 'O Mensch, bewein dein Sünde groß' ultimately becoming the closing movement of the first part of the Matthew Passion, and perhaps also why Keiser's Mark Passion was performed in 1726.

The second piece of evidence relating to the early planning of the Matthew Passion is found on the verso of the viola part of the *Sanctus* (BWV 232/III) in the set of parts prepared for Count Sporck towards the end of 1726.[41] At the bottom right corner, upside down, is a sequence of notes found in several places in the first violin part of the aria 'Mache dich, mein Herze, rein' in the Matthew Passion (No. 65). The notes were crossed out but the sheet was not discarded; it was later inverted and re-used for the viola part of the *Sanctus*. Although no text appears with the crossed-out notation, it is unlikely to have been associated with another text since the poetry of this aria in the Matthew Passion libretto is unusual. As Joshua Rifkin observes: 'The poem ends with a line isolated both in its syntax and its meaning from the preceding verses and Bach's setting faithfully preserves this unusual articulation.'[42] Since the aria appears near the end of the libretto, Rifkin concludes that the early version of the Matthew Passion was nearing completion towards the end of 1726.[43]

Another piece of evidence supporting the earlier dating of the Matthew Passion is a passion libretto by the poet Christian Friedrich Henrici, *alias* Picander, that appeared with instalments of cantata libretti during the liturgical year 1724–5. The complete anthology of libretti was re-published in book form in 1725, with the title *Sammlung Erbaulicher Gedancken über und auf die gewöhnlichen Sonn- und Fest-Tage*. Picander was also the poet who wrote the Matthew Passion libretto, and three items of this later libretto (Nos. 39, 49 and 68) are poetic parodies of movements in the 1725 passion libretto; they share vocabulary, imagery and, in some cases, rhyming schemes.[44] In recent years Elke Axmacher has discovered that for about half of the arias in the Matthew Passion libretto Picander drew heavily from a series of eight passion sermons by the Rostock theologian Heinrich Müller, appended to the author's collection of sermons entitled *Evangelisches Praeservativ wider den Schaden Josephs, in allen dreyen Ständen*, first published in Frankfurt and Rostock in 1681.[45] Bach had a copy of this work in his personal library, and it seems quite likely that the composer drew the attention of the poet to these sermons.[46] Using elements from the recently published 1725 passion libretto, and drawing on the passion sermons of Müller, Picander presumably worked with Bach in creating the libretto of the Matthew Passion, which was later published in the poet's *Ernst-Schertzhaffte und Satyrische Gedichte, Anderer Theil* (Leipzig, 1729).[47]

That the early version of the Matthew Passion was first performed on Good Friday, 11 April 1727 is confirmed by the movements of the Matthew Passion that Bach parodied for a memorial service. Prince Leopold of Anhalt-Köthen, Bach's former employer, died on 19 November 1728 at the age of thirty-three. The funeral ceremonies and burial were postponed until 23–4 March the following year so that the necessary preparations could be made. Bach was commissioned to compose two pieces of music: an unidentified work performed in Köthen on the eve of the funeral, 23 March,[48] and the four-sectioned cantata *Klagt, Kinder, klagt es aller Welt* (BWV 244a), which framed the funeral oration in the Reformed Jakobskirche on the following day. The score and parts are lost but the original libretto by Picander has survived.[49] Various Bach scholars have established that the music of ten of the twenty-four movements of the funeral cantata was essentially the same as Nos. 6, 8, 13, 20, 23, 39, 49, 57, 65 and 68 of the Matthew Passion. One of the reasons why the 1729 date for the first performance of the Matthew Passion was upheld for so long was because of a principle, almost a religious tenet, that Bach's music for the church was inviolable, and although some 'secular' music could find a more appropriate place in a 'sacred' work, the composer would never parody a 'sacred' work for a 'secular' purpose[50] – though in this particular instance the funeral rites could hardly be called 'secular'. Since only three weeks separated the performance of the funeral cantata and Good Friday in 1729, and because he was certain of the priority of BWV 244a, Schering proposed 1731 as the year of the first performance of the Matthew Passion. The 1731 proposal was quickly refuted, because the Mark Passion is known to have been performed that year (see below), but the view that the funeral music antedated the Matthew Passion persisted.[51] More recent research has clearly shown, however, that the passion music was composed first,[52] therefore supporting the current consensus that the Matthew Passion was first performed in 1727.

For many, a theological problem remained: to parody such a sublime work that sensitively portrays the death of the Son of God for a work that merely honours the death of an earthly prince borders on sacrilege. But, as suggested earlier, this is a problem of a later age rather than Bach's. In particular, there was in the Lutheran tradition an evangelical *ars moriendi* that saw in the Crucifixion, in addition to its fundamental redemptive nature, a significant reminder of human mortality. For example, in *Ein Betbüchlin, mit eyn Calender und Passional*, Wittenberg, 1529, Luther introduces the Passional, which presents the unfolding details of the Crucifixion, with his 'Sermon on preparing to die'.[53] The logic is simple: because Christ has died we can now face death. It is a thought that is expressed in many passion and other hymns, such as the ninth stanza of Paul Gerhardt's *O Haupt voll Blut und Wunden*, which Bach used immediately following the death of Jesus in the Matthew Passion (No. 62):

| | |
|---|---|
| Wenn ich einmal soll scheiden | When one day I must depart, |
| so scheide nicht von mir, | do not depart from me, |
| wenn ich den Tod soll leiden, | when I must suffer death, |
| so tritt du denn herfür! | come forth thou then to me. |
| Wenn mir am allerbängsten | When in my fears |
| wird um das Herze sein, | thou hast my heart possessed, |
| so reiß mich aus den Ängsten | then snatch me from anguish |
| kraft deiner Angst und Pein! | by the power of thy fear and pain! |

**Table 7.5** *Examples of structural patterns in the Matthew Passion*

| | |
|---|---|
| Narrative: | 4ᵉ. Evangelist: 'Da das Jesus merkete' |
| Comment: | 5. Recit.: 'Du lieber Heiland' |
| Prayer: | 6. Aria: 'Buß und Reu' |
| Narrative: | 11. Evangelist: 'Er antwortete und sprach' |
| Comment: | 12. Recit.: 'Wiewohl mein Herz in Tränen schwimmt' |
| Prayer: | 13. Aria: 'Ich will dir mein Herze schenken' |
| Narrative: | 21. Evangelist: 'Und ging hin ein wenig' |
| Comment: | 22. Recit.: 'Der Heiland fällt vor seinem Vater nieder' |
| Prayer: | 23. Aria: 'Gerne will ich mich bequemen' |

The funeral cantata for Prince Leopold also included three movements parodied from the *Trauer-Ode*, the funeral cantata *Laß, Fürstin, laß noch ein Strahl* (BWV 198), honouring the deceased Electress, Christiane Eberhardine, on 17 October 1727. These same movements, together with two others from BWV 198, were almost certainly parodied for Bach's Mark Passion (BWV 247), performed on Good Friday, 23 March 1731. As with BWV 244a, the music for the Mark Passion is no longer extant but the printed Picander libretto survives,[54] from which some of the music can be reconstructed.[55] There was therefore no inconsistency, from Bach's perspective, in adapting passion music for a funeral, or re-working funeral music for a passion, since in both human mortality is understood in light of the death of Christ.

The Matthew Passion begins with a large-scale chorale fantasia for double chorus, each one with its own supporting instruments: 'Kommt, ihr Töchter, helft mir klagen, Sehet den Bräutigam, Seht ihn als wie ein Lamm' (Come, O daughters, help my crying, see the Bridegroom, see him like a Lamb). This magnificent music seems complete in itself yet there is more: at bar 30, the ringing notes of the chorale *O Lamm Gottes unschuldig*, sung by ripieno sopranos, sound out over the double choral and orchestral resources. The text of the chorale is the metrical paraphrase of the Agnus Dei that had concluded the morning Hauptgottesdienst on Good Friday. With this powerful statement, 'Behold the Lamb of God, who takes away the sin of the world', the Biblical narrative of the passion can begin.

The components of the unfolding passion are often developed within a logical sequence (examples of this pattern are given in Table 7.5):

1. Biblical narrative
2. Reflective comment on the Biblical narrative in a recitative
3. The comment is turned into a prayer in the following aria

**Table 7.6** *Symmetrical structure of Part II of the Matthew Passion*

```
 ┌ 36ᵇ. Chorus I + II: 'Er ist des Todes schuldig'
 │ └ 36ᵈ. Chorus I + II: 'Weissage uns Christe, wer ists'
 │   ── 37. Chorale: 'Wer hat dich so geschlagen'
 │   ┌ 38ᵇ. Chorus II: 'Wahrlich, du bist auch einer'
 │   │  39. Aria: 'Erbarme dich, mein Gott'
 │   └ 41ᵇ Chorus I + II: 'Was gehet uns das an'
 │    ── 45ᵇ. Chorus I + II: 'Laß ihn kreuzigen'
 │       ┌ 46. Chorale: 'Wie wunderbarlich'
 │       └ 49. Aria: 'Aus Liebe will mein Heiland sterben'
 │    ── 50ᵇ. Chorus I + II: 'Laß ihn kreuzigen'
 │   ┌ 50ᵈ. Chorus I + II: 'Sein Blut komme über uns'
 │   │  51. Recit: 'Erbarm es Gott'
 │   └ 53ᵇ. Chorus I + II: 'Gegrüßet seist du, Jüdenkönig'
 │    ── 54. Chorale: 'O Haupt voll Blut und Wunden'
 │   ┌ 58ᵃ. Chorus I + II: 'Der du den Tempel Gottes zerbrichst'
 └── └ 58ᵈ. Chorus I + II: 'Andern hat er geholfen'
```

Although the Matthew Passion is structured somewhat differently from the John Passion – principally because of the differences between the Matthean and Johannine narratives – various chiastic patterns can be discovered. Again Smend's analyses have proved informative, though not as persuasive overall as his work on the John Passion.[56] In much the same way as the John Passion is centred on the quasi-chorale, 'Durch dein Gefängnis, Gottes Sohn', the Matthew Passion is focused on the aria 'Aus Liebe will mein Heiland sterben' (From love my Saviour dies; see Table 7.6[57]).

The Matthew Passion is by any standards a remarkable composition. It is the culmination of the Lutheran tradition of liturgical passions written for performance within Good Friday Vespers. Thereafter, the performance of such works would move outside the confines of church worship; indeed, elsewhere in Germany such non-liturgical oratorios were already being composed and performed.

## Music as *ordinarium*

Bach's cantatas and passions were written essentially as *proprium* music, that is, music composed for the individual Sundays and festivals of the church year. Such liturgical pieces were therefore restricted to the occasion for which they were written, because they were closely related to the Propers of a given day or celebration. But if movements from various cantatas were re-worked into settings of the Ordinary, then the music could be heard several times in any year, because concerted settings of the *Missa* – the Kyrie and Gloria – were required in Leipzig at major festivals. Moreover, similar settings of other parts of the Ordinary, such as the Credo, Sanctus and Agnus Dei, were also sung at various times throughout the church year. Thus from the 1730s Bach was concerned to transform some of his finest music from *proprium* to *ordinarium*. But he was already familiar with the concept of a setting of the Ordinary that could be repeated on a variety of occasions: the Magnificat, composed during his first year in Leipzig, a concerted setting of the Ordinary canticle at Vespers.

## The Magnificat

Until quite recently, the prevailing view has been that there were just three occasions during the church year when a concerted setting of the Latin Magnificat was performed within Vespers during Bach's tenure as Thomaskantor: Christmas Day, Easter Day and the Feast of Pentecost.[58] But the researches of Robert Cammarota have demonstrated that there were many more occasions on which such a setting would have been performed, not only in Leipzig but elsewhere in Lutheran Germany. For example, he draws attention to the twenty-two larger settings of the Magnificat that Johann Philipp Krieger directed in the Weissenfels court chapel during the year 1684–5.[59] Cammarota has computed, on the basis of the extant liturgical evidence, that instead of just three there was a minimum of sixteen occasions during the church year when Bach would have been required to direct a concerted setting of the Magnificat at Vespers. This suggests that Bach had access to a significant repertoire of Magnificat settings, by various composers, available for use throughout the church year. This manuscript corpus, as Cammarota has convincingly argued, was substantially dispersed by Breitkopf during the final quarter of the eighteenth century. Two manuscripts in Bach's hand have survived, comprising Magnificat settings and movements by other composers: one by Antonio Caldara, copied sometime between 1740 and 1742 (BWV 1082), and another by an anonymous composer (BWV Anhang 30) copied sometime after 1735.[60] There are other manuscript copies of a variety of Magnificat settings compiled by Bach's pupils and copyists during Bach's Leipzig years. We therefore now have a somewhat better understanding of the context within which Bach wrote his Latin Magnificat. It is clearly the most significant of perhaps thirty or forty different settings that Bach used in Leipzig.

Bach's Latin Magnificat exists in two basic forms. The first in E♭ was performed in Leipzig at Christmas Day Vespers in 1723. The Christmas

**Table 7.7** *The structure of the Christmas Magnificat (BWV 243a)*

```
 ┌ 1. Chorus: 'Magnificat'
 │  ┌ 2. Solo: 'Et exultavit'
 │  │  ┌ A. Chorus: 'Vom Himmel hoch'
 │  │  │  ┌ 3. Solo: 'Quia respexit'
 │  │  │  │     4. Chorus: 'Omnes generationes'
 │  │  │  └ 5. Solo: 'Quia fecit mihi magna'
 │  │  └ B. Chorus: 'Freuet euch und jubiliert'
 │  └ 6. Duet: 'Et misericordia'
 └ 7. Chorus: 'Fecit potentiam'
 ┌ C. Chorus: 'Gloria in excelsis Deo'
 │  ┌ 8. Solo: 'Deposuit'
 │  └ 9. Solo: 'Esurientes'
 │     D. Duet: 'Virga Jesse floruit'
 │  ┌ 10. Trio: 'Suscepit Israel'
 │  └ 11. Chorus: 'Sicut locutus est'
 └ 12. Chorus: 'Gloria Patri'
```

connection is established by the fact that this first version of the Magnificat includes four Christmas interpolations performed at specific points within the setting.[61] But did Bach write the Magnificat with Christmas in mind, or had there been an earlier performance? For Spitta and others, the Christmas connection is conclusive, since there would not have been an earlier opportunity for it to have been performed in 1723, but Cammarota's researches now put that conclusion in some doubt. The four Christmas interpolations do not occur in sequence within the manuscript but are appended at the end, with indications as to where they would have been inserted within the Magnificat. It is therefore possible that the Magnificat could have been performed earlier, without the interpolated movements. The most likely occasion would have been at Vespers on the First Sunday in Advent, 28 November 1723. If so, the version with additional movements would reflect a second performance a month later, at Vespers on Christmas Day 1723.

Bach was careful not to disturb the largely symmetrical tonal plan of the original twelve movements by the insertion of the Christmas interpolations.[62] Indeed, by inserting them at non-traditional locations within the text of the Magnificat, Bach created a thoughtful bipartite structure, the first part symmetrically centred on the chorus 'Omnes generationes', and the second framed by the two liturgical Glorias: the 'Gloria in excelsis Deo' and the 'Gloria Patri' (see Table 7.7).[63]

Sometime between 1732 and 1735 – most probably during the first half of the year 1733, when he was also working on the *Missa* (BWV 232/I; see pp. 112–16 below) – Bach produced a new version of his Magnificat. It remains essentially the same work, but is transposed down a semitone from E♭ to D major, the customary key for celebratory music employing trumpets and timpani. In the process of transposition a number of revisions and adjustments were made: for example, transverse flutes replacing recorders, the substitution of two oboes in place of the trumpet for the *tonus peregrinus* melody in the 'Suscepit Israel' movement (No. 10), and the omission of the four Christmas interpolations. The frequently made argument that he did so in order to make the work usable for the other two principal festivals is now seen to be a *non sequitur*. Since the E♭ version had the interpolations appended at the end, they could easily have been omitted, and, to judge from the fruits of Cammarota's research, had probably been performed several times over the years. The D major version of the Magnificat – the one almost universally performed today – is to be seen, therefore, in the same light as the fair copy of the Matthew Passion Bach made around 1736, or the fair copy of the John Passion Bach began around 1739, that is, part of the composer's intention to produce definitive versions of his finest music.

## Sanctus

In Vopelius's *Neu Leipziger Gesangbuch* three different settings of the Sanctus are given: two in chant, for use on regular Sundays, and one in six voices for festal use.[64] Between 1723 and 1746 Bach made use of at least six different concerted settings of the Sanctus: three (BWV 239–41) by other composers and three of his own composition. He wrote the Sanctus in C major (BWV 237) by the beginning of July 1723 and probably performed it on the feast of St John the Baptist, 24 June, in the same service that the cantata *Ihr Menschen, rühmet Gottes Liebe* (BWV 167) was first heard. It is scored for four-part choir, trumpets, timpani, oboes, strings and continuo (including organ). Before the end of the same year he wrote another Sanctus (BWV 238), a four-part fugal chorus with strings and continuo accompaniment, first performed on Christmas Day 1723. For Christmas Day 1724 Bach composed the large-scale setting of the *Sanctus* (BWV 232/III) that was later incorporated into the B minor Mass. Like Vopelius before him, Bach chose to write for six voices, but he was probably as much directly influenced by the Biblical background of the Sanctus as by the setting of the editor of the Leipzig *Gesangbuch*. Isaiah 6:1–2 reads: 'I saw the Lord . . . about him were attendant Seraphim, and each had six wings; one pair covered his face and one pair his feet, and one pair was spread in flight. They were calling ceaselessly to one another . . .' Bach's *Sanctus* abounds in sixes, threes and twos, not only illustrating the Isaiah 6 passage but also symbolising the traditional interpretation of the Sanctus as a

Trinitarian hymn in which each 'Sanctus' is addressed to each of the three Persons of the Trinity in turn. The movement is the only six-part writing in his ecclesiastical choral works and, in addition to timpani and continuo, calls for an orchestra made up of three trumpets, three oboes, and three strings. Further, it makes emphatic use of triplets, especially in the opening bars; it often calls for three vocal parts to be contrasted against the full six-part texture; and on two occasions – both for the duration of three bars – the three highest voices and the three lowest voices call back and forth to each other, imitating the Seraphim of Isaiah's vision. It is a truly magnificent, 'visionary' movement, and it is not surprising that later in life Bach wanted to incorporate it into the grander scheme of the B minor Mass.

## Missae

Bach sent a packet containing a set of twenty-one orchestral and vocal parts of the *Missa* (BWV 232/I; the Kyrie and Gloria of what later became the B minor Mass) to the new Elector of Saxony, Friedrich August II, with a covering letter, dated 27 July 1733, in which he sought the honorary title of Saxon Court Kapellmeister. Bach did this in order to establish his rights in a series of disputes with Leipzig officialdom concerning his duties in the city. Whatever Bach's intentions regarding performance of the *Missa* in the Catholic court chapel of Dresden (the parts he sent show no signs of ever being used), distinctive Lutheran influences can be detected within the *Missa*, especially the Kyrie; these might point towards its use in Leipzig sometime prior to July 1733.

Following Luther's *Deutsche Messe* of 1526, Bach employs a threefold *Kyrie*. It is a simple symmetrical structure in which the soprano duet is framed by two choral fugues:

| | | |
|---|---|---|
| 1. Kyrie eleison I | | choral fugue, single theme |
| | 2. Christe eleison | soprano duet, homophonic variety of themes, with canonic imitation, etc. |
| 3. Kyrie eleison II | | choral fugue, single theme |

Instead of starting out directly with the fugal theme, Bach makes a majestic four-bar announcement at the beginning of the first Kyrie. The soprano motif of these bars is clearly derived from the Kyrie of Luther's *Deutsche Messe*, as is the theme of the following fugue. Robert Marshall has argued that these opening bars were added after the fugue had been composed, since they contain typical compositional errors and corrections, whereas the choral fugue appears to have been copied from a pre-existing draft.[65] Christoph Wolff has demonstrated that this Kyrie I–Christe–Kyrie

II section of the *Missa* was influenced by the Kyrie of the *Missa* by the late composer to the Palatine Electoral court, Johann Hugo von Wilderer (c. 1670–1724), a *Missa* that Bach had copied out some time around 1730.[66]

The Kyrie is a Trinitarian prayer for mercy and the Gloria a Trinitarian hymn of praise. Thus in Vopelius's *Neu Leipziger Gesangbuch* the *Missa* is included within the section of Trinitarian hymns.[67] The same hymnal also divides the *Missa* into the same basic sections, 'Kyrie', 'Gloria in excelsis, et in terra . . .' and 'Laudamus te', as are found in Bach's *Missa* of 1733. The liturgical text of the Gloria is derived from two sources: the angelic hymn of Luke 2:14, to which was added, sometime during the early liturgical development of the Christian church, the hymn beginning 'Laudamus te'. Bach divided the 'Gloria in excelsis' into its component parts by effectively separating the Biblical hymn of the angels from the liturgical hymn of the early church:

**A  Biblical hymn**

> 4. 'Gloria in excelsis Deo' – chorus
> 5. 'Et in terra pax' – chorus

**B  Liturgical hymn**

> ⌐ 6. 'Laudamus te' – soprano aria
> └ 7. 'Gratias agimus' – chorus
> ⌐ 8. 'Domine Deus' – soprano and tenor duet
>       9. 'Qui tollis peccata mundi' – chorus
> └ 10. 'Qui sedes ad dextram' – alto aria
> ⌐ 11. 'Quoniam tu solus' – bass aria
> └ 12. 'Cum Sancto Spiritu' – chorus

The transition from the close of Kyrie II to the opening of the 'Gloria in excelsis Deo', the Biblical hymn, involves more than a change of mood. For Bach it also meant a change in compositional technique. Whereas at the end of Kyrie II the orchestra simply doubles the voice parts, in the Gloria there is independent instrumentation, complete with trumpets and timpani. Some speculate that the movement may have been parodied from a purely instrumental piece. Other movements are certainly parodied. The chorus 'Gratias agimus' (movement 7) is a reworking of the second movement from the cantata *Wir danken dir, Gott, wir danken dir* (BWV 29), written in 1731 for the inauguration of the Leipzig city council, here transformed into a dignified ascription of glory and praise – a double fugue. At the heart of Bach's setting of the liturgical hymn is the chorus 'Qui tollis peccata mundi' (movement 9), a parody of the first movement of the cantata *Schauet doch und sehet* (BWV 46), written for Trinity 10 in 1723. Here in the Gloria the movement is analogous to the 'Crucifixus', the central movement of the later *Symbolum Nicenum*, by focusing on the 'Lamb of God, who takes away the sin of the world', a theological and structural emphasis found in the other *Missae* of Bach (see further below). The final chorus, 'Cum Sancto Spiritu' (movement 12), is an ascription of fugal praise that echoes the opening 'Gloria in excelsis Deo'; indeed, the beginning of the fugal theme resembles an inversion of the opening 'Gloria'. By any standard BWV 232/I is a remarkable example of a Lutheran concerted *Missa*.

During the ten years between 1737/8 and 1747/8 Bach is known to have written a further five *Missae* (BWV 233–6, and the *Missa* in C minor BWV Anh. 29 which is known only in a fragmentary form). Did Bach turn to these settings of the *ordinarium* because his five cycles of *proprium* music, the cantatas, were nearing completion? Did he choose to parody music from the cantatas because he wanted the *Missa* and cantata on a special occasion to be thematically related, such as the *Missa* in G major (BWV 236) and the cantata *Gott der Herr ist Sonn und Schild* (BWV 79), with two movements in common, which could have been performed together in the same service on Reformation Day? Does this concentration on *ordinarium* music only represent Bach's own concerns, or was it also a primary concern of the Leipzig clergy? Although there are many unanswered questions, these *Missae* are more significant in Bach's total output than earlier Bach scholarship was ready to admit.[68]

Of the twenty-four movements of the four *Missae* (BWV 233–6), nineteen are parodies from ten cantatas written between July 1723 and January 1727 (see Table 7.8).[69] The first movement of BWV 233 was taken from an earlier work (BWV 233a), perhaps the opening movement from a now-lost cantata,[70] and two movements from BWV 233 and two from BWV 234 are also likely to be parodies, although the original movements are not known.

Structurally these four *Missae* are very similar, which seems to suggest that they were composed in close proximity to each other. But the 1733 *Missa*, written some years earlier, also has a similar structure, though on a larger scale, which would suggest that the similarities may have more to do with theology than with a particular period of composition. The four *Missae* each begin with a Kyrie movement and continue with a chiastic, five-movement Gloria in which a central aria is framed by two arias and two choruses. The central Gloria movements of two of the *Missae*, are, respectively, settings of the words 'Domini Fili unigeniti' ('Of the only-begotten Son' of the Lord) BWV 235/4, and 'Domine Deus, Agnus Dei' ('O Lord God, Lamb of God') BWV 236/4; the central Gloria movements of the other two (BWV 233/4 and BWV 234/4), as well as that of the 1733 Gloria (BWV 232/I/9), are settings of 'Qui tollis peccata mundi' ('Who takest away the sins of the world'), the relative clause of 'Domine Deus,

**Table 7.8** *Sources of the* Missae *(BWV 233–236)*

| Missae | BWV 17 | BWV 40 | BWV 67 | BWV 72 | BWV 79 | BWV 102 | BWV 136 | BWV 138 | BWV 179 | BWV 187 |
|---|---|---|---|---|---|---|---|---|---|---|
| *Missa* in A (BWV 234) | | | | | | | | | | |
| 1 Kyrie | | ? | | | | | | | | |
| 2 Gloria | | | 6 | | | | | | | |
| 3 Domine Deus | | ? | | | | | | | | |
| 4 Qui tollis | | | | | | | | | 5 | |
| 5 Quoniam | | | | | 2 | | | | | |
| 6 Cum Sancto Spiritu | | | | | | | 1 | | | |
| *Missa* in G (BWV 236) | | | | | | | | | | |
| 1 Kyrie | | | | | | | | | 1 | |
| 2 Gloria | | | | | 1 | | | | | |
| 3 Gratias | | | | | | | | 4 | | |
| 4 Domine Deus | | | | | 5 | | | | | |
| 5 Quoniam | | | | | | | | | 3 | |
| 6 Cum Sancto Spiritu | 1 | | | | | | | | | |
| *Missa* in G minor (BWV 235) | | | | | | | | | | |
| 1 Kyrie | | | | | | 1 | | | | |
| 2 Gloria | | | | 1 | | | | | | |
| 3 Gratias | | | | | | | | | | 4 |
| 4 Domini Fili | | | | | | | | | | 3 |
| 5 Qui tollis | | | | | | | | | | 5 |
| 6 Cum Sancto Spiritu | | | | | | | | | | 1 |
| *Missa* in F minor (BWV 233) | | | | | | | | | | |
| 1 Kyrie | 233a | | | | | | | | | |
| 2 Gloria | | ? | | | | | | | | |
| 3 Domine Deus | | ? | | | | | | | | |
| 4 Qui tollis | | | | | | 3 | | | | |
| 5 Quoniam | | | | | | 5 | | | | |
| 6 Cum Sancto Spiritu | | 1 | | | | | | | | |

Agnus Dei'. In two of the *Missae* the focus is on Christ, 'the Lord God', the 'only-begotten Son', who is the 'Agnus Dei', the sacrificial Lamb; in the other three the turning-point, the literal *crux*, is the work of Christ, 'who takest away the sins of the world'. The meaning of the Eucharist is therefore underscored by the anticipation of the petition to be sung during the distribution of communion: sometimes 'Qui tollis peccata mundi' from the Latin Agnus Dei, or, more frequently, 'der du trägst die Sünd' der Welt' from the German Agnus Dei, 'Christe, du Lamm Gottes'. That all five of the central Gloria movements are known parodies in no way diminishes either the creativity of the composer or the integrity of his liturgical music. Indeed, the care and consistency he demonstrated in the (re-) composition of the four *Missae* is surpassed only by the B minor Mass, the pinnacle of Bach's vocal works.

## B minor Mass[71]

Despite innumerable performances and intensive musicological investigation over the past century or so, there is much about the origins of the B minor Mass that remains unknown or problematic. What is now known as Bach's B minor Mass is made up of music composed between 1714 and 1749, that is, music that spans almost all of Bach's compositional career. However, the now familiar form of the work dates from sometime between 1748 and 1749. Bach arranged his music in four distinct sections: 1. *Missa* (BWV 232/I), 2. *Symbolum Nicenum* (BWV 232/II), 3. *Sanctus* (BWV 232/III), and 4. *Osanna* to *Dona nobis pacem* (BWV 232/IV).

What exactly Bach's motives were in preparing this *Missa tota* has been the subject of much speculation. On the one hand, there are those who have noted that in the inventory of C. P. E. Bach's estate, published in 1790, the work is described as 'Die große catholische Messe' (The Great Catholic Mass). This has been taken as J. S. Bach's own description of the work and that he had therefore self-consciously set out to compose a complete Mass for the Roman liturgy. On the other hand, the forms of the Latin texts that Bach employed reflect Lutheran rather than Catholic usage, and the division of the Mass into four, rather than the traditional five Catholic sections, underscores its Lutheran origins. But these points of view, rather than being mutually exclusive, underline the probability that Bach created a work that stands in the general tradition of Catholic masses, by setting the complete Ordinary, but which nevertheless grows out of a particular Lutheran liturgical usage. Although the complete work was far too long for performance at a Lutheran Mass – or a Catholic Mass, for that matter – each of its constituent sections could have been performed in a Lutheran Mass.

What is known of the origins of this *Missa tota* can be summarised as follows. First, sometime between around 1743 and August 1748 the 1724 *Sanctus* in D (BWV 232/III) was performed again in Leipzig. Secondly, the Latin cantata *Gloria in excelsis Deo* (BWV 191), a parody of music from the *Missa* of 1733 (BWV 232/I), was performed at Christmas within the same period that the *Sanctus* was re-performed, that is, sometime between 1743 and 1746. Gregory Butler has recently made a persuasive case for Cantata 191 having been performed in the University church (Paulinerkirche), rather than in either the Thomaskirche or the Nikolaikirche, at Christmas 1745.[72] Thirdly, in the early 1740s Bach made manuscript copies of a number of masses by Catholic composers, such as

Lotti, Caldara and Palestrina. In particular, he performed the Kyrie and Gloria from Palestrina's *Missa sine nomine* in Leipzig in 1742, and, apparently, similar movements from six Masses by Giovanni Battista Bassani were copied for performance sometime between 1735 and 1742. Thus the re-performance of music from the 1733 *Missa* and the 1724 *Sanctus*, together with his recent experience of Catholic masses, may well have been the inspiration for Bach to create the *Missa tota*, beginning sometime around 1746. Significantly the copies of the Bassani masses included not simply the Kyrie and Gloria but also the Credo. Thus it would seem that during the late 1730s and early 1740s concerted settings of the Nicene Creed were perhaps becoming more frequent in the Leipzig liturgy. In the Bassani Credos Bach incorporated into the existing music the first line of the text that was missing in these Catholic masses – because it was customarily sung by the priest – 'Credo in unum Deum', which in Bach's *Symbolum Nicenum* (BWV 232/II) is the first movement.

In recent years a manuscript of the 'Credo' movement of the *Symbolum Nicenum* in the hand of Johann Friedrich Agricola has been discovered.[73] Agricola was one of Bach's leading students in Leipzig between 1738 and 1741, who remained close to the Bach family in later years. After Johann Sebastian's death Agricola collaborated with C. P. E. Bach in writing the Thomaskantor's *Nekrolog*. What is significant about this manuscript is that it is a careful copy, almost identical with that found in Bach's holograph score of the B minor Mass, except that it is in the key of G major, that is, a whole tone lower than Bach's A major version. Examination of the movement in Bach's autograph score reveals that there are a number of errors suggesting that the composer was transposing from an existing score, rather than simply copying the movement from a draft into the final score.[74] This seems to suggest that there was an earlier version of the *Symbolum Nicenum*, from which Agricola copied this first movement and which Bach transposed into the score of his *Missa tota*. What cannot be known is whether the 'Credo' Agricola copied from was a complete setting of the Nicene Creed, a working draft, or a single movement.[75] The date of Agricola's manuscript copy of the 'Credo' movement has not yet been positively established, but it seems to have been completed around the time he made copies of other Bach works, that is, c. 1748.[76] Since it is now known that Bach entered the remainder of the work, from the 'Credo' to the end, into the original score during the period between August 1748 and October 1749,[77] the discovery of this Agricola manuscript suggests that an earlier form or draft of the *Symbolum Nicenum* existed in the period immediately prior to Bach's completion of the manuscript score of the B minor Mass.

The Nicene Creed, sequentially the next part of the Ordinary after the Kyrie and Gloria, was treated as an independent section (BWV 232/II).

During the process of compilation and composition of this *Symbolum Nicenum* Bach changed his mind over the structural relationships of the individual movements. This is evident from his manuscript score. Bach originally planned to set the Creed in eight movements, possibly conceiving it as a musical counterpart of Luther's threefold, Trinitarian, exposition of the Creed in his Large and Small Catechisms.[78]

1. 'Credo in unum Deum'
2. 'Patrem omnipotentem'

3. 'Et in unum Dominum' (including 'Et incarnatus est')
4. 'Crucifixus'
5. 'Et resurrexit'

6. 'Et in Spiritum sanctum'
7. 'Confiteor'
8. 'Et expecto'

Just how far Bach had proceeded with this plan is difficult to say, but at some later date – certainly after he had written out some, or all, of the 'Crucifixus' into the manuscript score – he decided to change the whole structure of the *Symbolum Nicenum*. Instead of the original eight movements he apparently decided on a symmetrical structure of nine, with the 'Crucifixus' at the centre. There was an obvious theological reason for doing so, since the work of Christ on the cross stands at the centre of Christianity and also at the centre of the classic confession of faith, and similar symmetrical patterns are a marked feature of Bach's mature compositions (see above).

In order to create this focal point of the *Symbolum Nicenum* Bach first re-wrote the voice parts of the duet 'Et in unum Dominum', to eliminate the words 'Et incarnatus est', and included the newly written parts in an appendix given at the end of the manuscript score of the *Symbolum Nicenum*. He then composed the now familiar meditative 'Et incarnatus est', written out on a separate sheet and inserted into the score before the 'Crucifixus':

1. 'Credo in unum Deum' – chorus
2. 'Patrem omnipotentem' – chorus
3. 'Et in unum Dominum' – duet
4. 'Et incarnatus est' – chorus
5. 'Crucifixus' – chorus
6. 'Et resurrexit' – chorus
7. 'Et in Spiritum sanctum' – solo
8. 'Confiteor' – chorus
9. 'Et expecto' – chorus[79]

As with the four Lutheran *Missae*, the *Symbolum Nicenum* is largely the product of parodied movements. The 'Credo in unum Deum' is an obvious exception, a masterpiece of contrapuntal engineering, an eight-part – five voices, two upper strings, and continuo – movement in the *stile antico*. The feeling of antiquity is reinforced by the fugal theme which is developed from the intonation, the opening melodic phrase of the Gregorian chant 'Credo in unum Deum'. The second movement, 'Patrem omnipotentem', is an adaptation of the first movement of Cantata 171, *Gott, wie dein Name, so ist auch dein Ruhm*, written for New Year's Day 1729, and associated with the text of Psalm 48.10: 'O God, according to thy Name, so also is thy glory to the ends of the world', a confession of faith in the Creator, and thus akin to the opening statements of the *Symbolum Nicenum*. Bach therefore, with understandable logic, uses the same music he had originally composed to glorify God's name, almost twenty years earlier, to extol the specific name of God, 'Patrem omnipo-tentem', but not without some substantial recomposition.

In the symmetrical structure of the *Symbolum Nicenum* a pair of choral movements occur at the beginning and at the end. The first move-ment of the concluding pair, 'Confiteor unum baptisma', has many links with the opening 'Credo in unum Deum'. It is apparently newly composed in the *stile antico*, and the associated Gregorian melody is heard within the counterpoint. Musically the word 'Confiteor' is stressed, together with 'in remissionem peccatorum', thus implying the correlation that to believe is to be forgiven.

Following the 'Confiteor', the text 'Et expecto resurrectionem mortuo-rum' is heard twice: first in an Adagio section emphasising 'death' fol-lowed by a Vivace e allegro depicting 'resurrection'. This repetition of the text blurs the distinction between the two movements 8 and 9, and paral-lels the close relationship between movements 1 and 2. Movement 9, like movement 2, is a re-working of an earlier piece from a cantata. Bach took the second movement of Cantata 120, *Gott, man lobet dich in der Stille*, a Ratswahl cantata performed in 1728, and substantially recomposed it for the final statement of the *Symbolum Nicenum*.[80]

Movements 3 and 4 are paired together in Bach's chiastic structure, but not as closely as movements 1 and 2. 'Et in unum Deum', like 'Christe eleison', is a duet in which the differences and similarities of the Father–Son relationship are depicted. This is appropriate since the words of the text stand at the beginning of the second paragraph of the Nicene Creed, which centres on the person and work of God the Son. 'Et in unum Deum' is followed by the 'Et incarnatus est' movement, inserted as something of an afterthought, although it is anything but superficial. The downward motion of the upper strings and the voice entries symbolise the 'downward' movement of the Incarnation, God taking human form.

The two movements that immediately follow the central movement are 6 and 7: 'Et resurrexit' and 'Et in Spiritum Sanctum'. The first is a virtuoso, concerto-like movement which calls for the full orchestral and vocal resources for the first time in the *Symbolum Nicenum*. The second (movement 7) is calm, tranquil and light in comparison with the previous movement.

At the centre of Bach's monumental setting of the *Symbolum Nicenum* is the 'Crucifixus'. The music is a parody of the opening section of the first movement of the Weimar cantata, written for the Third Sunday after Easter in 1714, *Weinen, Klagen, Sorgen, Zagen* (BWV 12). This cantata libretto deals with the significance of the cross in the Christian life, but does so in a rather oblique, almost hidden, way. For example, the second part of the first movement speaks of 'the sign of Jesus' but does not actually use the term 'cross', although the implied meaning is clear. Thus in the original cantata there was already a 'crucifixion' motif, and therefore it is easy to see why Bach chose to re-use this particular music in this pivotal position in the *Symbolum Nicenum*. Bach reworked this music in small but significant ways, such as the addition of a four-bar introduction in which the repeated passacaglia theme in the continuo is clearly stated, and the modification of the upper voice parts to intensify the declamation of 'Crucifixus'.

Although the B minor Mass was written in separate sections, there are nevertheless clear signs that the composer viewed it as a unified whole. Thus 'Crucifixus' (BWV 232/II/5) has links with 'Qui tollis peccata mundi' (BWV 232/I/9). Significantly both are pivotal movements in the centre of chiastic structures (see diagrams above); they are the only two movements in the Mass in which the normal five-voice choral writing is reduced to four (with no part for first soprano); and both have pulsating, anxious note-repetitions in the continuo. These connections are not arbitrary, for he 'who takes away the sin of the world' did so by the work of the cross.

Although the Osanna and Benedictus occur at the beginning of the fourth section (BWV 232/IV) they belong to the *Sanctus*. The separation of the Osanna and Benedictus from the latter is to be explained by Lutheran usage in Leipzig. From evidence found in Vopelius's *Neu Leipziger Gesangbuch* (1682) it appears that when the Sanctus was sung monodically the Osanna and Benedictus were included, but if a polyphonic or concerted setting of the Sanctus was sung they were customarily omitted.[81] Thus the original *Sanctus* in D (BWV 232/III) did not include the Osanna and Benedictus. But for his *Missa tota* Bach included both, and in doing so underlined his unitive understanding of the work. Although these final movements of the B minor Mass exist in a separate, fourth section, they could not be performed as a separate unit, as the first three sections could. There is the possibility that this final section is to be considered *musica sub communione*, that is, music performed during the distribution of communion. The Agnus Dei was certainly *musica sub communione*, but to perform the Osanna and Benedictus at this point, isolated from the *Sanctus* to which they liturgically belong, does not make any sense. The implication is that by including these additional pieces associated with the *Sanctus*, Bach intended that the two final sections of the B minor Mass (BWV 232/III–IV) should form one unit. If this is correct it would also mean that although the *Missa tota* physically comprises four distinct parts, conceptually the composer regarded it as a work in three sections, a chiastic arrangement centring on the Nicene Creed:

I.   Kyrie–Gloria (BWV 232/I)
II   Symbolum Nicenum (BWV 232/II)
III  Sanctus–Agnus Dei (BWV 232/III–IV)

The final, double section Sanctus-Agnus Dei, has a distinctive chiastic structure:

```
┌ Sanctus
│  ┌ Osanna in excelsis
│  [   Benedictus
│  └ Osanna in excelsis
└ Agnus Dei⁸²
```

There are a few signs of hurried work in the final section (BWV 232/IV). The Benedictus appears on spare staves following on from the Osanna, and there is no indication which obbligato instrument Bach had in mind. Almost certainly the composer intended a flute rather than violin, but there is no indication in the score. This is a reminder that the B minor Mass is an incomplete work, in the sense that no performing parts exist for three of the sections (BWV 232/II–IV), parts that would have clarified some of the problems found in the score.

Most of the final movements are parodies of earlier music. The repeated Osanna (BWV 232/IV/1 & 3) is almost certainly a parody of the first movement of the celebratory cantata in honour of August of Saxony, *Es lebe der König, der Vater im Lande* (BWV Anh. 11), performed on 3 August 1734.[83] The central Benedictus (BWV 232/IV/2) may well be a parody, but Kobayashi has argued, from the fact that there are traces of the composer's drafts in the manuscript score that were later notated in dark ink, that it is an original composition.[84]

The final two movements of the B minor Mass, setting the text of the Agnus Dei, are both parodies. The first, 'Agnus Dei' (BWV 232/IV/4) is an astonishing piece of careful recomposition,[85] and the final movement (BWV 232/IV/5), 'Dona nobis pacem', is not only the conclusion of the Agnus Dei but also the coda of the *Missa tota*. For this final petition of the Agnus Dei Bach re-used the music of the 'Gratias agimus tibi' (BWV 23/I/7), which was itself a parody of the second movement of the Ratswahl cantata *Wir danken dir* (BWV 29). Again the unity of the B minor Mass as a whole is emphasised, and the concept of 'danken'/ 'gratias'/Eucharist/thanksgiving, the very essence of the Mass – Lutheran or Catholic – is both underscored and reiterated at the end of the manuscript score of the work. Opinion is divided on whether the composer intended the B minor Mass to be performed as a complete whole. Whatever his intentions, Bach himself never heard his massive B minor Mass in a single performance.

The B minor Mass, like other mature vocal works of the composer, is a composite entity with much of the music having been written at an earlier time for other contexts. But these works are anything but disjointed amalgams of earlier composed music. They are consummate masterworks in which the master-composer has, with superlative skill, created musical expositions of two fundamental Christian doctrines: Incarnation in the Christmas Oratorio, Atonement in the Passions, and both doctrines together in the profound B minor Mass.

# 8  The instrumental music

*Werner Breig*

## The repertory

The Bach literature shows no unified approach to the categorisation of the instrumental music: while some writers describe the entire repertory as 'chamber music', others speak of 'chamber and orchestral music'. The reason for this uncertainty lies in the historical change in the meaning of the terms 'chamber music' and 'orchestra'. For Bach's contemporaries, the term 'chamber music' covered all types of music written for the court and for domestic consumption, but excluded music intended for the church and theatre.[1] In his letter releasing Bach from his service in 1723, the composer's employer in Köthen could write, therefore, that Bach had served him as 'Kapellmeister and director of our chamber music'.[2] According to our contemporary understanding of the term, it is now restricted to 'music written for and performed by a small ensemble, usually instrumental, with one performer on a part'.[3]

The word 'orchestra' was occasionally used in Bach's day to refer to a relatively large body of players,[4] or so it would appear to be used by Silvius Leopold Weiss in a letter to Johann Mattheson of 1723: 'But to accompany on the lute in the orchestra, that would of course be too weak.'[5] In general, however, it may be said that neither Bach nor his contemporaries drew a distinction in principle between an 'orchestra' and an ensemble that performed 'chamber music'.

The list below provides an overview of the whole repertory and the various possible ways of subdividing it (an asterisk indicates those works that were collected together by Bach himself to form a self-contained set).[6]

| | | |
|---|---|---|
| a | 1001–6 | * 6 sonatas and partitas for solo violin |
| b | 1007–12 | * 6 suites for solo cello |
| c | 1013 | Partita for solo flute |
| d | 1014–19 | * 6 sonatas for harpsichord and violin |
| e | 1021, 1023 | Sonatas for violin and continuo |
| f | 1025 | Suite for violin and harpsichord after S. L. Weiss |
| g | 1026 | Fugue in G minor for violin and continuo |
| h | 1027–9 | Sonatas for harpsichord and viola da gamba |
| i | 1030–2 | Sonatas for harpsichord and flute |

| | | | | |
|---|---|---|---|---|
| j | 1033–5 | Sonatas for flute and continuo | | |
| k | 1038 | Sonata for flute, violin and continuo | | |
| l | 1039 | Sonata for 2 flutes and continuo | | |
| m | 1079/3 | Sonata for flute, violin and continuo | | |
| n | 1041–2 | Concertos for violin and strings | | |
| o | 1043 | Concerto for 2 violins and strings | | |
| p | 1044 | Concerto for flute, violin, harpsichord and strings | | |
| q | 1046–51 | * 6 Brandenburg Concertos | | |
| r | 1052–7 | * 6 concertos for harpsichord and strings | | |
| s | 1058–9 | Concertos for harpsichord and strings | | |
| t | 1060–2 | Concertos for 2 harpsichords and strings | | |
| u | 1063–5 | Concertos for 3 or 4 harpsichords and strings | | |
| v | (deest) | Concertos that can be reconstructed from transcriptions[7] | | |
| w | 1066–9 | Overtures (Orchestral suites) | | |

| | BWV | BG, MGG 1 | BC | BWV | NBA, New Grove |
|---|---|---|---|---|---|
| a | 1001–6 | | Chamber works for a solo instrument | | |
| b | 1007–12 | | | | |
| c | 1013 | | | | |
| d | 1014–19 | | | | |
| e | 1021, 1023 | | | | |
| f | 1025 | | | | |
| g | 1026 | | Chamber works for duo or trio | Chamber works | Chamber works |
| h | 1027–9 | | | | |
| i | 1030–2 | | | | |
| j | 1033–5 | Chamber works | | | |
| k | 1038 | | | | |
| l | 1039 | | | | |
| m | 1079/3 | | | | |
| n | 1041–2 | | Chamber works for larger ensemble | Concertos & sinfonias | Orchestral works |
| o | 1043 | | | | |
| p | 1044 | | | | |
| q | 1046–51 | | | | |
| r | 1052–7 | | | | |
| s | 1058–9 | | | | |
| t | 1060–2 | | | | |
| u | 1063–5 | | | | |
| v | (deest) | | | | |
| w | 1066–9 | Orchestral works | | Overtures | |

Adopting historical terminology, the old Bach-Gesellschaft edition (*BG*) describes virtually all these works as 'chamber works'. Only the four orchestral suites are treated as 'orchestral works', perhaps because three of them are scored for groups of strings and winds.[8] (Alternatively, the historical origins of the overture in theatre music may have encouraged the editors to categorise them in this way.) The work-list appended to Friedrich Blume's article on Bach in the first edition of *MGG* (*MGG* 1) follows the categorisation of the old complete edition. More recently, the *Bach Compendium* (*BC*) has reverted to the earlier terminology and drawn a distinction between 'chamber music for one solo instrument' (M), 'chamber music for duo or trio' (N) and 'chamber music for larger ensemble' (O).[9] The last of these three groups also includes the four orchestral suites.

In the first edition of his *Bach-Werke-Verzeichnis* (1950), Wolfgang Schmieder used the term 'chamber music' in its modern sense and applied it to works scored for forces no greater than those required for trio sonatas; works for larger forces were arranged generically under the headings 'Concertos and Sinfonias' and 'Overtures'. A similar division is adopted by the *Neue Bach-Ausgabe* (*NBA*, series VI and VII) and by the article on Bach in the *New Grove dictionary*: both consistently use the modern categories of 'chamber music' and 'orchestral music'.

The present essay does not opt for one or other of these terms but seeks, wherever possible, to go back to the titles that Bach himself used, namely, solo, sonata, concerto and overture. Yet we cannot ignore the fact that, within the works under discussion, there is a distinction regarding Bach's treatment of the instruments at his disposal, one that occurs at precisely the point where the line is customarily drawn between chamber and orchestral music, namely, between a work written in three-stave, and one written in five-stave, score (unlike his contemporaries, Vivaldi, Handel and Fasch, Bach did not write four-stave scores – i.e., for two violins, viola and continuo – for entire works; he only used this scoring for a few individual movements).[10]

Scores of up to three staves are a faithful reflection of what might be termed the musical 'texture', whereas in scores of five or more staves, the instrumental part is not identical to the 'voice' of the polyphonic texture, which means that 'composition' in the narrower sense and 'instrumentation' are now two separate stages in the compositional process. (This is true even if the composer writes out the full score at the outset, without first preparing a 'texture sketch'.)

A simple example may help to explain this distinction. The full score of the Violin Concerto in E major BWV 1042 is on five staves (violino concertato, violini I and II, viola and continuo). The dual function of the solo violin was self-evident in Baroque violin concertos: on the one hand, it formed part of the ripieno in the tuttis, playing in unison with the first violins, while, on the other, it went its own way in the solo sections. Even within the ripieno, however, the relationship between texture and full score is flexible. In the first movement, bars 53–6 have a four-part texture, with the figurations in the solo violin accompanied by a three-part ripieno texture; but in the full score the two ripieno violins, playing the topmost voice in unison, retain their individual staves. Similar findings may be observed elsewhere in the piece: thus, in bars 23–4 of the first movement the bass line (B–A♯–G♯–C♯–F♯) is divided between the continuo and the viola, with the latter presenting a syncopated repetition of the continuo line a quaver later; and in bars 5–6 of the second movement, the four-part ripieno score displays a four-part texture that shortly becomes monophonic.

That the relationship between texture and score becomes increasingly complex the more instruments that are involved (particularly if those instruments are strings and winds) is self-evident. (A glance at the opening bars of the twelve-stave full score of the first Brandenburg Concerto will suffice to illustrate the complexity of the relationships.)

Attempts to define Bach's 'orchestral style' by reference to today's orchestral practice have proved to be problematical.[11] Yet it is perfectly possible – without the need to become embroiled in the controversies surrounding performance practice – to distinguish between musical structures in which texture and score are identical and those in which the clarification of instrumentation takes precedence over texture in the score. To describe structures of the second kind as 'orchestral' is surely legitimate, even if it does not reflect the terminology in use in Bach's own time.

## Solo works

The title-page of Bach's autograph fair copy of the six Sonatas and Partitas for unaccompanied violin includes the words 'Libro Primo' after the actual title, *Sei Solo à Violino senza Basso accompagnato*. These words clearly imply that Bach intended to continue the series with a 'Secondo libro' of works for unaccompanied cello, as indeed he did. But it is also worth asking whether, in describing this collection as 'Primo libro', Bach may not also have planned to write a whole series of similar sets of instrumental works: a 'Terzo libro' might have followed in the form of six partitas for unaccompanied flute (only one such work survives); and perhaps, in turn, these three volumes of solo works would have launched a whole series of instrumental works for various forces.

Such considerations necessarily remain within the realm of speculation, yet it is clear that, as a collection, the six pieces for unaccompanied violin show all the signs of careful overall planning, as one would expect at the beginning of any large-scale project. Of the two different types of work concerned – the four-movement sonata and the partita (suite) consisting largely of dance movements – there are three examples each. The six works as a whole are based on a unifying series of tonalities (G minor – B minor – A minor – D minor – C major – E major), the tonics of which can be interpreted either as the notes of the hexachord from G to E or as a circle of fifths from C to B; moreover, the fundamentals are arranged symmetrically around a palindromic series of intervals: third, second, fourth, second, third.

The six works for unaccompanied cello survive only in copies. The collection as a whole is less rounded and, in contrast to his practice elsewhere, Bach uses two of the tonic notes twice (C and D): G major – D minor – C major – E♭ major – C minor – D major. Nor are the six works written for a single type of cello: Suite no. 5 requires the use of scordatura (the top string is tuned down to g), while Suite no. 6 is scored for a five-stringed instrument. Klaus Hofmann has suggested that the set originally comprised three works (nos. 1–3) and that Bach later added three more works which, although already written, were not initially intended for the collection.[12] (We could perhaps go on from these considerations and, picking up our initial speculations, argue that other groups of works, such as the sonatas for viola da gamba and those for flute, both with continuo and with obbligato harpsichord, were similarly intended to be completed as six-part collections.)

As a compositional model for unaccompanied solo works, the suite must have seemed fundamentally more suitable than the sonata, since the sonata tradition demanded at least one fugal movement. In consequence, the suite-like partita is represented by no fewer than ten out of a total of thirteen pieces for solo instrument.

For three of his works for solo violin, Bach nonetheless ventured into the field of the sonata, with fugal second movements that exploit the violin's capacity for polyphonic effects. Although these fugues include longer episodes in which performer and listener can recover from the rigours of the polyphonic writing, these episodes certainly do not overshadow the fugal sections. On the contrary, the composer seems determined to prove that a violin fugue is not necessarily inferior to a fugue written for an ensemble. A glance at the structure of the fugue from the C major Sonata BWV 1005, for example, reveals the extent to which the whole weight of the composition rests on its elaborately developed fugal structure, with a ratio between the fugal and non-fugal sections of around five to two.

*Structure of C major fugue BWV 1005/2*

| | |
|---|---|
| 0–66 | Exposition |
| 66–92 | Transition, 1st episode (C major – A minor) |
| 92–165 | Stretto exposition |
| 165–201 | 2nd episode: figuration, sometimes with quotations of fugue subject; closing pedal point on D, with subject above it, involving *Fortspinnung* (E minor – G major) |
| 201–45 | Exposition in inversion ('al riverso') |
| 245–88 | 3rd episode with thematic figuration; closing pedal point on G, with subject above it, involving *Fortspinnung* as in episode 2 (C major – dominant of C major) |
| 288–354 | Da capo of bars 0–66 |

Apart from the polyphonic movements (including the Chaconne at the end of the Second Partita), in which Bach explores the very limits of the instrument's capabilities, we also find a large number of predominantly monophonic movements with relatively little multiple stopping. Yet, as solutions to a compositional problem, they command our respect no less than the fugues, constituting, as they do, a successful attempt to convey to the listener a sense of the harmonies underlying the unaccompanied melodic line. For Ernst Kurth, Bach's works for unaccompanied violin and cello were prototypes of a linear approach to composition: in his analyses of them, he insisted that even in lines that appear to be based on broken chords, it is the melodic element that is essential to our understanding. 'Bach's line never becomes bogged down in a feeble playing with harmonies.' He compensates for the chordal effects with 'increasing melodic strength'.[13] The utmost effort to reconcile that which actually conflicts is thus characteristic not only of the polyphonic but also of the monophonic movements.

## Ensemble sonatas

Bach's contribution to what might be called the ensemble sonata embraces works scored for the most varied combinations of instruments, but with a clearly recognisable centre of gravity: the works written for a melody instrument and obbligato harpsichord; in other words, sonatas of a type that Bach himself created as a modified version of the traditional trio sonata. A few general observations may not come amiss.

The trio sonata for two melody instruments and continuo arose in Italy in the seventeenth century and counts as one of the principal genres of Baroque instrumental music. The basic idea behind such works is the rivalry between two upper voices of equal status, over a bass line that alternately supports those voices and actively participates in the musical argument. This approach to music-making may be viewed as a residue of the texture of bichorality, now divorced from its spatial dimension. Whereas the vitality of this tradition is still evident in Handel's twenty-five trio sonatas, Bach's attitude to the trio sonata was rather more ambiguous. On the one hand, he retains three-part polyphony for two treble voices and bass as the starting-point for the vast majority of his sonatas, while, on the other, such works are rarely scored for the traditional combination of instruments found in trio sonatas, namely, two treble instruments and a continuo group. Central to Bach's interest was a type of sonata in which the keyboard instrument is not limited to the role of continuo but partici-pates in the performance of the obbligato treble voices (as in the sonatas for melody instrument and obbligato harpsichord) or even assumes responsibility for the entire three-part texture (as in the organ sonatas for two manuals and pedal). The fact that Bach wrote a trio sonata with con-tinuo as part of his *Musical Offering* as late as 1747 is no doubt bound up, above all, with the traditionalist approach to music-making that obtained at the court of Frederick II of Prussia, to whom the piece is dedicated.

Bach's preferred type of instrumental combination – melody instru-ment and obbligato harpsichord[14] – is represented by six surviving sonatas for violin and harpsichord (which Bach himself collected as a set), together with three sonatas for flute and harpsichord,[15] and three for viola da gamba and harpsichord.

Among the works with obbligato harpsichord, there is one – the viola da gamba sonata BWV 1027 – that also survives as a 'genuine' trio sonata for two flutes and continuo (BWV 1039). (It is generally assumed that the version with obbligato harpsichord is the later of the two.[16]) It is entirely conceivable that other sonatas with obbligato harpsichord are transcrip-tions of lost sonatas for two melody instruments and continuo.

Such conjectures become irrelevant, of course, when we turn to those sonatas in which Bach did not restrict himself to imitating trio textures but exploited the harpsichord's potential for full-toned sonorities. Slow movements in particular lend themselves to this treatment: in the six violin sonatas BWV 1014–19, the writing in half the slow movements is in more than three parts.[17] In the introductory Adagio of the E major Sonata BWV 1016, Bach even goes so far as to imitate the texture of a slow con-certo movement: the violin traces a melodically wide-ranging, richly ornamented cantabile line, while the harpsichord adds a polyphonic accompaniment, the three upper voices of which (rather like two violins and a viola) are taken by the right hand, with the left hand taking a bass line in which the doubling of the lower octave, written out in full, implies a cello and violone.

With his set of six sonatas for violin and harpsichord, Bach plainly planned a systematic exploration of the possibilities inherent in the sonata with obbligato harpsichord. This is particularly clear from their fast movements, which, viewed as a whole, constitute a veritable compendium of the formal possibilities of fugue within a trio sonata texture.

Apart from the violin, it was the viola da gamba and flute that Bach considered most suited to partnership with the harpsichord. Christoph Wolff regards it as pure chance that the flute is the only woodwind instrument that Bach used in any of his surviving sonatas: 'In addition to the flute, the oboe and recorder hold such an important place in the scoring of Bach's vocal works that their absence from his sonatas is simply inconceivable.'[18] Although one cannot deny the possibility that large numbers of works have gone missing, it is also conceivable that Bach drew a distinction between concertos and orchestral suites on the one hand and sonatas on the other, in other words, that he preferred to use the oboe as a solo instrument in works scored for larger forces, while favouring the flute in the intimate sonata on account of its tender tone and its capacity for subtle nuance.

The possibilities of the flute and harpsichord as a combination are explored in particularly impressive fashion in the B minor Sonata BWV 1030, a work described by Spitta as 'the best sonata for the flute that has ever existed'.[19] It probably dates from around 1736 and, with the single exception of the trio sonata from *The Musical Offering*, was the last, and perhaps the most important, of Bach's sonatas. It reveals that reflective approach to traditions which we find so frequently in Bach's works from the 1730s onwards. Formally speaking, its opening movement adopts the basic model of a fast concerto movement, but, in keeping with its expressive thematic writing, it is marked 'Andante'. The middle movement, headed 'Largo e dolce', is cast in the form of a flute solo with harpsichord accompaniment, an accompaniment that takes the form, in part, of a written-out thorough-bass, but which is also enlivened by figural writing whenever the flute falls silent or is required to play sustained notes. The final movement, headed 'Presto', is particularly surprising and, indeed, unique in its overall structure, inasmuch as it comprises two heterogeneous sections, an *alla breve* fugue and a gigue-like second section in 12/16 time. Bach has created an ingenious link between them by developing their opening phrases from the same five-note sequence, B–D–C♯–G–F♯. Hans Eppstein has sought to interpret the curious form of this final movement as the result of a two-stage creative process: according to him, the gigue (which is self-contained from the standpoint of its tonality) was written first, 'but was felt to be too lightweight as a counterbalance to the first movement' and was made weightier, therefore, by adding the fugal section before it.[20] But the fugal principle is so intimately bound up with Bach's conception of the sonata as a genre that it is difficult to imagine him planning a work as ambitious as the B minor Sonata without a fugal movement. Be that as it may, the Presto, with its combination of fugal textures and dance-like virtuosity, represents an original and highly effective solution to the problem of the final movement.

## Concertos

The immense formal variety of Bach's concertos emerges from a relatively small number of works. Although the *Bach-Werke-Verzeichnis* lists no fewer than twenty-five concertos under numbers 1041 to 1065, a third of these are not original concertos in the strict sense of the term. Four works are later versions of earlier surviving concertos by the composer (BWV 1054 is based on BWV 1042, BWV 1057 on BWV 1049, BWV 1058 on BWV 1041 and BWV 1062 on BWV 1043); BWV 1065 is a transcription of Vivaldi's Op. 3 no. 10;[21] the single-movement BWV 1045 is now believed to be the sinfonia of a lost cantata;[22] the Triple Concerto in A minor BWV 1044 is adapted from the two-movement keyboard work, BWV 894, and from the Trio Sonata BWV 527/2; and the Double Harpsichord Concerto BWV 1061, having, in essence, no string ripieno, may be seen as related to the Italian Concerto BWV 971. We are left with seventeen works, of which nine have survived in their original instrumentation, together with eight harpsichord concertos whose initial versions are no longer extant:

> BWV 1041–3 (concertos for 1 or 2 violins)
> BWV 1046–51 (6 Brandenburg Concertos)
> BWV 1052, 1053, 1055, 1056, 1059[23] (concertos for 1 harpsichord)
> BWV 1060, 1063, 1064 (concertos for 2 or 3 harpsichords).

Bach's most important model in this respect was Antonio Vivaldi, whose concertos, to quote from a recent monograph on the Italian composer, became 'the very embodiment of the new Italianate concerto and of a new language of instrumental music for the whole of musical Europe in the years around 1710'.[24] From Vivaldi, Bach took over not only the three-movement structure of the cyclical concerto but also ritornello form, which was of central significance to him in fashioning his outer movements.[25]

No less important, of course, was the independence Bach maintained from his model. What he learned from the Vivaldian concerto – the varied, yet regular, alternation between ritornello and episodes, and the progressive exploration of a circle of tonalities between the two outer tonic pillars – was combined with a new formal structure that sought greater rigour and regularity.

The opening movement of the First Brandenburg Concerto may serve to illustrate this point. Three formal elements may be distinguished here. The first is the alternation between ritornello or fragments of a ritornello and episodes. The ritornello entries draw on all the available forces (strings and woodwind choir, sometimes horns too), whereas the episodes are reduced to trio forces in varying combinations. It is clear from this episode that the interplay between ritornello and episode is not tied to any firm distinction between ripieno and solo: what functions as 'tutti' and 'solo' changes constantly within the course of the movement, without, however, calling into question the formal functions of 'ritornello' and 'episode'. A second formal component is the use of the two outer sections to hold together the movement as a whole: at the end we again hear the ritornello in its entirety (Vivaldi is generally satisfied with a fragment of the ritornello at this juncture), as a result of which the entire movement acquires a pronounced framework. To the formal principles of alternation and the profiling of the frame can be added a third: the use of recapitulation. This is achieved by means of the two seven-bar sections in genuine eight-part polyphony in bars 36–42 and 65–71, which are related to each other transpositionally. The first of these sections cadences exactly halfway through the movement on the fifth degree of the scale, while the second moves towards the tonic and leads directly into the final repeat of the ritornello. I have chosen this movement to illustrate my point since the First Brandenburg Concerto is believed to be one of Bach's earliest concertos, at least in its preliminary version, BWV 1046a.[26] If this is so, it would show that Bach had already placed his personal seal on the ritornello concerto style even during his time in Weimar.

In its narrower sense, ritornello form is the form found most frequently in Bach's fast concerto movements,[27] in addition to a single example from among his slow middle movements.[28] Two variants of ritornello form achieved a certain independence as formal types. They are, first, the type imitating a large-scale da capo form (ABA), with ritornellos beginning and ending the A sections[29] and, secondly, the concertato fugue, in which the ritornello is treated fugally.[30] More rarely we find dance-like movements in final position.[31] Rarest of all is a rondo.[32]

One of the characteristic features of Bach's instrumental concertos is the great emphasis given to the slow middle movements on account of their length and elaborate structure. Short movements of intermezzo-like character, as often found in Vivaldi, are alien to Bach's conception of the three-movement concerto. Three main types of slow middle movement may be distinguished:[33] (i) movements that set out from a characteristic bass model (the ostinato principle);[34] (ii) movements characterised by a cantabile melody in the upper voice (the arioso principle);[35] and (iii) imitative movements.[36] Ritornello form is not part of the formal repertory of Bach's slow movements, which, rather, stick to a central musical idea and spin it out at length.[37]

There is little sign that Bach carefully planned the assembly of his various sets of concertos. Certainly the Brandenburg Concertos (which were put together in a presentation score in 1721) form a collection of the usual scope of six pieces and although we can describe them as an instantly recognisable and 'meaningful set',[38] they lack at least one of the characteristics of a planned collection, namely, diversity of tonality. The fact that two of the concertos are in F and two in G major suggests that, whatever the purpose for which Bach collected this group of works together, they were originally independent pieces. At some later date around 1738 Bach compiled a further set of six concertos – the harpsichord concertos BWV 1052–7[39] – but since these works are, without exception, transcriptions of earlier works for melody instruments, it is impossible to speak of a planned entity here either. Of course, we can see from the fact that they were collected together as a six-part set that Bach regarded the revised versions not just as *ad hoc* transcriptions but as works that were valid in their own right, yet the manner in which his concertos have come down to us suggests in general that they are isolated pieces that cannot be marshalled into groups.

## Orchestral suites (overtures)

Bach's contribution to the genre of the French overture or orchestral suite is as qualitatively important as it is quantitatively limited. Unless we are to assume that works have been lost (and there is no real basis for such an assumption), we must consider the external and/or inner reasons for the small number of such works. The external reasons may perhaps be sought in the fact that Bach had few opportunities to perform such suites – but since we do not even know when the four existing works were performed (it is a matter of conjecture whether they were written for the court at Köthen or for performances in Leipzig), it must remain an open question whether such reasons exist at all.

It is easier to imagine the internal reasons for Bach's reserved approach to the genre. If we set out from the premise that Bach was invariably keen to write works of unmistakable originality within each genre, rather than merely exploring nuances within a constant type, we cannot avoid the fact that it was particularly difficult for him to fulfil this requirement in the context of the orchestral suite. This is because the elaborate opening movement, dominating the impression of the entire work, was strictly predetermined as a type. Even Johann Adolph Scheibe remarked that 'all overtures start in the same way, with the result that one misses a certain variety that is otherwise always necessary in music, if all pieces are not to sound the same'.[40] That 'a certain variety' was necessary was wholly in keeping with Bach's own credo as a composer, hence, perhaps, his reservations concerning the orchestral suite.

The sources of all four of Bach's orchestral suites (a fifth, BWV 1070, is generally deemed inauthentic) date from his years in Leipzig. The principal source of Suite no. 1 in C major BWV 1066 almost certainly dates from his first year in office; in its original form, Suite no. 4 in D major BWV 1069 must have been completed before Christmas 1725, since Bach used its opening movement in Cantata 110; Suite no. 3 BWV 1068 (also in D major) survives in a set of orchestral parts dating from 1731; and Suite no. 2 in B minor BWV 1067 survives in a manuscript from around 1738/9.

Bach's attempts to invest each work with an individual profile are clear from the fact that each is scored for different forces, which has important implications for its structure and character. Although the four-part string writing – in the normal distribution for two violins, viola and continuo – provides the essential backbone of each of the four works in question, Bach also makes provision for winds, the nature, number and function of which vary from work to work.

Suite no. 1 BWV 1066 is most closely associated with the French tradition of instrumentation and adds a woodwind group of two oboes and bassoon to the string orchestra. This trio serves, in part, to reinforce the tuttis and lend them a distinctive colour, but it also assumes independent functions in the episodic passages in the middle section of the Overture and in Gavotte II, Bourrée II and Passepied II. The writing for unison strings in Gavotte II is a delightful idea on the composer's part: the fanfare-like melodic line appears to spring from a desire to compensate the listener for the absence of trumpets in the piece.[41]

We may continue this brief survey by considering the second of the orchestral suites to have come down to us, Suite no. 4 in D major BWV 1069. It is scored for three choirs of instruments, namely, trumpets (with timpani), woodwind and strings. The winds comprise three oboes and bassoon and thus form a self-contained group that combines with the strings in four of the movements (the middle section of the Overture, Bourrée I and II and Gavotte) to produce a double-choir texture. The trumpet choir, which Bach appears to have added later, invests the work with a certain splendour and colour, but is not structurally independent: the piece could be performed without it.

Suite no. 3 in D major BWV 1068 is likewise scored for three instrumental choirs: two oboes, three trumpets and timpani, and strings. Such lavish resources notwithstanding, it is the string orchestra that is solely responsible for sustaining the weight of the musical argument. Possibly the piece was originally scored for strings alone, a scoring retained only in the second movement (Air); if so, this would be the only known instrumental work by Bach to be scored purely for four-part strings. It is probable that, as with BWV 1069, Bach would have considered it legitimate to perform the work in its 'fundamental' scoring.

Suite no. 2 in B minor BWV 1067 is the only one of the four in a minor tonality. Its instrumentation, too, sets it apart, the appearance of a flute in addition to the usual complement of strings suggesting nothing so much as a flute concerto. The flute is used as a concertante instrument in the middle section of the Overture, in the second couplet of the Rondeau, in the double of the Polonaise (where it adds a figurative upper voice to the polonaise melody in the bass) and in the final Badinerie. That the work may have been written around 1738/9, the date of its earliest source, is eminently conceivable.[42]

The structure of the opening movement finds the composer adopting a highly unusual solution: the fugal middle section is followed not by the expected repeat of the introductory section in common time but, somewhat surprisingly, by a variation in a slower 3/4 metre. Equally unusual for dance movements are the contrapuntal devices such as the canon at the lower fifth in the outer voices of the Sarabande and the migration of the upper voice of the Polonaise to the bass line in the double. All these features attest to Bach's reflective attitude towards tradition, an attitude clear from other works of this period.[43]

*Translated by Stewart Spencer*

# 9 The keyboard works: Bach as teacher and virtuoso

*Richard D. P. Jones*

According to J. G. Walther's *Musicalisches Lexicon* (Leipzig, 1732), Bach 'learned the first *principia* on the clavier from his eldest brother, Mr. Johann Christoph Bach, formerly organist and schoolmaster at Ohrdruf'.[1] No mention is made here (or in Bach's Obituary, which gives a similar account) of composition, and Johann Christoph is not known to have been a composer.[2] In answer to a query of J. N. Forkel's, Bach's son Carl Philipp Emanuel wrote in 1775: 'The instruction received by [J. S. Bach] in Ohrdruf may well have been designed for an organist and nothing more.'[3] The clear implication is that composition was largely excluded.

Here we have a fact of great importance for the understanding of Bach's early development as a composer: unlike his great contemporary G. F. Handel, he seems to have received no formal tuition in the rudiments of composition.[4] His early compositions, most of which are for keyboard, had dual roots: in his own rapidly growing skill as an organist and harpsichordist ('In a short time he had fully mastered all the pieces his brother had voluntarily given him to learn'[5]); and in his 'observation of the works of the most famous and proficient composers of his day and . . . the fruits of his own reflection upon them'.[6]

To judge by the character of Bach's early keyboard works, both the improvisatory and virtuoso aspects of his playing acted as spurs to his creativity. Improvisation was essential to the keyboard player's training in Bach's day, and numerous passages in the early keyboard works no doubt had an extempore basis, notably the free fantasy interludes in the sonata BWV 963 and in the toccatas BWV 910–15 or the ruminative elaborated chord sequences in the preludes BWV 921–3 and in the third section of the toccatas BWV 910 and 913. In addition, many pieces may have originated, at least in part, as material for the exercise of Bach's own virtuosity. In this light one can view the brilliant fugues in gigue rhythm that end the toccatas BWV 912 and 915, fugues in continuous semiquaver motion such as BWV 914 (last section) and 944/2, and the cadenzas that form a climactic conclusion to many of the early fugues (e.g. BWV 895/2, 948, 949 and 993).

However, these virtuoso and improvisatory elements, the urge 'to run or leap up and down the instrument, to take both hands as full as all the five fingers will allow and to proceed in this wild manner till he by chance finds a resting place',[7] represent only one side of the musical make-up of the young Bach. Just as strong, and eventually predominant, was the impulse to create order in sound, to excel in the art of musical construction.[8] Here Bach appears to have been very largely self-taught. His search for compositional models is illustrated in the story of his illicit copying during the Ohrdruf years (1695–1700) of a book of keyboard pieces belonging to his elder brother Johann Christoph.[9] This book, which is no longer extant,[10] contained music by three seventeenth-century South German composers – J. J. Froberger, J. C. Kerll and J. Pachelbel – two of whom (the second and third) were linked with Johann Christoph in a direct teacher–pupil line.

While studying at the Michaelisschule in Lüneburg (1700–2) Bach must have encountered the music of Georg Böhm, organist at the Johanniskirche. And we are told in the Obituary that 'From Lüneburg he journeyed now and again to Hamburg, to hear the then famous Organist of the Catharinen-Kirche, Johann Adam Reincken.'[11] During this period too he probably first became acquainted with the works of Dietrich Buxtehude, organist at the Marienkirche, Lübeck. The keyboard works of these and other North German composers, some perhaps brought south by Johann Sebastian, were copied out by his brother Johann Christoph in two large volumes – the Möller Manuscript (1704–7) and the Andreas Bach Book (1707/8–13).[12]

C. P. E. Bach mentions not only Böhm, Reincken and Buxtehude (see Chapter 6, p. 82 above) but also Frescobaldi, J. C. F. Fischer, N. A. Strungk and Nicolaus Bruhns as early influences upon his father.[13] Describing these 'favourites' as 'all strong fugue writers', he observes that his father 'Through his own study [of their works] and reflection alone [i.e. without formal tuition] . . . became even in his youth a pure and strong fugue writer.' It was presumably the more reflective side of Bach's musical personality, the passion for order, that attracted him at an early age to the art of fugue and counterpoint. While the immaturities of the earliest fugues are patent, some of the contrapuntal procedures that later became characteristic are already evident: the systematic use of stretto and inversion (Fugue in A major BWV 896/2); the play on direct and inverted forms of the subject (Fugue in A major BWV 949); the regular countersubject as strongly characterised as the subject itself (the posthorn motif in the last movement of the Capriccio in B♭ major BWV 992); and the combination in triple counterpoint of three subjects in contrasting modes of rhythmic movement (Fantasia in G minor BWV 917, Fugue in D minor BWV 948).

When playing these early fugues one is often struck by their awkwardness – they do not always fall easily under the hands. This might seem somewhat surprising, for the works of virtuosos are usually nothing if not idiomatic to their instrument. But C. P. E. Bach, in an illuminating reply to Forkel, divides his father's work into two classes: 'those for which he took the material from improvisations at the keyboard'; and those which were 'composed without instrument, but later tried out on one'.[14] It is a reasonable conjecture that works in which various contrapuntal devices are employed systematically belong for the most part to the second category. At this early stage, Bach's compositional technique being relatively unformed, there is a perceptible dichotomy between the two types, between what one might term the active and the reflective modes. In terms of musical structure these opposites coincide to a certain extent with strict and free forms.[15] The toccatas BWV 910–15 and the sonata BWV 963, with their alternation of free fantasias and fugues, represent early attempts to unite the strict and the free within a broad encompassing framework.

In addition to North German keyboard music, the Möller Manuscript and the Andreas Bach Book contain numerous early compositions of the young Bach, keyboard transcriptions of ensemble works, French and Italian pieces, and keyboard works by such South and Middle German composers as J. C. F. Fischer and Johann Kuhnau. Since this music is largely in the hand of Bach's brother Johann Christoph and since Johann Sebastian himself made a number of entries,[16] it is a reasonable assumption that the latter was for the most part familiar with this repertory.

Five of Johann Kuhnau's celebrated sonatas from the collection *Musicalische Vorstellung einiger Biblischer Historien* (Leipzig, 1700) form the opening items in the Andreas Bach Book. Kuhnau is not included in C. P. E. Bach's list of early influences, but his presence can nonetheless be felt in one of Bach's earliest suites, the *Praeludium et Partita del Tuono Terzo* BWV 833,[17] in his composition of sonatas for solo keyboard (BWV 963 and 967)[18] and in programmatic pieces – the closing fugue of BWV 963, based on a 'Thema all'Imitatio Gallina Cuccu' (theme imitating the hen and cuckoo), and the *Capriccio sopra la lontananza del [suo] fratro dilettissimo* (Capriccio on the absence of his most beloved brother) BWV 992. In later years Bach adopted Kuhnau's *Neue Clavier-Übung* (Leipzig, 1689 and 1692) as a model in the conception of his own *Clavier-Übung* I of 1726–31, which testifies to the value he continued to attach to the older composer's keyboard works. A similarly strong and lasting influence was exerted by the keyboard music of the Baden Kapellmeister J. C. F. Fischer, some of which Bach is known to have possessed:[19] for the early period we have the testimony of C. P. E. Bach;[20] and in Bach's maturity a key model in the conception and composition of *The Well-tempered Clavier* Books I and II (1722 and 1742) was Fischer's *Ariadne Musica* of 1702, a collection of short preludes and fugues in twenty different major and minor keys.[21]

Many of Fischer's instrumental works reflect the French taste of the Baden court. In the seventeenth and early eighteenth centuries German composers of every generation responded afresh to the two most influential national styles of the time – the French and the Italian. J. J. Froberger and Georg Muffat (to name only the best-known examples) were equally at home writing in both styles. In the case of J. S. Bach the issue is complex,[22] for successive waves of French and Italian influence can be felt throughout the course of his life, and no less significant are his indirect encounters with the two leading national styles via the work of various influential German contemporaries.

As a student at Lüneburg Bach already 'had the opportunity to … listen to a then famous band kept by the Duke of Zelle, and consisting for the most part of Frenchmen; thus he acquired a thorough grounding in the French taste'.[23] Moreover, C. P. E. Bach numbers among the composers admired and studied by the young Bach 'some old and good Frenchmen';[24] the Möller Manuscript contains five suites from Lebègue's *Les Pièces de Clavessin* (Paris, 1677); and, together with the Andreas Bach Book, it is today the principal source for the keyboard suites of Georg Böhm, who seems to have acted as an important intermediary in Bach's early encounter with the French style.[25] Among the first fruits of this encounter are the keyboard suites in A and B♭ major BWV 832 and 821.[26]

French influence was not restricted to French-style keyboard music. The orchestral overture-suite, extracted from opera, was not only transcribed for keyboard by German musicians but cultivated as an independent genre, both in orchestral (as in J. C. F. Fischer's *Le Journal du printems*, Op. 1, 1695) and keyboard garbs (as in Fischer's *Les Pièces de Clavessin*, Op. 2, 1696). The Möller Manuscript and the Andreas Bach Book contain not only suites from operas but seven examples of the keyboard variety, including Georg Böhm's exceptionally fine Ouverture in D. To this genre the young Bach contributed the Ouvertures in F and G minor, BWV 820 and 822.[27]

With regard to Italian keyboard music, Bach is known to have studied the works of Frescobaldi as a young man,[28] and to have made a copy of his *Fiori musicali* (Venice, 1635) in 1714.[29] Moreover, according to Franz Hauser, he copied out a Toccata and Passacaglia by Bernardo Pasquini.[30] But at least as strong in its effect upon the keyboard works of the young Bach was the impact of Italian instrumental music. His early fugues on themes from Italian trio sonatas – by Albinoni (BWV 946, 950 and 951), Corelli (BWV 579) and Legrenzi (BWV 574) – indicate that he had a wide

knowledge of this repertory. He also encountered the Italian style indirectly via the work of North German composers – in particular, Georg
Böhm, who had experienced the interaction of the French and Italian
styles at the Hamburg opera in the 1690s, and J. A. Reincken.[31] In his
*Hortus musicus* (Hamburg, 1687) Reincken unites the Italian *sonata da
chiesa* and *sonata da camera*: typically, the movements Grave–Allegro–
Adagio–Presto are immediately followed by Allemande–Courante–
Sarabande–Gigue. Three sonatas from this collection (nos. 1, 6 and 11)
were, in whole or in part, reworked by Bach for solo keyboard in his Sonatas
in A minor and C major BWV 965–6 and his Fugue in B♭ major BWV 954.

Expansion of Bach's range of style went hand in hand with refinements
in his compositional technique. Thus, in absorbing Italian instrumental
style, he learnt a new clarity of theme and structure and a more differentiated use of episode and sequence.[32] One of the earliest keyboard pieces in
which these gains are perceptible is the Fugue in A minor BWV 947,
which is close in style to some of Handel's early keyboard compositions.
Actual Italian themes are employed not only in the Albinoni fugues but in
the closing fugue of the Toccata in E minor BWV 914,[33] and perhaps also
in the *Aria Variata* BWV 989.[34] The six Toccatas BWV 910–15 represent
an early synthesis of the Italian and French styles (in conjunction with the
North German examples of Buxtehude and Böhm) as well as of strict and
free forms. The fugal Allegros are, on the whole, Italianate, but the elaborate Adagios often have a French flavour (see, for example, the third
movement of BWV 914, with its extended use of the *style brisé*).

Further significant encounters with French and Italian music are documented during the Weimar years (1708–17). Between about 1709 and 1714
Bach copied out François Dieupart's *Six Suittes de clavecin* (Amsterdam,
1701), the table of ornaments from Jean-Henri d'Anglebert's *Pièces de
clavecin* (Paris, 1689) and Nicolas de Grigny's *Premier Livre d'Orgue* (Paris,
1699).[35] Around the same time, perhaps, he composed the Suite in F minor
BWV 823, whose three movements, Prélude–Sarabande–Gigue, possibly
represent the closest approach he ever made to pure French style, and
the lute Suite in E minor BWV 996, in which a *Praeludio*, consisting of a
free fantasy and a Presto fughetta, introduces the French dances
Allemande–Courante–Sarabande–Bourrée– Gigue.

During this period, in connection with his duties as court musician at
Weimar, Bach became acquainted with the Italian-style concerto. Around
1709 he wrote out the parts of Concerto no. 2 in E minor from Albinoni's
*Sinfonie e concerti a cinque* (Venice, 1700) and of a Concerto in G major
for two solo violins, strings and continuo by G. P. Telemann.[36] A few years
later he transcribed Telemann concertos in F major and G minor, respectively for organ (lost) and harpsichord (BWV 985).[37] Bach's parts of

Telemann's G major Double Concerto were subsequently owned and copied by the celebrated German violinist J. G. Pisendel, who became acquainted with Bach in 1709.[38] Pisendel, a pupil of Giuseppe Torelli, may have introduced Bach to Torelli's concertos, one of which (a Concerto in D minor for violin, strings and continuo) was subsequently transcribed by Bach for harpsichord (BWV 979).[39]

Bach's many concerto transcriptions for organ (BWV 592–6) and harpsichord (BWV 972–87) probably originated in 1713–14 at the Weimar court as a commission from Prince Johann Ernst.[40] The prince returned in July 1713 from a tour of Holland, during which he may have heard the blind Amsterdam organist J. J. de Graaf playing solo keyboard transcriptions of 'the latest Italian concertos'.[41] The prince brought back from Amsterdam a large collection of new music, which no doubt included Antonio Vivaldi's newly published *L'estro armonico* Op. 3 (Amsterdam, 1711). From this celebrated collection Bach is known to have transcribed five concertos, as well as four from early versions of Vivaldi's Opp. 4 and 7, four by Prince Johann Ernst himself, two by Telemann and one each by Torelli and the Marcello brothers (BWV 974 and 981).

The impact upon Bach of this encounter with the Italian concerto was profound, providing him not only (in transcribed form) with vehicles for his own keyboard virtuosity but with compositional models that further extended his stylistic range and refined various aspects of his technique. The presence of the earlier Italian concerto can be felt in various keyboard works of the period c. 1709–14,[42] notably the Toccata in G major BWV 916, which is laid out like a three-movement concerto and employs Torellian short-ritornello form in its opening Allegro,[43] and the Fugue in A minor BWV 944/2, in which certain thematic and structural links with Torelli have been observed.[44] As for the later, Vivaldian concerto, Forkel informs us that Bach 'began to feel . . . that there must be order, connection and proportion in the [musical] thoughts; and that, to attain such objects, some kind of guide was necessary. Vivaldi's concertos for the violin, which were then just published [i.e. Op. 3] served him for such a guide.'[45] The act of transcribing them for keyboard, Forkel adds, 'taught him to think musically'.[46] In the light of this remark, it cannot be merely coincidental that the period of the transcriptions – 1713–14 – is also that in which the characteristics of Bach's mature style first become fully manifest.[47]

Vivaldian ritornello structure, treated with great freedom and resource, became a recurring feature of Bach's works in all genres after 1714. Examples for clavier range from the highly symmetrical and compact Fantasia in A minor BWV 904/1[48] to the lengthy and brilliant first movement of the Prelude and Fugue in A minor BWV 894. This work is designed like the opening Allegro and closing Presto of a concerto, and was in fact later arranged as such, forming the outer movements of the Concerto in A minor for flute, violin, harpsichord and strings BWV 1044. In the Préludes of English Suites nos. 2–6 BWV 807–11, Vivaldian ritornello form is united with the structure of the da capo aria,[49] a procedure that Bach adopts elsewhere in certain instrumental concertos (e.g. BWV 1042, 1054 and 1053). To this already rich design Bach adds fugue in the Prélude to no. 5 in E minor and prelude-and-fugue (or overture) in that of no. 6 in D minor. The closing gigues are brilliant and – in nos. 3–6 – fugal, so that a pair of virtuoso pieces frames a series of French dances (with the traditional ordering Allemande–Courante–Sarabande–optional lighter pair, played *alternativement*). The English Suites thus represent a second major synthesis, within the corpus of Bach's keyboard music, of the French and Italian styles.

Concerto-related works such as the English Suites and BWV 894 no doubt served as material for Bach's own virtuoso performances on the harpsichord during the period c. 1714–20. The Bach–Marchand contest of 1717, proposed (according to Bach's Obituary) by Jean Baptiste Volumier, Konzertmeister at the Dresden court, indicates that by the late Weimar years Bach was already famous as a keyboard virtuoso. And since composer-performers such as Bach no doubt played in large measure their own compositions, it is probably no mere coincidence that in the same year the first reference to Bach in print – in Johann Mattheson's *Das beschützte Orchestre*[50] – praises his keyboard works as well as his church compositions.

On 1 March 1719 Bach travelled to Berlin to acquire a splendid new harpsichord for the Köthen court – 'The great harpsichord or *Flügel* with two keyboards, by Michael Mietke'.[51] It has been suggested that he may have had this instrument in mind when he conceived two of his most brilliant harpsichord works – Brandenburg Concerto no. 5 in D major BWV 1050, and the Chromatic Fantasia and Fugue in D minor BWV 903.[52] The latter gives a good impression of Bach's middle-period keyboard improvisations. According to Forkel, 'When he played from his fancy, all the 24 keys were in his power ... His *Chromatic Fantasy* ... may prove what I here state. All his extempore fantasies are said to have been of a similar description ... ' However, elsewhere Forkel writes of BWV 903, 'I have taken infinite pains to discover another piece of this kind by Bach, but in vain. This fantasia is unique, and never had its like.'[53] These two passages are perhaps not as contradictory as they sound: it is possible that only in BWV 903 did Bach deliberately set down in permanent form the best and most characteristic substance of his middle-period improvisations.

On 22 January 1720, when Bach dedicated the first *Clavierbüchlein* to his nine-year old son Wilhelm Friedemann, a vital new element entered the conception of his keyboard works, namely instruction. Bach had, of course, taught numerous pupils since c. 1706/7 (most notably J. C. Vogler and J. T. Krebs), but it seems that not until 1720 did he compose keyboard works specifically for instruction.[54] The *Clavier-Büchlein vor Wilhelm Friedemann Bach* contains early versions of the Inventions and Sinfonias and of certain preludes from *The Well-tempered Clavier* Book I. A further impetus to Bach's keyboard composition was his marriage (on 3 December 1721) to Anna Magdalena Wilcke, a court singer at Köthen. To her he dedicated the first five French Suites (*Clavierbüchlein* for A. M. Bach, 1722) and the Partitas in A minor and E minor BWV 827 and 830 (*Clavierbüchlein* for A. M. Bach, 1725).

There are certain significant analogies between Wilhelm Friedemann's musical education, as reflected in the *Clavierbüchlein* of 1720, and Johann Sebastian's own early musical experience. First, composition and performance are united through the medium of the keyboard. The *Clavierbüchlein* contains not only early compositional studies of W. F. Bach's (BWV 836–7, 924a, 925 and 932) but models of ornamentation and fingering (the *Explication*, the *Applicatio*, the Prelude in G minor BWV 930, etc.). And the Inventions and Sinfonias, according to the 1723 title-page, show how 'to arrive at a singing style in playing and at the same time to acquire a strong foretaste of composition'.[55] Secondly, W. F. Bach learns, as his father had learned, by copying out the works of established composers – primarily, of course, his father's preludes and inventions, but also suites by German contemporaries, G. P. Telemann, G. H. Stölzel and J. C. Richter. Thirdly, W. F. Bach's earliest experience of composition, like his father's, has roots in keyboard improvisation – both series of preludes that served as composition models open with arpeggio preludes (BWV 924 and 926; BWV 846a, 847 and 851), which demonstrate how to elaborate upon improvised chord progressions (the young W. F. Bach attempts the same in his BWV 924a).[56]

Nevertheless, Wilhelm Friedemann's musical education, unlike his father's, is systematically directed towards composition as well as keyboard playing. The earliest stages of Bach's composition course, as recorded by C. P. E. Bach[57] – four-part thoroughbass and chorales – are not reflected in the *Clavierbüchlein*. But within the genre of prelude, which represents the first stage of free composition, there is a clear progression from the arpeggiated type to a motivic-contrapuntal style. Moreover, C. P. E. Bach informs us that, 'In teaching fugues, [Bach] began with two-part ones, and so on.' The reference is presumably to the two-part Inventions, which, as preliminaries to the study of fugue, were to be followed by the three-part Sinfonias. These, in turn, paved the way for *The Well-tempered Clavier*.

'Since [Bach] himself had composed the most instructive pieces for the clavier', writes C. P. E. Bach in the same passage, 'he brought up his pupils on them.' Thus the Köthen keyboard works, originally written in part for Wilhelm Friedemann and Anna Magdalena, became, alongside the English Suites, Bach's standard teaching material during the period c. 1720–5. This broadening use is reflected not only in the preparation of autograph fair copies (*The Well-tempered Clavier* Book I, 1722; the Inventions and Sinfonias, 1723), whose title-pages clearly formulate their didactic purpose, but in the numerous pupils' copies that originated around the same time. The pupils most closely involved in the early history of the Köthen clavier works are 'Anon 5', who may be identical with Johann Schneider, organist of the Nikolaikirche, Leipzig,[58] and Heinrich Nicolaus Gerber, who studied under Bach in Leipzig between 1724 and 1727.[59] According to Gerber's son Ernst Ludwig, 'At the first lesson [Bach] set his Inventions before him. When he had studied these through to Bach's satisfaction, there followed a series of suites, then the *Well-tempered Clavier*.'[60]

'In composition', C. P. E. Bach observes, '[Bach] started his pupils right in with what was practical, and omitted all the dry species of counterpoint that are given in Fux and others.'[61] Playing and composition, practice and theory, instruction and delectation: all are integrated within the great middle-period keyboard works. The Inventions, according to Bach's title-page, are intended for 'lovers of the clavier, and especially those desirous of learning'.[62] On the one hand, they encourage cantabile playing in all the most commonly used keys and help to develop independence of the hands in two- and three-part contrapuntal playing; on the other, they provide models of good *inventiones* and their development (an *inventio* is defined by Forkel as 'a musical subject which was so contrived that . . . the whole of a composition might be unfolded from it'[63]). *The Well-tempered Clavier* Book I is designed 'For the use and profit of the musical youth desirous of learning as well as for the pastime of those already skilled in this study'.[64] Here students are taught to read and play in all keys and in a wide variety of styles, ranging in the preludes from elaborate aria (C♯ minor, E♭ minor, F minor, G minor and B♭ minor) to brilliant toccata (B♭ major) and, in the fugues, from a relatively archaic five-part *alla breve* style (C♯ minor, B♭ minor) to the *stile francese* (D major) or a modern Italianate manner (G major). At the same time, they are taught how to handle the essential contrapuntal techniques – the systematic use of stretto (C major, D♯ minor, F major, A minor, B♭ minor), of double (E minor, F♯ minor), triple (C minor, C♯ major, C♯ minor, G♯ minor, B♭ major) and quadruple counterpoint (F minor), of inversion (D minor, D♯ minor, F♯ minor, G major, A minor, B major) and augmentation (D♯ minor) – and are provided with a comprehensive collection of compositional models in both strict and free forms. These opposites, already conjoined in the early toccatas, achieve in the mature prelude-and-fugue design of *The Well-tempered Clavier* Book I their most perfect balance.[65] There are signs that this was a hard-won achievement. Twelve of the first fifteen preludes (all but nos. 9, 11 and 14) were substantially enlarged around 1721–2 in order that they should form equal partners to their companion fugues. The equality sought was not only of scale and substance but also of technical demands, hence the often brilliant or quasi-improvisatory style of the interpolations – the prestos (C minor, E minor), the cadenzas (D major, D minor) and the toccata-like bars 63–98 of the Prelude in C♯ major.[66]

On 1 November 1726 the first Partita of Bach's *Clavier-Übung* I was announced in the Leipzig press.[67] Henceforth publication was fundamentally to influence the conception of the majority of Bach's major keyboard works. Already famed as a virtuoso organist and harpsichordist, Bach was now in a position to command a much wider audience for his own keyboard compositions. Accordingly, there is a marked contrast between the relatively intimate, didactic works of c. 1720–5 and the more outwardly oriented *Clavierübung* I–IV (1726–41), the series of works by which Bach chose to be represented before the musical public of his time.

In the six Partitas of *Clavier-Übung* I (1726–31) Bach – no doubt with publication in mind – returns to the grand scale and virtuoso technical demands of the English Suites. Moreover, within the limits of his standard overall design, he elevates diversity of style into a structural principle in order to display publicly the full range of his stylistic resources. This intention is most obvious in the preludes and in the optional dances or 'intermezzi' (termed 'galanterien' on the original title-pages). Whereas in the preludes of English Suites nos. 2–6 Bach set out with the fixed plan (however modified in execution) of the da capo-cum-ritornello structure, in the Partitas he explores the full range of forms at his disposal. Only the Sinfonia of Partita no. 2 (Grave adagio – Andante – Allegro) lacks precedent; the Praeludium of no. 1 is related to certain preludes in *The Well-tempered Clavier* Book I (F♯ major, A♭ major, B major), the Fantasia of no. 3 to the Inventions and Sinfonias (the latter were originally entitled 'fantasias'), the Ouverture of no. 4 to the French overture-suite (cf. BWV 820 and 822), the Praeambulum of no. 5 to the Torellian short-ritornello form (cf. BWV 916),[68] and the Toccata of no. 6 to the toccata-and-fugue design of BWV 852/1, 910–15, etc. The intermezzi of the English Suites are, without exception, a pair of French dances (minuets, bourrées, gavottes or passepieds) played *alternativement*. In the

French Suites Bach drew from a larger range of dance types, adding air, anglaise, loure and polonaise. Moreover, he increased the number of intermezzi during both composition and revision (French Suites nos. 2–5, in revised form, have three; no. 6, four). In the Partitas he returns to the earlier plan of two intermezzi (except in no. 2) but uses the *alterna-tivement* design only once (in no. 1) and diversifies the types still further by drawing from outside the French dance – the newcomers are Rondeaux, Burlesca, Scherzo, Tempo di Minuetto and Tempo di Gavotta.

No doubt with the public reception of the Partitas in mind, Bach uses colourful titles, particularly in the preludes and intermezzi, to reflect their diversity of content. Moreover, he deliberately highlights the con-junction of French and Italian styles – in itself, already a significant feature of his earlier suites – by linguistic differentiation. These opposites are united in a fresh synthesis, the French style acting as an upholder of tradition, the Italian as a vehicle of innovation. From this point of view it is highly significant that the Corrente and Tempo di Gavotta from Partita no. 6 originated as unnamed movements within an instrumental sonata (BWV 1019a),[69] for, like many movements in the Partitas, they are not so much dances as character pieces in dance time. In this connection it is also worth noting that the three solo violin suites of 1720 are entitled 'Partia', which is synonymous with 'Partita', and contain predominantly Italian movement titles (nos. 1 and 2), including the formula 'Tempo di...', or a mixture of Italian and French (no. 3). Thus the new freedom in Bach's handling of the keyboard dance, which is exhibited in the Partitas, seems to have roots in Italian-style instrumental music.

With the publication of *Clavier-Übung* I in 1726–31 Bach built up a formidable reputation as a composer, as well as a virtuoso performer, of keyboard music. In his *Musicalisches Lexicon* of 1732, J. G. Walther praises Bach's 'excellent clavier works', drawing particular attention to the six Partitas of *Clavier-Übung* I which had just appeared in print.[70] And Forkel remarks that *Clavier-Übung* I 'in its time made a great noise in the musical world. Such excellent compositions for the clavier had never been seen and heard before. Anyone who had learnt to perform well some pieces out of them could make his fortune thereby . . .'[71] On the other hand, it is clear from comments by Johann Mattheson (1731), Louise Gottsched (1732) and Lorenz Mizler (1738)[72] that the Partitas quickly gained a reputation for their technical difficulty. Bach had made them as attractive as possible to purchasers through colourful stylistic contrasts, but neither here nor elsewhere did he make any concession to the demand for easy music for amateurs. His published keyboard works were designed to reflect and display fully his own supreme technical abilities both as a composer and performer.

In 1735, four years after the complete edition of the keyboard Partitas, Bach published *Clavier-Übung* II, which has close links with the earlier publication. In *Clavier-Übung* I Bach intermingled movements with French and Italian titles; in *Clavier-Übung* II he took the further, logical step of juxtaposing complete works in the French and Italian styles. Not long before, his friend G. P. Telemann had published a keyboard work based upon the same principle: Telemann's *Fantaisies pour le clavessin* (Hamburg, 1732–3; TWV 33:1–36) contains three sets of twelve pieces; the first and third sets in the Italian style, the second set French.

In *Clavier-Übung* II the contrast between national styles is highlighted by presenting them in keys at opposite ends of the tonal spectrum – F major and B minor – with the Italian work in a major key with a flat signature and the French in a minor key with a sharp signature. The chief orchestral genre of each nation – the Italian solo concerto and the French overture-suite – is here transferred to the keyboard. On the title-page Bach specifies a two-manual harpsichord in order to permit keyboard imitation of tutti–solo contrasts and orchestral colour effects. Both the *Concerto nach Italiaenischen Gusto* BWV 971, described by J. A. Scheibe as 'a perfect model of a well-designed solo concerto',[73] and the *Ouverture nach Französischer Art* BWV 831, have partial precedents among Bach's earlier works: in the one case, the Weimar concerto transcriptions, the préludes to the English Suites, BWV 894, etc.; in the other, the overture-suites BWV 820 and 822 and the Ouverture to Partita no. 4 (1728). But they remain the only thoroughgoing representatives of their type among Bach's mature keyboard works. Like the keyboard transcriptions of the Weimar years, they no doubt served as vehicles for Bach's own virtuoso performances. The *Collegium musicum* concerts, which he directed from 1729, in all probability gave him the opportunity of playing these works, as well as the Partitas, before the Leipzig public.

The seven years or so (1735–42) that followed the publication of *Clavier-Übung* II are, as far as keyboard music is concerned, among Bach's richest and most productive. During this period he not only published new collections of organ and harpsichord music – *Clavier-Übung* III (1739) and IV (1741) – he also returned to his pre-Leipzig works, revising most of the 'eighteen chorales' from the Weimar years BWV 651–68, and compiling a sequel to the greatest keyboard work of the Köthen period, *The Well-tempered Clavier* Book I.

The 1730s saw further expansion of Bach's range of style to incorporate both archaic and modern elements. On the one hand, he showed a particular interest at this time in Latin church music (hence his own *Missa* settings BWV 232–6) and in classical vocal polyphony.[74] On the other, he was capable of writing music 'entirely in accordance with the latest taste',[75] having himself remarked in 1730 that 'The *gusto* has changed astonish-ingly, and accordingly the former style of music no longer seems to please our ears.'[76] Both stylistic extremes inform *Clavier-Übung* III and *The Well-tempered Clavier* Book II. In the organ collection, the three large Kyries BWV 669–71, 'Aus tiefer Not' BWV 686 and the first section of the closing Fuga a 5 BWV 552/2 are written in the pseudo-Palestrinian *stile antico*.[77] In stark contrast, writing 'in the latest taste' is found in the opening Praeludium BWV 552/1, and in the *pedaliter* setting of 'Vater unser im Himmelreich' BWV 682. In *The Well-tempered Clavier* Book II, three suc-cessive major-key fugues – D, E♭, E – form a triptych of stretto fugues in a relatively archaic, pseudo-vocal, polyphonic style, culminating in the purest example of *stile antico* in the E major fugue. At the other extreme are the ten binary-sonata preludes, whose roots are to be sought in the greatly expanded keyboard dances of *Clavier-Übung* I. This form had already been detached from dance in the Praeludium in G major BWV 902/1 (c. 1726/7), and in the Fantasia in C minor BWV 906/1 (c. 1729). The successors to these pieces among the preludes of *The Well-tempered Clavier* II tend to reflect the aesthetic aims of the more progressive styles of the day: natural grace, elegance and simplicity. In particular, the pathos of the Preludes in F minor and G♯ minor seems to embody Bach's personal response to the *empfindsamer Stil* of his eldest sons.

In the autumn of 1741,[78] while still working upon *The Well-tempered Clavier* Book II, Bach published the final work in the *Clavier-Übung* series, the *Aria mit verschiedenen Veraenderungen* or 'Goldberg Variations' BWV 988. Within the variation structure of this work – a form that Bach had apparently not employed since the early *Aria variata* BWV 989 and *Partite diverse* BWV 766–8 – three essential characteristics of his keyboard music are united: stylistic diversity, virtuosity and strict counterpoint. These elements correspond with the tripartite grouping of the variations (except nos. 1–3 and 28–30) as character piece – virtuoso piece – canon. The canons increase progressively in interval (from unison to ninth), the virtuoso pieces in brilliance, while the character pieces include two trios, a stretto, a gigue, a fughetta, two arias, an over-ture, an alla breve and a quodlibet. Styles range from the relatively archaic (as in the alla breve) to Bach's most up-to-date manner in the arias, particularly in the highly chromatic and poignant minor-key varia-tion no. 25. A novel element is the use of popular tunes in the Quodlibet, as in the roughly contemporary *Cantate burlesque* or 'Peasant Cantata' BWV 212 (1742).

The extreme brilliance and wit of the virtuoso variations recalls the 'ingenious jesting with art' of Domenico Scarlatti,[79] whose *Essercizi per gravicembalo* had appeared in 1738–9 (it is not known whether Bach was acquainted with it). However, similar attributes can be ascribed to such earlier pieces as the Capriccio from Partita no. 2 (1727) or the Praeambulum from Partita no. 5 (1730). And there are precedents for the crossed-hands technique with which the Goldberg Variations begin (nos. 1 and 5) in the Giga from Partita no. 1 (1726), the Fantasia in C minor BWV 906/1 (c. 1729; revised c. 1738) and the Prelude in B♭ major (c. 1740) from *The Well-tempered Clavier* Book II. It is but a small step from here to crossed-hands writing for two keyboards – Part IV of the *Clavier-Übung*, like Part II, calls for 'a harpsichord with two manuals', and variation no. 5 is marked 'a 1 ovvero 2 Clav.' – in which twin hand-parts have equal access to the full range of the keyboard (variations nos. 8, 11, 14 etc.).

It is more than likely that the Goldberg Variations were first played by Bach himself at one of his last *Collegium musicum* concerts in 1741. The events recorded by Forkel[80] – the performance of the work by the brilliant young Bach pupil J. G. Goldberg (then only fourteen) for a patron of Bach's, the diplomat H. C. R. von Keyserlingk, in order to relieve the tedium caused by insomnia – probably took place shortly after publication,[81] for Bach is known to have stayed at Keyserlingk's Dresden home in November 1741.[82]

Around 1742, shortly after the appearance of *Clavier-Übung* IV and roughly when he completed the compilation of *The Well-tempered Clavier* Book II, Bach prepared much of the autograph score of *The Art of Fugue* BWV 1080.[83] This close temporal proximity casts a revealing light on the nature of the work, for it unites the conceptual principles of its two immediate predecessors: on the one hand, the didactic fugal writing for keyboard; on the other, the monothematic structure and the systematic use of canon.

As an instructive collection of fugues, *The Art of Fugue* is decidedly more schematic than its forebears, *The Well-tempered Clavier* Books I and II. Both the early manuscript version (c. 1742–6) and the later printed version (c. 1747–9; published posthumously in 1751) are ordered according to the underlying principle of progressively increasing contrapuntal complexity. Multiple schemes are in simultaneous operation: subject plain – subject varied; subject direct – inverted – direct+inverted; subject alone – subject combined with regular countersubjects; simple counterpoint – double counterpoint at the octave, tenth and twelfth – triple and quadruple counterpoint. The manner in which these schemes are carried through is demonstrably more logical and consistent in the later version.[84] But both versions might, with perhaps greater justice, have been entitled 'The Art of Counterpoint' rather than 'The Art of Fugue'.[85] In this regard it is significant that each fugue in its later, printed version was entitled not 'Fuga', but 'Contrapunctus'.

The didactic nature of the work is highlighted, both in the autograph and in the original edition, by notation in open score, which gives the student a clear visual impression of the contrapuntal structure. This notation, which Frescobaldi and Scheidt used for polyphonic keyboard music in the early seventeenth century, has in the past misled musicians into viewing *The Art of Fugue* as a purely theoretical work, an abstract contribution to musical philosophy. In reality, theory and practice are here integrated as indissolubly as in all Bach's didactic keyboard works. Numerous details attest to Bach's concern for practical considerations: the subsequent elaborations in the first version of the augmentation canon; the many performance marks (ornaments, slurs and staccato dots), particularly in the canons; the additional ornaments and articulation marks in the revised version; the subsequent halving of bars (nos. 1–3) and doubling of note-values (nos. 8–13 and 17) for increased legibility; the cadenza-like flourishes in Contrapunctus 8 and the provision for an improvised cadenza in the Canon alla Decima; and, finally, the re-working of the three-part mirror fugue in a more practicable form as a 'Fuga a 2 Clav.'. Nor should *The Art of Fugue* be considered a narrowly didactic work. The dual purpose of instruction and delectation announced on the title-page of *The Well-tempered Clavier* Book I (see above) no doubt applies with equal force to its late successor.

By the time Bach improvised at the court of Frederick the Great at Potsdam in May 1747, the earlier, manuscript version of *The Art of Fugue* was in all probability either complete or not far from completion. It is no surprise, therefore, that in *The Musical Offering* BWV 1079 – the considered fruit of his improvisation upon the theme presented to him by the king – Bach borrowed a fundamental principle from the work with which he had recently been preoccupied: the concept of monothematic contrapuntal variations, with fugue and canon as chief constituents.[86] To these elements he adds the trio sonata and instruments other than harpsichord, presumably as a tribute to the flute-playing king.

The cornerstones of the work are the two keyboard fugues or 'ricercars', which, more comprehensively than *Clavier-Übung* II, represent a conjunction of opposites, reconciling different sides of Bach's musical personality. In the deliberate contrast between the three- and six-part ricercars, short-score notation is set against open-score, *style galant* against traditional polyphonic style, perhaps fortepiano against harpsichord or organ,[87] and 'ricercar' in the sense of an extempore 'searching for harmonic . . . patterns that might be used in the finished product'[88] against 'ricercar' as an elaborately constructed fugue, successor to the imitative ricercar of former centuries (see Plates 2 and 3).

Plate 2 Ricercar a 3, from the the *Musical Offering* BWV 1079: first page of the original print (Staatsbibliothek zu Berlin-Preussischer Kulturbesitz)

**Plate 3** Ricercar a 6, from the the *Musical Offering* BWV 1079: first page of the original print (Staatsbibliothek zu Berlin-Preussischer Kulturbesitz)

We have come full circle. The opposing impulses that inspired Bach's earliest compositions – keyboard skills and the contrapuntal ordering of sound, representing the active and the reflective sides of his musical make-up – find, in the many-sided contrast between the two ricercars, an emblem of their duality, and in the united structure of this major work of his last years, a symbol of their reconciliation.

# 10  Composition as arrangement and adaptation

*Werner Breig*

At every period of his creative life Bach may be found altering, arranging and continuing to develop his own and other composers' works. For the young Bach, arranging other composers' works was a means of analysing and coming to terms with the various musical traditions that he was attempting to assimilate. Parody – the practice of re-using his own vocal works and providing them with new words in new contexts – became increasingly important to him during the Leipzig years 1723–50. His leadership of the local *Collegium musicum* from 1729 also resulted in a series of harpsichord arrangements of older concertos originally scored for solo melody instruments. And among the activities of his final decade, the compilation, completion and editing of earlier works occupies a not inconsiderable space: it is to this tendency that we owe collections such as the '18', the 'Schübler' Chorales and the second book of *The Well-tempered Clavier*. Even more far-reaching revisions may be found in two instrumental works that were redrafted during the 1740s, namely, the Canonic Variations and *The Art of Fugue*. In consequence, both these works survive in characteristically different versions. Nor should we forget in this context Bach's completion, towards the end of his life, of his Mass in B Minor (a completion substantially based on the use of parody) and, perhaps most surprisingly of all, his recourse to the work of a younger contemporary in the form of Giovanni Battista Pergolesi's *Stabat mater*, which he rewrote as a vocal composition with new words, *Tilge, Höchster, meine Sünden* BWV 1083/243a.

Although the two processes involved in these examples may be described as 'arrangement' and 'transcription', on the one hand, and as the preparation of new 'versions', on the other, both have a common origin in the composer's interest in continuing to work on pieces which were already compositionally formed and to explore the possibilities inherent in a finished work. These investigations on Bach's part have something of the appearance of a systematic search: they reveal his way of theorising, an approach that involved thinking about music not by means of concepts but through the musical material itself.

In view of the large number of works by Bach that are the starting-point or end-result of a process of arrangement, the present study must of necessity be selective. This selection is based on three guiding principles.

First, only arrangements of instrumental works will be considered.[1] The composer's extensive use of parody in his vocal music will not, therefore, be examined.[2] Secondly, we shall forgo any discussion of the different 'versions' of a work and limit ourselves to 'arrangements' (i.e. those pieces where the performing forces are changed). And, thirdly, we shall not consider individual, albeit fascinating, cases such as the relationship between the Triple Concerto BWV 1044 and its sources, but shall confine ourselves to related groups of works, in which the general tendencies and rules governing Bach's technique of adaptation are easier to observe.

Three groups of works from different periods of Bach's creative life will be considered in the light of these criteria:

1.  the arrangements of Johann Adam Reincken's *Hortus musicus*
2.  the transcriptions of concertos by other composers
3.  the concertos for harpsichord and strings.

## The arrangements of Johann Adam Reincken's *Hortus musicus*

The first group of works to be discussed consists of three of Bach's keyboard compositions based on works by Johann Adam Reincken: the B♭ major Fugue BWV 954 and the Sonatas in A minor BWV 965 and C major BWV 966. Bach's source was a volume of Reincken's chamber music published in 1687 under the title *Hortus musicus recentibus aliquot flosculis Sonaten, Allemanden, Couranten, Sarabanden, et Giguen cum 2. Viol., Viola et Basso continuo*, i.e., for two violins, viola da gamba and a continuo part that sometimes doubles the gamba and at other times plays an independent role as a fourth voice.

The numbering of the individual works and movements in the 1697 imprint is somewhat confusing, with the result that references to them in scholarly writings are frequently incorrect. The work as a whole comprises six sets of movements arranged according to tonality (I is in A minor, II in B♭ major, III in C major, IV in D minor, V in E minor and VI in A major). None of these sets has a generic title but each is made up of the five types of piece mentioned in the volume's overall title (sonata, allemande, courante, sarabande and gigue). The individual pieces are numbered continuously from 1 to 30, so that the first set of movements comprises Sonata 1ma, Allemande 2da, Courante 3tia, Sarabande 4ta and Gigue 5ta, the second set (in B♭ major) of Sonata 6ta and so on. The sonatas, in turn, contain a series of movements that are not separately numbered. The second movement of each sonata is invariably a fugue. For the sake of clarification, the group of dance movements that follows each sonata will be described hereafter as a 'suite', while each tonally closed group of movements will be described as a 'cycle' numbered from I to VI. The individual movements within each sonata will be distinguished by means of additional lower-case letters.

Bach's arrangements draw on only the first three cycles of Reincken's work. He arranged the first cycle in A minor in its entirety and from the third cycle in C major he chose the sonata and allemande;[3] in the case of the second cycle in B♭ major, his source was movement 6b or, to be more precise, its theme. The following diagram provides a synoptic overview of Reincken's cycles I–III and the corresponding BWV numbers:

[Cycle I in A minor]
1.  Sonata                                                        BWV
    a. Adagio                                                     965/1
    b. Allegro                                                    965/2
    c. Solo (Violin I). Largo (Adagio) – Presto   965/3
        Solo (Viola da gamba). Adagio – Allegro

[Suite]
2.  Allemande. Allegro                                    965/4
3.  Courante                                                   965/5
4.  Sarabande                                                965/6
5.  Gigue                                                        965/7

[Cycle II in B♭ major]
6.  Sonata
    a. Grave (Adagio)
    b. Allegro [Fuga]                                        954
    c. Solo (Violin I). Adagio – Presto
        Solo (Viola da gamba). Adagio – Presto
7.  Allemande. Allegro
8.  Courante
9.  Sarabande
10. Gigue

[Cycle III in C major]
11. Sonata
    a. Lento (Adagio)                                        966/1
    b. Allegro [Fuga]                                        966/2
    c. Solo (Violin I). Largo – Allegro              966/3
        Solo (Viola da gamba). Adagio – Allegro
12. Allemande. Allegro                                   966/4
13. Courante
14. Sarabande
15. Gigue. Presto

**Example 10.1** Reincken, Sonate 11<sup>ma</sup>
Bach, Sonata BWV 966

Bach's transcriptions of Reincken raise fundamental questions that have yet to be answered with any certainty: we do not know, for example, exactly when they were prepared and we cannot be sure what prompted Bach to undertake these arrangements. Before we consider these questions in greater detail, we may usefully say something about Bach's method of arranging them.

Reincken's originals have been arranged in three different ways, two of which represent the two extremes of his practice, while the third represents an attempt to mediate between these:

1. Bach retains the basic substance of his source, which he ornaments and condenses. This first type of arrangement is found in all the non-fugal movements, with Bach remaining especially close to his source in the first three movements of each suite (Allemande, Courante and Sarabande). Here the arrangement consists, above all, of a more rhythmically animated bass line and more pronounced motivic working-out of the inner voices. Bach's interventions are most far-reaching in the introductory slow movements, where Reincken's simple structures are replaced by a network of figures often linked by imitation. A particularly revealing example is Bach's arrangement of the opening bars of Reincken's third cycle, namely, BWV 966 (Example 10.1). Reincken's violin figure in bar 2 provides the basis for a diminution motif that appears no fewer than five times in the two bars quoted here. Whether or nor we choose to describe this type of arrangement as 'overworked', as David Schulenberg has done,[4] it implies an artistic ambition that goes beyond the mere deployment of playful mannerisms and contains elements of actual 'composition'.

2. Bach uses only the subject, which is independently reworked, so that, strictly speaking, it is no longer possible to speak of an arrangement. He

adopts this approach in the fugal Allegro movements that come second in each sonata. Reincken's sonata fugues all follow the same basic pattern, one that is striking in its simplicity: each of the three voices has only two positions for the subject, one on the first degree of the scale, the other on the fifth. There are no octave transpositions (even though the compass of the instruments would have allowed them). In the B♭ major fugue from Reincken's second cycle, for example, the subject enters in the violins on b♭ (dux) or f′ (comes), and on the viola da gamba on B♭ or f. In the course of the movement the entries migrate successively from first to second violin and thence to viola da gamba. Since all possible combinations have already been exhausted after two entries on each instrument, the whole sequence of entries is then repeated, thereby resulting in four expositions (in the sense used by later writers on fugal theory). Since the countersubject entries are largely arranged along similar lines, the result is highly repetitive. The A minor fugue from the first cycle is similarly structured, while the C major fugue from the third cycle has two repeats, resulting in six expositions in all.

The type of fugue that Bach encountered here is essentially that of the permutation fugue, i.e., 'a type of fugue . . . in which every voice enters with the same succession of a number of ideas, the second idea in each voice serving to accompany the first in the succeeding voice, etc.'.[5] Bach himself, of course, wrote a whole series of movements using this particular type of fugue, beginning during his residence at Mühlhausen (probably for the first time in Cantata 196).[6] There seems little doubt that Reincken's sonata fugues were among his models. In his *Hortus musicus* arrangements, however, Bach did not simply imitate this particular type, but wrote unmistakably independent fugues inspired by Reincken's subjects. His independence emerges, first, from the large part played by the episodes (between 42 and 57 per cent of each piece) and, secondly, from the greater number of positions in which the subject enters: in both the C major Fugue BWV 966/2 and B flat major Fugue BWV 954, six degrees of the scale are used as the starting note (not only the tonic and dominant, but also the second, third, fourth and sixth degrees).[7]

3. Bach uses the subject from his source while retaining other formal features. Although this third type of arrangement is found in only a single movement, namely, Bach's transcription of the Gigue from Reincken's first cycle, it is nevertheless of fundamental importance as a source of inspiration for the gigues in Bach's own keyboard suites.

Reincken modifies the principles of the permutation fugue by using a form comprising two repeated sections, ‖: A :‖: B :‖. In the second part the subject appears in inversion, with the same (descending) order of entries. Bach not only takes up the idea of thematic inversion, but applies the principle of inversion to other aspects of the work. First, the order of voices is not repeated after the first four entries of the subject: instead of descending from soprano to bass again, the voices now enter in reverse order; and, secondly, the second part is an exact mirror of the first in terms of the order in which the subject enters. The following diagrams may serve to illustrate the way in which the subjects are arranged ('D' = 'dux', 'C' = 'comes'):

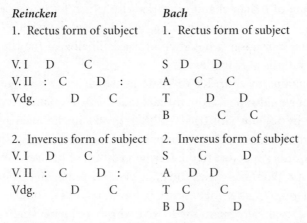

| *Reincken* | | | | *Bach* | | | |
|---|---|---|---|---|---|---|---|
| 1. Rectus form of subject | | | | 1. Rectus form of subject | | | |
| | | | | | | | |
| V. I | D | C | | S | D | D | |
| V. II | : C | D | : | A | C | C | |
| Vdg. | | D | C | T | | D | D |
| | | | | B | | C | C |
| | | | | | | | |
| 2. Inversus form of subject | | | | 2. Inversus form of subject | | | |
| V. I | D | C | | S | C | | D |
| V. II | : C | D | : | A | D | D | |
| Vdg. | | D | C | T | C | | C |
| | | | | B | D | | D |

This 'mirror' principle was to have considerable repercussions for the structure of the gigues in Bach's own suites, finding its most elaborate expression in the final movement of the Sixth English Suite.[8]

In the light of the foregoing summary, we may now attempt to draw a number of more general conclusions beginning with Bach's choice of models (it is assumed that no arrangements have been lost). The choice appears inconsistent, inasmuch as Bach neither arranges complete cycles, as he was later to do in his concerto transcriptions, nor restricts himself to fugal movements, as in his fugues based on Albinoni's trio sonatas. Presumably, he originally intended to arrange Reincken's *Hortus musicus* in its entirety, perhaps hoping that, in the act of transcription, he could broach the problem raised by the keyboard sonata as a genre. He may have asked himself, as Johann Kuhnau did, 'Why should one not be able to treat the same things on a keyboard as on other instruments, since no single instrument has ever disputed the keyboard's claims to perfection?'[9] To explore this problem by transcribing a set of sonatas could have seemed as obvious to Bach as his related procedure in the case of the concerto. And the fact that he did not ultimately carry through his plan to fruition might be explained in terms not dissimilar to those that apply to the *Orgelbüchlein*, of whose 164 planned chorales Bach noted down only 44: after a certain point, to have continued would have brought no new rewards, the problem that he had set himself having already been resolved.

It still remains unclear, of course, what persuaded Bach to choose Reincken's work in the first place and why he should have taken it as the starting-point of his attempts to come to terms with the keyboard sonata as a genre, since, unlike the Italian concertos, Reincken's collection of 1687 could scarcely have pointed him in a new stylistic direction. Perhaps Reincken's somewhat simple compositional style offered greater scope for Bach's elaboration than Albinoni's Op. 1 set of sonatas – to name a collection of Italian chamber works with which Bach was demonstrably familiar.[10] Or was Bach thinking of a kind of homage to the elderly Hamburg composer, who, after all, was still alive at the time that these transcriptions were made?

It remains to consider the date at which these arrangements were made. It would appear from the fact that the two sonatas have survived in a copy by Johann Gottfried Walther, P 803 in the Staatsbibliothek in Berlin, that these pieces cannot postdate Bach's years in Weimar.[11] In the list of works appended to the German edition of his *New Grove* article,[12] Christoph Wolff has picked up an idea advanced in an earlier article and suggested a hypothetical dating '? before 1705', but it could be objected to this that, as already mentioned, two of the three fugues (in B♭ major and C major) have a wide harmonic ambit and are thus comparable to organ fugues such as BWV 536, 543, 550 and 564 – in other words, works unlikely to have been written before Bach's visit to Buxtehude in Lübeck. While the lack of autograph sources from Bach's early years scarcely allows us to date his works with any certainty, it should still be possible to adduce analytical arguments in an attempt to advance a chronology of these works within the context of the composer's early keyboard music.

## The Weimar concerto transcriptions

Unlike the first group of works discussed in the present article, the second group can be dated with some accuracy and assigned to a particular period in Bach's life. These are his transcriptions of solo concertos by Italian composers or by German composers working under Italian influence. They were undertaken midway through his Weimar period or, to be more precise, in 1713–14.[13]

Among the various types of composition from the European musical tradition on which Bach drew, the Italian solo concerto was the most recent. Prince Johann Ernst of Saxe-Weimar (1696–1715) clearly played an important role in bringing these works to Bach's attention: he undertook a study trip to the Netherlands (principally Utrecht) between 1711 and 1713 and, in the course of his visit, bought up vast quantities of scores for the Weimar court orchestra (Amsterdam was at that time one of the leading centres of music publishing in Europe). Among the works he brought back to Weimar were Antonio Vivaldi's twelve Op. 3 concertos published in Amsterdam around 1712 under the title *L'estro armonico*. Prince Johann Ernst had clearly developed a particular enthusiasm for the Italian concerto, an enthusiasm which led to a positive burgeoning of the genre at the Weimar court between his return from the Netherlands in July 1713 and his renewed departure a year later.[14] The prince himself contributed to the orchestra's repertory with a number of works of his own, and Bach, in his capacity as court organist, was required to perform keyboard transcriptions of concertos.

Of the large number of transcriptions – five for organ (BWV 592–6) and sixteen for harpsichord (BWV 972–87),[15] it will be sufficient to cite a mere handful to illustrate Bach's creative approach to his sources. The opening ritornello of the first movement of Vivaldi's Violin Concerto in D major RV 208[16] (described in one manuscript as *Il grosso Mogul*[17]) contains an arpeggiated motif that is passed to and fro, imitatively, between first violins and basses. A direct transcription for organ would have produced Example 10.2. Bach's version of this passage is guided by a desire to retain for as long as possible the continuous semiquaver movement built up in the previous section and to provide an independent line for the player's left hand. Both these aims are achieved by the addition of a semiquaver figuration in the middle register, resulting in the version given in Example 10.3.

A similar aim may be observed in the concerto's final movement: in the episodes which, in the original, comprise passages for solo violin accompanied by continuo, Bach adds a richly agitated countermelody in the left hand, thus producing a polyphonic two-part setting for solo keyboard (from bar 32).

Finally, we may consider a passage from the G major Concerto BWV 592, which is an arrangement of a concerto by Johann Ernst of Saxe-Weimar.[18] The skill with which the seventeen-year-old prince was able to express himself in imitating the form, technique and thematic language of the Vivaldian solo concerto after only a short period of study with the Weimar town organist, Johann Gottfried Walther, attests to musical gifts that were far from negligible, although, of course, a certain dilettantism is undeniable.

It is interesting to note that Bach's approach to the prince's compositions is different from that which he adopted for works by Vivaldi, Torelli and Marcello. In his transcriptions of the latter pieces Bach altered the accompanying voices and figurations but left the main thematic lines untouched. In the G major Concerto BWV 592, by contrast, one sometimes

**Example 10.2**  Vivaldi, Violin Concerto in D major RV 208, first movement: literal transcription
for organ

**Example 10.3**  Vivaldi, Violin Concerto in D major RV 208, first movement: Bach's
transcription, BWV 594

has the impression that Bach was attempting – in the discreetest possible
way – to give the young prince an extra lesson in composition. A characteristic case of such a substantive 'correction' occurs in a passage towards the
end of the slow movement. In the prince's original, a brief motif is passed to
and fro between first violin and the lower voices; following an imperfect
cadence, the previous passage is repeated note for note, before being
rounded off with a perfect cadence. If Bach had remained true to his source
in transcribing this passage for the organ, the result would have read as in
Example 10.4.

Clearly Bach felt that, in its original form, this passage was stiff and
schematic. In his attempts to improve it, he began with the upper voice,

**Example 10.4** Johann Ernst of Saxe-Weimar, Concerto in G major, second movement: literal; transcription for organ

**Example 10.5** Johann Ernst of Saxe-Weimar, Concerto in G major, second movement: Bach's transcription, BWV 592

bridging the rests in the original with an expressive, long-breathed can-tilena. Moreover, the consequent is no longer a mechanical repeat of the antecedent but outdoes it with more expansive melodic gestures (espe-cially the diminished seventh rising to a high c‴), while the part-writing in the inner voices has been developed in a linear direction, thereby adding a new depth to the passage. As a result of these changes, Bach's version now runs as in Example 10.5.

Thanks to his biographer, Johann Nikolaus Forkel, Bach's interest in the Italian solo concerto is well known. At the start of chapter 5 of his life of the composer, Forkel writes that, after a number of earlier failures, Bach had felt that

> there must be order, connection, and proportion in the thoughts; and that,
> to obtain such objects, some kind of guide was necessary. Vivaldi's
> Concertos for the violin, which were then just published, served him for
> such a guide. He so often heard them praised as admirable compositions
> that he conceived the happy idea of arranging them all for his clavier. He
> studied the chain of the ideas, their relation to each other, the variations of
> the modulations, and many other particulars. The change necessary to be
> made in the ideas and passages composed for the violin, but not suitable
> to the clavier, taught him to think musically; so that after his labour was
> completed, he no longer needed to expect his ideas from his fingers, but
> could derive them from his own fancy.[19]

This account needs to be treated with some caution, not least because it is full of factual errors. Bach did not arrange 'all' Vivaldi's violin concertos – not even all that he knew; his knowledge of the Italian solo concerto extended to works by Alessandro and Benedetto Marcello, Giuseppe Torelli, Tomaso Albinoni and perhaps other Italian composers, too; and it scarcely needs to be added that, at the time that he got to know Vivaldi's concertos, Bach was by no means as inexperienced a composer as Forkel suggests. Nonetheless, we may well be right in assuming that Forkel's account is based on a report given to him by the composer's sons and that, ultimately, Bach himself recognised that his encounter with the Italian concerto, in particular with Vivaldi, was of seminal importance to him.

In this respect, the final sentence of the passage quoted above deserves particular attention. It is said here that Vivaldi taught Bach 'to think musically'.[20] Within the specific context of this passage, 'to think musically' means to grasp a musical shape independently of the guise that it assumes in terms of a particular instrument and to reduce it to what might be termed its 'purely musical' essence, an essence that can then be reproduced, in modified form, on another instrument. Yet Vivaldi must have taught Bach 'to think musically' not only on this specific point but in a far more comprehensive sense, as Forkel himself implies in the earlier part of the passage: 'He studied the chain of the ideas, their relation to each other, the variations of the modulations, and many other particulars.'

What could Bach have learned from Vivaldi's concertos in this respect?

The musical technique that is found in these works is based on a system of antitheses. Within the individual movements we find the contrast between tutti and solo, ritornello and episode, harmonic stability and modulation, clear-cut themes and flexible figurations. If we go beyond the confines of the individual movement, we find a further contrast between quick outer movements and a slow middle movement. The compositional deployment of such antitheses and the effective use of the basic tools of harmonic tonality ensured that Vivaldi's concertos have a high degree of musical plausibility and explain why Bach's encounter with these works altered his whole way of thinking about music.

It is notable that Forkel does not claim that Bach immediately began to write his own concertos under the influence of Italian models. His account was intended to show, essentially, that Bach's interest in Vivaldi was of direct benefit to his work as a keyboard composer. As such, it accords with what we know about the main areas of Bach's interest during his years in Weimar, when he concentrated in the main on keyboard music and, especially, on organ music. In other words, Bach's assimilation of the compositional technique associated with the Italian solo concerto was bound up from the outset with what might be called a 'dialogue between musical genres'. The all-embracing influence of the concerto continued to leave its mark in many ways even after Bach had left Weimar, and there is scarcely a single area of his output as a composer that was not affected by basic ideas of concerto form.

## The concertos for harpsichord and ripieno strings

However rich they may be in terms of their many details, it must be said of Bach's Weimar concerto transcriptions in general that their significance lies less in their artistic results than in the lessons that Bach learned from his interest in this repertory. This is no longer true, however, of that other great complex of works involving transcriptions of existing concertos, namely, the harpsichord concertos or, to be more precise, the concertos for between one and four concertante harpsichords with ripieno strings that Bach wrote during his years in Leipzig. These are almost all arrangements of his own works, the only exception being BWV 1065, in which Bach evidently wanted to write for the spectacular combination of four concertante harpsichords – an aim that could not be realised with any of his own works, with the result that he fell back once again on Vivaldi's *L'estro armonico* Op. 3, which had already played an important role at the time of his Weimar transcriptions and from which he now proceeded to select Concerto no. 10 RV 580.

The majority of Bach's fourteen harpsichord concertos BWV 1052–65 date from the time of his association with the Leipzig *Collegium musicum*, a group composed of students and middle-class citizens founded by Telemann in 1702 and superintended by Bach from the spring of 1729 until the summer of 1737 and, again, from the end of October 1739 until at least 1741. It would seem that Bach's work with the Leipzig *Collegium musicum* served to rekindle his interest in the instrumental concerto (although it would be wrong to exclude the possibility of other occasions for his performing concertos[21]). For the first time in the history of music, the harpsichord was now used on a grand scale as a concertante instrument. Bach evidently did not feel under any obligation to write new works for these new resources but based his harpsichord concertos on existing concertos for melody instruments (generally violin or oboe[22]), a circumstance which, for a time, led to a serious underestimation of these works.

It is clear from the surviving sources that, in writing his harpsichord concertos, Bach initially concentrated on works for several instruments.[23] This may have been bound up with the fact that in the years around 1730 Bach had several highly gifted harpsichordists among his pupils who could be called upon to take part in performances of these works: among potential players were his sons Wilhelm Friedemann and Carl Philipp Emanuel, who remained under the parental roof until 1733 and 1734 respectively, and Johann Ludwig Krebs, who studied with Bach between 1726 and 1735. It may have been these three students, together with the composer himself, who appeared as soloists in the first performance of his concerto for four harpsichords.

The following discussion will concentrate in the main on the concertos for the 'normal' forces of a single solo harpsichord (BWV 1052–9). It was with these works that Bach clearly concluded his involvement with the harpsichord concerto. The autograph score of these works is currently lodged in the Staatsbibliothek in Berlin (P 234) and has been dated by Yoshitake Kobayashi to the period 'around 1738'.[24]

The fact that these works did not reach their surviving form until towards the end of the 1730s does not necessarily mean, of course, that they had not already been performed on an earlier occasion. They did not need to be written down but could be performed from the original parts, especially if Bach himself played the solo part from the score, while making the necessary changes. The need to write the piece down arose only in the case of an artistically ambitious transcription, but not when the work was simply adapted for the practicalities of performance.

Bach seems to have been guided by just such an ambition when he set about preparing his series of eight concertos for harpsichord and strings.

Six of these works (BWV 1052–7) form a self-contained set in the full sense of the term: in keeping with Bach's normal practice, they are introduced by the letters 'J. J.' ('Jesu juva') and rounded off with 'Finis. S. D. Gl.' ('Soli deo gloria'). Apart from the six Brandenburg Concertos, this set of harpsichord concertos is the only self-contained cycle of concertos to be assembled by Bach himself.

The autograph volume P 234 contains not only these six concertos but, immediately after them, a further complete concerto in G minor (BWV 1058, a transcription of the A minor Violin Concerto BWV 1041) and a brief fragment of a concerto in D minor (BWV 1059) evidently based on a lost oboe concerto in the same key. The present order of the concertos in the manuscript does not, of course, reflect the sequence in which they were composed: the last two concertos in the manuscript – BWV 1058 and 1059 – were the first to be written down and were not placed after BWV 1057 until the manuscript was bound, an understandable ordering, since in this way the fragmentary BWV 1059 could be placed at the end.[25] Only when we take account of the order in which they were composed will Bach's transcriptions of these concertos be seen to reflect an artistic endeavour that was carried out with the greatest clarity of design.

Unlike the Brandenburg Concertos, Bach never prepared a fair copy of these concertos: the surviving autograph score, P 234, is a first draft containing an extraordinary number of corrections to certain passages. In consequence, not all the inconsistencies that arose during transcription have been removed, and there are also occasional problems in deciphering Bach's handwriting. On the other hand, the manuscript offers us an opportunity to examine in detail the problems with which Bach found himself faced when transcribing his various sources and to see the different solutions that he adopted. The following remarks represent just such an attempt to address these various problems.

1. Initially we find a method of transcribing the source which, in its simplicity, suggests something of an extempore process: the strings play the ripieno in the version found in the concerto for melody instrument, while the harpsichordist takes over the solo line (right hand) and continuo bass line (left hand), the latter ornamented in a manner suited to a keyboard instrument. This was the method adopted in the first of these transcriptions, the G minor Concerto BWV 1058, which is based on the Violin Concerto in A minor BWV 1041. The process of writing out the transcription allowed the composer to refine his technique: first, the violin concerto was transposed down a whole tone, thereby accommodating the solo part to the compass of the harpsichord, with its highest note of d′′′;[26] and, secondly, the harpsichord bass could now be more carefully notated, a task that Bach approached with undeniable ambition, as may be seen from a

whole series of corrections in the harpsichord's bass line. Since Bach did not plan to make any changes to the ripieno strings, he was able to adopt a very simple system when copying out the score: he began by notating all the string parts, then transcribed the solo violin as the harpsichord treble and finally added the harpsichord bass, the figurative working-out of which represents the only real addition of any substance.

It is clear from the entry 'J. J.' at the beginning of the score that Bach intended to start a new opus with Concerto BWV 1058. In retrospect, however, he seems not to have been satisfied with this transcription, no doubt because the new solo instrument is hardly in a position to assert its independence. After a fragmentary attempt to transcribe an oboe concerto in the form of BWV 1059,[27] he began work on a new opus, again introduced by the initials 'J. J.' At its head he placed the concerto BWV 1052, which is a transcription of a lost violin concerto in D minor. Here, too, Bach began by notating the complete string ripieno, before adding the solo part. The fact that the result differs considerably from that achieved in BWV 1058 is due to the source, which is believed to be one of Bach's earliest original concertos and which, in its immoderate virtuosity, is not unlike such works as Vivaldi's D major Concerto (*Il grosso Mogul*).[28] Unlike the densely textured A minor Violin Concerto, this early work offered ample scope for an extraordinarily virtuoso harpsichord part involving full-toned chordal harmonies and figurative developments.

2. The next work to be added to his new opus was the E major Concerto BWV 1053 (the lost source of which appears to be a concerto for solo woodwind and ripieno strings), for which Bach radically altered his method of transcription. Evidently it had become plain to him that the practice of leaving the ripieno untouched would lead to results as unsatisfactory as they had been in the case of BWV 1058. It is clear from several passages in the autograph score that he began by elaborating the harpsichord part and that only then did he add the string parts. Of immense importance in this context is his rewriting of the harpsichord bass, which for whole passages bears only the most general similarity to the continuo of his source. But this more subtle writing for the harpsichord bass can come into its own only if the simpler basic form is not simultaneously played in the string bass. For this reason, the ripieno bass falls silent during most of the solo sections, with the result that the harpsichordist's left hand is permanently occupied, either as part of the tutti or in a solo capacity, while the string bass generally appears only in the tutti passages. The upper string parts were likewise not simply taken over unaltered but were frequently modified to take account of the harpsichord treble.[29] For the first time, the harpsichord thus becomes an independent partner in its dialogue with the strings.

3. Bach retained one aspect of the method of transcription employed throughout the opening movement of BWV 1053 in the transcriptions that followed: namely the tendency to limit the involvement of the string bass to the tutti passages and the careful redrafting of the harpsichord bass. But when it came to rewriting the upper string parts, Bach appears to have felt that the amount of work involved in this task was greater than any possible artistic gain. At all events, he largely retained the three upper string parts in the second movement of BWV 1053.

This further change in the principle underlying his method of transcription led Bach to adopt yet another new procedure in copying out his source: he began by entering the three upper string parts in his score, then he added the harpsichord treble and bass, and finally he formed the string bass line. In this manner Bach arranged the second and third movements of BWV 1053 and the whole of the three following concertos, BWV 1054, 1055 and 1056.

4. When Bach decided to transcribe his Fourth Brandenburg Concerto BWV 1049 as the final concerto in the set (BWV 1057), he found himself faced by a particularly complicated problem, but one which also offered an opportunity for strikingly original solutions. In this case, his source was not a concerto for a melody instrument and ripieno strings but a triple concerto scored for violin and two recorders, which are used in a whole variety of different combinations in the original 'concert avec plusieurs instruments'. In the transcription, the harpsichord's basic function is to take over the original violin part. But Bach was inspired by the various instrumental groupings of his source to deploy the harpsichord in other ways, too. Thus in places it functions as a continuo instrument; it can engage in four-part polyphony with the recorders (here the harpsichord treble is totally new); and it replaces the original trio of recorders and violin in the slow movement. It appears that Bach consciously placed the F major Concerto at the end of the collection: it forms the culmination of the set not only by dint of its exceptionally effective harpsichord part but also by virtue of its wealth of timbres resulting from the interplay of three diverse instrumental families.

Earlier writers on Bach frequently undervalued the importance of the composer's harpsichord concertos. Arguably the crassest of their critics was Albert Schweitzer, who dismissed them out of hand: 'The arrangements are often made with quite incredible haste and carelessness; either time was pressing, or he felt no interest in what he was doing . . . We are under no special obligation to incorporate these transcriptions in our concert programmes.'[30] Our observations on Bach's working method show us, on the contrary, that Bach approached the question of instrumentally appropriate textures with immense conscientiousness.

That Bach was keenly interested in the harpsichord concerto is clear, moreover, from the fact that he evidently transcribed for the harpsichord all suitable concertos for melody instrument. We know of no solo concertos for one, two or three melody instruments that do not also exist as harpsichord concertos; conversely, we have a whole series of harpsichord concertos of which the sources for solo melody instrument are no longer extant (indeed, these represent the majority). Yet it is virtually certain that these concertos are arrangements, and in most cases the sources of the transcriptions can be reconstructed with some probability from the harpsichord concertos. In short, Bach's harpsichord concertos may be seen as a large-scale retrospective of his work in the field of the concerto. We cannot doubt that, for the composer himself, these later versions represented artistically viable alternatives.

*Translated by Stewart Spencer*

# 11  Bachian invention and its mechanisms

*Laurence Dreyfus*

Since the nineteenth century, the analysis of music has undertaken to provide accounts of musical structure by explaining musical events and patterns that lend coherence to an individual work as well as contributing to its beauty and meaning. Drawing on a variety of musical building blocks – whether harmonic, contrapuntal, melodic, rhythmic or sectional – analysts of various theoretical persuasions have asked their readers to set aside their first impressions in order to pay attention to the way a piece of music works by examining the details of its 'facture'. The 'truth-value' of such interpretations can of course never be divorced from the ideas an analyst holds about musical structure, since these notions or 'theories' largely determine which musical parameters count as structurally significant. Nonetheless within the realm of musical analysis – far different from, say, mathematics or physics – it has rarely been the elegance or grandiosity of a structural theory that has attracted adherents. Instead, successful analyses have always appealed to an inherently musical plausibility, fuzzy though such a concept must ultimately remain. For this reason, the seeming circularity of interpretation endemic to musical analysis will appear less troubling, especially when one realises that analysts – if they are to succeed – need to persuade a community of musicians that it is possible to hear a piece as proceeding 'so and not otherwise', to borrow a phrase of Theodor W. Adorno. And contrary to some popular perceptions, musicians are a famously hard-nosed lot when it comes to being told how to hear a piece with which they are intimate.

The issue of musical plausibility in an analysis can be taken a step further if one asserts that accounts of musical structure are really no more than reconstructions of a set of actions taken by a composer. Analysis in this sense is tantamount to a kind of de-composition, taking apart what was once put together. How, one may ask, could it be otherwise unless the composer is some kind of *idiot savant* taking dictation from an inaccessible muse? A discussion of this issue has been side-tracked for a long time by fears that analytical statements might all be taken to be identical to verbal statements composers might make (though they rarely do) about how they composed a piece of music. In the case of composers from the past, moreover, it has also seemed arrogant to claim that an analyst represents the sense of compositional acts, since the (usually) dead composer, conveniently absent, is unavailable to provide a definitive refutation. Still other analysts, tacitly echoing the announced 'death of the author' in the 1960s, have renounced the notion of compositional intentions and sought to reinforce the idea that analysis is not a form of 'decomposition' at all but rather a discipline concerned with the perception of listeners. This approach seems safely empirical but prematurely concedes an intellectual defeat to 'cognitive science': for what brought traditional analysts to masterworks of the European tradition in the first place was not a theory of psychology but rather the recognition of aesthetic meaning and value which demanded to be decoded.

The approach I take in the present essay is not especially bothered by these objections to 'intentionalist' analysis. Instead I suspect very much to the contrary that analysts' only hope of contributing to humanistic knowledge is to embrace the idea that they are in fact 'decomposing' the work of a primarily sentient and thinking composer. For if analysis makes claims about an art work that are only incidental to human action and agency – whether or not this agency is explicit and conscious or more subliminal and inchoate – who should possibly be interested in them? It is disingenuous, moreover, to sever the link between an analyst's readings and a composer's actions, for two reasons: (1) most musical composition is a highly conscious affair and there is every reason to think that analytical attempts to grasp a composer's working methods will actually yield insights into a high proportion of intentionally crafted musical events, and (2) analysts routinely cite any evidence of a composer's intentions that confirms analytical findings whenever this is available (as in compositional sketches, documented statements, letters or contemporaneous theoretical constructs), thus demonstrating that they are happy to succumb to a 'crypto-intentionalism' when it suits their purposes. Analysts ought therefore to come clean and acknowledge that they are keenly interested in a composer's idea of the work and might as well incorporate this explicit interest into their own methods and writing.[1]

The music of J. S. Bach has provided a fertile field for analysis ever since early Enlightenment authors such as Kirnberger and Marpurg began to treat Bach as a special fount of harmonic wisdom. Indeed, one of the pleasures in studying Bach's music is to grasp the complex construction so closely connected with its depth and beauty. On the other hand, the famous complexity of so much of Bach's music becomes remarkably transparent as soon as one discovers the relevant building blocks on which a particular genre of music is erected. Many kinds of Bach works – such as fugues, arias, choruses, concerto movements and so on – involve the crafting of musical ideas which are repeated and varied in relatively disciplined ways throughout an entire movement and it is the nature of this 'discipline' on which my attention is focused in this essay. While an exact repetition only duplicates a musical thought, the variation of an idea alters and inflects it so as to say something new. It is useful, moreover, to distinguish between two kinds of variation: (1) a decoration of the idea, in which the original meaning remains essentially intact beneath a mere embellishment, and (2) an inflection of the idea which alters its meaning, a meaning that could not be predicted without some serious mental effort.

Given this notion of repetition and variation, it makes sense – as a first analytical step – to dissolve a piece of music into its underlying 'common denominators' by bracketing all its exact repetitions and decorative variations, so as to isolate its set of core ideas. In the case of most Bachian genres, the set of significant ideas will be relatively small, which is to say that many related musical passages are best understood as *inflected variations* of one another. With Bach, moreover, one can go a step further in asserting that the composer's manipulation of musical ideas is less a matter of artful variation than an often coercive filtering of musical ideas through a grid of relatively mechanical procedures which comprise Bach's primary toolbox. It is these sets of procedures which 'operate' on the core ideas, thereby 'producing' the new, variant forms. Rather than adopt a lax attitude of tasteful association (common among his contemporaries) which produces elegant variations, Bach's compositional procedures often amount to an obsessive search for congruent musical relations. This quest for invention continually seeks to mechanise the compositional process and accounts for the fundamental complexity of Bach's textures at the same time that it makes his music especially susceptible to a structured analysis based on comparison and contrast. For this reason, I have used the term 'compositional mechanisms' rather than the more common early twentieth-century notion of organic connections in talking about congruent musical relations. The distinction between these two realms is not a binary one but rather constitutes a field within which I try to privilege conscious actions which the composer must have taken over purely analytical constructs which ignore human agency or elevate it to impossible superhuman heights.

For Bach and his German contemporaries, the act of thinking through the fundamental musical building blocks of a composition fell under the rhetorical rubric of *inventio*, which since ancient times had been concerned with the *discovery* of ideas. Invention is naturally tied to concrete genres of music – such as minuets, fugues, concertos, arias and so on – which themselves are ordered on a stylistic hierarchy according to the degree of artifice which they contain. The genres, in turn, are distinguished not only by the styles in which they are clothed, but also by the formal schemes, which, in the rhetorical language commonly found in German music theory of this period, were understood as the 'elaboration' or 'arrangement' of the composition. (Some authors, such as Johann Mattheson, go a step further to distinguish between the 'elaboration' of musical ideas and their actual 'disposition' within the form of a musical composition.) It is particularly advantageous to separate out 'inventions' from their 'arrangement' since the convention of 'musical form' for most large-scale genres remains a remarkably relaxed affair for this historical period: only in small-scale genres such as dances can the 'form' of a movement – in particular, the restricted length of its sections – be considered, as it were, a topic of invention. In fugues, concertos, arias and other related pieces, on the other hand, the conventions of form – topics of *disposition* in the language of rhetoric – usually shape only the beginnings and ends of movements, and have relatively little to say about what happens in which order in between. For this reason, it makes sense to allow the *inventa*, or the discovered ideas, a kind of priority in understanding a large-scale movement no matter where they are found and to observe how the Bachian mechanisms of invention structure both their various forms and the moments of their presentation in the piece as a whole.

In this essay, I will examine two pieces of music – the first fugal Allegro from the G major gamba sonata BWV 1027 (movement 2), and the opening chorus from Cantata 78, *Jesu, der du meine Seele* – from the vantage point of compositional mechanisms, and thereby hope to suggest methods of paradigmatic analysis that apply to a wide variety of Bach's works whose workings are loosely structured around the principles of fugue and concerto. (It will be useful to have at hand scores of BWV 1027/2 and BWV 78/1 while reading through the analyses that follow.[2])

It is revealing to focus first on BWV 1027/2, a trio sonata movement in Corellian style which Bach arranged (probably no earlier than the 1730s) for viola da gamba and obbligato harpsichord. The analysis of such sonata movements proves somewhat frustrating for most conventional methods, since apart from the opening fugal gestures of subject and answer (*dux* and *comes*) in the principal melodic voices, there are no known rules for how such movements should be conceived or how their principal ideas ought to be organised. Naturally there were conventional ideas of harmony that ensured that a movement began and ended in the same key, but apart from predictable modulations to closely related scale degrees, and an exclusion of certain cadences perched on remote scale degrees, there was no prescribed way in which the disposition or 'form' of such a movement could be conceived ahead of time. (It hardly needs mentioning that such unpredictability is at a great remove from the more strictly conceived set of tonal conventions that prevailed in later eighteenth-century music organised around the 'sonata principle', in which the invention of ideas was inextricably linked to their location within a schematic whole.) Given a fugal preoccupation with thematic subjects (and in this instance countersubjects), one also expects to find other fugal devices such as invertible counterpoint and perhaps even melodic inversion as well as passages of lesser importance in which the themes are absent, traditionally called episodes. In addition, because this is a *fugal sonata movement* rather than a *fugue* proper one expects to find the composer treating incremental musical ideas or inventions that are not part of the fugal ideas 'exposed' at the beginning of the movement, especially as sonata movements often tend to be longer and hence more discursive than fugues proper. The main point to stress here is that a recognition of the genre of the movement – a fugal allegro in a trio sonata – reveals very little about the nature of the compositional invention or the overall plan of the movement. Indeed, considered as a whole, the formal aesthetic of such a movement is guided not so much by the metaphor of drama as by the metaphor of invention or discovery itself: rather than imagine a piece as shaped by the twists and turns of fate, leading relentlessly towards a comic resolution or a tragic catharsis, one is challenged to make sense of a musical puzzle, whose entire solution cannot be really glimpsed until all the pieces have been assembled. Unlike a puzzle, however, in which all the pieces fit together in some contiguous juxtaposition on a two-dimensional plane, the Bachian puzzle works far more within a three-dimensional space in which individual pieces (that is, musical passages or inventions) are joined both above and below as well as next to one another, as both paradigms and syntagms. The result is that the phenomenal order of the piece as played or heard in performance is but a pleasing, if also privileged, way to encounter the puzzle. To come to grasp the sense and meaning of the puzzle entails, however, another project, that of reconstructing an ideal mental disposition whose object is the depth and subtlety of musical thought itself.

What signs of genre in the opening bars of the gamba sonata movement disclose the kinds of inventions we might expect to find in this work? Here the two fugal parts over a continuo bass signal the model of the Corellian Allegro taken from a four-movement *sonata da chiesa* (or trio sonata). Since the theme in the harpsichord treble is answered at the lower fourth by the gamba in b. 5, we are dealing with something related to fugue. But since the bass part does not participate in the fugal statements and answers – at least not at the outset – it is clear that this is not a fugue proper (as in a keyboard fugue) but rather a more informal sonata movement that will draw on aspects of fugue. Given this genre designation, we will therefore expect that relatively strict imitative manipulations of musical material will mingle freely with far less formal spinnings-out of melodic themes in a more expansive and relaxed environment than would be typical of a conventional fugue. An explicit equality of the two upper parts, moreover, ensures that thematic material will be balanced over the course of the movement: as soon as a particular exposition of thematic materials occurs in one of the two upper voices (here in the gamba part and in the right hand of the harpsichord part) one can be sure that the same material will occur in the other part as well.

If we nonetheless explore the specifically fugal aspects of the movement, we arrive at a set of core inventions that provide a clear overview of the kind of pre-compositional thinking in which Bach must have engaged as well as a heuristic beginning point for an analysis attuned to inflections of the basic paradigms. Examples 11.1, 11.2 and 11.3 display these inventions, which summarise the basic kinds of paces through which Bach puts his subject (labelled S). As can be seen, Example 11.1 traffics in doubly invertible counterpoint with a countersubject; given that voice-exchange is a *sine qua non* for a fugal trio sonata movement, we must consider this invention the primary motor behind the movement. Examples 11.2–11.3 depict inventions that show how very seriously Bach understood the possibilities of a fugal Corellian Allegro. He has imported two sets of arcane fugal devices that are usually foreign to the genre. In Example 11.2, he deals with two canons (or strettos), the first invertible at the upper and lower octave after a time interval of a dotted semibreve – represented as S + 8 (o·) and S – 8 (o·) – and the theme played against itself at the upper sixth simultaneously, represented as S + 6 (simul). Although the overlap between canonic voices in Example 11.2a extends only to the length of five crotchets and does not include the entire subject, it is worth considering this invention nearly on a par with the invertible counterpoint found in Example 11.1. This is so because Bach's work on the stretto, considered at an early enough stage in the overall invention, may well have influenced the form of the subject itself, especially when one considers the pronounced contrary motion that characterises the overlapping portions in the stretto. Example 11.3 focuses on the kinds of melodic invention found in counterfugues by displaying both a transposition of the subject into the minor mode – which I call a 'modeswitch' – and the two varieties of melodic inversion of the subject, that which preserves the exact intervals of the subject in a mirror image, labelled $SI_1$, and that which reverses the melodic direction but preserves the mode of the subject, here labelled $SI_2$.

**Example 11.1**  Main inventions in BWV 1027/2

(a)  $\frac{S}{CS}$

(b)  $\frac{CS}{S}$

**Example 11.2**

(a)  S ± 8 · (o.)

(b)  S + 6 (simul)

**Example 11.3**

S  (MODESWITCH)

(a)

SI₁ (preserves interval)

(b)

SI₂ (preserves mode)

(c)

**Example 11.4**  Main inventions in BWV 1027/2

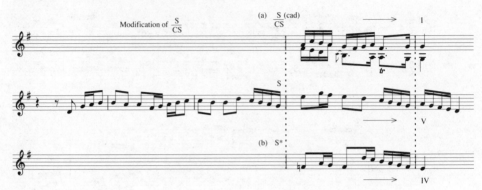

**Example 11.5**  'Continuity section'

**Example 11.6**  Harmonic progressions found in 'one-off' episodes

The 'modeswitch' works flawlessly on the entire subject, and hence was probably considered in an early stage of the invention of the subject itself, since not every theme – especially such a lengthy one – makes musical sense when its intervallic structure is so altered. The brevity of the melodic inversions, on the other hand, suggests that either they are less important in the overall inventive process or else they survive from a stage of invention in which the subject was only to have lasted the length of two bars. (If Bach had meant the melodic inversions to be more important, he would have devised themes that were completely invertible melodically, as he did in the counterfugues found in the *Well-tempered Clavier*, for example.)

As the raw materials for a hybrid double counterfugue the set of inventions contained in Examples 11.1, 11.2 and 11.3 might well have sufficed, although a more active and integrated imitative bass part would have been necessary as well as the usual episodes to link the disposition of the various inventions. For the purposes of a sonata movement, however, Bach imagined a somewhat more expansive texture, and, as a result, required various extensions of his inventions as well as episodic building blocks that could be repeated within the course of the composition. Over and above these repeatable episodes, one still expects to find 'one-off' episodic links that were part of a later stage of the composition's elaboration (see p. 183 below).

As for the expansions to the invention these were of two kinds, as shown in Example 11.4. In Example 11.4a, Bach crafted an invertible cadential modification of the primary fugal complex which permits a cadence in the local tonic, a feature of closure that would not be permitted in a normal keyboard fugue. (This cadential complex is labelled S(cad)/CS and is also invertible.) In Example 11.4b, Bach provides another reading of the first invention (labelled S*) which allows the harmony to modulate to the upper fourth scale degree. Notice here how the two alternatives in b. 4 are similar enough in melodic contour to permit Bach to draw on the two forms nearly interchangeably. As the directional arrows and roman numerals in Example 11.4 show, moreover, the three forms of the subject encourage contrasting tonal progressions by moving to the dominant, to the local subdominant or towards closure in the local tonic.

As for repeated episodes, one can turn to a longish passage that I term the 'continuity section' which occurs three times within the movement (bb. 21–8, 52–9 and 99–106). This passage is so highly structured that it must be seen as related closely to the primary invention of the composition, rather than to the elaboration, out of which such episodic material usually stems. A voice-leading reduction of the passage, given in

Example 11.5, begins with a sequence of 7–6 progressions, proceeds to a patch of imitation that aspires to be canonic – labelled X – 4 (o·) – and concludes each time by preparing a new reiteration of the primary subject (either in I or in V) that leads to a cadence. The structured aspect of the 'continuity section' lies in its ability not only to create a relatively stable section in which the subject is absent, but also to mimic the paradigmatic functions of the primary inventions themselves by displaying distinctly different invertible combinations at each occurrence. Indeed, Bach alludes to a triply invertible complex in the sequential opening of the three occurrences of the 'continuity section' when he arranges the permutations of the voices (including the bass line) in the order a/b/c, b/a/c and, finally, a/c/b. It is this depth of thought applied systematically to that which composers ordinarily considered the ornamental aspect of musical composition that largely distinguishes Bach from his contemporaries.

The final invention that requires an explanation is an elegant 'researched' relation between the subject and the countersubject itself, indicated by the arrow between the two voices found in Example 11.1a. By 'research' I mean the furthest extreme of invention, that aspect which seeks out the most subtle and arcane combinations extending far beyond a mere variation or inflection of a musical idea. 'Research' is an attempt to seek out relationships between subjects or segments of a subject in a way inexplicable by mechanism. That is, the human inventor of the machine toys around with the inventions to arrive at a particularly dazzling coincidental relationship that can only result from an intelligence and musicality attuned to the most extraordinary possibilities. In this example the researched relation occurs as a result of a seemingly trivial connection between the subject and countersubject. By substituting an f♯ for the g in the countersubject at the point indicated by the arrow, Bach is able to produce a completely seamless musical 'join' between the two voices (see bb. 106–11). This seemingly trivial alteration creates yet another possibility for inventive display in which the subject – already immodest in length – is miraculously heard to continue without needing to catch its breath. Thus subject and countersubject work together in a syntagmatic relation (i.e. linked in succession) as well as in the more usual paradigmatic relation (i.e. in various simultaneous combinations). I intentionally call this relation 'researched', since the term evokes the imposing historical genre of the ricercar (which Bach himself refers to in his *Musical Offering*), a work designed to display the results of research into musical ideas in an especially dignified setting. Seeking out such relations is of course part of the delight Bach takes in researching his material but his elevated approach to invention is evident even within relatively unpretentious genres such as the 'mere' trio sonata.

Although it is doubtful to suppose that all the processes I have detailed were explicitly pre-compositional – that is, that Bach thought of his inventions utterly apart from their ultimate placement within the disposition of the movement as a whole – it has been useful to detail their structure and mechanisms apart from the layout of the movement so as to observe the really remarkable depth of thought that is brought to bear on such a relatively small set of raw materials. This insight is easily captured statistically: the length of the movement is 113 bars and, without yet mentioning the 'one-off' episodes, we have already accounted for some 85 bars of music. This calculation suggests that, in a movement of this kind, the issue of disposition or form (1) cannot be detached from the specific discoveries of invention and (2) is ultimately concerned with a rational and pleasing ordering of the *inventa*.

Figure 11.1 depicts how this process of disposition might best be understood. Across the page following the directional arrows is the syntagmatic ordering of musical events with bar numbers above each event signifying the beginning of each invention or episode. Down the page are three columns which, in paradigmatic fashion, represent parallel kinds of musical events: column A contains the basic display of the main inventions, column B the elaborative episodes and column C the larger blocks all initiated by the 'continuity section' which lead to the main cadential articulations.

It is important to distinguish the Bachian logic of invention – which relies on predetermined compositional mechanisms that seek out possible treatments of the subject – from that of disposition, which is both more informal an arrangement and less demanding a compositional skill. For example, column A shows how Bach displayed inventions in three similar groupings: (1) the primary and the modulating fugal complex, (2) the two inversions and modal transposition of the subject and (3) the canonic devices. It should be pointed out that none of this ordering is remotely permutational or mathematical in any way. Neither a meaningful number of bars in each section nor any predetermined ordering for any one group of similar inventions is intended here. Consider, for example, the passage beginning in b. 33 which displays the melodic operations performed on the theme. It begins with $SI_2$ in the harpsichord treble 'answered' by $SI_1$ in the gamba and pursued wittily by the complete statement of S in the minor heard (this time) surprisingly in the bass line. Following a non-thematic cadence in VI and several bars of what I call a 'batterie episode' (which derives from the free voice in the gamba part in bb. 39–40 accompanying the 'continuo solo') Bach reintroduces $SI_2$ twice in a miniature exposition of the inversion (preserving mode), but this time fails to mention the inversion preserving interval ($SI_1$) before

**Figure 11.1** BWV 1027/2, paradigmatic map

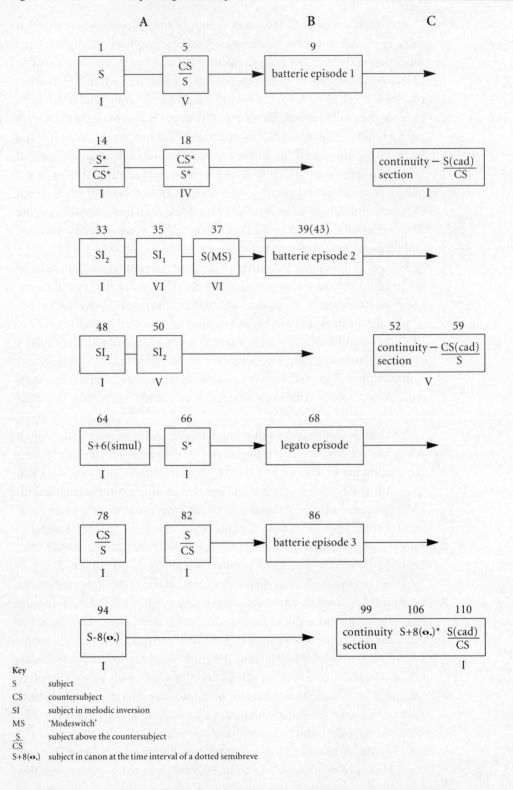

Key
S          subject
CS         countersubject
SI         subject in melodic inversion
MS         'Modeswitch'
$\frac{S}{CS}$   subject above the countersubject
S+8(o.)    subject in canon at the time interval of a dotted semibreve

moving into the 'continuity section'. A very pleasant arrangement to be sure, thematically as well as harmonically, but hardly an architectonic wonder. Similarly, the longish section involving the canonic devices at bb. 64 and 94 also takes time to recapitulate themes from the opening (at bb. 66ff., 78ff. and 82ff.), but not in any systematic fashion. This is not to say that Bach was never interested in symmetrical arrangements or numerically conceived dispositions, but that these were matters that only rarely infringed on the more intrinsically musical challenges of invention and its mechanisms.[3]

If there is an element of drama tied to the form of the piece, it is linked to the display of a further invention whose presence was not to be anticipated. I refer here to the final bars of the piece, in which one expects the 'continuity section' to lead back to the primary invertible complex. Instead of this, Bach introduces both the remaining canonic inversion of the subject played against itself, and then, in a true *tour de force*, miraculously transforms one device into another, so that at the downbeat of b. 110, the canonic device of S + 8 (o·) suddenly transforms itself into CS/S without any notice being given that this sleight-of-hand has taken place. The breathless and playful quality of this satisfying ending can be ascribed, then, to a final display of inventive wit whose artifice is almost entirely concealed.

Finally, a brief word about the episodes noted in column B of Figure 11.1, the 'one-off' links referred to earlier. Three of them play on the idiomatic technique of string-crossing called *batterie* mentioned above and are so labelled, while the fourth episode takes as its 'subject' a long legato figure that moves towards E minor before sequencing by descending step to a cadence in I. However effective and expressive these individual passages, the compositional effort expended on them must have been minimal, much more like play than work. For despite the surface resemblances in some melodic details, the underlying harmonic structure differs in each case, as Example 11.6 shows. For this reason, it is useful to think about these kinds of episodes as late accretions to the compositional process, as elaboration rather than invention.

If one thinks about the movement as a whole, it is striking how the playful character of the subject and the modest pretensions of the genre are grounded in a logic notable for its depth and rigour. To speak of the procedures of invention as mechanistic is, however, not to downplay the genius involved here, since it is the engagement of the man with the machine and the consequences drawn from this engagement that capture our musical interest. It is Bach, after all – and not an inanimate object – who not only selects the raw material to be fed into the compositional machines but also exercises great care in choosing the proper tools for the job at hand. All this takes a kind of ingenuity that is not easily replicable, particularly when the products of invention bear such a remarkably personal stamp. The musical result does indeed exude a kind of miraculous quality, which is surely why analyses modelled on the ideology of organicism have sometimes produced such interesting insights.

In the following discussion of a choral concerto movement from Cantata 78, I turn to another kind of analysis exemplifying some procedures of invention that begin with a pre-existent musical object, in this case the Lutheran chorale text and its accompanying melody.[4] Here the tools used for interpretation not only turn on the genre conventions but also bring into a play a realm of concepts and meanings signified by divinely inspired words. A question to bear in mind here is whether Bach's music figures in a merely supporting role to the words – its function according to all Christian theology – or whether Bachian processes of musical invention are able to interpret the sense behind the words in ways that both complement and eclipse the sense of the verbal text.

The first movement of this so-called chorale cantata from Trinity 1724 sets the opening eight-line strophe of Johann Rist's chorale text (1641), which is labelled alphabetically according to the distinct musical strains which set each line:

| | | |
|---|---|---|
| A | Jesu, der du meine Seele | Jesus, you who have taken my soul |
| B | hast durch deinen bittern Tod | Through your bitter death |
| A | aus des Teufels finstern Höhle | From the devil's dark den |
| B | und der schweren Seelennoth | And from the great agony of the soul |
| C | kräftiglich herausgerissen | Have wrested it forcibly, |
| D | und mich solches lassen wissen | And have let me know this much |
| E | durch dein angenehmes Wort, | Through your soothing words: |
| F | sei doch itzt, o Gott, mein Hort! | Be now, O God, my rock! |

Since the chorale tune is pre-existent, it is important to begin the analysis not at the beginning of the piece but rather with the chorale melody itself and the harmonic and contrapuntal possibilities it presented to the composer. It is obvious that Bach's conception for the work must have begun by taking stock of how, in the opening movement, the chorale tune was usable as a cantus firmus, a compositional procedure to which he devoted himself during his second Leipzig cantata cycle (1724–5). This particular movement, surely one of the best known and loved opening movements among the sacred vocal works, is indeed remarkable for its integration of cantus firmus, ritornello and fugal points of imitation. Thinking through a cantus firmus piece, after all, need not give rise to such an integrated perspective, since one can imagine a far less formal arrangement between the long notes and internal fugal tricks.

**Example 11.7** Main inventions in BWV 78/1

In the case of BWV 78/1, the invention underlying the movement proceeded from Bach's initial discovery that each of the six musical strains of
the chorale tune could be combined contrapuntally over forms of a chromatic chaconne bass representing the falling fourth of the traditional
lamento (G–F♯–F♮–E–E♭–D). This was a staggering discovery and a none
too obvious one at that, since the melodic character of strain A implied
closure in the tonic whilst Strain B concludes on an implied half cadence
on the dominant. In the first place (as Example 11.7 shows), although the
triple metre offered convenient ways to prepare and resolve chromatic
dissonances, in fact only two musical strains – A and B – worked flawlessly
over the prime form of the lamento, and in the case of strain F, the melody

had to begin a full bar later and needed to be embellished at bb. 3–4 to fit the bass line. Perhaps Bach's most brilliant observation was that strains C and D could be made to work together with transposed versions of the chaconne bass if the lamento underwent a 'modeswitch' into the major and was 'arrayed' (or transposed) onto scale degrees VII and III. Strain E, on the other hand, presented an initial fly in the ointment: although it could be matched with the pitch content of the lamento bass in G minor, the actual placing of the notes in the bass would have to be altered. (The original placing would have led to accented unprepared dissonances on the downbeats of the second and third bars of the bass line.) Given a rich enough contrapuntal fabric, however, this small adjustment would not be all that noticeable.

Of course the existence of two contrapuntal lines implied certain harmonic directions and, if one compares the differing sets of basso continuo figures, Bach went out of his way to chart a slightly different course in the thorough bass underlying each statement of the chorale tune. Naturally this consideration of harmony went hand in hand with creating a melody for the ritornello. From the small number of concordances between the prime form of the ritornello theme and the cantus firmus and the relative lack of strictness in the way Bach deploys the ritornello, it is reasonable to infer that the invention of the opening chaconne rondeau – with its grandiose and tragic associations with French courtly dance – occurred at a later stage, though perhaps prior to the setting of strain F whose pitch content, as mentioned, needed to be embellished in any case so as to match bb. 3–4 of the lamento bass.

If one had begun the analysis at the beginning of the piece with the chaconne itself, that is, taking the harmony and voice-leading of the opening as itself a primary determining structure, the analytic results would appear somewhat more haphazard, since the precise melodic shape of the theme is not maintained regularly throughout the movement. Indeed the chaconne theme is altered in ways only explicable when it is realised that the chaconne phrase as a whole (comprising its two parts labelled 'a' and 'b' in Example 11.7) is itself not an autonomous invention but rather was determined by its ability to combine with the lamento bass and with two strains of the cantus firmus chorale tune, A and F. (One can see, for example, how the phrase 'a' of the chaconne would have created parallel octaves with the melody of chorale strain B, and the lack of a good fit with other strains probably caused Bach to turn to contrasting elaborations in setting the remaining chorale strains.) The germ of the invention of the chaconne theme can perhaps best be gleaned from bb. 21–5, the first statement of strain A over the lamento bass. Here one comes closest to a threefold juxtaposition of the three inventive elements, although a comparison of b. 24 with b. 4 reveals that Bach was also willing to take a few liberties with the chaconne theme so as to give it a compelling independent shape at the beginning of the movement, the only moment within the movement when the 'a' phrase is heard on its own. The other statements of the chaconne are all clearly subsidiary to the chorale and the lamento, as for example at bb. 118–21 in the setting of strain E. A mechanical feature of Bach's invention, therefore, is that he takes his compositional hierarchies seriously, and, given the more subsidiary role of the chaconne theme, he will treat it more casually so as not to alter the more fundamental elements of structure: the chorale tune and the lamento bass.

Interestingly, when the chorale tune is absent, Bach takes the opportunity to elevate the 'b' phrase of the chaconne to the realm of invention by transposing it to the major mode in b. 85, as shown in the example. (A related 'modeswitch' occurs at bb. 99ff.) Here the 'modeswitch' follows directly upon a statement of the chorale tune strain in which the chaconne melody could not have been heard because of the poor counterpoint that would have resulted on the third beat in b. 81 and in b. 84. It is almost as if one is returned to the site of composition where an unusually obsessive composer routinely (and in this case vainly) tries to fit each of his musical discoveries into ever new moulds.

The remaining inventive work of the movement can be expressed in a series of canonic and fugal devices which treat the lamento bass individually and perform various operations on it to produce new points of imitation. As is usual with this aspect of Bach's workshop, the devices display Bach's further 'research' on his materials, and some operations are bound to be more successful than others. The first device, as shown in Example 11.8a, appears at bb. 9ff. and 13ff. and represents the invention of a countersubject in invertible counterpoint that can be rotated against the lamento. The other three devices, shown in Examples 11.8b, c, d and e, are canonic rather than fugal: (11.8b) in bb. 17ff., Bach attempts a canon at the lower fourth at the distance of a dotted minim (CANONIC LAMENT L − 4 (𝅗𝅥.)), which is aborted midstream to favour the entrance of the chorale strain A; (8c) in bb. 25ff., he melodically inverts the lament and plays this in a canon at the lower fifth (INVERTED CANONIC LAMENT L(inv) − 5 (𝅗𝅥.)); and (8d) in bb. 107–25, he is able to produce a brilliantly extended and recurrent point of imitation by altering the end of the lamento to create a perpetual canon alternating between the upper fourth and the lower fifth at the distance of a dotted semibreve (PERPETUAL CANONIC LAMENT* L + 4 (𝅝·) and L − 5 (𝅝·)), and concluding with a new canonic device, L* + 5 (𝅗𝅥.).

While elaborating and disposing these subsidiary inventions, Bach also makes a point of expanding the harmonic field of the movement by

**Example 11.8** Other inventions in BWV 78/1

(a) Lament with rotated countersubject

(b) Canonic lament L – 4 ($\downarrow$.)

(c) Inverted canonic lament L (Inv) – 5 ($\downarrow$.)

(d) Perpetual canonic lament

(e) Canonic lament *

focusing on the tonal array of scale degrees, so that across the movement as a whole, the lamento appears on five of the seven diatonic scale degrees: I, III, IV, V and VII. This interest in the array of tonal stations covered by inventions is not so much a matter of ingenuity (although it may have provided an impetus for the invention of the perpetual canon) but rather of disposition and form and is fundamental to the way in which Bach apparently thought through large-scale designs. To ensure that an invention is heard on a variety of scale degrees means not only that a large-scale movement occupies an appropriately broad tonal space but that the composer is actively seeking out forms of variation that are far less a matter of facile contrasts than integrated interpretations of a few well-chosen and well-designed discoveries.

The resulting saturation of this movement with inventions also means that there is precious little room for episodic work. Episodes occur only towards the end of the movement in three isolated passages (bb. 89–94, bb. 103–7 and bb. 125–36). In the first, having exhausted his musical invention, Bach turns to a more direct representation of the text in the highly declamatory motet style setting the line: 'und mich solches lassen wissen'. (The sequential harmonic structure of the passage, however, is not new and is taken from the continuo line in bb. 73ff. which therefore binds the setting of strains C and D together in an especially compelling way.) One can also observe Bach's decorative attempt to play with motivic resemblances in the episodes (the fifths in bb. 89ff., or the melodic contours of bb. 125ff., both derived from the chaconne melody), which have to be heard as the elegant and stylish play of decoration rather than the more severe work of compositional inventions.

Examining the movement as a whole, one might easily imagine – given the linked eight-bar structures of the chaconne phrases – that Bach could have crafted various symmetrical architectonic structures and hierarchies to give the piece a definitive shape. There is, however, no compelling evidence of an interest in this sort of architecture, with the exception of some important local forms of structural repetition. Consider the first seventy-two bars of the piece, which conclude with a modulation to the dominant. At the beginning, Bach is grouping the eight-bar phrases into periods of sixteen bars, setting up a large-scale formal pattern in the form of an ABAC structure[5] (although already within this opening section the chorale strains, for example, occur both at the beginning (b. 33) and in the middle (b. 21) of the eight-bar 'periods'). The passage at bb. 33–48, for example, is meant to be heard as structurally parallel to the passage at bb. 1–16, while bb. 49–64 are parallel to bb. 17–32. This bit of symmetry is hardly surprising in light of the conventional repetition of the *Stollen* (i.e. the As in an AAB form) in the chorale itself. But, with the setting of the line 'und der schweren Seelennoth' heard in the cantus firmus at b. 64, Bach pulls the rug from beneath his symmetrical design by adding an ungainly extra eight bars which prevent the lamento from returning to the tonic and, for the first time in the piece, moves to a dominant pedal which leads to the roving tonality of the next section. Whilst this break in the pattern creates an awkward asymmetry from a geometric standpoint, it produces excellent music, in that there is an immediate drive away from the formal courtly gestures of the sixteen-bar period towards the dramatic flight of the dactylic (♪♪♪ ♪♪♪ ♪♪♪) setting of the line 'kräftiglich herausgerissen' in bb. 73ff. While the impulse to design some aspects of the disposition according to simple geometric algorithms can therefore provide a useful component in the disposition of a work, it is rarely allowed to gain the upper hand. This becomes especially evident in the final section of the movement (from bb. 89ff.), where even the eight-bar structures are eclipsed by phrases of anomalous lengths: 10 bars + 4 bars + 4 bars + 11 bars + 7 bars + 4 bars and so on until the closing eight-bar phrase in b. 136.

Just as the analogy of music to rhetoric was surely understood more metaphorically than literally, so any analogy of musical form or disposition to architecture or mathematics can only be understood as partial and incomplete. In the end it is difficult to see how architectonic considerations of large-scale form can alone provide any deep understanding of the ways in which Bach's music actually functions. Bits of musical symmetry are certainly found in abundance in Bach's works, but they have to do more with his love of contrapuntal rotations and textural voice-exchanges related to the mechanical manipulation of invented ideas than with the overall 'form' of a composition. This kind of routine elaboration can be easily grasped by comparing parallel passages such as bb. 17–24 and bb. 49–56, in which the strings and oboes exchange parts.

The remarkable density and integration of the movement can thus be more precisely defined by separating out the relatively strict compositional elements from those that are more ornamental. In the realm of affect, the movement is profound precisely because of the emotional associations and meanings represented by the wealth of core inventions and especially by their own elaboration. The lamento bass is not some static sign of grieving but graphically depicts a recurring state of pathos and mourning by its varied repetitions of painful chromatic descents in equal pulses of crotchets. The repetitions are not so much literary (i.e. tied to the actual words) as gestural in the sense that they are experienced in combination with the most extended dance of French court ballet, the grand chaconne, which so often figures in Lullian lyric tragedy as a highly artificial choreography of summation and apotheosis. The rhythmic and metric impulse of this dance is such – with its unpredictable and heavily stressed binary subdivisions of a ternary bar – (♩♪) or (♩♩) – that the music projects no particular desire for closure beyond the eight-bar phrase and, on the contrary, is always rushing headlong into the new 'couplet'. Although the coincidence of lament and chaconne may seem eminently appropriate, the two musical elements are actually in conflict with one another in so far as the equally measured pulses and chromaticism of Bach's lament adversely affect the sweeping lilt of the chaconne phrases, rendering them ponderous, even morose. The special affect of the piece stems therefore not so much from synthesis but rather from creative solecisms and improprieties.

The deep thought with which Bach endows this movement therefore cannot be restricted merely to some rhetorical representation of individual lines of the chorale text, but rather goes much further in providing an unexpected musical gloss on the theological and poetic ideas that occur later in the cantata – the unbearable burden of the pain of sin in the tenor recitative, for example – as well as a unique gestural tableau (in a choreographic sense) which musically both depicts and enacts the ideas tied to the inventions. The inventions, as it were, give an interpretative shape to notions of empathy and suffering (the lamento and its melodic and contrapuntal permutations), to ideas of tragedy and the enactment of gestures associated with *les grands sentiments* (the chaconne) as well as to the assertion of faith and the hope for redemption (the chorale tune). And they do so both through the simultaneous projection of signs in which music – of all the arts – excels and through the prolongation and analysis of the experience, something which is elaborated over the time of the piece as a whole. This twofold approach to musical invention – metaphysical interpretation and temporal enactment – might even be understood as the ultimate ambition of the Bachian project itself.

To return to the issues raised at the beginning of this essay, one can see that mechanisms of Bachian invention have nothing to do with soulless and dry artifices opposed to musical expression but rather reflect an attempt to make music think about itself so as to be genuinely expressive, a method that treats musical materials with the utmost seriousness in order to say something that is both novel and true. And while it is fascinating to gain insights into Bach's phenomenal mastery of craft, it is also the case that none of his technical manipulations would be of the slightest interest if it did not reflect a living and breathing composer whose works are still saying remarkable things a quarter of a millennium after his death. Naturally the particular analytical readings I have presented are open to question, revision and refutation. One might even suggest that their interest lies perhaps less in their methodological novelty – which of course is indebted to time-honoured forms of musical analysis – than in the kinds of interpretative claims which they end up supporting about a very special composer writing very particular pieces of music. In the end, one is interested to make claims about the nature of Bach's compositional personality as a totality: its exploitation of raw materials, its obsession with rigorous mechanisms, its exaggerated respect for processes of strict counterpoint, its interest in unusual metaphors and gestures and, perhaps surprisingly, its lack of deep interest in geometry and symmetrical designs. The analyses also betray, I hope, the pleasure that attends the close examination of Bach's works, in which one aspires to glimpse the composer's dependence on talent and feeling as well as on arduous work and hard-won struggle. Far from some untouchable canonic icon of greatness, the image of Bach that emerges from the close examination of his compositional actions is a very human one, and for that reason alone, paints perhaps a more poignant portrait than do analyses accustomed to seeing only perfection and unity. The 'miracle' of the Bachian experience, finally, is not that music can evoke divine perfection, but rather that one confronts a composer aware of the fallibility of his art as well as the unusual power of his music to shape aesthetic experience in ways that forever alter one's sense of being alive.

PART III

# Influence and reception

# 12  Bach as teacher and model

*Stephen Daw*

Johann Sebastian Bach's activities as a teacher appear to have been both widespread and respected. Nevertheless, the substantial body of evidence concerning his teaching and methods is far from complete or authoritative. Furthermore, the circumstances of each individual pupil and Bach's own changing whim apparently led to a variability of approach. As in other areas of his activity, such inconsistency was probably also the result of the composer's continuing quest for improvement and his almost compulsive thirst for new challenges. Bach seems to have been a highly *creative* teacher, surprisingly so for his historical environment.

There are various ways in which we can identify Bach's pupils:

1　Recorded or preserved written evidence from Bach himself (say in a written testimonial) refers to personal instruction. It may also refer to collaboration in performance under his supervision (which is a rather different matter).

2　Written or reported evidence from an individual pupil may refer to study with Bach, sometimes with further comment concerning when and how the learning process was effected.

3　Sometimes music manuscripts compiled in collaboration with pupils demonstrate an educational purpose; but one needs to be careful here, since there may be many reasons why Bach required copying assistance without any specifically didactic intention.

4　Written reports by third parties, stating that others have been, are, or hope to become students of Bach.

5　The records of choir schools (the register of Thomasschule alumni, published by B. F. Richter in the *BJb* 1906 and subsequently destroyed, is useful, but it does not cover the *Externer* (day-pupils), including Bach's own sons).[1]

Bach had close relations only with those pupils who participated in the elaborate church music and he was only peripherally involved with the less musical pupils, delegating his responsibilities for teaching Latin (see Chapter 2, p. 24, above). The participation of boys as choral ripienists in the courts of Weimar and Köthen does not necessarily imply that they encountered Bach in a teaching capacity, but it cannot be excluded that some received personal instruction as a result of such contact.

It stands to reason that the better pupils would have been those most associated with Bach in rehearsal and performance, as copyists (particularly in Leipzig), occasionally as privately coached performers (in singing and keyboard continuo) and, in exceptional cases, as students of composition and solo keyboard performance. Johann Ludwig Krebs (1713–80) was accorded such favoured treatment and responded especially well, and there is little doubt that members of the Bach family and other relations were highly eligible to become Bach's students. Indeed relatives from the periphery of the Bach family lodged in Sebastian Bach's own quarters, whether in Weimar, Köthen or Leipzig.[2]

If we cannot be certain of the extent to which Bach was the teacher even of his Ohrdruf nephews, how much harder it is to be sure of any special pedagogic relationship with, say, his two busiest copyists during the early Leipzig years, Johann Andreas Kuhnau (who copied between February 1723 – for the *Probestück* (Bach's audition piece) – and 30 December 1725) and Christian Gottlob Meissner (also a copyist for the *Probestück*, but working until 1729 as an alumnus and even later – until 1731 – as a university student). Meissner, reportedly a capable singer and the librettist of the homage cantata to Leipzig, 'Apollo et Mercurius' (BWV 216a),[3] must have learned much of Bach's system of preparation for performance. Given that the jointly produced performing materials are the only surviving evidence of their cooperation, his profit may have been from Bach's example rather than his direct teaching. The concept of learning by immediate example (study by patterns) is, rather, the most ubiquitous form of discipleship revealed in the present study; indeed this seems to be the method by which Bach himself learned composition (see Chapter 10, pp. 136–40 above).

The closest report we have of a teaching process devised by Bach comes at second hand from the son (Ernst Ludwig) of Heinrich Nicolaus Gerber (b. 1702), who was a pupil of Bach for about two years, apparently from about November 1724. Ernst Ludwig reported (in the first published part of his *Historisch-Bibliographisches Lexicon der Tonkünstler*, Leipzig, 1790), that

> Bach accepted him with particular kindness ... and ... promised to give him
> the instruction he desired and asked at once whether he had industriously
> played fugues. At the first lesson he set his Inventions before him. When he
> had studied these through to Bach's satisfaction, there followed a series of
> Suites, then the *Well-tempered Clavier*. This latter work Bach played
> altogether three times through to him with his unmatchable art, and my
> father counted these among his happiest hours, when Bach, under the
> pretext of not feeling in the mood to teach, sat himself at one of his fine

instruments and thus turned these hours into minutes. The conclusion of
the instruction was thorough bass, for which Bach chose the Albinoni violin
solos; and I must admit that I never heard anything to surpass the style
in which my father executed these basses according to Bach's fashion,
particularly in the singing of the voices. This accompaniment was in itself
so beautiful that no principal voice could have added to the pleasure it
gave me.[4]

A student such as Heinrich Nicolaus Gerber probably paid quite hand-
somely for his tuition (which was probably not the case with Bach's inner-
most circle of pupils, i.e. family, sons of former associates, like Ludwig
Krebs, and a few pupils taught over a number of years, like Altnikol). The
teaching Gerber received seems to have been formally organised, probably with regular lessons. He had already learned something by witnessing
Bach at work in both secular and sacred music, since the *Lexicon* mentioned earlier that the young would-be student 'had heard much excellent
church music, and many a concert, under Bach's direction' during his first
half year in Leipzig, prior to his request for personal tuition.[5] There is also
the reference to Sebastian Bach's playing of *The Well-tempered Clavier*
'under the pretext of not feeling in the mood to teach'. It seems improba-
ble that the composer performed all the preludes and fugues consecu-
tively at one sitting; surely, the reference is to demonstrative playings on
many occasions, over the two years, possibly in cyclic groupings.

Bach's inquiry as to whether Gerber 'had industriously played fugues'
probably followed a request to hear the prospective pupil improvise;
upon hearing him elaborate a chorale or play dance-variations, it would
be perfectly reasonable to ask him if he had seriously studied extempore
fugue; what is even more interesting is that this expectation from
someone of Bach's background and type would have referred both to
musical practice (as in improvisation and its potential – though not
inevitable – development into notated composition) and to compositional theory (the enabling strategy, upon which any musical practice
would need to be securely rooted); perhaps Bach had already become
aware of the fascination with which the Gerbers would consider these
very relationships. What was probably a negative answer, or a rather
clumsy attempt to display ability, could well have resulted in Bach's deci-
sion to start work on the Inventions at the first lesson proper.

The reason for Bach's choice of the Inventions (whatever this title
actually signifies[6]) as a vehicle for preliminary study is their particularly
clear didactic purpose and availability, since Bach had already developed
them during the training of his extremely able eldest son Wilhelm
Friedemann. Their preface refers quite directly to their various educational applications:

A sincere guide through which lovers of keyboard music, and particularly those anxious to learn, are shown in a clear way not only (1) how to play without error in 2 parts, but also, upon further progress, (2) how to treat three obbligato parts correctly and well; and at the same time not only to be inspired with good inventions, but properly to develop them; and most of all to achieve a cantabile manner of playing and to gain a strong appetite to compose.[7]

The eager pupil must invent good musical figures (themes, structures, expressions or whatever cannot be excluded by that vital word, *Inventions*) and then develop them well. This applies equally to improvisation and composition, i.e. to any musical practice, but in his last few words, Bach implies that improvisation comes first, composition being but its (possibly main and ultimate) consequence. The student must play keyboard instruments so that the parts speak clearly and in a singing ('*Cantable*' – sic) way. These words are effectively re-used in the Gerbers' description of Bach's own playing and his teaching of thorough bass. They might allude to the subtle style of finger-attack, applicable to both harpsichord and clavichord, in which the digits are drawn backwards along the keys. Emanuel Bach describes this carefully in his *Versuch über die wahre Art das Clavier zu spielen*, part 1 (Berlin, 1753). It seems that those who listened carefully to Johann Sebastian Bach were specially impressed by his ability to preserve the cantabile sound in several voices (as, for example, in the accompaniments to Albinoni violin sonatas, recalled by Gerber).

Emanuel Bach, writing in reply to Forkel's enquiries in a letter dated 13 January 1775, described his father's learning programme thus:

In composition he started his pupils right in with what was practical, and omitted all the *dry species* of counterpoint that are given in Fux and others. His pupils had to begin their studies by learning pure four-part thorough bass. From this he went to chorales; first he added the basses himself, and they had to invent the alto and tenor. Then he taught them to devise the basses themselves. He particularly insisted on the writing out of the thorough bass in [four real] parts. In teaching fugues, he began with two-part ones, and so on . . . As for the invention of ideas, he required this from the very beginning, and anyone who had none he advised to stay away from composition altogether. With his children as well as with other pupils he did not begin the study of composition until he had seen work of theirs in which he detected talent.[8]

Surviving materials in the hand of Heinrich Nicolaus Gerber show that in the busy 1720s, at least, Sebastian Bach expected his pupils to copy out his own music. He added ornamentation and other details, though barely ever fingering.[9] It is also apparent that Bach gradually adjusted details of a textual nature as these supervised copies were completed; this he also did much later in the case of Johann Christoph Altnikol's copy of the second part of *The Well-tempered Clavier*. Thus the teacher's concern was not solely to instruct his pupil in the mastery of the techniques of performance and composition; it also gave occasion to introduce him to finer points of self-criticism and revision such as few composers have chosen ever to share with their more intimate assistants, let alone students.

A few examples survive which illustrate Bach's development of his pupils' harmonic abilities. The first movements of the Sonata in G major for flute, violin and continuo BWV 1038 and of that in F major for violin and continuo BWV 1022 are both apparently student studies over a bass line which Bach had earlier used (and probably even composed) for his own Sonata in G for violin and continuo BWV 1021. Both stem from shortly after the Gerber period, and neither has been seriously considered as Sebastian's own composition (above the bass) since the music of BWV 1021 and commentary upon it were both published in *NBA* VI/1 (1958). Each has its own sweet-toothed charm, as do sections of the flute sonata in E♭ BWV 1031. Perhaps all three were written by a young, fashion-conscious Leipzig student, such as Friedrich Gottlieb Wild or Christoph Gottlob Wecker[10] (both of whom were promising composers and useful players of the transverse flute). There survives from the 1740s an attempt, apparently by Johann Christoph Friedrich Bach, to set a bass line beneath a fragment of the Polonaise melody that Bach set in the Ouverture in B minor BWV 1067/6.

But, surely, most of this kind of learning would have been gained through practical work at keyboard instruments. It seems inevitable that students and alumni would have formed the corpus from which continuo keyboard players were developed for both church and secular use. Bach and his later students (from Christoph Nichelmann on) considered the study of composition to be best achieved through 'devising good ideas' and then developing them. The former was taught by example and exhortation, the latter by keyboard experiment, and by examination and experiment with figured bass.[11] Composition was often seen as a component of *Musica practica* in Lutheran Germany during the seventeenth century, but this association diminished quite rapidly subsequently.[12]

It is often difficult to discern which individuals studied thoroughly and individually with Bach in the earlier years. In Weimar, Philipp David Kräuter,[13] Johann Tobias Krebs (1690–1762)[14] and Johann Caspar Vogler (1693–1763)[15] all studied in a manner similar to Gerber, but using a rather different, less Bach-centred copying repertoire. Probably the same applied to members of the Bach family who joined Sebastian's household; moreover, pupils at the Thomasschule were presumably given tuition based on the contemporary 'usual' copying repertoire.

In 1737, Johann Elias Bach of Schweinfurt arrived in Bach's Leipzig household as a tutor and personal secretary in return for lodgings. This freed Sebastian to undertake more teaching, which was a happy coincidence, since from late May 1738 to 1741 Johann Friedrich Agricola and from 1739 to 1741 Johann Philipp Kirnberger (a former pupil of both J. P. Kellner and H. N. Gerber) both came to Leipzig University. The opportunity to study with Bach was apparently one of their major motives for coming.

The new repertoire they were to learn had broadened to include some of the organ works formerly learned by Tobias Krebs and Johann Caspar Vogler, new concertos, freshly arranged and/or copied by Bach for the *Collegium musicum* concerts, as well as ensemble sonatas and music by Bach's two eldest sons.[16]

From March 1744 until January 1748 Johann Christoph Altnikol came to the University with apparently very much the same purpose as Agricola and Kirnberger. He was even encouraged to copy a score of the early version of the St Matthew Passion and later to enjoy the composer's own supervision in the compilation (c. 1743–4) of a new version of *The Well-tempered Clavier* Book II.[17] Altnikol also copied out cantatas in score, perhaps partly so that Johann Sebastian could lend the originals or their copies to his son Wilhelm Friedemann in Halle,[18] or to others.

Of course, Agricola, Kirnberger and Altnikol all continued to copy music by J. S. Bach after their studies were over; they contributed in this way not only to the preservation of the music, but also (since copying was still probably considered to be largely a part of one's practical training in music, *Musica practica*) to its continued performance. The Berlin 'Bach circle' and central Saxony's shorter-lived pockets of Orthodox Lutheran church musicians were consequently enriched and afforded an opportunity to practise what was increasingly seen as a dying art, but nevertheless deserving of preservation in publications (such as Georg Friedrich Kauffmann's *Harmonische Seelenlust* and Bach's own late *Sechs Choräle von Verschiedener Art*) or manuscript anthologies suitable for reference (like J. G. Walther's manuscript preserved in the Hague, where settings of the same chorale by as many as ten different composers are grouped together, presumably for selection).[19]

The latest generation of prospective Bach students – the generation represented by Johann Gottfried Müthel (1728–88), Johann Christoph Kittel (1732–1809), Johann Christoph Oley (1738–89) and possibly even the somewhat older Johann Gottlieb Goldberg (?1728–56) – did not have time adequately to study with the master, given Bach's death in 1750; however, without copies made by Kittel, Oley and the Thomasschule student copyist Christian Friedrich Penzel (1737–1801), we should have lost important sources for a very wide range of Bach's music.

Many contemporary admirers of Bach were unable to establish a direct studying relationship with him, yet some of these were extremely active as copyists of his music. Some of them made copies in order to instruct their own pupils, some to pursue their own researches as students, and others for their own practical use. The tracing of lineages from the composer and his family outwards in these ways has been outstandingly well researched by Hans-Joachim Schulze.[20] The industrious Johann Peter Kellner (1705–72), for instance, was a practising organist, teacher and scholar working very much in the old-established tradition of *Musica practica*, and using his copies to assemble a wide repertoire of keyboard (mostly organ) and chamber music. His almost complete copy of Bach's unaccompanied cello suites – the oldest preserved source – is remarkable in that they are written partly in *scordatura* for an instrument he very probably did not play, and still contain what appear to be analytical markings to facilitate easy examination of Bach's way of developing 'good ideas'.[21]

Others who collected and in turn disseminated Bach's music through copying – or by commissioning copies – included Johann Gottfried Walther (1684–1748) and Johann Tobias Krebs (1690–1762), after both had ceased to see Bach regularly, Johann Christoph Preller (1699–1747) and Johann Nikolaus Mempell (1713–47). Kellner, in particular, developed quite an industry for mailing Bach copies from Gräfenroda, where it is easy to picture him sitting, in the rear first-floor window on a summer evening, copying the music with the help by the slowly sinking western sun, with the new Baroque church framing the view of the churchyard to the right.

Naturally there were other local pockets of interest in Bach's legacy, and it was inevitable that some of these would be based around copying, since that was a route through which Bach himself had learned and subsequently taught. There were lasting traditions in Berlin, Hamburg, Thuringia and, as the eighteenth century approached its close, in Vienna, where a circle of intellectuals fostered by Baron van Swieten stimulated Mozart's interest in both Bach and Handel.[22] Around the same time, the Nuremberg organist Lorenz Scholz (1720–98) was compiling an interesting collection of manuscripts, mainly of keyboard works by both Johann Sebastian and Carl Philipp Emanuel Bach. These included a number of fugues, several in alternative versions, besides a very interesting possible early version of the Italian Concerto BWV 971.[23]

The value and styles of Bach's oeuvre, which was not immune to criticism even during his lifetime (see Chapter 4, p. 55 above), became a focus for further controversy. Bach's excellence in harmony and in consistent industrious invention began to be used not simply as an example of good practice, but also as support for preferences to which he would probably never have dreamed of subscribing. Initially, this was mostly confined to disputes over musical theory. In one famous and protracted debate between Kirnberger and Marpurg,[24] he was quoted as a supporter of each opposing view. Forkel's biography of 1802 reveals a new preoccupation with Bach as a representative of the whole of German musical literature, and by the time of Philipp Spitta's biography (1873, 1880) Bach had become the foremost representative of the German – and, specifically, the German Lutheran – soul; to some, he was virtually a Protestant saint.

All of this might seem somewhat at odds with the clearly didactic style of some of his prefaces and dedications, but we are wrong to consider these out of context. Title-pages and dedications were usually couched in terms specifically relevant to the early eighteenth century, and Bach's were always scrupulously devout. His vision of resourcing those 'desirous of learning' was naturally restricted to students of his own time and, at best, the immediate future. Immortality, as Handel shows in his setting of *Semele*, is not something to which mortals should ever be inclined to aspire.

Yet from his very modesty and devotion sprang also an acutely self-critical capacity. His striving for greater perfection in preludes and fugues witnessed by his late association with Altnikol was remarkable. If a temporally bound attitude to his own oeuvre could inspire such refinement of technique, then we cannot guess how foreknowledge of a modern veneration of his music might have inhibited, or even – who knows? – further inspired his compositional processes. Perhaps mastery of both composition and instruction came to him as a matter of course, since his faith was so abundantly based on individual and communal discipleship. The best teachers – as well as those who most obviously set examples worth following – never feel that they themselves have nothing more to learn.[25]

# 13 Changing issues of performance practice

*George B. Stauffer*

The notion of consciously performing the works of Johann Sebastian Bach in a Baroque fashion, with Baroque forces, is a relatively recent development. Indeed, it is an idea that has taken firm hold only in the past fifty years. When we look back on the history of Bach's music – its birth in the Baroque, its eclipse in the Classical Period, its rediscovery in the Romantic era, and its canonisation in modern times – we find that musicians took many different approaches to playing it. The issues of what we now call 'performance practice' have constantly changed.

The Baroque era itself was a period of considerable stylistic self-consciousness, and this self-consciousness affected the way pieces were performed. As a German, Bach took an eclectic approach towards composition, calculatedly calling on aspects of at least five national styles: German, French, Italian, English and Polish. Each style implied particular forms, gestures, and – most importantly – modes of performance. For instance, the Overture in B Minor BWV 831, written in the French style ('nach Französischer Art' as Bach put it), contains rhythms in the opening section that attempt to record the sharply dotted 'French' performing style. When Bach revised the early, C minor, version of this Overture, BWV 831a, for inclusion in *Clavier-Übung* II (where it is paired with an Italian Concerto 'nach Italiaenischen Gusto'), he sharpened the rhythms to bring the execution more closely into line with the French manner of playing (Example 13.1).[1] That is to say, he intentionally bowed to the conventions of French performance practice.

To take a second example: when Bach composed the 'Domine Deus' of the B minor Mass ('arranged' might be a better word, since the music is surely derived from an earlier piece), he notated the opening melodic motive with even semiquavers. When Bach presented performance parts of the work to the Saxon elector, Friedrich August II, in 1733, he embellished the motive with lombardic rhythm, an Italian gesture that was extremely fashionable in Dresden in the 1730s (Example 13.2).[2] Still later, in the 1740s, when he used the 'Domine Deus' music for the 'Gloria Patri' of the Latin work *Gloria in excelsis Deo* BWV 191, he reverted to the even semiquavers for the opening motive. It would seem, then, that to curry favour with August II in the 1733 performance, Bach decided to

Example 13.1  The Overture from the French Overture in B minor, BWV 831
          (a)  in its early, C minor form (BWV 831a)
          (b)  as it appears in *Clavier-Übung* II

Example 13.2  The opening motive from the 'Domine Deus' of the B Minor, BWV 232
          (a)  as it appears in the autograph score
          (b)  as it appears in the Dresden parts

utilise Italian performance conventions that were popular at the Dresden court.

  That Bach and his Baroque colleagues were required to master such aspects of 'performance practice' as part of their training is clear from Bach's lament about the difficult lot of German musicians, who were not allowed the liberty of playing solely in an 'instinctive' way: 'It is somewhat odd, moreover, that German musicians are expected to be capable of performing at once and *ex tempore* all kinds of music, whether it comes from Italy or France, England or Poland.'[3] For guidance, the uninitiated could turn to the prefaces of Georg Muffat's *Florilegia* publications (1695–98) and the *Ausserlesene Instrumental-Music* (1701), the chapter 'Von der musicalischen Schreib-Art' in Johann Mattheson's *Der vollkommene Capellmeister* (1739) or similar sources that set forth detailed descriptions of native and foreign genres and the playing traditions that went with them. Such instructional aids were especially prevalent in Germany and England, the two European countries most receptive to foreign influence. For Bach, the chief issue of performance practice was undoubtedly the understanding and mastery of foreign styles.

  A newly international style emerged during the Classical era following

Bach's death. In the music of Haydn, Mozart and Beethoven, one finds national borders dissolved in a more cosmopolitan idiom, one in which natural, unaffected performance stood as the desired norm. The French philosopher Noel-Antoine Pluche praised the violin playing of his Parisian contemporary Jean Baptiste Anet, for instance, saying it was devoid of artifice and display and exhibited instead a sustained expressive line that resembled the lyricism of the human voice. Pluche associated this approach with *musique chantante* – lyrical music that was effortless and natural to the voice, that was without artifice and distortion.[4] Contrived overdotting and lombardic rhythmic alterations would have been anathema to this Classical aesthetic.

In Germany, however, many Baroque customs lingered in the second half of the eighteenth century, and in northern centres such as Berlin and Hamburg Viennese classicism seems to have had little effect on the way Bach's music was performed. Manuscript copies of the organ and keyboard works that circulated in Germany between 1750 and 1800 generally lack editorial accretions. They have an 'Urtext' appearance, and one suspects that the musicians who used them played Bach's music in much the same way it had been performed fifty years before (in addition, most of the manuscripts were owned by first- or second-generation Bach students, who were well schooled in his manner of performance). The vocal works, too, appear to have been approached from the earlier standpoint. When Carl Philipp Emanuel Bach presented the Credo of the B minor Mass at a Hamburg benefit concert in 1786, he added Baroque-style slurrings and ornaments and adjusted the instrumentation here and there (chiefly to compensate for the lack of oboes d'amore, which had become obsolete, and to supply *colla parte* doubling in the 'Credo in unum Deum' and 'Confiteor' movements, which may have been his father's intention in any case).[5] He also added a short Introduction of his own composition. But on the whole, he made no substantive changes in the score and treated the Credo as a Baroque chamber piece, using forces much like those available to his father.[6] Emanuel's older brother Wilhelm Friedemann took a similarly conservative approach in revising Cantata 80, *Ein feste Burg*, for his own use: when he added trumpets and drums to the first and fifth movements, he did so with such stylistic adroitness that the accretion was excised only with the editing of the *Neue Bach-Ausgabe* in recent times.[7]

In progressive Vienna, where the ties with Bach's practices were less direct, musicians were quicker to update his music. For Baron van Swieten's Sunday afternoon reading sessions of Bach and Handel, Mozart and others transcribed *Well-tempered Clavier* fugues for string ensemble (trio, quartet or quintet), a medium considered to be more voice-like and natural than the organ, harpsichord or clavichord. In addition, the fugue arrangements were sometimes prefaced with newly composed preludes in classical style[8] – a procedure analogous to C. P. E. Bach's use of his own Introduction for the Credo in Hamburg. When Mozart arranged *Acis and Galatea, Messiah, Alexander's Feast* and the Ode for St Cecilia's Day for performances by the Gesellschaft der associierten Cavaliers, he fleshed out Handel's scores, orchestrating the secco recitatives and adding clarinet, horn and other instrumental parts to other movements. One suspects he would have done the same with Bach's vocal music, if it had been available at the time.

The Romantic period brought a more extreme break with Bach's practices. Romantic musicians, with their passionate longing for the past, viewed Bach not just as an important historical figure – like Handel or Vivaldi – but as a kindred spirit, an isolated genius who laboured for a largely unappreciative audience. In Johann Nicolaus Forkel's seminal biography of 1802, we find Bach described in terms appropriate to Beethoven:

> He laboured for himself, like every true genius; he fulfilled his own wish, satisfied his own taste, chose his subjects according to his own opinion, and lastly, derived the most pleasure from his own approbation . . . He thought the artist could form the public, but that the public could not form the artist . . . [9]

As a consequence, nineteenth-century musicians readily claimed Bach's music for their own and did not hesitate to refashion his works in a highly Romantic style. When Mendelssohn resurrected the St Matthew Passion in 1829, he used the mixed chorus of the Berlin Singakademie (an amateur choral society which boasted almost 400 members), the orchestra of the Philharmonischer Verein (an ensemble of enthusiasts led by supplementary professionals) and a separate group of operatic soloists (including Anna Milder-Hauptmann, who had performed the part of Leonora in the 1805, 1806 and 1814 performances of Beethoven's *Fidelio*). To bring the St Matthew Passion into line with Romantic tastes, Mendelssohn replaced Bach's oboes d'amore with clarinets, added melodic phrasings, crescendos and diminuendos and other dynamic marks, and expressive tempo indications. He also made extensive cuts in the aria sections.

The year before, Gaspare Spontini, director of the Berlin Opera, had used similarly grand forces for a performance of the Credo portion (*Symbolum Nicenum*) of the B minor Mass in the Berlin Opera House. Spontini paired the Credo with the Kyrie and Gloria from Beethoven's *Missa solemnis*, and it was not long before the general public viewed the B minor Mass and the *Missa solemnis* as the two Great German Mass settings of the nineteenth century.[10] In this way, Bach and Beethoven became colleagues across time – similar, heroic figures struggling against similar, cruel destinies (Bach against blindness, Beethoven against deafness).[11]

The sharp change in performance practice initiated by the blossoming of Romanticism is strikingly visible in Czerny's editions of Bach's keyboard music. Franz Anton Hoffmeister's edition of *The Well-tempered Clavier* (Plate 4), issued between 1801 and 1803 – i.e., at the very end of the Classical period – preserves the unadulterated 'Urtext' appearance of Bach's eighteenth-century manuscript. Czerny's edition of 1837 (Plate 5) reflects a radically different approach, one paralleling Mendelssohn's reworking of the St Matthew Passion. Czerny has 'orchestrated' Bach's score by adding dynamic markings, phrasings, crescendos and diminuendos, rubatos and expressive tempo indications. In a review of the edition, Robert Schumann condoned Czerny's changes, noting that Bach's fugues were 'character pieces of the highest order, at times genuinely poetic creations, each demanding its own expression, its own particular lights and shadows'.[12] Czerny stated that his additions stemmed from his recollection of Beethoven's performances of *The Well-tempered Clavier*. Whether or not this is true, the claim demonstrates once again the Romantic desire to link Bach with Beethoven, and Czerny's editions stand as remarkable testimony to the Beethovenesque manner of Bach performance that was in vogue at the time.

As Romantic style reached full sway, the 'enhancement' of Bach's music increased to the point where composers added new parts to the scores almost as a matter of course. For an 1841 Gewandhaus performance with the violinist Ferdinand David, Mendelssohn produced a piano accompaniment for the Chaconne from the D minor Partita for unaccompanied violin. Schumann, perhaps inspired by Mendelssohn, composed piano accompaniments for all six unaccompanied violin sonatas and partitas and the six unaccompanied cello suites. The Chaconne in particular was later orchestrated by Joseph Joachim Raff and arranged for piano left hand by Johannes Brahms, in both instances with a certain amount of 'fleshing out'. Charles Gounod took Czerny's rendition of the Prelude in C Major from the first book of *The Well-tempered Clavier* and added a newly composed soprano melody over it to produce his kitsch classic *Ave Maria, mélodie religieuse adaptée au 1er prélude de J. S. Bach*. In so doing, he draped Bach's pedagogical work with the mystical cloak of nineteenth-century Catholic church music. In the *Melodisch-contrapunktische Studien* Op. 137a, Ignaz Moscheles augmented *Well-tempered Clavier* preludes with melodic cello lines. Franz Liszt and Ferruccio Busoni filled out Bach's organ works and transferred them to piano, the ideal

Plate 4 Franz Anton Hoffmeister's edition of *The Well-tempered Clavier*, issued between 1801 and 1803, first page of Book II

## Preludio I.

**Plate 5** Czerny's edition of *The Well-tempered Clavier*, 1837, first page of Book II

expressive instrument for the Romantics (together with the violin and cello, of course). And Max Reger added a third line to Bach's Two-part Inventions to produce organ trios for his *Schule des Triospiels* of 1903. In many cases, the additions reflected the Romantic desire for melody at all cost. Mendelssohn promoted the *Orgelbüchlein* chorales as organ music and performed them as such. But he also urged friends to try playing pieces such as *Ich ruf zu dir, Herr Jesu Christ* as a piano solo, with the melody in octaves, or as a violin–piano duet, with violin 'singing' the chorale tune above the piano.[13]

Schumann's critique of Mendelssohn's accompaniment to the D minor Chaconne reflects the attitude of the day:

> David played a Ciacona by J. S. Bach, a piece from the sonatas for solo violin about which it has been said, wrongly as it turns out, that one could not imagine another part being added. Mendelssohn Bartholdy refuted that idea in the most convincing manner by accompanying it at the piano, and so wonderfully that the old, immortal cantor seemed to have a hand in the performance himself.[14]

Nineteenth-century musicians evinced little desire to return to Baroque performance practices. Instead, they wished to bring Bach back to life as a born-again Beethoven, as a Romantic colleague taking direct part in the music-making.

Yet at that very moment, the seeds of modern 'authenticity' were being sown. Between 1844 and 1852 the Leipzig publisher C. F. Peters, spurred by the great interest in Bach's music created by the *Bachbewegung*, issued the complete organ works in eight volumes. The editor, Friedrich Conrad Griepenkerl, derived the text by comparing all available early manuscript sources of the pieces. This ground-breaking critical edition (its text is still used by Peters) was soon followed by the *Bach-Gesamtausgabe*, issued by the Bach-Gesellschaft between 1851 and 1899. Although the scholarly standards of the *Bach-Gesamtausgabe* were uneven by today's measure, the edition nevertheless represented a remarkable effort, in the midst of an era of great subjectivity, to present Bach's scores in an Urtext form. Like Griepenkerl, the editors of the *Bach-Gesamtausgabe* used early manuscripts and prints (which they described in critical commentaries) to produce as authentic a text as possible, and the 'clean' appearance of the music stood in marked contrast to the heavily edited scores of other contemporary editions (such as the complete edition of the Henry Purcell Society).

The monumental Bach biographies of Carl Heinrich Bitter (*Johann Sebastian Bach*, 1865) and Philipp Spitta (*Johann Sebastian Bach*, 1873–80) also played an important role in ushering in a new era of objectivity. Although their accounts were steeped in the spirit of German Romanticism, Bitter and Spitta presented archival documents that illuminated the nature of Bach's own music-making. For instance, both printed the text of the 'Short but most necessary draft for a well-appointed church music' of 1730, in which Bach outlined the performing forces needed for church music in Leipzig: twelve to sixteen singers and nineteen to twenty-five instrumentalists for the weekly church music.

Such figures were a far cry from the immense bodies of performers used in Romantic renditions of the sacred vocal works. Spitta, in particular, examined the precise nature of Bach's instruments and ensembles. More significantly, he discussed specific performance issues in a new, objective way, citing evidence both from the original Bach manuscripts and prints and from long-forgotten seventeenth- and eighteenth-century treatises. It was Spitta, for instance, who first pointed to the presence of lombardic rhythm in the Dresden parts of the 'Domine Deus' of the B minor Mass and pondered its possible interpretation.[15] Although Spitta's biography was not oriented toward performance per se, it was – and remains – a veritable compendium of documentary information on Baroque practices. Over half a century passed before equally valuable studies appeared: Charles Sanford Terry's *Bach's Orchestra* (1932), which focused on the nature of Bach's instruments and the constitution of his ensembles in Weimar, Köthen and Leipzig, and Arnold Schering's *Johann Sebastian Bachs Leipziger Kirchenmusik* (1936) and *Johann Sebastian Bach und das Musikleben Leipzigs im 18. Jahrhundert* (1941), which surveyed Bach's music practices in Leipzig.

The concept of using source work and archival information to recreate Bach's manner of playing evolved slowly, as the 'early music movement' itself gained ground. At the ancient Benedictine abbey of Solesmes in France, Dom Prosper Guéranger and Canon Augustin Gontier attracted considerable attention, from 1860 onwards, by attempting to recapture the barless performance of Gregorian chant. Thirty years later, in London, Arnold Dolmetsch unveiled the string fantasies of Jenkins, Simpson, Lawes and Locke and performed the works with a consort of reconstructed seventeenth-century viols. Dolmetsch's first clavichords and harpsichords, built in the 1890s, received wide acclaim. While the Solesmes performances and Dolmetsch's instruments were heavily influenced by nineteenth-century tastes, they nevertheless represented decisive steps away from Romantic introspective subjectivity and towards an historical dimension in performance.

Within the field of Bach scholarship and performance, the revival of early practices began as a longing for the past, a sentiment typical of late Romanticism. In 1904, in the first issue of the *Bach-Jahrbuch* (the journal of the recently formed Neue Bach-Gesellschaft), Arnold Schering lamented the loss of Baroque traditions and reasoned that their disappearance made it difficult – if not impossible – to recreate Bach's performance practices.[16] The rise of middle-class music-making, the advent of the public concert, the training of musicians in the Classical and Romantic schools and the disappearance of many Baroque instruments had created an immense gulf between Bach's time and the twentieth century. It was not simply a matter of wanting to return to Bach's performance style: Schering doubted that such a recreation could ever be accomplished. Tastes and practices had changed. The chasm seemed too large to be bridged.

Albert Schweitzer was similarly wistful about the past in *J. S. Bach, le musicien-poète* (1905), mourning the loss of sounds known to Bach, such as the oboe d'amore and the boys' voices. Like Dolmetsch, Schweitzer was a child of the nineteenth century and did not reject Romantic performances. But he began to lobby for restraint. With the B minor Mass, for instance, Schweitzer gently urged a reduction in the size of the chorus:

> Bach indeed never dreamed of a performance of the 'Gloria', the 'Et resurrexit', and the 'Osanna' of his B-Minor Mass by three or four hundred singers; nevertheless we may venture to perform in this way, and it has been done successfully. We ought to recognise, however, that it is all a matter of chance. Even with a choir of a hundred and fifty voices there is a danger of lines of the vocal polyphony coming out too thickly and heavily in a way directly opposed to the nature of Bach's music.[17]

During the course of the twentieth century, the instruments and ensembles of Bach's day have been recreated, one by one. With the organ, it was Schweitzer himself who called for a return to early precepts. In *Deutsche und französische Orgelbaukunst* (1906), Schweitzer accused German organ makers of compromising the sound of the instruments they built in favour of modern gadgetry. Schweitzer's personal ideal was the Romantic organ of Aristide Cavaillé-Coll. But in the Organ Reform Movement that followed, it was the North German Baroque organ of Arp Schnitger, especially, that was elevated as the perfect instrument for Bach's music.[18] It took some time to discern the precise principles behind Schnitger's instruments, however: existing historical instruments, such as the Scherer/Fritzsche/Schnitger organ in the Jakobikirche in Hamburg, were often restored poorly, and new instruments constructed in the Schnitger mould were at first pseudo-Baroque; quasi-North German stops, generally over-voiced, were combined with electro-pneumatic actions. In time, firms such as Marcussen, Flentrop and Beckerath began building organs based more accurately on Baroque ideals, with tracker action, slider chests, low wind pressure, and appropriately scaled and voiced pipework.[19] Further scrutiny of existing historical instruments produced further refinements, and by the 1970s Jürgen Ahrend, Charles Fiske, Gene Bedient and others were constructing reproductions of a wide variety of seventeenth- and eighteenth-century German organs (and of other prototypes as well), incorporating uneven wind, unequal temperament, consoles with short keys and flat, straight pedalboards, and other historical features. By the last quarter of the twentieth century,

a Baroque tracker organ, or a reproduction of one, is usually the instrument of choice for performances and recordings of Bach's organ music.

A similar evolution can be observed with the harpsichord. The harpsichord revival, initiated by Dolmetsch at the end of the nineteenth
century, was carried forth almost single-handedly in the early twentieth
by Wanda Landowska. Like the initial organs of the Organ Revival
Movement, Landowska's famous Pleyel harpsichords, first built to her
own specifications in 1912, were only a distant approximation of a
Baroque instrument (as were the Neupert firm's 'Bach disposition' harpsichords, with long treble scales, 16' registers and registration pedals).
But Landowska's spirited performances sparked interest in the use of
harpsichord – rather than piano – for Bach's clavier music and set the
stage for the more authentic reproductions built after World War II by
Martin Skowronek, William Dowd, Frank Hubbard and others.[20] By the
1970s, Bach's keyboard music was being performed as frequently on the
instrument for which it was conceived – the eighteenth-century harpsichord (or a reconstruction of one) – as on the instrument on which it was
revived, the piano.

With string, woodwind and brass instruments the return to historical
prototypes followed a similar course: well-intended pseudo-reconstruc-
tions gradually yielded to ever-more-accurate reproductions. With the
violin, for instance, replacing the modern steel strings with gut on surviving eighteenth-century instruments often proved to be insufficient:
during the nineteenth century, the necks of such instruments had often
been angled, the fingerboards lengthened, and the original bows replaced
by larger, convex Tourte models to produce a broader sound and longer,
legato melodic lines (the highly arched 'Bach' bow, capable of playing
legato multiple stops, was a purely modern invention).

In time, it became increasingly apparent that to produce an historically
true Baroque sound, all instruments in an ensemble had to be constructed
according to eighteenth-century precepts. Retrospective performances
of Brandenburg Concerto No. 2 in the 1960s, for instance, sometimes substituted alto recorder (the *flauto* of the original score) for the more
commonly used Böhm transverse flute. But the recorder made little
headway when paired with a modern trumpet in the concertino passages.
To achieve proper balance, one needed a lighter-toned, valveless Baroque
trumpet. Writing with remarkable clairvoyance in 1937, Friedrich Smend
convincingly demonstrated the inherent equality (and interchangeabilty)
of Bach's melodic lines – an equality he believed could be realised only
through the delicately matched voices of a Baroque chamber ensemble.[21]
Only thirty years later, with the resurrection of all the instruments in
Bach's instrumentarium, could such an equality be achieved.

With Bach's vocal music, the return to original forces came more slowly, perhaps because of the vested interest of choral societies and mixed church choirs in maintaining nineteenth-century traditions. The Bach Cantata Club of London was one of the first groups to take Schweitzer's message on Bach's vocal forces to heart and perform Bach's choral music with a new degree of historical fidelity. The Club often used a modest-sized, mixed chorus of thirty-six voices with a chamber orchestra. In America, Arthur Mendel's Cantata Singers presented Bach's cantatas, passions and Latin church music with similarly small forces, and Robert Shaw's 1961 recording of the B minor Mass with thirty-three professional singers and twenty-nine instrumentalists represented an earnest effort to break away from the choral-society tradition. In Germany, Wilhelm Ehmann experimented with practical issues of Baroque performance with his Westfälische Kantorei at the Hochschule für Kirchenmusik in Münster. But these groups continued to use mixed choirs and modern instruments. Even to as mainstream a musician as Paul Hindemith, however, it was clear, by 1950, that reducing the size of the forces or making other token adjustments no longer sufficed:

> It is not enough for us to use a harpsichord as continuo instrument. We must string our string instruments differently; we must construct our wind instruments with the scalings of the time; and we must even recreate the relationship of choir pitch and chamber pitch in the tuning of our instruments.[22]

Implicit in this, of course, was the belief that modern musicians could learn how to play early instruments, and that scholars could provide them with guidance about the nuances of Baroque performance. Dolmetsch had taken the first step in both areas, through his own performances and with his 1915 publication, *The interpretation of the music of the XVII and XVIII centuries*, the first modern guide to Baroque performance practice. After World War II, Dolmetsch's findings were refined and greatly expanded by Robert Donington, whose *Interpretation of early music* (dedicated to Dolmetsch) provided performers with detailed discussions on matters concerning style, embellishment and accompaniment. Frederick Neumann, Michael Collins, David Fuller and other Baroque specialists subjected bowing, articulation, fingering, tempo and other aspects of performance to further scrutiny.

Within the field of Bach studies, the editorial work on the *Neue Bach-Ausgabe* (1954–) and the intense source investigations of Alfred Dürr, Georg von Dadelsen, Robert Marshall, Christoph Wolff and others were soon providing the type of performance-related information that

**Example 13.3** The *Applicatio* in C major BWV 994, from *Clavier-Büchlein vor Wilhelm Friedemann Bach*

Hindemith envisioned.[23] The musical texts of Bach's works were re-evaluated, and new consideration given to details like the placement of slurs, the use of dots, altered rhythms and instrumental terminology. Renewed examination of the original performance parts revealed much about the pragmatic nature of Bach's music making, and often complemented the discoveries of instrument builders. For instance, Marshall's detailed study of dynamic marks in the autograph scores showed that Bach used only three indications on the *forte* side of the spectrum (*forte, poco forte* and *mezzo forte*) but many refinements on the *piano* side (*piano, sempre piano, piano piano, piu piano, poco piano* and *pianissimo*).[24] The emphasis on the quieter end of the dynamic range parallels the findings of instrument builders about the structure of Baroque violins and bows: that they were designed for subtle dynamic nuances rather than the forceful projection of a loud tone.

Or to take another example: the few surviving fingering indications in the extant keyboard manuscripts show that even as a mature player, Bach maintained, on occasion at least, the seventeenth-century practice of playing substantial parts of white-note scales with two-finger patterns.[25] The right-hand fingering (3–4–3–4–3–4) for the opening C major scale in the well-known *Applicatio* from the *Clavier-Büchlein vor Wilhelm Friedemann Bach* (Example 13.3) facilitates frequent mordents and shakes and is more naturally (and easily) rendered on the small, short keys of an early keyboard instrument, particularly the clavichord, than on the wide, long keys of a modern piano (the smaller key-dip of the former would also aid the execution). Interestingly enough, John Butt's extensive study of articulation markings in all the Bach original materials has shown that the composer's favourite slur, from a statistical standpoint, was this very type of two-note grouping.[26] When the Baroque organ of the Jakobikirche in Hamburg was restored shortly after World War II, it was provided with modern keyboards and pedalboard because these were thought to facilitate the performance of Bach's works. That the organ has now been restored to its original condition, with its modernised console removed, demonstrates how far thinking on historical performance practices and instrument building has changed in the last twenty years.

The editing of the *Neue Bach-Ausgabe* has also illuminated the many inconsistencies of Bach's own approach to marking his performing scores, and one of the most controversial issues to emerge is slurring. In unison passages, for instance, Bach not infrequently assigned different slurrings to different instruments playing the same notes. Were the differentiated slurrings accidental, and as a consequence should they be regularised – the general policy of the *Neue Bach-Ausgabe*?[27] Or were they introduced intentionally to produce a type of subtle, articulatory heterophony, and should they thus be retained, as Dene Barnett has proposed?[28] Or were they evolutionary, refined by Bach as he worked through a score, and should they then be regularised according to the last entry, as Georg von Dadelsen has suggested?[29] Such issues are not settled easily, by scholarship or performance.

Scholarly debate and editorial policy were put into practice in a culminating way in the complete recording of Bach's church cantatas and other vocal works by Nikolaus Harnoncourt and Gustav Leonhardt. This series, begun in 1971, served as a testing ground for ideas on historical performance that had been gestating since the turn of the century. These performers set a new standard for interpreting Bach's ensemble music through renditions that combined scholarship, performance practice and even instrument building (Bach's oboe da caccia was rediscovered during the course of the cantata cycle, for instance, and reconstructed from Leipzig prototypes).[30] To critics accustomed to the lush sounds of nineteenth-century-oriented groups, Harnoncourt's recordings at first seemed shocking: 'The Baroque horn is afraid of its own shadow . . . and a mixed chorus is infinitely preferable to the combination of men, falsettists, and boys', Paul Henry Lang declared.[31] But by 1980 or so, the new approach was emulated throughout Europe and the United States, bringing the 'original forces' movement to complete fruition.

What direction will performance practice take in the future? However close the historical instruments and practices used by today's performers may be to Bach's own, it is clear that many matters remain open to further interpretation. Much needs to be learned about the Thuringian organ, which may be a better guide to playing and registering Bach's organ works than the Schnitger instruments that received such attention in the Organ Revival. Thuringian instruments typically contained an abundance of flue stops at 8' and 4' pitch, suggesting that a more 'orchestral' sound, one with a certain amount of foundation doubling, might be more appropriate for Bach's organ music than previously thought.[32] The same is true of Bach's harpsichord: obviously, Bach would have encountered mainly

Central German harpsichords rather than the French or Flemish type of instruments most usually built today. Thuringian and Saxon harpsichords were distinctly eclectic in design, combining elements of French, Flemish, Italian and German construction. In addition, they were sometimes strung in brass, which produces a clear, penetrating sound ideal for Bach's dense counterpoint.[33] And it has been questioned whether Bach's harpsichord concertos were written for harpsichord at all: Eva Badura-Skoda has made a strong case for Bach's extensive use, in Leipzig at least, of the fortepiano, which he helped to perfect (and market) for his colleague Gottfried Silbermann.[34]

Even the nature of Bach's chorus is open to debate: Did Bach's choir normally consist of no more than a quartet, with just one voice per part, as Joshua Rifkin has proposed (and demonstrated with several recordings), or should it be a larger group of twelve to sixteen singers, as Bach himself seems to have indicated in the 'Short but most necessary draft'?[35] Whether or not Rifkin's approach will gain wide acceptance remains to be seen. Complicating the picture further are developments typified by Harnoncourt's second recording of the B minor Mass (1986), in which he retreats somewhat from the 'original forces' concept by using an enlarged Concentus Musicus ensemble with the Arnold Schoenberg Chor, a professional choir of men and women. In an interview, Harnoncourt explained that he used a mixed chorus instead of a boys' choir because women's voices 'bring the sensuous flair of adults to the music'.[36] Subsequent recordings by other ensembles have confirmed the return of a subjective element in performance practice and may represent the beginning of a new era, one in which performers knowingly – and unabashedly – seek a middle ground between what they know of Bach's conventions and their own personal tastes. Whether or not this is true, if the past two-and-a-half centuries are any indication, the issues of Bach performance practice will continue to change.

# 14 Bach reception: some concepts and parameters

*Martin Zenck*

'One follows a great example most faithfully by not following it . . .'

(*F. Busoni*)[1]

## Questions – parameters – possible solutions

To raise objections about the very topic one has been asked to write about is surely unusual; perhaps it would be better not to address the topic at all. But that would be far too simple a solution. It makes more sense to formulate the discontent, not as a disclaimer soon to be forgotten, but rather as a critical undercurrent that will run throughout both this chapter and the next.

Three fundamental objections can be raised against the assigned topic. First, much of the material is ubiquitous, given that there is hardly a composer of the nineteenth or twentieth century who has not occupied himself with Bach, whether it be by choice or requirement. Perhaps it would therefore be more feasible to investigate those who have given Bach a wide berth. Delimiting the material in this manner would serve as a corrective to the unattainable goal of comprehensively listing and critically interpreting all forms of Bach reception. Secondly, there is the danger of mythologising Bach by producing yet another historiographically outmoded description of great heroes, a monocausal, linear music history delineated by monuments, Bach – Beethoven – Brahms – Schoenberg – Boulez. Thirdly, there is the historical and ontological difference between Bach's horizon of expectation and that of the present day;[2] the ubiquity of Bach's music and the mythologising of Bach today contradict the situation in his own time.

It would be wrong simply to proceed with the task in hand as if the objections had not been raised at all, as if as a result of expressing them, the author would be immune from accusations of insufficient self-criticism about the absurdity and the presumptuousness of the project. A more meaningful approach is to understand the three objections (pp. 219–24 below) not as established facts but rather as problems which one can at least attempt to solve (pp. 224–5). By reflecting on these problems, the material, which is simply too extensive to examine compre-hensively, can be better organised and selected.

## Criteria for selection and organisation

Given that almost every important composer has encountered Bach in the course of learning a musical instrument, in studying harmony and counterpoint, and further through arrangements and transcriptions, compositions upon the name B-A-C-H or free works about Bach cast as improvisations or tone-poems,[3] a list of composers influenced directly or indirectly by Bach would be a long one. If we were also to add theoretical, literary, historical, artistic and philosophical reflections about Bach to this list, we would arrive at a 'bad infinity', the term Hegel used to describe the arbitrariness of purely quantitative research.

A complete list of all of the works on the name B-A-C-H could, for example, be omitted because these works are usually merely an expres-sion of admiration. Many also evidence the intention of an historical self-aggrandisement by associating with the historical figure 'Bach', but without contributing substantially to new interpretations of Bach's com-positions, as Liszt and Busoni so productively did.

A further limitation arises from the categorisation of the material relat-ing to the history of Bach's influence.[4] This *history of influence* highlights those Bach works which have affected subsequent music history (the influence of the St Matthew Passion on Mendelssohn is a good example of this[5]). In *reception history*, on the other hand, Bach's works are an object mastered by composers (Busoni's revision of Bach's famous *Chaconne* is not a respectful transcription, like that of Brahms, but rather a transfor-mation whereby a new original is created). Even in those borderline cases where they only differ slightly from one another, the history of influence and the history of reception are nonetheless very well suited as initial cate-gories to organise the entire body of work before other criteria can be used to subdivide further this overwhelmingly large amount of material.

Thus, one can place the history of the transmission of Bach's works in the category of the history of influence, understood as the preservation of the Bach tradition. Reception history, on the other hand, pertains to instances where Bach's works are no longer seen within the context of that tradition, but instead are, at least partly, fundamentally changed within the understanding and interpretation of a particular compositional and performing environment. The goal is not the reproduction – after all imaginary – of the original but rather a transformation which always views Bach through the lens of new developments in music.

If the distinction between the histories of influence and reception is of significant influence in organising the entire material, further criteria pertain to reception itself. These are defined according to the extent and intensity of the distance between the original Bach work and the revision or new composition: the keyboard reduction (for example, the *partition du piano* in the Lisztian sense of a Bach motet for organ); the transcription (from organ to piano, for example), which adheres relatively closely to the Bach original; the 'translation', which, like a translation from one language to another, transfers the Bach work from his horizon of expectation to that of the later composer; the revision with significant interventions; works upon B-A-C-H; improvisations and free compositions on a Bach theme or on an entire work by him; compositions which result from listening to or reading Bach's music; and, finally, tone-poems based on a composer's image of Bach.

Furthermore, there is the treatment of Bach in music theory and above all in compositional theory, which fosters a decisive connection between a composer's revisions of Bach and the composer's own works, in which Bach's general influence can be perceived (compare, for example, Beethoven, Liszt, Busoni, Webern, Stefan Wolpe, Erich Itor Kahn, Karel Goeyvaerts, etc.[6]).

The distinction between the histories of influence (transmission history) and reception structure the entire body of material on Bach in the nineteenth and twentieth centuries. This, together with the formation of various paradigmatic works 'after' Bach, makes possible a further evaluation of the materials. Thus in the late nineteenth century and at the turn of the century, transcriptions of various kinds provide the characteristic picture of Bach, while instrumentations and orchestrations of Bach's 'speculative' late works are significant for the structural image of Bach in the New Music of the 1920s and 1950s. From the perspective of a structural history,[7] the composition, selection, and prioritising of reception materials are shaped by history and the historian together, so that historical reconstruction and aesthetic construction of the material interact productively with one another.

## The mythologising of Bach: Nietzsche's critique

The second objection to the prescribed topic is more serious than the first since it concerns the omnipresence of Bach's oeuvre and the German nationalist elevation of history through the monumentalisation of Bach. Friedrich Nietzsche wrote generally about this problem with regard to the writing of history ('Historie') and more specifically in reference to Bach.

In his second 'Untimely meditation' on 'The uses and abuses of history for life', Nietzsche differentiates three types of history: 'a monumental, an antiquarian and a critical type of history'.[8] The extreme elevation of the past, which is 'indistinguishable from a mythical fiction',[9] renders one incapable of a clear understanding of either the past or the present and, for that reason, becomes a 'disadvantage' for that which is active and living. I can only underscore Nietzsche's insight; the typical, retrospective elevation of the image of Bach among historians has become 'a mythical fiction', against which subsequent history has no chance of asserting itself, except as the history of decline, the complementary opposite of 'monumental history'. For, based on its *point de perfection* (seen, in this case, as the actual time and environment in which Bach worked and composed) anything that follows can only decline from the perfect. To the extent then that the elevated image of Bach is relativised and takes on variable and human characteristics, reception history has the opportunity to transform the old image of Bach, to crystallise its multi-faceted potential.

Elsewhere Nietzsche discusses the concrete problem of 'monumental history' with reference to Bach. He thus contrasts 'German music' and its 'Dionysian foundations' with enlightened 'Socratic culture' and states that from the perspective of Socratic culture, German music 'is perceived as the terrible-inexplicable, the overpowerful-hostile: German music as we have generally come to understand it in its mighty course from Bach to Beethoven, and from Beethoven to Wagner'.[10]

Although Nietzsche speaks of a 'mighty course', the succession of heroes Bach – Beethoven – Wagner appears odd to him, principally because it cannot be explained rationally or by a concept of beauty. This is surprising, because he initially assigns the 'arithmetical abacus of fugue', i.e., mathematical beauty, to Bach's music, only later to maintain that this is not an adequate explanation of its mysterious foundations. In his early work *The birth of tragedy*, Nietzsche does not fall prey to the myth of the numerically determined rationality of Bach. He senses something more behind Bach's music but at the same time does not want to mythologise this inkling. Two aphorisms from the later book *Human, all too human*, in the chapter entitled 'From the souls of artists and writers', pick up once again where this earlier reflection left off.[11] Although aphorism 218 addresses architecture and music in general, the connection to Bach (together with Palestrina) becomes clear in aphorism 219. Behind ancient architecture and the 'modern' music brought into being by these composers, behind the beauty of their artifice, one can detect a 'higher order of things', 'the feeling of inexhaustible significance'. Thus Nietzsche emphasises that without 'that profoundly religious conversion, without that resounding of the deeply agitated heart, music would have remained scholarly or operatic'.

It is significant for the following discussion of historical and ontological difference that Nietzsche reclaims this fundamental distance from Bach's horizon of expectation: it is located within his artistic metaphysics and aesthetic religion, and seems retrievable only through the 'profoundly religious conversion'. Although the 'mighty course' from Bach to Beethoven and then to Wagner may at first sound like a mythologising of Bach, with Nietzsche it is characterised by the realisation of the difference between the eras and thus should rather be understood as the intentional recovery of the mythological in Bach's music.

## The historical and ontological difference: Hans Blumenberg's *Matthäus-Passion*

With the phrase 'profoundly religious conversion', Nietzsche emphasised the distance between his concept of music and that of Bach. Bach's music resides far back in the past and is not accessible to an ear schooled directly on Wagner. In a later aphorism, Nietzsche reflects fundamentally on the historical location of Bach in relation to Goethe, pointing forward to Albert Schweitzer's belief that Bach signals an endpoint in history or, as Heinrich Besseler suggested,[12] a point of departure for classical music, one which made this epoch possible and which was, in turn, re-thought by it:

> *Sebastian Bach.* – In so far as one does *not* listen to Bach's music as a complete and experienced expert in counterpoint and every species of fugal style, and must consequently do without the actual artistic pleasure it affords, it will seem to us when we hear his music as though (to employ a grandiose expression of Goethe's) we were present *as God was creating the world.* That is to say, we feel that here something great is in the process of coming into being: our *great* modern music. It has already conquered the world by conquering the church, national characteristics, and counterpoint. In Bach there is still too much crude Christianity, crude Germanism, crude scholasticism; he stands on the threshold of European (modern) music, but from here looks back towards the Middle Ages.[13]

Together with the earlier aphorism, the one quoted here, No. 149, and the following one on Handel (both from 'The wanderer and his shadow') convey the difficulty of situating Bach historically. On the one hand, a 'religious change of heart', i.e., synchronising present-day reception with Bach's own understanding of himself, is necessary for the understanding of his music in its historical essence; this includes Bach's backward-looking perspective on what still survived from the Middle Ages, on

Christianity, Scholasticism and German nationalism. On the other hand, he broke with this retrospection and transformed it instead into something which signals the beginning of modern music and points to the future (to Wagner, for example, in *The birth of tragedy*, an idea which Ernst Bloch later took up[14]). Nietzsche did not comment more specifically on the multiple perspectives of Bach's music. Above all, he did not address the question of how – its permanent 'difference' notwithstanding – Bach's music has continued to be relevant to our understanding of music and composition at each historical stage.

Before we can answer questions about the possible realising – and the merging – of various musical concepts and horizons of expectation, the points which contribute to the notion of distance or difference must be outlined. In his famous work on the St Matthew Passion, Hans Blumenberg underlined the ontological and historical difference between us today and Bach:

> Within this conceptual framework one can think about the person listening to the Passion according to Matthew, the person that Bach had in mind, so as not to overlook him. We also think about the listener many years later from whose horizon the images and analogies, the holy stories and sermons, the words and hymns of Bach's parishioners have vanished, without being substituted by anything comparable.[15]

Blumenberg addresses two problems here which are central to the discussion of Bach in the nineteenth and twentieth centuries: first, Bach's unequivocal 'occupation of a horizon' of understanding so that he could reach his listeners and congregation; and secondly, the 'implied listener' (with reference to Wolfgang Iser[16]), i.e., the listener written into the score, who possibly perceives the Passion from a different horizon of expectation than Bach's. Here Blumenberg emphasises the new reception history: we are too late to understand Bach as he understood himself; this lapse of time is irretrievable; no simultaneity is possible between our horizon and that of Bach because the 'images' of the Matthew Passion have become foreign to us.

Whether the vanished images are so fundamental that we can no longer understand Bach's Passion remains open and will be discussed presently. For now, it seems more important to address the question of what exactly has become foreign to us in the Passion. First, there is the religious purpose and the sacred liturgical function of Bach's music, which was composed to honour God and performed at a particular location at a specific time in the church year. Secondly, along with the vanished images, there is the loss of rhetorical knowledge caused by the 'decay of the doctrine of musical figures',[17] so that we are confronted with topoi that we do not understand. Thirdly, there is the 'mathematical ontology'[18] of Bach's work, which is expressed cosmologically and theologically, independently of the symmetrical concepts of architecture. Thus the music contains not only a numerical principle of 'unconscious counting' (Leibniz),[19] but also the meaning that stands behind a numerically determined proportion.

These are, then, the three areas which constitute the historical and ontological difference and which, according to Blumenberg, make an understanding of Bach difficult. If, however, we speak of the implied listener and the possible 'shift' of perspective during the nineteenth and twentieth centuries, there must also have been a process of reinterpreting Bach's music which was detached from Bach's own understanding. Otherwise, there would be only two possibilities: not to perform Bach's music at all owing to its absolute foreignness, or to receive Bach's music only according to strict historical performance practice (and with the theological understanding of Bach's parishioners). The following analysis will show that the history of Bach reception – far from banning performance or prescribing only the understanding that Bach had of himself – has led to a constant reinterpretation of Bach's music.

## Partial dissolution of the difference

The two views of Bach as either the end of an epoch or as the beginning of modern music and the forerunner of classical music evidence two approaches to history: on the one hand, the radical rupture in 1750 beyond which there extends no Bach tradition,[20] so that Bach's music must remain substantially inaccessible to us today; on the other hand, the historical, stylistic, compositional and semantic potential first realised through the history of influence and reception – not a loss of meaning over time, but rather a constantly transformed growth in meaning which progresses not in a linear fashion but rather as a result of paradigm shifts.

According to Thomas S. Kuhn it is these new paradigms that fundamentally change understanding.[21] 'Scientific revolutions' are brought about not by scientific inventions or new methods of investigation but rather by changes in the overarching perspective through which the world and history are suddenly perceived. At first it might seem as if the continuity of the Bach tradition would enable one perspective to move on to the next so as to keep Bach's music alive to the present day. Paradoxically, the opposite is the case.

The fundamentally transformed view of music that emerged in the late eighteenth, nineteenth and twentieth centuries brought about a substantial reinterpretation of Bach's music. It was not the preservation of Bach's music in its original historical-aesthetic meaning that fostered its influence and vitality, but rather the transformation of the Bachian form into new ways of thinking about form and structure. Through the reinterpretation of Bach the separate horizons approach and merge with one another, their historical distance having been recognised. Consequently, the music is brought into the present.

One of the paradigms is the concept of music which held sway after the beginning of the modern period and which established new periods, phases and developments, such as the 'classic', the 'romantic', and 'classicism'.[22] Further paradigms are the new syntactic, harmonic and formal categories such as periodisation and prose, functional harmony and dodecaphonic atonality, anti-architectonic formal principles such as developing variation, and open and free forms. Other possible paradigms are visualisations of Bach's music, where the implicit dramaturgy is realised in choreography and staging. Finally there is the paradigmatic shift in the function of music to that of aesthetic autonomy whereby Bach's keyboard and instrumental works take on a new, historically conditioned, meaning with the shift from the eighteenth to the nineteenth centuries.[23]

In the following chapter, Bach reception will be discussed according to the historical-stylistic paradigms which led to the reinterpretations of Bach's work. The point of departure is the 'adoption' and 'classical reinterpretation of Bach' including Mozart's reception of Bach in the late eighteenth century,[24] which forms the basis of the 'romantic interpretation of Bach'[25] – the 'classical', 'neo-romantic', and 'late romantic image of Bach' – in the nineteenth century.

In Liszt's interpretation of Bach lies the origin of the modern period of Bach reception, which leads through Reger and Schoenberg in the twentieth century to the neoclassicism of Stravinsky on the one hand and to the 'Young Classicism' of Busoni on the other. These three directions, the free atonal style, neoclassicism and the 'Young Classicism' are, from the perspective of the 1920s, the starting point for understanding Bach through dodecaphony, serial and post-serial music, and through to the minimalist and neo-romantic music of the eighties and nineties.

## 15 Reinterpreting Bach in the nineteenth and twentieth centuries

*Martin Zenck*

### The second half of the eighteenth century: 'adoption' – 'classical' rephrasing – Mozart's image of Bach

The historical location of Bach in the music of the nineteenth and twentieth centuries and the accompanying radical changes are determined by his position in the second half of the eighteenth century.[1] The caesura '1750' could indicate a break in the influence of Bach's music, or the beginning of a tradition where it and his understanding of it are transmitted to his sons, students and future generations in a linear, undisturbed fashion, or, conversely, the beginning of the process of reinterpretation that is more familiar after the turn of the nineteenth century. Each of these three positions has consequences for the writing of music history in the second half of the eighteenth century and for the development of a 'Romantic Bach interpretation' in the early nineteenth century. In the first case, the phase 1750–1800 can be portrayed without Bach, which, given the minor influence of Bach's music on the general public, would be correct. In the second case, the preservation of the Bach tradition, there is the danger that the 'shift' of the divergent horizons of expectation, in Blumenberg's sense, would be exaggerated and the historical portrayal would be focused too much on the monument 'Bach'. The third position has the advantage of differentiating between the ideas of breaking with the past and continuity and sees the process of reinterpretation during the eighteenth century as the decisive precondition for the means whereby Bach's music, once functional and rhetorical, now becomes autonomous.

The notion of integrating Bach into the historiography of the eighteenth century is grounded in the esoteric influence of his music in compositional theory, in music theory, in instrumental performance particularly on organ and keyboard, and within the practice of composition, above all in the work of Mozart. Even if the influence of Bach's music in the public sphere was relatively limited, there is no pressing reason why we should ignore the significance of its esoteric impact. One already sees the consequences of the strict style in Mozart's transcriptions of Bach's fugues and trio movements for string quartet and trio,[2] in the trio-sonata

**Example 15.1** 'Song of the armed men' from Mozart, *Die Zauberflöte*

texture sometimes found in Mozart's string quartets (above all in the slow introduction to the 'Dissonance Quartet' KV 465)[3] and in the cantus firmus 'Ach Gott, vom Himmel sieh darein' from Bach's cantata of the same name, BWV 2, which Mozart employs in the 'Song of the armed men' in the *Magic Flute*[4] (see Example 15.1). The esoteric influence on music aesthetics and the writing of music history is another decisive prerequisite for the reinterpretation of Bach's keyboard and instrumental music in the poetics of Romanticism, in which it was understood as 'absolute' music.[5]

Three areas form the basis for the 'development of the Romantic interpretation of Bach':[6] first, J. N. Forkel's division of Bach's music into
periods;[7] secondly, Mozart's adaptation of slow middle movements by
Bach, above all those from the organ sonatas (BWV 527, II and BWV 526,
II and III) in KV 405a, and their integration into the quartet style of KV
465 (in the 'Song of the armed men' he is able to imitate the *stile antico* so
well that he represents the old and unchangeable law in this sphere);
thirdly, the new aesthetic of *Empfindsamkeit* and the *Sturm und Drang*,
enabling a 're-occupation' of Bach's music.[8] These are then the decisive
reasons why, at the beginning of the nineteenth century, Bach's music
finally moves beyond an esoteric function into the public eye.

## Bach at the outset of the modern period: Franz Liszt

Backward-looking sentimentalism and the tendency to monumentalise:
these are characteristic nineteenth-century attitudes towards Bach. With
Liszt these attitudes changed fundamentally with consequences that
extend to the neoclassicism of Stravinsky and to the 'Young Classicism' of
Busoni. When Liszt draws on Bach, he does not sink into a bygone age,
losing sight of the present. Nor does he support the monumentalisation of
Bach's work in the nineteenth century in order to elevate himself historically. Bach is simultaneously distanced from and near to him: distanced
because he does not see Bach as the embodiment of absolute counterpoint, but emphasises totally different elements of his music, above all the
free and improvised ones; near in the sense that Liszt adheres very precisely to Bach's text. These new attitudes become clear in the context of his
Bach revisions, his works on Bach and his original compositions.

As in the case of the transcriptions of Schubert *Lieder* which are precur-
sors to Liszt's own piano *Lieder*, Liszt's Bach 'revisions' directly relate to his
entire oeuvre and its development. Early on there are the Six Preludes and
Fugues for organ (BWV 543–8) arranged for piano (1842–50). While these
transcriptions remain very close to the original (the pedal part is doubled
in octaves in the left hand to recreate the low register of the organ), the
later compositions on the theme *B-A-C-H* (1870) and *Weinen, Klagen,
Sorgen, Zagen* (based on BWV 12/2 and BWV 232 II/5) are already 'music
about music' in the Nietzschean sense,[9] in other words, compositions for
which the distinction between original and arrangement would be irrelevant. These are new works which, by means of their distance from the
original works, both fundamentally change Bach's compositions and
bring Liszt's compositional status to a qualitatively different level.

Characteristic of this is the fact that there are in each case many different versions, with the later ones more distanced from Bach. Significantly, Liszt made arrangements of other Bach works between these versions, which illuminate the direction of the later ones. Examples are: *Einleitung und Fuge aus der Motette 'Ich hatte viel Bekümmernis'* BWV 21 (1862–3) and the chorale arrangement 'Aus tiefer Not schrei ich zu dir' BWV 38 (1860), both transcriptions for organ; and the piano transcriptions of the Adagio from the violin sonata in C minor BWV 1017 and of the Fantasia and Fugue in G minor BWV 542. To the extent that a greater degree of freedom was possible in these transcriptions, the later versions become works *sui generis* in spite of the explicit relation to Bach models. If one recalls that Liszt, the great concert pianist and improviser, gave public performances of the Chromatic Fantasia and Fugue, the six preludes and fugues that he had transcribed, and the Goldberg Variations, then the close relationship between interpretation in performance as a variant of the Bach text and transcription and transformation as a further variant of the model becomes clear. Thus, for Liszt, both works from the Bach tradition and his own compositions turn into a 'Score of variants' ('Partitur von Varianten').[10]

To this composer of the 'modern'[11] period neither the works of Bach nor the songs of Schubert nor his own works are self-contained and organic works in contrast to which all musical realisations and interpretations would be variations; rather, they are already variations of a '*Livre*' in the sense of Boulez's interpretations of Mallarmé, and that of later 'concept art'; i.e. crystallisations of a developing conception of art. This is clearly seen in the later versions of *Weinen, Klagen, Sorgen, Zagen* and *B-A-C-H*. Whereas Liszt's other Bach arrangements follow the sequence of the originals, here Liszt strives, in the course of revisions, for the principle of structural isolation.[12] This became extremely important, for example, in the late piano works *Unstern* and *Nuages gris*. In *Weinen, Klagen* Liszt changes the time frame of the original (BWV 12). The chromatic chaconne bass of the opening chorus is already an object for development in the introductory 'Lento' of Liszt's organ version, particularly in the middle voice (see Example 15.2), from its first appearance in b. 8. The chorale 'Was Gott thut, das ist wohl gethan' appears at a different place in Liszt's work and fulfils a different function.[13]

In addition to this decontextualisation of quotations, Liszt also accentuates the logic of the sequences by submitting Bach's chaconne bass as it occurs in the 'Crucifixus' from the Mass in B Minor to the process of developing variation. On the one hand, then, there is structural isolation; on the other, structural intensification of the process and connections. Next to this stands the poetic programme of the *Réminiscences*[14] as the intensification of the compositional dialectic.[15] Liszt's artistic-religious reading of Bach's cantata and the 'Crucifixus' must be read with this in mind.

**Example 15.2**  Franz Liszt, Fantasia on *Weinen, Klagen, Sorgen, Zagen*, bb. 1–29

## Liszt and his influence; Ferruccio Busoni

**(For the outstanding Busoni and Wolpe performer, G. D. Madge)**

New aspects of a Bach image which was also significant in the development of the 'New Music' are often associated with the Bach transcriptions of Ferruccio Busoni and Max Reger which appeared soon after 1890.[16] The epochal significance of Liszt's readings of Bach were often overlooked as a result. Nevertheless, Busoni played Liszt's works in concert and, in several works, pointed to the significance of Liszt the pianist, interpreter and composer. Busoni dedicated a major portion of his second book on musical aesthetics, *Von der Einheit der Musik*, to Liszt.[17] The latter is seen in this book as being closely related to Mozart, who along with J. S. Bach provides a point of orientation for Busoni's conception of 'Young Classicism'.[18] Moreover, Liszt's oeuvre stands as the pinnacle at the end of Busoni's *Beiträge zu einer Hochschule des Klavierspiels*.

In the foreword to the first edition of the transcriptions of the two organ toccatas in C major (BWV 564) and D minor (BWV 565), Busoni announced the plan for his twelve-volume *Hochschule des Klavierspiels*. In this programme of a rejuvenated classicism which proceeded from Bach to modernity he expressly included Liszt: not the Bach transcriptions but rather those works which were significantly influenced by his reading of Bach: the Fantasia and Fugue on 'Ad nos, ad salutarem undam' and the *Mephisto Waltzes*, the two works that Busoni designated as volumes 11 and 12 in the proposed series, accompanied by this significant concluding remark:

> In my opinion, a critical-pedagogical edition of the most important piano works by Franz Liszt (which are still misunderstood even by pianists) should be erected as a monument. Owing to the scattered nature of Liszt editions, however, it would be necessary to undertake the difficult task of obtaining the agreement of the original publishers.[19]

The *Hochschule des Klavierspiels* was to be independent of the twenty-five-volume edition of J. S. Bach's collected keyboard works that Busoni edited with Mugellini and Petri,[20] and was to present a *Gradus ad Parnassum* which ranged from Cramer's Studies, through the annotated editions of the Inventions, the Sinfonias and *The Well-tempered Clavier* and a piano score of the Concerto in D minor, to Busoni's transcriptions of the organ chorales, organ preludes and fugues, two toccatas, the Chaconne from the D minor partita for unaccompanied violin and both the Liszt pieces mentioned above. Busoni's intensive work on the edition of Bach's works and its pianistic commentary, and his analysis within the context of his programmatic conception of 'Young Classicism', with its literary and poetic interpretations, reveal the decisive difference between him and Liszt.

Although Liszt had performed Bach's works in concert, for which purpose he had transcribed the six preludes and fugues for piano, and although he expressed interest in the publication of Bach's collected works, his concern with Bach is mainly limited to the works on *B-A-C-H* and *Weinen, Klagen* and their 'variants'. Busoni's engagement with Bach, on the other hand, lasted his entire life, as a presence that often threatens to be all-consuming (for example in the powerful music of the *Fantasia contrappuntistica* and the opera *Doktor Faustus*). One can see traces of Bach in a few further works by Liszt (the late piano works, for example). Busoni's entire piano ouevre, by contrast, is permeated with Bachian insertions and additions. Busoni always takes a position vis-à-vis Bach: he explains the purpose of the new annotated edition of Bach's works; he gives reasons for the necessity of Bach transcriptions; he even gives thought to a staged production of the St Matthew Passion, for which he drew up an outline.[21]

Busoni's introduction to the first part of *The Well-tempered Clavier* is significant for his new image of Bach. First, Bach's utopian potential justifies the expansion and 'modernisation' of Bach's works. Busoni, as both editor and composer, realises Bach's intentions in a way that had not been possible in Bach's own time. Secondly, the affinity between turn-of-the-century modernism and Bach facilitated the radically interventionist edition (in the preface of which Busoni pointed out that classical music 'was in fact more distant' than Bach's). Thirdly, Busoni's edition was used in the intensive training of pianists, who would come to perform Bach's piano works adequately through the 'pre-school' of the Inventions and the 'high-school' of the *Well-tempered Clavier* and through the concert arrangements of the organ fugues, the toccatas, the Goldberg Variations and the violin Chaconne. That is to say, they were to be enabled to 'play them extemporaneously' as if Busoni himself were improvising them in performance. Although the strictness and order of Bach's music might lead the performer to believe that he should play the music according to the exact notes, paradoxically Busoni used Bach as an example of how the pianist should become released from a merely reproductive role and assume the status of creator.

Busoni wrote about the problem of reproduction and production in the essay 'Wert der Bearbeitung' ('The value of arrangement'). When he states that 'every notation is already the transcription of an abstract idea'[22] he recognises – in the sense of more recent structuralist theories of text[23] – that each reading or musical reproduction is a further transcription of an original that exists only in the imagination but not in the actual notes on the page. In this essay he nonetheless adheres to the notion of an ideal 'original' that can be affected but not destroyed by each execution: 'The performance of a work is also a transcription which – no matter how free it is – can never eliminate the original.'[24]

For Busoni, performance, revision, and composition represent graduated levels of the indivisible creative process and not three distinct entities. This insight guides not only his writings but also his entire oeuvre, above all the works for piano. Kindermann's catalogue of Busoni's works and the recording of the complete piano works by Geoffrey Douglas Madge[25] show how fluid the transition is between transcription, which is relatively close to the performance, and the more distancing revision of, or free fantasy on, one of Bach's works. It is as if, for Busoni, all of the aspects of the topic 'Bach' are permeated by a fundamental idea that extends from the 'abstract idea', through the musical imagination, and then to the actual performance, transcription and composition. A significant parallel can be seen with Liszt's conception of the 'Score of variants' (see p. 229 above), where there is neither an original and a final version nor an eternally binding autograph copy, but instead only variations and actualised perspectives of an 'abstract idea'. Bach is for Busoni a point of departure from which all works emanate.

If one thinks of a system of concentric circles in the sense of Hegel, those works which are closest to the centre are closest to Bach. Those on the outer periphery reveal a greater distance and are refracted through the new points 'Mozart' and 'Liszt'. Busoni pointed to 'Liszt' as an important centre facing 'Bach' when he declared in Old-Testament idiom: 'Truly, Bach is the alpha of the keyboard piece and Liszt the omega.'[26]

Several of these circular motions are followed here from the inside outwards: from the Goldberg Variations, the *Chaconne*, the *Sonatina brevis*, the *Fantasia contrappuntistica*, to the significance of the Toccata in C major (BWV 564) for Busoni's own 1920 *Toccata*. The importance of the editions and the revisions for pianoforte performance (various modes of touch and articulation) and for the improvisational capacity of the pianist have already been pointed out. These are also of central importance for musical interpretation and the organisation of the formal structure. The edition of the Goldberg Variations by Egon Petri (in the twenty-five-volume comprehensive edition of Bach's keyboard works which he co-edited with Busoni), is one which, with Busoni's preface, provides key interpretative insights into this variation cycle. Not only is it essential for the phrasing and articulation of the individual variations, their character and tempo; it also contains important insights into the grouping of the variations and the architecture of the entire work.

Like Josef Rheinberger in his 1883 revision of the Goldberg Variations for two pianos, further revised by Max Reger in 1914/15, Busoni wanted to 'save' Bach's work for the concert hall with his new version of 1915. The receptivity of both performer and listener was to be heightened through judicious cuts, 'rewritings' and a new grouping of the variations. These interventions – obviously contrary to the original architectonic structure – are characteristic of Busoni's reinterpretation of Bach.

Although the tripartite and symmetrical structure of the entire cycle is clear to him, as the preface shows,[27] he subordinates the regularly arranged formal principle centred on the overture (No. 16) on the one hand to an anti-climactic one, with the slow movements Nos. 13 and 25 ending the first and second groups, and on the other to a dynamic one, with Nos. 29 and 30 together with the Aria conceived as a continuous unit, as an 'Allegro finale'. A pianist playing according to Busoni's edition would have to perform the twenty variations (ten having been cut) in the following manner: group 1, from the Aria to No. 13, which, due to the exclusion of the three canons, is now No. 10; group 2, from No. 14 (= No. 11) to the great funeral sarabande No. 25 (= No. 17); group 3 doubly reordered with variations 26 and 28 coming together as the 'pianistic' variations (= 18 and 19) and the closing group including the *da capo* as a final unit (now variation 20). Between the variations Busoni would like to see very precise interpretative principles: separation, connection, greater caesuras and closer connections indicated by pauses and 'attacca' signs.

Although Busoni does not assume (except in the two Adagio variations) that there is necessarily any connection with the Diabelli Variations,[28] the entire conception is oriented towards Beethoven's cumulative dynamism of form (especially in the remarks about the structure of the conclusion):

> Reaching the climax here (with the profound Adagio, No. 25), everything that follows must unfold in the manner of a finale. Thus, the canon at the ninth (number 27) comes at the wrong moment and is omitted.
>
> For the prescribed repetition of the complete Aria at the end of the work, the editor thought it appropriate to reduce the theme to its original melodic outline (simplified and free of ornamentation), ringing out like a hymn and – owing to the shift to the lower octave – with a more powerful sound. This is done in such a way that the initial appearance of the theme can be heard as its first variation.
>
> This division of the groups does not only mean a chance to catch one's breath, an ordering, an overview. It personifies three specific conditions of creativity: change within the circle, internal deepening, and external elevation.

Busoni worked time and again on the indexing of his works. The index he appended to his book *Von der Einheit der Musik* (1922) is instructive, since one can clearly see how pervasive are the categories edition, revision and composition. Thus, under section VI, entitled 'Revisions, transcriptions, studies and compositions for the pianoforte after J. S. Bach by F. Busoni', one finds the category 'revisions' which contains both 'Lehrstücke' and 'Meisterstücke' (the latter including the *Chromatic Fantasy and Fugue*, the 'piano' concerto in D minor and the Goldberg

**Example 15.3** Goldberg Variations, return of the aria in Busoni's version

Variations). There is also a volume of 'Transcriptions' (including, among other things, the organ toccatas and the chaconne for violin, which is dedicated to Eugène d'Albert). Finally, there is a volume entitled 'Compositions and Transcriptions' which includes the 'Chorale prelude on a Bach fragment', the *Sonatina brevis* and the *Fantasia contrappuntistica*.

Although Busoni makes a strict distinction between 'revision' and 'transcription', the two principles are comparable in such performance editions as the 'Goldberg Variations' and the Chaconne. The changes are so significant in both works that – even without the deletions and the change of instrument – one must speak here of new and original works by Busoni. In these cases there would be no point in distinguishing between authentic Bach and Busoni's own manner of composition.

This point is clearly to be seen in Busoni's concert arrangement for pianoforte of Bach's D minor Chaconne. Busoni maintains that he has simply realised the possibilities already inherent in Bach's music, which until now, owing to historical conditions, could not be put into action. Yet this obscures the fundamental opposition between Bach and Busoni. Bach's conception of music in the 'Ciaccona' (BWV 1004, V) is as a mathematical discipline (as in the quadrivium); he uses a total of 257 bars, that is, the four-bar bass pattern to the power of four (= 256) and a final bar on the open D. Busoni, on the other hand, often combines the groups of four bars into larger units: he extends the ninth chord (bar 77) by an extra bar (see Example 15.4) and adds another four bars with a voice exchange variation (bb. 86–9 = 82–5), thus extending the total to 262 bars. More significant than the change in the numerical disposition are those in the harmonic texture and figuration. The voices are doubled (in octaves) and monophonic texture is harmonised. At the same time, prominent notes in the figuration are accentuated by register changes and chord concentrations (divided up almost in the manner of Beethoven, bb. 33–7), in the sense of Ernst Kurth's contemporaneous concept of pseudo-polyphony.[29] Busoni also creates free voices: either contrapuntal countersubjects (bb. 82ff., left hand) or a melody in sarabande rhythm on Bach's figuration (bb. 158ff., left hand). Finally, in bars 182ff., contrary to Bach, he continues the semiquaver figuration, thereby creating a more cumulative form. Thus Busoni takes further what was already evident in the performance edition of the Goldberg Variations: instead of Bach's numerical proportions and tripartite grouping of the variations, he subjugates the entire form to an ultimate dynamic.

If until now we have remained in the inner circle, which stands relatively close to the centre (i.e. original Bach works), we will now approach the outer circle, far from the centrepiece 'Bach', with the categories of 'Free rendering' and 'Fantasy'. To these belong, in chronological order, the *Fantasia nach Johann Sebastian Bach* (1909), the *Fantasia contrappuntistica* (1910) and the *Sonatina brevis* (1918–19), which have consequences for Busoni's own works (e. g. the 'Toccata' of 1920), and for specific stylistic tendencies of neo-classicism and the 'New Objectivity' of the 1920s and 30s.

At the centre of the *Fantasia nach J. S. Bach* (K 253) are the chorale variations on 'Christ, der du bist der helle Tag' (BWV 766). The relatively free improvisation approaches the chorale and its 'Partite diverse' and then moves away, going back and forth between Bach, Wagner's *Tristan*, Scriabin's preludes and Busoni. Although two other chorale variations are included (BWV 600 and BWV 602) the 'Partite diverse' remain the hidden centre: hidden because the introductory prelude freely transforms the framework of the chorale into harmonically far-reaching arpeggios; hidden because the extensions depart greatly from the original, the order of the three 'quoted' variations is not maintained (Busoni selected three of seven) and because the conclusion takes up the beginning in expanded form, not in order to confirm and elevate the basic

**Example 15.4** Bach's 'Ciaccona', in Busoni's arrangement, bb. 73–81

# Plan des Werkes

## A. Analytischer:

1. Choral - Variationen (Einleitung — Choral und Variationen — Übergang)
2. Fuga I. 3. Fuga II. 4. Fuga III. 5. Intermezzo. 6. Variatio I. 7. Variatio II.
8. Variatio III.   9. Cadenza.   10. Fuga IV.   11. Corale.   12. Stretta.

## B. Architektonischer:

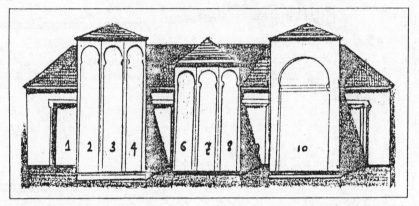

**Plate 6**  Ferruccio Busoni, *Fantasia contrappuntistica* (1910), analytical and
architectural plan

theme, but rather to dissolve the form in the darkness of the beginning.
For Busoni the significant idea is that composing is in essence not only a
fitting-together, but a fitting-in whereby the proportions of the original
are significantly altered. This insertion takes place organically in the
genre of 'Fantasie', fusing together – as syncretism – all that is heterogeneous.

This work leads directly to the 'Große Fuge'[30] of the *Fantasia contrappuntistica*, a year later, and, in other ways, to the *Sonatina brevis*. While the
*Fantasia nach J. S. Bach* is freer in its interpretation, imaginatively
realigning the notes of the melody, the later two works are stricter in their
development. Busoni himself pointed to the precedence of fantasy and
'instinct' over the 'intellect': 'It (intellect) wins one over and leads one
astray. It helps a person repress his own instincts and tolerate the imper-
sonal. It always has good reasons to make one blind to the extraordinary.'[31] Busoni searched for the 'extraordinary' as he moved with ever new
impulses towards the 'definitive' edition of his 'Kunst der Fuge'. The
*Fantasia contrappuntistica* has often been misunderstood as hubris.

Busoni's goal was not to complete something which Bach left incomplete, but rather to revise the work so that it would reflect the state of composition in 1910. It is no accident that the following sentence is found in the 'Selbst-Rezension', the central purpose of which is to legitimise the *Fantasia*: 'One follows a great example most faithfully by not following it: for an example becomes great when it deviates from the one preceding it.'[32] Bach's *Art of Fugue* is thus a model to the extent that through Busoni it gives rise to a new one. The latter is not confined within the limits of the former, however, for then it would simply be an 'imitation' and not a 'creation' through which 'unintentionally a new law emerges'.

Most significant is the connection between Busoni's justification of 'difference' in relation to Bach in the 'Selbst-Rezension' and the function of the text as a whole. It reviews a concert in which Schoenberg gave a lecture on the unknown as an object of composition. In the same concert, Busoni's *Fantasia contrappuntistica*, the *Berceuse élégiaque*, and the Concerto for piano, orchestra and male choir were performed. The 'Selbst-Rezension' can be interpreted with reference to Busoni's own understanding of the *Fantasia contrappuntistica*. Five elements can be emphasised. First, the contradiction between Busoni's deviation from Bach which he considers a prerequisite for remaining faithful to him and his later statement concerning the continuation of that which is present in Bach's model: Busoni vacillates between the idea that a music of the future can be derived in a straight line from tradition and the notion that it is gained from the radical reinterpretation of a model that, in the moment of transformation, becomes a new paradigm. Secondly, he sees the breakup of tonality in the *Fantasia contrappuntistica* – which borders on the 'free atonality' of Schoenberg – as resulting from voice leading. He touches upon Schoenberg's concept of harmonic theory, in which the step towards the dissolution of tonality arises not from the connection of sounds, but rather from the logic of the voice leading. Thirdly, he understands his 'Große Fuge', as Bach did his own *Art of Fugue*, as a portrayal of absolute composition detached from actual instrumentation, and he designates his versions for piano, for two pianos, for organ, and his proposed orchestration only as means of portraying the absolute relationships of notes. Fourthly, he separates himself from Debussy's horizontal-parallel conception of harmony by claiming for himself a multi-linear and 'multiversal' way of thinking which is reminiscent of Schoenberg's concept of 'musical space' with its dimensions of above and below and depth. Here one might also recall Busoni's idea of architecture as frozen music, when he precedes the *Fantasia* not only with an analytical chart but also with an architectonic one (Plate 6). Fifthly, in contrast to Bach, Busoni varies the intervals of the basic theme – in Schoenberg's sense of 'developing variation' – a means which enables him

to engage with the 'denial of the difference between consonance and dissonance', and thus with Schoenberg's programme of the 'emancipation of
dissonance'. In spite of the difference between Busoni's extensive and
Schoenberg's 'concise' style[33] – as seen, for example, in the latter's Op. 11,
the second movement of which Busoni revised – a comparison of the two is
possible, showing how extensively Busoni had appropriated Bach in 1910
from the viewpoint of the New Music.

With the *Sonatina brevis in signo Joannis Magni for Pianoforte*, of
1918–19, Busoni completed his move to a more rigid form of presentation. In this 'free imitation of Bach's small Fantasia and Fugue in D minor'
(BWV 905) the logic of the voice leading, through the isolation of the sus-
pended ninth D–E♭, increasingly dissolves the horizontal development in
the middle part of the three-voice fugue through counter-movements
and chromatic octave progressions, and the end of the work returns to the
beginning of the fantasia (Example 15.5). This fugue, with its harsh passages, and its chiselled and chilled counter-movements emanating from
the chromatic fantasy section, points already to the neoclassicism and
'New Objectivity' of the 1920s. It appears to be closer to the early
Hindemith, Stravinsky, Stefan Wolpe, Eisler and Weill than to Busoni's
own stylistic ideal of the 'Young Classicism'.

## The influence of Busoni's 'Bach': Stefan Wolpe's analysis of Bach's Passacaglia BWV 582 and its significance for his music of the 1930s and 1940s

Busoni's comprehensive reinterpretation of Bach's works through annotated editions, transcriptions, and revisions led to a significant paradigm
shift in twentieth-century Bach reception: Bach was viewed neither from
his own perspective nor from the perspective of eighteenth-century
music, but rather through Busoni's transformation of his music. The use
and appropriation of the knowledge of Bach's music in the area of composition showed that 'Bach' could still be a fruitful model for the development of the 'New Music'. Busoni's compositional oeuvre demonstrates
this even though his extreme orientation towards 'Bach' and his 'Entwurf
einer neuen Ästhetik der Tonkunst'[34] led to a polarisation which, for
example in the case of his operas, was not always resolved in favour of
music of the future. There are, however, numerous examples where Bach
reception functioned productively for an emphatically 'New Music': the
two most significant examples are the *Fantasia contrappuntistica* discussed above and the revision of Bach's organ Toccata in C major (BWV
564) in the form of Busoni's own Toccata for piano from 1920.[35]

**Example 15.5**  Busoni, *Sonata brevis* (1918–19), conclusion

The parallel with Max Reger has already been pointed out, and indeed the meaning that Busoni's Bach image had taken on for Reger is particularly significant. The mutual interest of Schoenberg and Busoni in each other's work has also been noted: Busoni's in Schoenberg's piano piece Op. 11/2, and Schoenberg's critical remarks on Busoni's programmatic and futuristic tract, 'Entwurf einer neuen Ästhetik der Tonkunst'. Less well known is the fact that two of the three Bach works that Schoenberg revised had already been transcribed for piano by Busoni. The first work is the chorale prelude 'Komm, Gott, Schöpfer, heiliger Geist' BWV 667 which Busoni had presented in two versions in 1898 and which Schoenberg arranged for orchestra in 1922.[36] The second work is the Prelude and Fugue in E♭ major (BWV 552), which Busoni 'freely revised for the pianoforte for concert-use' in 1916/20, and which Schoenberg arranged for orchestra in 1928. The premiere was conducted by Schoenberg's student Anton Webern in 1929.

By this time, then, the seeds of Bach reception were directly or indirectly planted by Busoni and extended far into the twentieth century: within the Schoenberg school to Alban Berg and Anton Webern;[37] among Busoni's students in Berlin of the 1920s directly or indirectly to Hermann Scherchen, Wladimir Vogel and above all to Stefan Wolpe. On the one hand, it was Bach's later, speculative works that, through Busoni's arrangements,[38] had such a great influence on performance practice and composition during the twentieth century. On the other hand, Bach's improvisational work was also brought to light through Busoni's transcriptions. The fantasy of extemporaneous performance led to many extensive preludes and fantasies whose figuration and harmony were freed from the dictates of strict composition.

Of the many composers that were influenced by Busoni, I have chosen to focus here on one who is relatively unknown in the area of Bach reception. It is well known that when the nineteen-year-old Stefan Wolpe studied – with little enjoyment – at the Berlin Conservatory of Music under Paul Juon, he was an ardent admirer of Busoni.[39] This was not unusual in Berlin during the early twenties since all the young enthusiasts who were interested in the 'New Music' felt drawn to Busoni. Moreover, the young Stefan Wolpe, as Hans-Heinz Stuckenschmidt shows,[40] was a considerable pianist, so was naturally drawn to a performer of Busoni's status.

For the neo-classicists of the 1920s – Stravinsky, Krenek and Hindemith – Bach was the point of departure for the motorisation of contrapuntal progressions. At this time, Wolpe's attention was focused not on Bach's music but rather on the political goals of the 'November Group', on interaction with the 'Bauhaus' group and with the Dadaist

Kurt Schwitters, whose poem 'An Anna Blume' Wolpe set as a chamber opera. The first and intensive encounter with Bach possibly came through Anton Webern, under whom Wolpe studied composition for a short time in 1933.

When Wolpe arrived in Vienna, Webern had already made a name for himself as an outstanding conductor of Bach's works.[41] Before transcribing Bach's 'Ricercare a sei voci' for orchestra in 1935, Webern had already made explicit references to Bach in his own works of that period, the Symphony Op. 21, the Concerto for nine instruments and the String Quartet Op. 28.[42] While studying with Webern,[43] Wolpe composed a 'Passacaglia', a compositional genre of the strictest style which had also served for Webern's Op. 1. It is no coincidence that variation form played a decisive role in Wolpe's later works: the *Passacaglia*, the fourth part of *Studies on basic rows*, of 1936, and in the *Dance in form of a Chaconne* of 1938.[44]

Also germane is the relationship – in terms of content and chronology – of these works to Wolpe's arrangement (1938) of Bach's Concerto for two keyboards, BWV 1062,[45] and to three essays in which his reflections on Bach are explicitly related to his own compositional production: first, the handwritten 'Zur Passacaglia in Cmoll von Bach' (New York, 1939), secondly, the typescript 'Über Dance in the form of a Chaconne' (New York, 1938), which already anticipates the later text, and thirdly, 'Über das Prelude und Fuge, fmoll, Das Wohltemperierte Klavier, Bd. II, J. S. Bach' (New York, c. 1940).[46]

Here Wolpe's close relationship with – and deviation from – Busoni and Webern becomes clear. Like them, Wolpe revised Bach's work, but his main engagement with Bach took place on an exclusively theoretical level before it led to actual compositions. Furthermore, Wolpe's compositions are not based overtly on a specific Bach work or the theme *B-A-C-H*. In the manuscript on Bach's 'Passacaglia' there is a compositional and structural way of thinking that was to be decisive for Hermann Scherchen, René Leibowitz, Henri Pousseur and Pierre Boulez. In the following paragraphs I will critically discuss Wolpe's text in order to show how it can function as a document of the structural image of Bach held by the generation standing between the dodecaphony and neoclassicism of the 1920s and 30s and the serialism of the 1950s and 60s.

Wolpe wrote this manuscript in New York in 1939 after his emigration from his Palestinian exile. Although it was intended as a lecture in German, there are sections with interlinear translations into English and some parts written completely in English. Wolpe had not yet completely mastered English but was feeling more and more secure in the language and wanted to be able to speak freely in it.

The unpublished manuscript is divided into four chapters: 1. The problem of the ostinato and repetition in music generally; 2. An analysis of three aspects of Bach's 'Passacaglia' theme: (a) regularity of the 8 strong beats; (b) two centres of gravity with regard to prolongation; (c) articulation of the component motifs; 3. The relationship of the variations to one another and 4. The modern version of the Passacaglia in Schoenberg, Hindemith, Bartók, Copland, and Wolpe.

Wolpe's analysis is a transcription of the Bach text. It triggers a compositional transfer which leads to a new work: a work in which the original analysis is fully absorbed and which can only be traced back to the corresponding Bach work because Wolpe makes reference to the analysis in the later text on his Chaconne. Although Wolpe's manuscript does not discuss the historical context of its theoretical aspects, his insights are historically significant: for instance, his reflection on the 'varied' repetition of the bass theme; the relationship between the invariance of the theme and the 'variance' of the variations; the historical-philosophical speculation on the concept of time as 'constellation' that was so important to Wolpe; and the implicit reference to architecture as frozen music.

Throughout, Wolpe looks at Bach's score as if for the first time. His view is, in the best sense, simple and elementary, and thus fundamental. His discussion of the problem of repetition in ostinato forms soon proves to be far-reaching; when the author attempts to answer the question as to whether Bach's 'Passacaglia' describes a process or a condition, he comes to the paradoxical conclusion that it characterises a 'condition of variability' which emanates from compositionally motivated 'repetitions'. Wolpe states: 'There is nothing so ludicrous as to repeat something, to insist on a repetition without understanding why something is being repeated.' He knows from rhetoric that a single repetition strengthens an idea but that the repetition of the repetition only weakens the clarity of the idea that has been repeated. Bach must therefore justify the repetitions of the bass theme, because on the surface they simply reflect a proportional scheme of 21 repetitions of eight bars and a fugue. Bach wrote the Passacaglia in order to provide proof not of a numerical relationship but of a procedure: to set in motion a particular sequence of varied repetitions.

To explain the tension between invariance and variance is thus Wolpe's first significant concern. The repetitions are variants of an invariant part of the theme. It is not, however, that the process gives the theme these possibilities of development but rather that the eight-bar bass contains these perspectives already within itself. Thus Wolpe arrives at the notion of the 'constellation'[47] and 'simultaneity' of the theme and its variations.

In reality, the composition develops in the succession of theme, twenty

**Example 15.6** Bach, Passacaglia in C minor, BWV 582, theme and variation 1

variations and the 'thema fugatum'. Ideally, however, the 'subjectum' is the 'totum simul praesens' of the whole work. The 'varied repetitions' confirm the motivic profile of the theme and do not change it, as they do, for instance, in Beethoven's op. 120,[48] where the theme is destroyed through the process of retrospective force. With the seemingly contradictory concept, 'the condition of variability', Wolpe reveals then, in the first chapter of his work, a significant insight into the architecture of Bach's music: the bass theme is variable without losing the status of a firm condition; the 'accidents' develop in succession, but are, however, a fixed part of the 'substance'; the 'varied repetitions' are necessary to establish the substance of the theme in various ways. Thus the basic premise of the 'the serial' is paralleled, whereby music must coagulate in a static 'image of an essence' in which the construction of a composition is completely contained and no longer bound to a projection in time.

In the second chapter of his work, Wolpe addresses the concrete characteristics of Bach's bass theme, which lead to corresponding compositional elements in the variations and fugue. Wolpe draws attention to the opposition between the fixed and regular bass which emphasises the first beat and the first variation which dissolves this metrical pattern (see Example 15.6). He then examines a further characteristic of the theme, the 'two centres of gravity of the phrase' that are reached with the ascending movement to a♭, the highest note, and, with the descending movement, to the lowest note, C. Just as the eight strong beats have an ordering function for the structuring of each respective variation, the 'two centres of gravity' of a♭ and C determine the upper and lower limit within which the theme and counterpoints move. At the same time, these limits are always being expanded. One must add that the counterpoints do not always orient themselves to these cornerstones of movement, but instead are frequently shifted so that, as Wolpe maintains – with good reason – 'the bass consists of two equal parts upon which there are forms that go through a completely different process of development'. Thus there are compositional elements here which prevent a literal repetition without changing the substance of the theme.

A third topic in the second chapter pertains to the 'similarity of the component motifs which articulate the movement of the line' in the theme and the derivation of the counterpoints from these component motifs. 'Through the unity of the motivic material . . . the theme lives transformed to a new level of its own self.' Wolpe demonstrates this union of the bass theme with the other voices by showing that the counterpoints are either derived from the rotation around the top note a♭ (g–a♭–f) or from the pieces cut out of the bass line e♭–f–g–a♭–f. Bach employs the contrapuntal devices of diminution, augmentation, abbreviation and inverted extension to engender within the the compositional processes a sense of variation on the static substance of the theme.

Without question, the most important topic is introduced in the third chapter. This pertains to the 'relationship of the variations to one another', the basis of the individual 'rhythmic variation'. The focus here is on how the form constitutes itself note-for-note from the inside out. Variations 9 and 13 and 18–20 are emphasised. The process of condensation in variations 6, 7 and 8 is a prerequisite for variation 9 which, for Wolpe, is the decisive turning point of the movement. Here the figuration of the bass permeates the other voices for the first time, something which causes the 'dissolution of the gravity' of the bass. It is not this that is decisive, though, but rather the 'progress' of 'bringing together'; that now the 'antithetical elements' of theme and counterpoints are dissolved in favour of equal presentation by all the voices. The continuity associated with the main voice is dissolved here through the equalising of the voice functions (see Example 15.7).

This decentralisation continues in variation 10 where the hitherto continuous line of the theme is interrupted with rests. In variations 11 and 12 it causes a change in register (the bass theme is heard now in the soprano), and, in the subsequent numbers, particularly variation 13, it results in the 'disappearance' of the theme.

In Wolpe's interpretation centralisation and 'decentralisation' are an expression of Bach's attempt to thematise the register and octave positions. These positions are not simply thematically occupied in new and unmediated ways. Instead, this process is prepared in advance and,

**Example 15.7** Bach, Passacaglia in C minor, BWV 582, variations 8 and 9

after var. 9, has consequences for the subsequent development. The thematisation of various levels, the dimensions of above and below together with the laws of gravity and their displacement, are decisive for Wolpe's own compositional perspective of 'musical space':

> The reason is not only that all of the levels eventually become
> thematised, that that which was first formally attempted in No. 9 . . . as a
> sign of the permeation of all levels with the thematic material, is carried

**Example 15.8**  Bach, Passacaglia in C minor, BWV 582, variations 19 and 20

through in variations 11, 12 and 13 as a process of development. In variation 9 the material is not complete. There fragments of the theme, presenting themselves in different ways, variously continue the theme in an individual way on another level. But in variations 11, 12 and 13, however, the various levels are thematised into an authentic sense of the theme. Until the theme has reached its old position as bass, until it is reconstituted as the bass theme, it must cover the distance through all the phases of the musical space; as when something falls, it ultimately reaches the ground.

**Example 15.9** Stefan Wolpe, *Dance in form of a Chaconne*, bb. 1–20 (Reproduced with kind permission of the copyright owners)

Variation 16 is thus for Wolpe the end of the 'restoration of the bass ground' and introduces what will be important in variations 19 and 20: the principle of 'the piling-up of movement'.

At this point something utterly central occurs for Wolpe: the arresting of the fluid onward movement of music through the concentration of chords, something to which Wolpe alludes with the title of his piano piece 'Stehende Musik' ('stationary music'), of 1925.

> Variation 18 is created to show the unyielding repetitions as unyielding as possible. Here the content stands very still, and because everything is so obstinate and is repeated so stubbornly (*a type of stationary music*), the theme suddenly seems (precisely for that reason) so full of movement, so fluid, to flow so peacefully. (see Example 8)[49]

The direct reference to a past work reveals the close relationship between analysis and composition. In his lecture, written only a little while later, on his own Chaconne composition ('Über Dance in the Form of a Chaconne, 1938') Wolpe once more demonstrates the relationship between compositional practice and theory when he refers to his text on Bach's Passacaglia.[50]

The following aspects of Bach's music and its analysis are productive for Wolpe's Chaconne (and also, in part, for his earlier 'Passacaglia' of 1936): first, the tension between the stability of the bass theme and the transformative power of the counterpoints, which, for Bach, led to the *restitutio ad integrum* and for Wolpe to the 'repetition' of the theme on an entirely different level; secondly, the attempt to individualise a relatively abstract and general theme through variations; thirdly, with the thematisation and opening up of the levels to show the bass theme in the fanning out of spatial perspectives (for Wolpe this irresistible progress towards the extreme octave-positions results in the collapse of the thematic process); fourthly, the C minor tonality which Wolpe unequivocally took over from Bach but which for Wolpe is ruptured from within through the dissolution of the borders of musical space; and fifthly, the principle of chorale variation, that Wolpe, taking his cue from Busoni's revisions of Bach's chorale variations, transformed in his own way into the 'Dance in form of a Chaconne' (Example 15.9).[51] Bach was for Wolpe, as for other composers of the twentieth century, a model that, in Busoni's sense, functioned most productively when it was not faithfully followed. Those composers, on the other hand, who followed Bach to the letter, fell far behind Bach or fell prey to the historicism of neo-romanticism or 'New Objectivity'.

*Translated by Linda M. von Hoene, revised by the editor*

# Notes

## Introduction

1   G. von Dadelsen, *Beiträge zur Chronologie der Werke Johann Sebastian Bachs* (Trossingen, 1958); and A. Dürr, *Zur Chronologie der Leipziger Vokalwerke J. S. Bachs*, 2nd edn (Kassel, 1976).

2   The most famous polemic promoting criticism above positivism is J. Kerman's *Musicology* (London, 1985) (*Contemplating music* is the American title).

3   See Susan McClary, 'The blasphemy of talking politics during Bach year', *Music and society: the politics of composition, performance and reception*, ed. R. Leppert and S. McClary (Cambridge, 1987), pp. 13–62. McClary's approach, showing Bach as a proto-enlightened commentator on the contingency of worldly hierarchies, has been modified by Michael Marissen, in his study *The social and religious designs of J. S. Bach's Brandenburg Concertos* (Princeton, 1995), who shows that Bach's critique reflects an orthodox Lutheran standpoint.

4   T. W. Adorno, 'Bach defended against his devotees', *Prisms*, ed. and trans. S. and S. Weber (Cambridge, Mass., 1981), pp. 133–46; Edward Said, *Culture and imperialism* (London and New York, 1993); *Musical elaborations* (London, 1991; New York, 1993).

5   See Suzanne G. Cusick, 'On a lesbian relation with music: a serious effort not to think straight', *Queering the pitch: the new gay and lesbian musicology*, ed. P. Brett, E. Wood and G. C. Thomas (New York and London, 1994), pp. 67–83. Philip Brett's article in the same volume, 'Musicality, essentialism, and the closet', pp. 9–26, is a rare example of a direct attack on Bach and his achievement, particularly with regard to his influence and reception as a teacher. Brett makes it clear that he sees Bach as an abstracting meddler, appropriating for instance the 'simple, defenseless tunes' of the chorale repertory. It seems to me that Brett's opinion can easily be dismantled even from his own viewpoint: chorales, as one of the most potently ideological and successfully politicising musical repertories of all time, can hardly be associated with the simple, pure and defenceless; unison singing (the traditional manner of performance) is nothing if not patriarchal and monolithic; Bach's harmonisations, by the musical conventions of their own age, are supremely – even excessively – expressive, hardly abstract; and, surely, far from being patriarchal, they 'feminise' a patriarchal tradition, festooning with 'embarrassing' ornament the iron rule of unison song. Yet what is valuable about Brett's approach is the fact that the target of his attack is the *reception* of Bach, the way Bach has been appropriated as an instrument of repressive musical thinking over the last two centuries or so.

6　E. Chafe, *Tonal allegory in the vocal music of J. S. Bach* (Berkeley and Los Angeles, 1991).

## 1  The Bach family

1　*Dok* I, p. 68; *BR*, p. 126. All translations here are the author's own.

2　See G. Kraft, 'Neue Beiträge zur Bach-Genealogie', *Beiträge zur Musikwissenschaft* 1 (1959), pp. 29–61.

3　*Dok* I, p. 184; *BR*, p. 203.

4　The 'Hungarian' origin of the Bach family has often been disputed by those who argue that Veit was returning home to Thuringia after a period in 'Ungarn', but it is attested in at least two documents that predate the Genealogy. One of these is a letter dated 24 April 1728 from Johann Nicolaus Bach (1699–1753) to his pupil Nikolaus Alexis Príleský (see H.-J. Schulze, '"Die Bachen stammen aus Ungarn her". Ein unbekannter Brief Johann Nikolaus Bachs aus dem Jahre 1728', *BJb* 75 (1989), pp. 213–20); the other is the entry on J. S. Bach in the *Musicalisches Lexicon* (Leipzig, 1732), p. 64, by Bach's kinsman J. G. Walther. For the most recent research on the origins of the Wechmar line, according to which Veit Bach arrived in Wechmar with his son Hans in the 1590s, see Knut Kreuch, *Die Urväterheimat der Musikerfamilie Bach* (Wechmar, 1994).

5　J. N. Forkel, *Über Johann Sebastian Bachs Leben, Kunst und Kunstwerke* (Leipzig, 1802; English trans., London, 1820), p. 5.

6　*Nun ist alles überwunden*, an 'aria' for SATB and organ, has been attributed to either Johann Christoph or Heinrich Bach (1615–92); see A. Basso, *Frau Musika: la vita e le opere di J. S. Bach*, 2 vols. (Turin, 1979–83), vol. I, p. 278. Basso lists ninety-four extant works by members of the Bach family before J. S. on pp. 278–82 of his book.

7　Bach copied parts for *Der Gerechte, ob er gleich* by Johann Christoph Bach (one of the works in the *Alt-Bachisches Archiv* in 1743–6); see Y. Kobayashi, *Die Notenschrift Johann Sebastian Bachs. Dokumentation ihrer Entwicklung* (Kassel, 1989) (*NBA*, IX/2), p. 212. For further information about the *Alt-Bachisches Archiv* and its chronology, see especially D. R. Melamed, *J. S. Bach and the German motet* (Cambridge, 1995), pp. 161–88.

8　Basso, *Frau Musika*, vol. I, p. 714.

9　J. S. Bach's father, Ambrosius (1645–95), was a twin with Johann Christoph (1645–93); another Johann Christoph (1642–1703) and his wife Maria Elisabetha *née* Wedemann produced twins in 1685; J. S. Bach's own twins were born (and died) in 1713; and among later generations twins were born to Johann Bernhard (1700–43) and his wife Johanna Dorothea *née* vom Hofe in 1732.

10　Ambrosius's unfortunate younger sister Dorothee Maria (1652–79) was born deformed and imbecile.

11　The tendency towards intermarriage among the Bachs reached its closest point of consanguinity in 1817, when Ernst Carl Christian Bach (1785–1859) married his first cousin Sophie Charlotte (1781–1868), daughter of

Augustinus Tobias Bernhard Bach (1740–89); see Basso, *Frau Musika*, vol. I, pp. 737 and 739.

12   The Genealogy mistakenly gives 1704 as the date of Bach's Arnstadt appointment.

13   *Dok* I, p. 67; *BR*, p. 125.

## 2  *Bach and the domestic politics of Electoral Saxony*

1   This essay is based upon the articles by the author cited in the bibliography. In addition, it presents some previously unpublished research on Bach's income, based particularly on the Leipzig City Archives, and on the relationship between the territorial history of the Electorate of Saxony and the city history of Leipzig; this was supported by a fellowship from the Volkswagen-Stiftung during 1989–90.

## 3  *Music and Lutheranism*

1   See W. Blankenburg, 'Church music in Reformed Europe', in F. Blume, *Protestant church music: a history* (London, 1974), pp. 507–90, especially pp. 509–64.

2   See R. A. Leaver, 'The Lutheran Reformation', *The Renaissance: from the 1470s to the end of the 16th century*, ed. I. Fenlon, Music and society 2 (Englewood Cliffs, N.J., 1989), pp. 263–85.

3   C. S. Terry, *Joh. Seb. Bach: cantata texts, sacred and secular with a reconstruction of the Leipzig liturgy of his period* (London, 1926; reprinted 1964); A. Robertson, *The church cantatas of J. S. Bach* (London, 1972).

4   *The Book of Concord: the confessions of the Evangelical Lutheran Church*, trans. and ed. T. G. Tappert (Philadelphia, 1959).

5   In Leipzig, Bach composed a sequence of three cantatas celebrating the bicentenary of the presentation of the Augsburg Confession in June 1730, BWV 190a, 120b and Anh. 4; see W. Neumann, *Sämtliche von J. S. Bach vertonte Texte* (Leipzig, 1974), pp. 180–1. An annual Reformation festival, celebrating Luther's posting of the Ninety-Five Theses in Wittenberg on 31 October 1517, was observed in Leipzig, for which Bach composed cantatas BWV 79 and 80.

6   German, Latin and English versions of the Visitation Articles can be found in *Triglott Concordia: the symbolical books of the Ev. Lutheran Church* (St Louis, 1921), pp. 1150–7.

7   *Dok* II, pp. 99–100 (a facsimile of the document is given facing p. 177); *BR*, pp. 92–3.

8   *Dok* II, p. 101.

9   *Dok* III, pp. 630–1.

10   *Book of Concord*, p. 30 (German text).

11   *Book of Concord*, p. 478.

12   Augsburg Confession, Art. II; *Book of Concord*, p. 29 (Latin text).

13  Two recent discussions of the theology of Bach's music are particularly important, though not all their conclusions have been accepted. The first was written by an ecclesiastical historian and the other by a musicologist: J. Pelikan, *Bach among the theologians* (Philadelphia, 1986), and E. Chafe, *Tonal allegory in the vocal music of J. S. Bach* (Berkeley, 1991).

14  G. von Dadelsen, *Beiträge zur Chronologie der Werke Johann Sebastian Bachs* (Trossingen, 1958); A. Dürr, *Zur Chronologie der Leipziger Vokalwerke J. S. Bachs*, 2nd edn (Kassel, 1976).

15  F. Blume, 'Outlines of a new picture of Bach', *ML* 44 (1963), pp. 214–27, p. 218; reprinted in W. Hays, ed., *Twentieth-century views of music history* (New York, 1972), pp. 225–38.

16  The basic literature is: C. Trautmann, '"Calovii Schrifften. 3. Bände" aus Johann Sebastian Bachs Nachlass und ihre Bedeutung für das Bild des lutherischen Kantors Bach', *MuK* 39 (1969), pp. 145–60, translated as 'J. S. Bach: new light on his faith', *Concordia Theological Monthly* 42 (1971), pp. 88–99; G. Herz, 'Towards a new image of Bach', *BACH* 1/4 (1970), pp. 9–27 and 2/1 (1971), pp. 7–28, reprinted in G. Herz, *Essays on Bach* (Ann Arbor, 1985), pp. 149–84; G. Herz, *Bach sources in America* (Kassel, 1984), pp. 187–95; R. A. Leaver, *J. S. Bach and Scripture: glosses from the Calov Bible Commentary* (St Louis, 1985); H. H. Cox, ed., *The Calov Bible of J. S. Bach* (Ann Arbor, 1985); see also *Dok* III, pp. 636–7.

17  D. Arnold, *Bach* (Oxford, 1984), pp. 58–9.

18  See T. Wilhelmi, 'Bachs Bibliothek: eine Weiterführung der Arbeit von Hans Preuß', *BJb* 65 (1979), pp. 107–29; and R. A. Leaver, *Bachs theologische Bibliothek; eine kritische Bibliographie/Bach's theological library; a critical bibliography* (Neuhausen-Stuttgart, 1983). Much of this work has been done by various members of the Internationale Arbeitsgemeinschaft für theologische Bachforschung (IATB), founded by Walter Blankenburg in 1976; see 'Editor's introduction', G. Stiller, *Johann Sebastian Bach and liturgical life in Leipzig*, ed. R. A. Leaver (St Louis, 1984), pp. 13–15; and the *Bulletin* of the IATB, Heidelberg 1988–, which includes up-dated bibliographies of the writings of the members.

19  See Leaver, *Bachs theologische Bibliothek*, Nos. 2, 3, 1, 6, 4, 7 and 28 respectively.

20  See Chapter 7, pp. 116ff. below.

21  The basic study in German remains O. Söhngen, *Theologie der Musik* (Kassel, 1967), in which Luther's understanding of music is contrasted with that of Zwingli and Calvin. Some of Söhngen's conclusions have been questioned, most recently by J. L. Irwin, *Neither voice or heart alone: German Lutheran theology of music in the age of the Baroque* (New York, 1993). See also L. Steiger and R. Steiger, *Sehet! Wir gehn hinauf gen Jerusalem. Johann Sebastian Bachs Kantaten auf den Sonntag Estomihi* (Göttingen, 1992), pp. 11–14 and such English studies as W. E. Buszin, 'Luther on music', *MQ* 32 (1946), pp. 80–97, in essence an abbreviated translation of K. Anton, *Luther und die Musik* (Zwickau, 1916; 3rd edn 1928); P. Nettl, *Luther and music* (Philadelphia, 1948), in which no sources are documented; C. Schalk, *Luther on music: paradigms of praise* (St Louis, 1988).

22   *LW* LIII, pp. 321, 323; *WA* L, pp. 368, 370–1; all translations of Luther are
      taken from *LW*. See also W. Blankenburg, 'Überlieferung und Textgeschichte
      von Martin Luthers "Encomion musices"', *Lutherjahrbuch* (1973), pp. 80–104.

23   *LW* XLIX, p. 428; *WA Br* V, p. 639.

24   *WA Tr* No. 7034; see also Nos. 968 and 3815.

25   Bach owned a copy of the work, most probably a later imprint; see Leaver,
      *Bachs theologische Bibliothek*, No. 4.

26   *WA Tr* No. 816.

27   *WA Tr* No. 1258; *LW* LIV, pp. 129–30.

28   *LW* LIII, p. 333.

29   *WA Tr* No. 4441.

30   This connection is explored further in Chapter 7.

31   Leaver, *Bach and Scripture*, p. 95.

32   Leaver, *Bach and Scripture*, p. 97.

33   See F. Krummacher, 'Luthers Musikbegriff und die Kirchenmusik Bachs',
      *Luther: Zeitschrift der Luther-Gesellschaft* 56 (1985), pp. 136–51.

34   *WA Tr* No. 6248. See also Luther's comment in his lectures on Titus of 1527
      (on Titus 1:13): 'They want to be teachers but they cannot even sing', *WA*
      XXV, p. 29.

35   See J. Rautenstrauch, *Luther und die Pflege der kirchlichen Musik in Sachsen*
      (Leipzig, 1907; reprinted Hildesheim 1970); J. Butt, *Music and the art of
      performance in the German Baroque* (Cambridge, 1994); Schalk, *Luther on
      music*, pp. 28–30.

36   *Die Thomasschule Leipzig zur Zeit Johann Sebastian Bachs. Ordnungen und
      Gesetze 1634, 1723, 1733*, ed. H.-J. Schulze (Leipzig, 1987). For example, under
      the rubric 'Von der Musik', the 1733 *Ordnung* states (p. 22): 'Our forefathers
      ordered that music should be studied in the Thomasschule so that the alumni
      should serve the musical needs of all the town churches [in Leipzig].'

37   See, for example, *The journals of Henry Melchior Muhlenberg*, trans. T. G.
      Tappert and J. W. Doberstein, 3 vols. (Philadelphia, 1942–58), vol. I, p. 85.

38   See the 1634 Thomasschule *Ordnung*, sig. H4r. Early in Bach's cantorate there
      was a misunderstanding regarding his non-musical teaching; see *Dok* II,
      pp. 136–8; *BR*, pp. 95–6.

39   See B. Spinks, *Luther's liturgical criteria and his reform of the Canon of the
      Mass* (Bramcote, Nottingham, 1982); R. A. Leaver, 'Theological consistency,
      liturgical integrity, and musical hermeneutic in Luther's liturgical reforms',
      *The Lutheran Quarterly* 9 (1994), pp. 117–38.

40   *WA* XII, pp. 205–20; *WA* XIX, pp. 72–113; *LW* LIII, pp. 19–40; *LW* LIII,
      pp. 61–90.

41   Later Lutheran usage of the Ordinary is discussed in Chapter 7.

42   See Art. 24 of the Augsburg Confession: 'The mass is retained among us and
      is celebrated with the greatest reverence. Almost all the customary ceremonies
      are also retained, except that German hymns are interspersed here and there
      among the parts sung in Latin'; *Book of Concord*, p. 56 (Latin text); see note 4
      above.

43   *Book of Concord*, p. 34 (German text).

44    See D. Gojowy, 'Kirchenlieder im Umkreis von J. S. Bach', *Jahrbuch für Liturgik und Hymnologie* 22 (1978), pp. 79–123.

45    R. A. Leaver, 'Bach and hymnody: the evidence of the Orgelbüchlein', *EM* 13 (1985), pp. 227–36.

46    E.g. BWV 675–7, 711, 715, 717, 771.

47    R. A. Leaver, 'Bach's "Clavierübung III": some historical and theological considerations', *OY* 6 (1975), pp. 17–32, pp. 20–1.

48    E.g., BWV 437, 740, 765, 1098; there were also two further settings of the melody in the Catechism part of *Clavier-Übung* III (BWV 680 and 681); see further below.

49    There is some confusion over the number of main sections of the small catechism, in some sources cited as five and in others as six; see Leaver, 'Bach's "Clavierübung III"', p. 31, n. 36.

50    *Ibid.*, pp. 21–7.

51    On the three Reformation festivals held in Leipzig in 1739, *ibid.*, pp. 17–18.

52    *Geistliche lieder / auffs new gebessert und gemehrt / zu Wittenberg* (Leipzig, 1539).

53    See E. Sehling, ed., *Die evangelischen Kirchenordnungen des XVI. Jahrhunderts*, 15 vols. (Leipzig and Tübingen, 1902–80), vol. I, pp. 264–81. Its liturgical provisions are summarised in L. D. Reed, *The Lutheran liturgy* (Philadelphia, 1959), pp. 101–2.

54    The most accessible survey of the period from Luther to Bach is found in Blume, *Protestant church music*, pp. 1–315; see also R. A. Leaver, 'Lutheran Vespers as a context for music', *Church, stage, and studio: music and its contexts in seventeenth-century Germany*, ed. P. Walker (Ann Arbor, 1990), pp. 143–61.

## 4  Bach's metaphysics of music

1    See H. H. Cox, ed., *The Calov Bible of J. S. Bach* (Ann Arbor, 1985), p. 419: 'NB Bey einer andächtigen Musig [*sic*] ist allezeit gott mit seiner Gnaden-Gegenwart.'

2    G. van der Leeuw, *Sacred and profane beauty: the holy in art*, trans. D. E. Green (Nashville and New York, n.d.), p. 4; quoted in J. A. Martin, *Beauty and holiness* (Princeton, 1990), p. 87.

3    See G. Stiller, *Johann Sebastian Bach and liturgical life in Leipzig*, ed. R. A. Leaver (St Louis, 1984), p. 210.

4    See J. L. Irwin, *Neither voice nor heart alone: German Lutheran theology of music in the age of the Baroque* (New York, 1993), especially pp. 134, 141–53.

5    The so-called Neumeister model for cantatas in Bach's own environment, with its absorption of da capo arias and recitatives, is merely the latest flowering of this process.

6    F. Kalb, *Theology of worship in 17th-century Lutheranism*, trans. H. P. A. Hamann (St Louis, 1965), p. 149.

7    *Ibid.*, p. 141.

8    Irwin, *Neither voice nor heart alone*, especially pp. 12–22, 112–34.

9   See R. Dammann, *Der Musikbegriff im deutschen Barock* (Cologne, 1967; revised 1984), pp. 62–5.

10  This latter point might be one way in which the new 'expressive' music of the Italian Baroque explicitly fulfilled Luther's intention that music should promote well-being and banish the Devil (a line of thought that can be traced right back to Pythagorean times; see J. Butt, *Music education and the art of performance in the German Baroque* (Cambridge, 1994), pp. 12–13).

11  Irwin, Neither voice nor heart alone, pp. 21–2, 31–3, shows that Frick was extreme in arguing that scorn and ignorance of music were just cause of divine punishment and the abuse of music was tantamount to blasphemy.

12  *Ibid.*, pp. 40 and 199.

13  This is echoed in the writings of the Orthodox music theorist A. Werckmeister, e.g. in his annotations to Steffani's *Send-Schreiben* (1699); published by J. L. Albrecht (Mühlhausen, 1760), p. 31. A concern for the spiritual disposition of the musicians is also expressed by the Pietists.

14  For a description of one prominent figure who opposed instrumental music from within Orthodoxy, Grossgebauer, see Kalb, *Theology of worship*, pp. 143–4.

15  Stiller, *J. S. Bach and liturgical life*, pp. 144–8; Butt, *Music education*, pp. 25–9.

16  See B. F. Richter, 'Eine Abhandlung Joh. Kuhnaus', *MMg* 34 (1902), p. 149.

17  For the origins of this division in Italian theory and practice at the turn of the seventeenth century, see C. Palisca, 'The genesis of Mattheson's style classification', *New Mattheson studies*, ed. G. Buelow (Cambridge, 1983), pp. 409–23.

18  *Ibid.*, p. 410, for this translation and original text.

19  *Ibid.*, p. 421.

20  Irwin, *Neither voice nor heart alone*, pp. 145–7.

21  See A. Forchert, 'Polemik als Erkenntnisform: Bemerkungen zu den Schriften Matthesons', *New Mattheson studies*, ed. G. Buelow (Cambridge, 1983), pp. 199–212, especially pp. 209–11.

22  *Dok* II, pp. 196–7; *BR*, p. 441.

23  See also *MGG* IV, col. 1130.

24  *Dok* II, p. 153; *BR*, p. 229.

25  Irwin, *Neither voice nor heart alone*, pp. 130–4, claims that sacred and secular music are not placed on an equal level theologically before the writings of the Breslau theologian Gottfried Scheibel (*Zufällige Gedancken von der Kirchenmusic* (Frankfurt and Leipzig, 1721)). Stiller, *J. S. Bach and liturgical life*, thus somewhat oversimplifies the issue with his general attitude that the sacred and secular are not separated in Orthodox Lutheranism (see e.g. p. 210).

26  As Irwin notes, *Neither voice nor heart alone*, p. 142, this practice hardly distinguishes Bach from his contemporaries. While it is certainly indicative of a religious disposition it does not single Bach out for particular piety.

27  'Denen Liebhabern zur Gemüths Ergoezung verfertiget'.

28  See H.-J. Schulze, *Studien zur Bach-Überlieferung im 18. Jahrhundert* (Leipzig and Dresden, 1984), pp. 125–7.

29  German text in *Dok* II, p. 334; translation by author. See also the new
    annotated translation, by P. L. Poulin, *J. S. Bach – Precepts and principles for
    playing the thorough-bass or accompanying in four parts* (Oxford, 1994),
    pp. 10–11.

30  *Dok* II, p. 334 for Niedt's German text.

31  See W. Blankenburg, 'J. S. Bach und die Aufklärung', *Bach Gedenkschrift* 1950,
    ed. K. Matthaei (Zurich, 1950), pp. 25–34, especially pp. 27–9.

32  See A. Dürr, *Studien über die frühen Kantaten Johann Sebastian Bachs* (1951);
    rev. edn (Wiesbaden, 1977), pp. 223–4; and W. H. Scheide, 'Bach vs. Bach –
    Mühlhausen dismissal request vs. Erdmann letter', *Bachiana et alia
    musicologica – Festschrift Alfred Dürr zum 65. Geburtstag*, ed. W. Rehm (Kassel,
    1983), pp. 234–42.

33  *Dok* I, pp. 60–4; *BR*, pp. 120–4.

34  See Butt, *Music education*, pp. 30–3; see also Chapter 2 above, for the political
    situation in Leipzig. That Bach saw his position within the church as a sacred
    duty is suggested by his highlighting of a passage concerning 'justifiable
    anger', in his copy of Calov's Bible commentary (see Cox, *The Calov Bible*,
    p. 445, facsimile 218). Anger is justified 'for the sake of your office and for
    God's sake', which is not to be confused with anger for one's own sake, as
    proscribed by Christ in his sermon on the mount.

35  E.g. the cancelled Passion of 1739, *Dok* II, pp. 338–9; *BR*, pp. 162–3. For
    references to the sorry state of the choir during the last years of Bach's life, see C.
    Fröde, 'Zu einer Kritik des Thomanerchores von 1749', *BJb* 70 (1984), pp. 53–8.

36  Irwin, *Neither voice nor heart alone*, p. 143, goes even further, in suggesting
    that the call for a 'well-appointed' church music refers not to liturgical order,
    but merely to artistic excellence. I suspect, rather, that Bach saw liturgical
    order and artistic excellence as two sides of the same coin.

37  Cox, *The Calov Bible*, p. 418, facsimile 110.

38  *Ibid.*, p. 418, facsimile 111.

39  *Ibid.* 419, facsimile 112. The Biblical text reads: 'And when the voice arose
    from the trumpets, cymbals, and other string players and from the praising of
    the Lord that He is good and that His mercy endures forever, the house of the
    Lord was filled with a cloud.'

40  *Dok* II, pp. 461–4.

41  See H. J. Kreutzer, 'Johann Sebastian Bach und das literarische Leipzig der
    Aufklärung,' *BJb* 77 (1991), pp. 7–31, pp. 28–9, for a refutation of the received
    wisdom that Birnbaum was a lecturer in rhetoric.

42  G. J. Buelow, 'In defence of J. A. Scheibe against J. S. Bach', *PRMA* 101
    (1974/5), pp. 85–100; G. Wagner, 'J. A. Scheibe – J. S. Bach: Versuch einer
    Bewertung', *BJb* 68 (1982), pp. 33–49; C. Wolff, '"Die sonderbaren
    Vollkommenheiten des Herrn Hofcompositeurs". Versuch über die Eigenart
    der Bachschen Musik', *Bachiana et alia musicologica – Festschrift Alfred Dürr
    zum 65. Geburtstag*, ed. W. Rehm (Kassel, 1983), pp. 356–62; trans. '"The
    extraordinary perfections of the Hon. Court Composer": an inquiry into the
    individuality of Bach's music', *Bach: essays on his life and music* (Cambridge,
    Mass., 1991), pp. 391–7.

43   *Dok* II, pp. 286–7; *BR*, p. 238.

44   Wagner, 'J. A. Scheibe – J. S. Bach'.

45   Furthermore, Scheibe's favourable description of a musical style close to Bach's in another issue of his *Critischer Musicus*, under the heading of 'tropischer' or 'verblühmter Ausdruck' (Wagner, 'J. A. Scheibe – J. S. Bach', p. 37), does not mean that he thought this style should be applied indiscriminately to all musical genres; it is one of several styles, each with its appropriate uses.

46   Kreutzer, 'Johann Sebastian Bach und das literarische Leipzig', pp. 13, 29.

47   *Dok* II, pp. 360–3; *BR*, pp. 249–51.

48   See, for example, Mizler's statement at the end of Bach's 1754 Obituary: 'Our lately departed Bach did not, it is true, occupy himself with deep theoretical speculation on music, but was all the stronger in the practice of the art.' *BR*, p. 224; *Dok* III, p. 89.

49   *Dok* II, pp. 296–306; *BR*, pp. 239–47.

50   Wolff, '"The extraordinary perfections"', p. 393.

51   Birnbaum continues this reasoning in his second defence of Bach in 1739: singers and instrumentalists could overcome the difficulties of Bach's music with practice and industry. *Dok* II, p. 356.

52   *Dok* III, p. 340; *BR*, p. 291.

53   *Dok* III, pp. 523–4; *BR*, p. 455.

54   *Dok* III, p. 285; *BR*, p. 277.

55   See Wolff, '"The extraordinary perfections"', p. 395; text in *Dok* II, p. 397; *BR*, p. 290.

56   Luther himself took a similar approach to nature, when he commented that 'when natural music is sharpened and polished by art, then one begins to see with amazement the great and perfect wisdom of God in his wonderful work of music'. *WA Tr* 2362.

57   *Dok* II, p. 485; translation by author.

58   *Dok* III, pp. 14–15; *BR*, p. 267.

59   Marpurg proceeds to use blatantly gendered imagery to describe his notion of music history: the timeless contrapuntal basis of music is the stable *manly* element, something which the modern composer should assimilate in order to 'set himself against the spreading rubbish of womanish song'. In other words, the dictates of fashion and taste are to be seen as unstable, ephemeral and feminine, while the solid foundation of music is masculine.

## 5   'A mind unconscious that it is calculating'?

1   For a summary of studies making connections between Leibniz and Bach, see A. Luppi, *Lo specchio dell'armonia universale: estetica e musica in Leibniz* (Milan, 1989), pp. 158–68. Among the writings not reviewed by Luppi is E. E. Lowinsky's essay 'Taste, style, and ideology in eighteenth-century music' (written in 1963), in *Music in the culture of the Renaissance and other essays*, ed. B. J. Blackburn, 2 vols. (Chicago, 1989), vol. I, pp. 67–86. For the most recent application of Leibniz's principles to Bach, see U. Leisinger, 'Forms and

functions of the choral movements in J. S. Bach's *St. Matthew Passion*', *Bach studies* 2, ed. D. R. Melamed (Cambridge, 1995), pp. 70–84, especially pp. 80–4.

2   W. Blankenburg, 'J. S. Bach und die Aufklärung', *Bach Gedenkschrift* 1950, ed. K. Matthaei (Zurich, 1950), p. 26.

3   The only example I have managed to trace of a previous author relating Bach and Spinoza is W. Mellers, *Bach and the dance of God* (London, 1980), which contains a few scattered references to the philosopher.

4   This is the 'optimistic' view of the theologian Blankenburg, 'J. S. Bach und die Aufklärung'.

5   See Chapter 4, note 48 above.

6   This is essentially the approach taken by H. H. Eggebrecht, 'Bach und Leibniz', *Bericht über die wissenschaftliche Bachtagung der Gesellschaft für Musikforschung* (Leipzig, 1951), pp. 431–47. Here Eggebrecht is critical of previous writers who tend to connect Leibniz's philosophical terms to specific musical devices.

7   Much of the following summary of Wolff's aesthetics is drawn from J. Birke, *Christian Wolffs Metaphysik und die zeitgenössische Literatur- und Musiktheorie. Gottsched, Scheibe, Mizler* (Berlin, 1966).

8   *Ibid.*, p. 1.

9   *Leibniz – philosophical writings*, ed. G. H. R. Parkinson (London, 1973), p. 50.

10  Birke, *Christian Wolffs Metaphysik*, p. 7.

11  *Ibid.*, pp. 10–11.

12  *Ibid.*, p. 17.

13  *Leibniz – philosophical writings*, p. 188.

14  Leisinger, 'Forms and functions', especially pp. 80–4.

15  *Leibniz – philosophical writings*, p. 142.

16  *Johann Gottfried Walther – Praecepta der musikalischen Composition*, ed. P. Benary, *Jenaer Beiträge zur Musikforschung* vol. II, ed. H. Besseler (Leipzig, 1955).

17  See note 6 above.

18  For a fascinating study of the antecedents for most of the components of Spinoza's *Ethics*, see H. A. Wolfson, 'Behind the geometrical method', *Spinoza – a collection of critical essays*, ed. M. Grene (New York, 1973), pp. 3–24.

19  All translations of Spinoza's *Ethics* are taken from *A Spinoza reader*, ed. and trans. E. Curley (Princeton, 1994).

20  Leibniz did not deny the ontological argument, but believed it needed to be supported by other arguments.

21  Leibniz also equated perfection with the degree of positive reality, in a letter to Wolff of 1715; see D. Blumenfeld, 'Perfection and happiness in the best possible world', *The Cambridge companion to Leibniz* (Cambridge, 1995), pp. 382–410, especially pp. 394–5.

22  For an outline of this distinction in the concepts of perfection, see W. Kaufmann, *Critique of religion and philosophy* (Princeton, 1958; reprinted 1978), p. 164

23  See R. L. Marshall. *The compositional process of J. S. Bach*, 2 vols. (Princeton,

1972), vol. I, p. 15: 'It would seem that Bach did not have the patience or inclination – or ability – merely to copy any vocal work on a larger scale ... in a purely mechanical manner without introducing – at least occasionally – improvements of detail. For copying meant literally writing music, which meant in turn for such a musical talent as Bach a constant stimulus to the critical imagination and fantasy.'

24  See, in particular, L. Goehr, *The imaginary museum of musical works* (Oxford, 1992), especially pp. 113–15.

25  E.g. the Christmas Oratorio, *Well-tempered Clavier* Book II, *Art of Fugue*, and Mass in B Minor.

26  *Dok* I, pp. 220–1; *BR*, p. 86.

27  To be candid, this is not a good example, since such calculations surely rely more simply on memory.

28  It may be no coincidence that the favourable reception of Spinoza, or at least the period of his strongest influence, begins with figures such as Goethe and Kant, precisely the time of Bach's 'rediscovery'. For a fascinating study of Spinoza's influence, see Y. Yovel, *Spinoza and other heretics – the adventures of immanence* (Princeton, 1989).

29  I am grateful to many long-suffering colleagues and friends in my efforts to write Chapters 4 and 5. The following deserve particular mention: Karol Berger, Lydia Goehr, Joseph Kerman, Robin Leaver and Anthony Newcomb. I am also most grateful for the assistance of Jennifer Griesbach and Kevin Bazzana, to whom I assigned the tasks of exploring Bach's relationship to Leipzig and Spinoza in a seminar at the University of California, Berkeley, Spring 1992.

## 6  The early works and the heritage of the seventeenth century

1  J. N. Forkel, *Über Johann Sebastian Bachs Leben, Kunst und Kunstwerke* (Leipzig, 1802); trans. in *BR*, p. 336.

2  M. Boyd, *Bach* (London, 1983), p. 27.

3  P. Williams, review of C. Wolff, ed., *The Neumeister collection of chorale preludes from the Bach circle* and *Organ chorales from the Neumeister collection*, in *EM* 15 (1987), p. 95.

4  A. Dürr, *Studien über die frühen Kantaten Johann Sebastian Bachs*, rev. edn (Wiesbaden, 1977).

5  C. Wolff, 'The identity of the "Fratro Dilettissimo" in the Capriccio in B-Flat Major and other problems of Bach's early harpsichord works', *The harpsichord and its repertoire*, Proceedings of the International Harpsichord Symposium, Utrecht 1990, ed. P. Dirksen (Utrecht, 1992), p. 150. An alternative view has been advanced by Robert Marshall ('Johann Sebastian Bach', *Eighteenth-century keyboard music*, ed. R. L. Marshall (New York, 1994), pp. 68–123), who argues that 'the decade 1703–1713 ... is best regarded as constituting a single creative period in Bach's life' (p. 72).

6   Christoph Wolff proposed this period of time by analogy with the age at which Handel and Bach's own sons began composing: 'Pachelbel, Buxtehude und die weitere Einfluß-Sphäre des jungen Bach', *Das Frühwerk Johann Sebastian Bachs*, ed. K. Heller and H.-J. Schulze (Cologne, 1995), pp. 21–32. I am grateful to Professor Wolff for allowing me to read this essay in advance of its publication.

7   P. Williams, 'BWV 565: a Toccata in D Minor for organ by J. S. Bach?', *EM* 9 (1981), pp. 330–7. Williams suggests that it may originally have been composed as a violin piece by 'one of the talented organists of the J. L. Krebs/ J. C. Kittel generation around 1750' (p. 335). Alternatively, it has been proposed that the work originated with J. P. Kellner, a Thuringian organist and cantor with close ties to Bach; see D. Humphreys, 'The D Minor Toccata BWV 565', *EM* 10 (1982), pp. 216–17.

8   C. Wolff, 'The identity of the "Fratro Dilettissimo"'.

9   W. H. Scheide, 'Johann Sebastian Bachs Sammlung von Kantaten seines Vetters Johann Ludwig Bach', *BJb* 46 (1959), pp. 52–94.

10   G. Herz, 'BWV 131: Bach's first cantata', *Studies in eighteenth-century music: a tribute to Karl Geiringer on his seventieth birthday*, ed. H. C. Robbins Landon and R. E. Chapman (London and New York, 1970), pp. 272–91; reprinted in G. Herz, *Essays on J. S. Bach* (Ann Arbor, 1985), pp. 127–45.

11   A. Glöckner, 'Zur Echtheit und Datierung der Kantate BWV 150 "Nach dir, Herr, verlanget mich"', *BJb* 74 (1988), pp. 195–203.

12   These include four organ pieces (an early version of the Prelude and Fugue in G minor BWV 535a; two settings of the chorale 'Wie schön leuchtet der Morgenstern' BWV 739 and 764; and a newly authenticated Fantasia in C minor BWV Anh. 205) and three vocal works (the cantatas *Gott ist mein König* BWV 71 and *Aus der Tiefe rufe ich, Herr, zu dir* BWV 131, and the Quodlibet BWV 524).

13   The sporadic transmission of the early works testifies to Bach's own lack of interest in them. The higher level of technical competence and the increased sophistication of his later compositions rendered many of the earlier attempts obsolete. See Wolff, 'The identity of the "Fratro Dilettissimo"', p. 150; and F. Blume, 'J. S. Bach's youth', *MQ* 54 (1968), pp. 29–30.

14   Occasionally, even works for which autographs survive have been rejected on stylistic grounds. For instance, the two organ settings of the chorale 'Wie schön leuchtet der Morgenstern' (BWV 739 and 764) were excluded from the *NBA* volume of the singly transmitted organ chorales (H. Klotz, ed., *NBA* IV/3). In 'Bach's earliest autograph', *MQ* 71 (1985), pp. 235–63, Russell Stinson argues convincingly that these two pieces are indeed authentic Bach, and reports that they are scheduled to appear in a supplementary volume of the *NBA* (p. 237, nn. 7 and 9). For a fascinating account of the early twentieth-century origins of the prevailing 'climate of doubt concerning the authenticity of Bach's early . . . works', see R. S. Hill, '*Echtheit angezweifelt*: style and authenticity in two suites attributed to Bach', *EM* 13 (1985), pp. 248–55, especially pp. 249–50.

15   H.-J. Schulze, *Studien zur Bach-Überlieferung im 18. Jahrhundert* (Leipzig,

1984), pp. 30–56. For an important complementary biographical study, see Schulze, 'Johann Christoph Bach (1671–1721), "Organist und Schul Collega in Ohrdruf", Johann Sebastian Bachs erster Lehrer', *BJb* 71 (1985), pp. 55–81.

16  The Fantasia in C minor (BWV deest) in the Andreas Bach Book is transmitted anonymously, but it has recently been identified as an autograph. See D. Kilian, 'Zu einem Bachschen Tabulaturautograph', *Bachiana et alia musicologica – Festschrift Alfred Dürr zum 65. Geburtstag*, ed. W. Rehm (Kassel, 1983), pp. 161–7. Robert Hill has presented evidence suggesting that a number of Bach's early keyboard works were originally notated in tablature. See R. S. Hill, 'Tablature versus staff notation: or, why did the young J. S. Bach compose in tablature?' *Church, stage, and studio: music and its contexts in seventeenth-century Germany*, ed. P. Walker (Ann Arbor, 1990), pp. 349–59.

17  R. S. Hill, ed., *Keyboard music from the Andreas Bach Book and the Möller Manuscript* (Cambridge, Mass., 1991), p. xxiii.

18  *Ibid.*, pp. xxii–xxiii.

19  The piece on which this composition is based, Legrenzi's trio sonata Op. 2 No. 11 ('La Mont'Albana'), was identified by Robert Hill ('Die Herkunft von Bachs "Thema Legrenzianum"', *BJb* 72 (1986), pp. 105–7).

20  D. Humphreys, 'A Bach polyglot: the A major prelude & fugue BWV 536', *OY* 20 (1989), pp. 72–87, (quotation on p. 78).

21  George Stauffer, the Pastorale's most vigorous advocate, suggests that it may have been composed in 1723–6, a period when Bach penned a number of pastoral-derived movements in his cantatas; 'Bach's Pastorale in F: a closer look at a maligned work', *OY* 14 (1983), pp. 44–60, especially p. 59. Russell Stinson points out that the *galant* style of the third movement might indicate that it dates from as late as the 1730s; *The Bach manuscripts of Johann Peter Kellner and his circle: a case study in reception history* (Durham, N.C. and London, 1990), pp. 111–14.

22  D. Schulenberg, *The keyboard music of J. S. Bach* (New York, 1992).

23  A short but substantial discussion of two of them is found in Stinson, *The Bach manuscripts*, pp. 123–5, where it is argued that two compositions in a Berlin miscellany (Staatsbibliothek zu Berlin-Preussischer Kulturbesitz, shelf mark P 804), the Suite in B♭ major (BWV 821) and the Prelude and Fugue in A minor (BWV 895), are both authentic early Bach works. For an exemplary discussion and inventory of P 804, an important source that includes a number of compositions by the young Bach, see R. Stinson, '"Ein Sammelband aus Johann Peter Kellners Besitz": Neue Forschungen zur Berliner Bach-Handschrift *P 804*', *BJb* 78 (1992), pp. 45–64.

24  The Bach compositions were published in Johann Sebastian Bach, *Orgelchoräle der Neumeister-Sammlung / Organ chorales from the Neumeister collection*, ed. C. Wolff (New Haven and Kassel, 1985). A facsimile of the entire manuscript appeared as C. Wolff, ed., *The Neumeister collection of chorale preludes from the Bach circle (Yale University manuscript LM 4708)* (New Haven, 1986). The extensive introduction to the facsimile is reprinted in Wolff, 'The Neumeister collection of chorale preludes from the Bach circle', *Bach: essays on his life and music* (Cambridge, Mass., 1991), pp. 107–27.

Among the many reports of this find and reviews of these editions, some of the most important include: C. Wolff, 'Bach's organ music: studies and discoveries', *MT* 126 (1985), pp. 149–52; W. Krumbach, 'Sechzig unbekannte Orgelwerke von Johann Sebastian Bach? Ein vorläufiger Fundbericht', *NZM* 146 (1985), no. 3, pp. 4–12, and no. 5, pp. 6–18 (see also Wolff's reply in no. 6, p. 2); A. Dürr, 'Kein Meister fällt vom Himmel: Zu Johann Sebastian Bachs Orgelchorälen der Neumeister-Sammlung', *Musica* 40 (1986), pp. 309–12.

25   The compiler and probable scribe of the manuscript was Johann Gottfried Neumeister (1756–1840), a schoolteacher and organist who had studied music with one of Bach's colleagues in the Society of the Musical Sciences (Correspondierende Societät der musicalischen Wissenschaften), the composer and theorist Georg Andreas Sorge; see Wolff, *The Neumeister collection*, pp. 108–11.

26   W. Schmieder, ed., *Thematisch-systematisches Verzeichnis der musikalischen Werke von Johann Sebastian Bach. Bach-Werke-Verzeichnis (BWV)*, 2nd edn (Wiesbaden, 1990).

27   *NBA* IV/3. If the *Bach-Gesellschaft* edition in the nineteenth century was sometimes too inclusive, the *Neue Bach-Ausgabe* has sometimes been too exclusive. See note 14, above.

28   See C. Wolff, 'Chronology and style in the early works: a background for the Orgel-Büchlein', *Bach: essays on his life and music* , pp. 297–305; and R. Stinson, 'Some thoughts on Bach's Neumeister chorales', *JM* 11 (1993), pp. 455–77, and 'The compositional history of Bach's *Orgelbüchlein* reconsidered', *Bach perspectives* 1 ed. R. Stinson (Lincoln, Nebr. and London, 1995), pp. 43–78.

29   Most notably, Günter Hartmann has insisted that BWV 1096 ('Christe, der du bist Tag und Licht' or 'Wir danken dir, Herr Jesu Christ'), a fragment of which was in a lost manuscript compiled by Johann Gottfried Walther, is by Pachelbel. See G. Hartmann, 'Authentischer Bach-Elbel. Marginalie zu einem der angeblichen Bach-Choräle der Neumeister-Sammlung', *NZM* 147 (1986), no. 4, pp. 4–6. Wolff, however, believes that the fragmentary version is a corruption (*The Neumeister collection*, p. 118).

30   As Krumbach has put it, 'Who else could have composed the pieces that are attributed to him there?'; Krumbach, 'Sechzig unbekannte Orgelwerke', no. 5, p. 10.

31   W. Breig, 'Textbezug und Werkidee in Johann Sebastian Bachs frühen Orgelchorälen', *Musikkulturgeschichte. Festschrift für Constantin Floros zum 60. Geburtstag*, ed. P. Petersen (Wiesbaden, 1990), pp. 167–82, especially pp. 175–6.

32   These include the borrowing of elements from the North German chorale fantasy (e.g. frequent changes of metre, the migration of the cantus firmus from one voice to another and the placement of the cantus firmus in an interior voice) and a distinctive harmonic formula used for the final cadence of a movement (the diminished seventh chord as a substitute for the dominant, leading to the tonic). See Stinson, 'Some thoughts on Bach's Neumeister chorales', pp. 455–67.

33   See Johann Michael Bach, *Sämtliche Orgelchoräle mit einem Anhang*

(*Orgelchoräle des Bach-Kreises, hauptsächlich aus der Neumeister-Sammlung*) /
*The complete organ chorales with an appendix* (*Organ chorales of the Bach
circle, mainly from the Neumeister collection*), ed. C. Wolff (Kirchheim-Teck,
1988).

34   Wolff, *The Neumeister collection*, p. 116. These points have been disputed by
Dominik Sackmann ('Der "Yaler" Bach. Beobachtungen zur Handschrift US-NH
(Yale) LM 4708 und deren Umfeld', *BzBF* 9/10 (1991), pp. 165–72), who argues
that 'it would be wrong to see in the organ chorales of Johann Michael Bach the
principal and decisive models for the chorales of Johann Sebastian Bach' (p. 169).
He notes that the style of the Neumeister chorales involves 'the union of
conventional vocal and organistic formal means' and therefore urges that the
vocal music of the older members of the Bach family (e.g. the motets and
cantatas of J. M. and J. C. Bach) also be explored as a source of influence (p. 170).

35   E. May, 'The types, uses, and historical position of Bach's organ chorales',
*J. S. Bach as organist: his instruments, music, and performance practices*, ed.
G. Stauffer and E. May (Bloomington, 1986), pp. 81–101.

36   Although their manuscript transmission is far from impeccable, the
authenticity of these chorale partitas has never been seriously questioned.
BWV 771, on the other hand, appears to be the work of Nicolaus Vetter
(1666–1734). See P. Williams, *The organ music of J. S. Bach*, 3 vols.
(Cambridge, 1980–4), vol. II, pp. 328–9.

37   R. S. Hill, 'The Möller manuscript and the Andreas Bach Book: two keyboard
anthologies from the circle of the young Johann Sebastian Bach', 2 vols. (Ph.D.
dissertation, Harvard University, 1987), vol. I, pp. 432–3. The piece is
transcribed in Appendix G (vol. II, pp. 750–1). See also B. Cooper, 'An
unknown Bach source', *MT* 113 (1972), pp. 1167–9.

38   Schulenberg, *Keyboard music*, p. 397, n. 30.

39   F. Morana, 'The "Dobenecker" Toccata, *BWV-Anh*. II 85: an early Bach work?'
*BACH* 24/2 (1993), pp. 26–37.

40   For an account of the development of this paradigm, see S. A. Crist, 'Beyond
"Bach-centrism": historiographic perspectives on Johann Sebastian Bach and
seventeenth-century music', *CMS* 33/34 (1993–4), pp. 56–69.

41   H.-J. Schulze, 'Johann Sebastian Bach und die Tradition', *Bach-Händel-Schütz-
Ehrung der DDR 1985. V. Internationales Bachfest in Verbindung mit dem 60.
Bachfest der Neuen Bachgesellschaft, Leipzig, 19. bis 27. März 1985*, ed. W. Felix
et al. (Leipzig, 1985), pp. 33–7, p. 36. See also A. Forchert, 'Johann Sebastian
Bachs Verhältnis zur Tradition', *51. Bachfest der Neuen Bachgesellschaft in
Berlin (West) vom 25. bis 30. August 1976* (Berlin, 1976), pp. 5–16.

42   K. Heller, 'Norddeutsche Musikkultur als Traditionsraum des jungen Bach',
*BJb* 75 (1989), pp. 16–17.

43   W. Breig, 'Der norddeutsche Orgelchoral und Johann Sebastian Bach.
Gattung, Typus, Werk', *Gattung und Werk in der Musikgeschichte
Norddeutschlands und Skandinaviens*, ed. F. Krummacher and H. W. Schwab
(Kassel, 1982), pp. 79–94.

44   F. Krummacher, 'Bach und die norddeutsche Orgeltoccata. Fragen und
Überlegungen', *BJb* 71 (1985), pp. 119–34, especially pp. 123–6.

45   Heller, 'Norddeutsche Musikkultur', p. 16.

46   C. Wolff, 'Buxtehude, Bach, and seventeenth-century music in retrospect', *Bach: essays on his life and music*, pp. 54–5. F. Krummacher's 'Dietrich Buxtehude. Musik zwischen Geschichte und Gegenwart', *Dietrich Buxtehude und die europäische Musik seiner Zeit. Bericht über das Lübecker Symposion 1987*, ed. A. Edler and F. Krummacher (Kassel, 1990), pp. 9–30, includes a number of important observations and insights about the relationship between Buxtehude and Bach.

47   See H.-J. Schulze, 'Bach und Buxtehude. Eine wenig beachtete Quelle in der Carnegie Library zu Pittsburgh/PA', *BJb* 77 (1991), pp. 177–81; and D. O. Franklin, 'The Carnegie Manuscript and J. S. Bach', *BACH* 22/1 (1991), pp. 5–15. If the unknown hand is indeed Sebastian's, this would be the earliest known example of his music writing.

48   J.-C. Zehnder, 'Georg Böhm und Johann Sebastian Bach. Zur Chronologie der Bachschen Stilentwicklung', *BJb* 74 (1988), pp. 74, 90.

49   *Dok* III, p. 82; *BR*, p. 217.

50   The article on Reincken in *NG* (vol. XV, pp. 717–18) lists about twenty.

51   Two notable exceptions are C. Wolff, 'Johann Adam Reinken und Johann Sebastian Bach. Zum Kontext des Bachschen Frühwerks', *BJb* 71 (1985), pp. 99–118; English trans., 'Bach and Johann Adam Reinken: a context for the early works', *Bach: essays on his life and music*, pp. 56–71; and R. S. Hill, 'Stilanalyse und Überlieferungsproblematik. Das Variationssuiten-Repertoire J. A. Reinckens', *Dietrich Buxtehude und die europäische Musik*, pp. 204–14.

52   Wolff, 'Bach and Johann Adam Reinken', especially pp. 64–6.

53   Unlike a normal fugue, a 'permutation fugue' contains no free material, but instead consists of several discrete subjects that are continually combined with one another in many different ways.

54   P. Walker, 'Die Entstehung der Permutationsfuge', *BJb* 75 (1989), pp. 21–41; English trans., 'The origin of the permutation fugue', *Studies in the history of music*, vol. III, *The creative process* (New York, 1993), pp. 57–91. Permutation fugues are further discussed in Chapter 10 below, pp. 158–9.

55   At present, the standard study of Bach's organ compositions, including the early works, is Williams, *Organ music* (see n. 36); for the keyboard works without obbligato pedal, it is Schulenberg, *Keyboard music* (see n. 22). Both books frequently point out ways in which Bach's youthful music is indebted to works by earlier composers. The best survey of Bach's organ chorales is May's article (see n. 35). Finally, Dürr's volume on the early cantatas (see n. 4) contains much useful information, especially about the manuscript transmission of this repertory. But the style-critical portions, which were originally written around 1950 and were reprinted virtually unaltered in the 1977 edition, are badly out of date.

56   G. B. Stauffer, *The organ preludes of Johann Sebastian Bach* (Ann Arbor, 1980), and 'Fugue types in Bach's free organ works', *J. S. Bach as organist*, pp. 133–56. See also W. Breig, 'Formprobleme in Bachs frühen Orgelfugen', *BJb* 78 (1992), pp. 7–21; English trans., 'Form problems in Bach's early organ fugues', *A Bach tribute: essays in honor of William H. Scheide*, ed. P. Brainard and R. Robinson (Kassel and Chapel Hill, N.C., 1993), pp. 45–56.

57    K. Heller, 'Die freien Allegrosätze in der frühen Tastenmusik Johann Sebastian Bachs', *BzBF* 9/10 (1991), pp. 173–85.

58    F. Krummacher, 'Bachs frühe Kantaten im Kontext der Tradition', *Mf* 44 (1991), pp. 9–32. Miriam Whaples has focused even more specifically on the arias in Bach's Mühlhausen cantatas (1707–8) in an effort to illuminate the origins of his earliest Italianate arias, those in the 'Hunt' Cantata (BWV 208). See M. K. Whaples, 'Bach's earliest arias', *BACH* 20/1 (1989), pp. 31–54.

59    C. Oefner, 'Eisenach zur Zeit des jungen Bach', *BJb* 71 (1985), pp. 43–54.

60    The library's holdings included motets by Senfl, Obrecht, Isaac, Pierre de la Rue, Josquin and Mouton, as well as collections of works by Hammerschmidt and Niedt. See M. Schiffner, 'Johann Sebastian Bach in Arnstadt', *BzBF* 4 (1985), pp. 5–22, especially p. 13.

61    *Ibid.*, p. 18. See also Schiffner's detailed study of the Arnstadt court *Kapelle* (M. Schiffner, 'Die Arnstädter Hofkapelle – regionales Zentrum der Musikpflege im historischen und zeitgenössischen Umfeld des jungen Bach', *BzBF* 6 (1988), pp. 37–53), which touches on Bach only briefly.

62    Boyd, who believes that Bach must have known something of the library's contents, notes that by 1696 the collection contained some 1,100 manuscripts by approximately 175 different composers and a large number of prints. Included were 'Latin polyphony by Lassus, Monteverdi, Carissimi, Rovetta and others, and sacred works by the greatest German masters of the seventeenth century: Buxtehude, Hammerschmidt, Kerll, Scheidt, Schein, Schütz, Tunder etc.', as well as works by two of Bach's relatives (his great-uncle, Heinrich, and his uncle, Johann Christoph) and Georg Böhm, organist at the Johanniskirche in Lüneburg. See Boyd, *Bach*, pp. 12–13.

63    M. Petzoldt, '"Ut probus & doctus reddar". Zum Anteil der Theologie bei der Schulausbildung Johann Sebastian Bachs in Eisenach, Ohrdruf und Lüneburg', *BJb* 71 (1985), pp. 7–42.

64    G. Fock, *Der junge Bach in Lüneburg. 1700 bis 1702* (Hamburg, 1950).

65    E. Chafe, *Tonal allegory in the vocal music of J. S. Bach* (Berkeley, 1991), pp. 91–123 (quotation on p. 123).

66    *Ibid.*, p. 121.

67    R. L. Marshall, 'Organ or "Klavier"? Instrumental prescriptions in the sources of the keyboard works', *The music of Johann Sebastian Bach: the sources, the style, the significance* (New York, 1989), pp. 271–93, especially p. 283. This essay originally appeared in Stauffer and May, eds., *J. S. Bach as organist*, pp. 193–211.

68    Wolff, 'The identity of the "Fratro Dilettissimo"', pp. 154–5.

69    The research for this essay was completed with the support of a Fellowship for University Teachers from the National Endowment for the Humanities.

## 7  *The mature vocal works and their theological and liturgical context*

1    *Leipziger Allgemeine musikalische Zeitung*, July 1818; facsimile in *NBA* II/1 *KB*, p. 215.

2    *BR*, p. 383.

3    R. L. Marshall, 'On Bach's universality', *The universal Bach: lectures celebrating the tercentenary of Bach's birthday* (Philadelphia, 1986), pp. 50–66; also in R. L. Marshall, *The music of Johann Sebastian Bach: the sources, the style, the significance* (New York, 1989), pp. 65–79, here pp. 68–69. On the homiletic character of Bach's vocal music, see also R. A. Leaver, *J. S. Bach as preacher: his Passions and music in worship* (St Louis, 1984); W. Böhme, ed., *Johann Sebastian Bach Prediger in Tönen* (Karlsruhe, 1985); and Chapter 3 of this volume.

4    See Chapter 3. Some additional and corrective information is found in M. Petzoldt and J. Petri, *Johann Sebastian Bach Ehre sei dir Gott gesungen. Bilder und Texte zu Bachs Leben als Christ und seinem Wirken für die Kirche* (Göttingen, 1988), but there is the need for a new study that re-examines the source material in the light of Bach research over the past thirty years. A useful summary of liturgical forms of Bach's time can be found in P. Williams, *The organ music of J. S. Bach*, 3 vols. (Cambridge, 1980–4), vol. III, *A background*, pp. 1–15.

5    See Chapter 3, pp. 42–5, for Luther's liturgies, and P. Graff, *Geschichte der Auflösung der alten gottesdienstlichen Formen in der evangelischen Kirche Deutschlands*, 2 vols. (Göttingen, 1937–9), for an account of the decline of liturgical forms within Lutheranism.

6    *Dok* III, p. 86; *BR* p. 221.

7    See Chapter 3, note 14.

8    *Dok* I, pp. 248–9, 251.

9    See Chapter 3, notes 44–5.

10   The *Leipziger Kirchen-Staat* (1710) indicates that from time to time there was concerted music 'after the sermon' immediately before the *Verba Institutionis* (see W. Herbst, ed., *Evangelischer Gottesdienst. Quellen zur seiner Geschichte* (Göttingen, 1992), p. 147). This should not be misinterpreted as meaning that the second part of a two-part cantata was sung at this juncture: the reference is clearly to a concerted setting of the Sanctus.

11   See the excellent survey article by H.-J. Schulze, 'The parody process in Bach's music: an old problem reconsidered', *BACH* 20 (1989), pp. 7–21; W. Neumann, 'Über Ausmaß und Wesen des Bachschen Parodieverfahrens', *BJb* 51 (1965), pp. 63–85. K. Häfner, *Aspekte des Parodieverfahrens bei Johann Sebastian Bachs. Beiträge zur Wiederentdeckung verschollener Vokalwerke* (Laaber, 1987) is a conjectural and overstated consideration of Bach's use of parody; see the review by H.-J. Schulze, *BJb* 76 (1990), pp. 92–4.

12   P. Spitta, *Johann Sebastian Bach: his work and influence on the music of Germany, 1685–1750*, trans. C. Bell and J. A. Fuller-Maitland, 3 vols. (1889; reprinted New York, 1951), vol. II, pp. 576–7; see also vol. I, p. 569.

13   L. Schrade, 'Bach: the conflict between the sacred and the secular', *Journal of the History of Ideas* 7 (1946), pp. 151–94; see also J. Pelikan, *Bach among the theologians* (Philadelphia, 1986), pp. 130–40.

14   See O. Söhngen, *Theologie der Musik* (Kassel, 1967); G. Stiller, *Johann Sebastian Bach and liturgical life in Leipzig*, ed. R. A. Leaver (St Louis, 1984),

p. 149; C. Wolff, *Der stile antico in der Musik Johann Sebastian Bachs. Studien zu Bachs Spätwerk* (Wiesbaden, 1968), p. 9.

15  See W. Neumann, *Handbuch der Kantaten Joh. Seb. Bachs*, 5th edn (Wiesbaden, 1984); and A. Dürr, *Die Kantaten von Johann Sebastian Bach*, 5th edn (Kassel, 1985) for the most reliable treatment.

16  Two other works are given the designation 'Oratorio' following the example of the Christmas Oratorio: *Oratorium Festo Paschatos*, the Easter Oratorio (BWV 249), originally written in 1725 as a cantata for Easter Day but not titled *Oratorium* until sometime around 1738; and *Oratorium Festo Ascensionis Christi*, the Ascension Oratorio (BWV 11), which includes a number of parodied movements, first performed on 19 May 1735.

17  Basic literature includes: R. Steiger, 'Die Einheit des Weihnachtsoratorium von J. S. Bach', *MuK* 51 (1981), pp. 273–80 and 52 (1982), pp. 9–15; W. Blankenburg, *Das Weihnachts-Oratorium von Johann Sebastian Bach* (Kassel, 1982).

18  See the facsimile in W. Neumann, *Sämtliche von Johann Sebastian Bach vertonte Texte* (Leipzig, 1974), pp. 448–55.

19  See E. Chafe, '"Hercules auf dem Scheidewege" and the Christmas Oratorio', *Tonal allegory in the vocal music of J. S. Bach* (Berkeley, 1991), pp. 255–73.

20  *Dok* II, p. 241.

21  See further, E. Koch, 'Tröstendes Echo. Zur theologischen Deutung der Echo-Arie im IV. Teil des Weihnachts-Oratoriums von Johann Sebastian Bach', *BJb* 75 (1989), pp. 203–11; R. Steiger, '"Fallt mit Danken, fallt mit Loben Vor des Höchsten Gnaden-Thron". Zum IV. Teil des Weihnachts-Oratoriums von Johann Sebastian Bach', *Ars et musica in liturgia: celebratory volume presented to Casper Honders on the occasion of his seventieth birthday*, ed. F. Brouwer and R. A. Leaver (Utrecht, 1993), pp. 198–211.

22  See O. von Holst, 'Turba Chöre des Weihnachts-Oratoriums und der Markuspassion', *MuK* 38 (1968), pp. 229–33.

23  That the melody had primary passion associations is evident from Bach's use of its opening melodic line, repeated six times, in the basso continuo of the opening movement of Cantata 127, written for *Estomihi*, the Sunday before Lent, which was celebrated at that time as a kind of Passion Sunday. Significantly this first movement of Cantata 127 was later used in the *Passionspasticcio*, incorporating the music of Telemann and others, as the opening movement of the second part, following Part I which had ended with the same 'Passion Chorale' melody; see J. W. Grubbs, 'Ein Passions-Pasticcio des 18. Jahrhunderts', *BJb* 51 (1965), pp. 10–42, especially pp. 25–6. On the connections between *Estomihi* cantatas and Good Friday performances of passion music, see L. Steiger and R. Steiger, *Sehet! Wir gehn hinauf gen Jerusalem. Johann Sebastian Bachs Kantaten auf den Sonntag Estomihi* (Göttingen, 1992), *passim*, especially pp. 136–41.

24  Such connections between Incarnation and Atonement may support the hypothesis of von Holst (see note 22 above), since Bach may have deliberately chosen to parody the *turbae* choruses from the Mark Passion in the *Christmas Oratorio* as much for theological as musical reasons.

25   G. Vopelius, *Neu Leipziger Gesangbuch* (Leipzig, 1682), pp. 179ff. and 227ff. respectively.

26   See A. Glöckner, 'Bach and the Passion music of his contemporaries', *MT* 116 (1975), pp. 613–16; and 'Johann Sebastian Bachs Aufführungen zeitgenössischer Passionsmusiken', *BJb* 63 (1977), pp. 75–119.

27   BWV 246a; see Y. Kobayashi, 'Zu einem neu entdeckten Autograph Bachs. Choral: Aus der Tiefen', *BJb* 57 (1971), pp. 5–12; see also Glöckner, 'Johann Sebastian Bachs Aufführungen', pp. 91–9, 108.

28   See Glöckner, 'Johann Sebastian Bachs Aufführungen', p. 91.

29   Arthur Mendel leaves open the possibility that parts of the work had been prepared in earlier years; see *NBA* II/4 *KB* (1974), p. 67, n. 1, and the article cited in the following note. Don Franklin has more recently speculated that there might have been at least an earlier form of the 1724 John Passion, perhaps even two; see D. O. Franklin, 'The libretto of Bach's John Passion and the doctrine of reconciliation: an historical perspective', *Das Blut Jesu und die Lehre von der Versöhnung im Werk Johann Sebastian Bachs*, ed. A. A. Clement (Amsterdam, 1995), pp. 179–203.

30   See A. Mendel, 'Traces of the pre-history of Bach's St John and St Matthew Passions', *Festschrift Otto Erich Deutsch zum 80. Geburtstag*, ed. W. Gerstenberg et al. (Kassel, 1963), pp. 31–48.

31   F. Smend, 'Die Johannes-Passion von Bach. Auf ihren Bau untersucht', *BJb* 23 (1926), pp. 105–28; reprinted in F. Smend, *Bach-Studien. Gesammelte Reden und Aufsätze*, ed. C. Wolff (Kassel, 1969), pp. 11–23.

32   Smend's analysis has been generally accepted, though sometimes slightly modified, and used to interpret other parts of the Passion: see, for example, R. A. Leaver, *J. S. Bach and Scripture: glosses from the Calov Bible Commentary* (St Louis, 1985), pp. 131–5; E. Chafe, *Tonal allegory*, pp. 307–15, especially p. 312; see also W. Breig, 'Bemerkungen zur zyklischen Symmetrie in Bachs Leipziger Kirchenmusik', *MuK* 53 (1983), pp. 173–9.

33   Based on Smend, *Bach-Studien*, p. 22, but with movement numbers changed to those of *NBA*.

34   See Mendel *NBA* II/4 *KB*, pp. 163–4.

35   The term 'Gnadenthron', used here, or its equivalent 'Gnadenstuhl', itself conceptualises an image of the crucifixion; see H. Werthemann, 'Jesus Christus, vorgestellt zu einem Gnadenstuhl durch den Glauben in seinem Blut. Der Sühnedeckel der alttestamentlichen Bundeslade und seine Erfüllung in Christus', *Das Blut Jesu*, ed. Clement, pp. 63–78.

36   See further discussions such as: A. Dürr, *Die Johannes-Passion von Johann Sebastian Bach. Entstehung, Überlieferung, Werkeinführung* (Munich and Kassel, 1988), and Chafe, *Tonal allegory*, pp. 275–335.

37   See J. Rifkin, 'The chronology of Bach's Saint Matthew Passion', *MQ* 61 (1975), pp. 360–87.

38   E. Chafe, 'J. S. Bach's St. Matthew Passion: aspects of planning, structure, and chronology', *JAMS* 35 (1982), pp. 49–114, especially pp. 104–7.

39   *Ibid.*, p. 111. Such a connection was actually made between Cantata 127 and

the second version of the John Passion in 1725 with Bach's use of *Christe, du Lamm Gottes* in the first movement of the cantata and in the last movement of the passion; see R. A. Leaver, 'Bach and the German Agnus Dei', *A Bach tribute: essays in honor of William H. Scheide*, ed. P. Brainard and R. Robinson (Kassel, 1993), pp. 163–71.

40   Chafe, 'J. S. Bach's St. Matthew Passion', p. 110.

41   See F. Smend, *NBA* II/1 *KB* (1956), pp. 172–3 and 225.

42   Rifkin, 'Chronology of Bach's Saint Matthew Passion', p. 361, note 6.

43   Rifkin's conclusion is based on Bach's known technique of composing cantatas sequentially, in order of the movements. Chafe, while accepting 1727 as the year of the first performance of the Matthew Passion, thinks it unlikely that Bach would have composed such a complex work in a strict linear progression; see Chafe, 'J. S. Bach's St. Matthew Passion', p. 50.

44   The complete 1725 passion libretto is found in P. Spitta, *Johann Sebastian Bach*, 2 vols. (German version only; Wiesbaden, 1964), vol. II, pp. 873–81. See also Chafe, 'J. S. Bach's St. Matthew Passion', pp. 55–7; E. Axmacher, '*Aus Liebe will mein Heyland sterben*'. *Untersuchungen zum Wandel des Passionsverständnisses im frühen 18. Jahrhundert* (Neuhausen-Stuttgart, 1984), pp. 166–9.

45   E. Axmacher, 'Eine Quellenfund zum Text der Matthäus-Passion', *BJb* 64 (1978), pp. 181–91; Axmacher, '*Aus Liebe will mein Heyland sterben*', pp. 170–96; E. Axmacher, 'Die Deutung der Passion Jesu im Text der Matthäus-Passion von J. S. Bach', *Luther: Zeitschrift der Luther-Gesellschaft* 56 (1985), pp. 49–69.

46   See R. A. Leaver, *Bachs theologische Bibliothek; eine kritische Bibliographie / Bach's theological library; a critical bibliography* (Neuhausen-Stuttgart, 1983), No. 19. After Luther and the orthodox theologian August Pfeiffer, Müller was Bach's next preferred author — in his library there were four other titles by Müller; Leaver, *Bachs theologische Bibliothek*, Nos. 8, 20, 41 and 42.

47   The libretto, which appeared without the biblical narrative and most of the chorales, is given in facsimile in Neumann, *Johann Sebastian Bach vertonte Texte*, pp. 321–4.

48   See *Dok* II, pp. 190–1.

49   This is given in facsimile in Neumann, *Johann Sebastian Bach vertonte Texte*, pp. 398–401. The libretto was later reprinted in Picander's third collection of libretti, *Ernst-Schertzhaffte und Satyrische Gedichte, Dritter Theil* (Leipzig, 1732); given in facsimile in Neumann, *Johann Sebastian Bach vertonte Texte*, pp. 344–5. Smend discovered a manuscript copy of the libretto, containing several significant variants, which is probably the earliest form; see F. Smend, *Bach in Köthen* (Berlin, 1951), pp. 209–19.

50   See A. Schering, 'Kleine Bachstudien', *BJb* 30 (1933), p. 37, and 'Zur Markus-Passion und zur "vierten" Passion', *BJb* 36 (1939), p. 5.

51   See D. Gojowy, 'Zur Frage der Köthener Trauermusik und der Matthäuspassion', *BJb* 51 (1965), pp. 86–134.

52    See P. Brainard, 'Bach's parody procedure and the St. Matthew Passion', *JAMS* 22 (1969), pp. 241–60; H. Streck, *Die Verskunst in den poetischen Texten zu den Kantaten J. S. Bachs* (Hamburg, 1971), pp. 132–53; Rifkin, 'Chronology of Bach's Saint Matthew Passion', pp. 376–82.

53    In between the two items is the Prayer of Manasseh, but since this is a prayer of confession, it is clearly intended as an appendix to Luther's sermon; see the facsimile, ed. F. Schulz (Kassel, 1982).

54    It is found in Picander's *Ernst-Schertzhaffte und Satyrische Gedichte, Dritter Theil*; given in facsimile in Neumann, *Johann Sebastian Bach vertonte Texte*, pp. 326–32.

55    F. Smend, 'Bachs Markus-Passion', *BJb* 37 (1940–8), pp. 1–35, reprinted in Smend, *Bach-Studien*, pp. 110–36; and A. Dürr, 'Bachs Trauer-Ode und Markus-Passion', *NZM* 124 (1963), pp. 459–66. In addition to the parodied movements from BWV 198, the first movement of Cantata 54 was also re-worked for the passion. More recently, various editors have suggested that movements from BWV 7, 120a, 204, 234, as well as the bass aria 'Himmel reiße', composed for the second version of the John Passion in 1725 but later excluded, may also have been parodied in the Mark Passion.

56    F. Smend, 'Bachs Matthäus-Passion: Untersuchungen zur Geschichte des Werkes bis 1750', *BJb* 25 (1928), pp. 1–95; reprinted in Smend, *Bach-Studien*, pp. 24–83; but compare the more detailed discussion in Chafe, *Tonal allegory*, pp. 337–423.

57    Based on Smend, *Bach-Studien*, p. 44, with *NBA* movement numbers.

58    See, for example, A. Dürr, in *NBA* II/3 *KB* (1955), p. 7.

59    R. M. Cammarota, 'The repertoire of Magnificats in Leipzig at the time of J. S. Bach: a study of the manuscript sources' (Ph.D. dissertation, New York University, 1986), p. 96.

60    *Ibid.*, p. 240.

61    In incorporating these Christmas interpolations Bach was following Leipzig tradition, as did his predecessor Kuhnau; see R. M. Cammarota, 'The sources of the Christmas interpolations in J. S. Bach's Magnificat in E-flat major (BWV 243a)', *CM* 36 (1983), pp. 79–99; see also Cammarota, 'Magnificats in Leipzig', pp. 297–341.

62    See R. L. Marshall, 'On the origin of Bach's Magnificat: a Lutheran composer's challenge', *Bach studies*, ed. D. O. Franklin (Cambridge, 1989), pp. 3–17, also in R. L. Marshall, *The music of Johann Sebastian Bach*, pp. 161–73, especially pp. 168–9.

63    See Cammarota, 'Magnificats in Leipzig', p. 325. The bipartite structure of the early version of the Magnificat may mean that the sermon at Christmas Vespers, 1723, was preached after 'Fecit potentiam' and before 'Gloria in excelsis Deo'.

64    Vopelius, *Neu Leipziger Gesangbuch*, 1084–5, 1092–8; see J. Grimm, *Das 'Neu Leipziger Gesangbuch' des Gottfried Vopelius (Leipzig, 1682). Untersuchungen zur Klärung seiner geschichtlichen Stellung* (Berlin, 1969), pp. 97–8.

65    R. L. Marshall, 'Beobachtungen am Autograph der h-moll-Messe. Zum

Kompositionsprozess', *MuK* 50 (1980), pp. 230–9; English trans., 'The Mass in B Minor: the autograph scores and the compositional process', in Marshall, *Music of Johann Sebastian Bach*, pp. 175–89, especially pp. 175–6.

66   C. Wolff, 'Zur musikalischen Vorgeschichte des Kyrie aus Johann Sebastian Bachs Messe in h-Moll', *Festschrift für Bruno Stäblein zum 70. Geburtstag*, ed. M. Ruhnke (Kassel, 1967), pp. 316–26; English translation by A. Mann, 'Origins of the Kyrie of the Kyrie of the B Minor Mass', in C. Wolff, *Bach: essays on his life and music* (Cambridge, Mass., 1991), pp. 141–51.

67   Vopelius, *Neu Leipziger Gesangbuch*, pp. 421–3; see Grimm, *Das 'Neu Leipziger Gesangbuch'* , p. 65.

68   Recent literature includes: E. Platen and M. Helms, *NBA* II/2 *KB* (1982); A. Mann, '"Missa Brevis" and "Historia": Bach's A Major Mass', *BACH* 16/1 (1985), pp. 6–11; R. A. Leaver, 'Parody and theological consistency: notes on Bach's A-Major Mass', *BACH* 21/3 (1990), pp. 30–43.

69   In chronological order the cantatas are: BWV 136, 179, 138, 40, 67, 79, 187, 102, 17 and 72.

70   The present author has suggested that it may have been an *Estomihi* cantata (see Leaver, 'Bach and the German Agnus Dei', p. 170). But if Hofmann's recent reconstruction of the chronology of Bach's cantatas in Weimar (BWV 233a appears to have originated in Weimar) is correct, Bach did not have occasion to compose an *Estomihi* cantata at the Weimar court; see K. Hofmann, 'Neue Überlegungen zu Bachs Weimarer Kantaten-Kalender', *BJb* 79 (1993), pp. 9–29.

71   Important recent literature includes: W. Blankenburg, *Einführung in Bachs h-Moll-Messe BWV 232* (Kassel, 1974; reprinted 1986); H. Rilling, *Johann Sebastian Bach's B-minor Mass* (Princeton, 1984), a translation of the German edition (1979), which has been subsequently revised and expanded (Stuttgart, 1986); J. Butt, *Bach: Mass in B Minor* (Cambridge, 1991) includes a bibliography of important recent articles.

72   See G. G. Butler, 'Johann Sebastian Bachs Gloria in excelsis Deo BWV 191. Musik für ein Leipziger Dankfest', *BJb* 78 (1992), pp. 65–71.

73   This discovery is the subject of a paper by Peter Wollny, 'Ein Quellenfund zur Entstehungsgeschichte der h-Moll-Messe', *BJb* 80 (1994), pp. 163–9.

74   Rifkin (review in *Notes* 44 (June 1988), p. 789) had already come to this conclusion before the existence of the Agricola manuscript was known.

75   The movement made a strong and lasting impact on Agricola. At the end of his life the former student of Bach made reference to it, in a posthumously published book review: 'From recent times . . . there is a setting of the words *Credo in unum Deum*, from a great Mass by the blessed J. S. Bach, with eight obbligato parts, namely, 5 vocal parts, two violins, and Generalbass . . .'; *Allgemeine deutsche Bibliothek* (Berlin) 25/1 (1775), p. 108; *Dok* III, p. 294.

76   See A. Dürr, 'Zur Chronologie der Handschrift Johann Christoph Altnickols und Johann Friedrich Agricolas', *BJb* 56 (1970), pp. 44–63.

77   Y. Kobayashi, 'Zur Chronologie der Spätwerke Johann Sebastian Bachs. Kompositions- und Aufführungstätigkeit von 1736 bis 1750', *BJb* 74 (1988), pp. 7–72.

78   The sections on the Creed of Luther's Small and Large Catechisms are given in *The Book of Concord: the confessions of the Evangelical Lutheran Church*, trans. and ed. T. G. Tappert (Philadelphia, 1959), pp. 344–5 and 411–20 respectively.

79   Eric Chafe has proposed a different, 'audible' structure; see E. T. Chafe, 'The St John Passion: theology and musical structure', *Bach studies*, ed. D. O. Franklin (Cambridge, 1989), pp. 75–112, p. 92, note 37. He suggests that Bach adopted an asymmetrical tripartite structure – following Luther's expositions of the Creed in his catechisms – by creating a 2 + 4 + 3 grouping of movements. While Chafe is perceptive in drawing attention to the influence of Luther's catechetical exposition of the Creed, this influence was more likely to have been on the original ground-plan rather than the later modification. If the original eight movements were patterned after Luther's expositions of the Creed, in a 2 + 3 + 3 structure, the 'Crucifixus' and 'Confiteor' form the central movements of the second and third articles of the Creed. Perhaps it was just this asymmetricality that caused Bach to modify the structure of the *Symbolum Nicenum*. Thus by creating the new 'Et incarnatus est' movement, the overall structure became Trinitarian (9 = 3 × 3), and the centrepoint of the second article of the Creed remained the 'Crucifixus', which now became the centre of gravity of the entire *Symbolum Nicenum*. Although Chafe argues persuasively that his solution is 'dynamic' in contrast to the 'more abstract' symmetrical structure, such chiastic relationships nevertheless appear to have been an important element in Bach's compositional process.

80   Ratswahl (lit. 'council election') cantatas were written to celebrate changes of the town council. Bach probably used this cantata as his model, though it is theoretically possible for him to have used the earlier manifestations of the music in BWV 120a and BWV 120b, of which the former is incomplete and the latter is lost.

81   See Grimm, *Das 'Neu Leipziger Gesangbuch'*, pp. 97–8.

82   The 'Sanctus' and 'Agnus Dei' both have a threefold content.

83   The same music was used again for the first movement for another congratulatory cantata for August of Saxony: *Preise dein Glücke, gesegnetes Sachsen* (BWV 215), performed on 5 October 1734.

84   Y. Kobayashi, 'Die Universalität in Bachs h-moll-Messe. Eine Beitrag zum Bach-Bild der letzten Lebensjahr', *MuK* 57 (1987), pp. 9–24, especially p. 19; English trans. by J. W. Baxter, 'Universality in Bach's B Minor Mass: a portrait of Bach in his final years', *BACH* 24/2 (1993), pp. 3–25, especially pp. 17–19. It is on this kind of evidence that Dürr argues against the tendency to see parodies everywhere in Bach's later works; see A. Dürr, *Johann Sebastian Bach. Seine Handschrift. Abbild seines Schaffens* (Wiesbaden, 1984), pp. 46–8, 72, and 'Schriftcharakter und Werkchronologie bei Johann Sebastian Bach', *Bericht über die Wissenschaftliche Konferenz zum V. Internationalen Bachfest der DDR in Verbindung mit dem 60. Bachfest der Neuen Bachgesellschaft* (1985), ed. W. Hoffmann and A. Scheiderheinze (Leipzig, 1988), pp. 283–9.

85   See C. Wolff, 'The Agnus Dei of the B Minor Mass: parody and new
composition reconciled', in Wolff, *Bach: essays on his life and music*, pp. 332–9;
R. A. Leaver, '*Agnus Dei* compositions of J. S. Bach: some liturgical and
theological perspectives', *Das Blut Jesu*, ed. Clement, pp. 233–49.

## 8  The instrumental music

1   On the history of this term, see E. Reimer's article 'Kammermusik' in
*Handwörterbuch der musikalischen Terminologie* (1971).

2   Dok II, p. 93; *BR*, p. 89.

3   See the entry on 'Chamber music' in *The new Harvard dictionary of music*, ed.
D. M. Randel (Cambridge, Mass., 1986), p. 146.

4   On the history of this term, see M. Staehelin's article 'Orchester' in
*Handwörterbuch der musikalischen Terminologie* (1981).

5   Quoted by H. Becker in his article, 'Orchester', in *MGG*, vol. X, col. 173.

6   As with all other areas of Bach's creative activities, this repertory has no
clearly defined boundaries: there is a whole series of works whose
authenticity is not universally acknowledged. In order not to extend the
discussion unduly, we shall accept the findings reflected in the most
recent list of Bach's works, namely, the German edition of Christoph
Wolff's *New Grove* article (C. Wolff et al., *Die Bach-Familie* (Stuttgart and
Weimar, 1993)). The trio sonata from *The Musical Offering* BWV 1079 is also
included in the present table since it belongs here generically, even though all
lists and editions of Bach's works place it in the context of the original edition
of 1747.

7   The question of the reconstruction of lost works on the basis of transcriptions
has been discussed in various contexts in writings on Bach; see, for example,
U. Siegele, *Kompositionsweise und Bearbeitungstechnik in der
Instrumentalmusik J. S. Bachs* (dissertation, University of Tübingen, 1957);
published as Tübinger Beiträge zur Musikwissenschaft, vol. III (Stuttgart,
1975); W. Fischer, *NBA* VII/7 *KB*; W. Breig, 'Bachs Violinkonzert d-moll.
Studien zu seiner Gestalt und seiner Entstehungsgeschichte', *BJb* 62 (1976),
pp. 7–34; and W. Breig, 'Zur Gestalt von Johann Sebastian Bachs Konzert für
Oboe d'amore', *Tibia* 18 (1993), pp. 431–48.

8   Under this criterion, the first Brandenburg Concerto, too, would come under
the heading of 'orchestral music'.

9   *BC*, I/1 (Leipzig, 1985), p. 13. The volumes dealing with the instrumental
music have yet to appear.

10  The pieces in question are the Polacca from the first Brandenburg Concerto
and the Air from the Orchestral Suite BWV 1068; but see below for a
discussion of the forces used in the latter.

11  For two recent controversial articles on this subject, see H.-J. Schulze, 'Johann
Sebastian Bach's orchestra: some unanswered questions', *EM* 17 (1989),
pp. 3–15; and J. Rifkin, 'More (and less) on Bach's orchestra', *Performance
Practice Review* 4 (1991), pp. 5–13.

12    K. Hofmann, 'Überlegungen zum Aufbau Bachscher Suiten- und Sonatensammlungen', *Johann Sebastian Bach. Schaffenskonzeption, Werkidee, Textbezug*, ed. W. Felix, A. Schneiderheinze and H.-J. Schulze; *BzBF* 9/10 (Leipzig, 1991), pp. 85–94, especially pp. 93–4.

13    E. Kurth, *Grundlagen des linearen Kontrapunkts. Einführung in Stil und Technik von Bachs melodischer Polyphonie* (Berne, 1917), p. 260.

14    The most detailed examination of this particular group of works may be found in Hans Eppstein's authoritative *Studien über J. S. Bachs Sonaten für ein Melodieinstrument und obligates Cembalo*, Studia musicologica Upsaliensia (new series) II (Uppsala, 1966).

15    Of these, the authenticity of BWV 1031 has often been called into question.

16    See Hans Eppstein's study 'Zur Problematik von J. S. Bachs Sonate für Violine und Cembalo G-dur (BWV 1019)', *AfMw* 21 (1964), pp. 217–42.

17    The movements concerned are BWV 1014/1, 1016/1, 1016/3, 1018/1, 1018/3 and 1019/2. That it is also possible to speak of independent functions of the obbligato keyboard in other cases, too, has been amply demonstrated by Eppstein, *Studien über J. S. Bachs Sonaten*, pp. 33–44.

18    C. Wolff, 'Bach's Leipzig chamber music', *EM* 13 (1985), pp. 165–75, especially p. 166.

19    P. Spitta, *Johann Sebastian Bach*, 2 vols. (Leipzig, 1873–80; reprinted Darmstadt, 1979), vol. I, p. 730; trans. C. Bell and J. A. Fuller-Maitland as *Johann Sebastian Bach: his work and influence on the music of Germany*, 3 vols. (1889; reprinted New York, 1951), vol. II, p. 122.

20    Eppstein, *Studien über J. S. Bachs Sonaten*, p. 89.

21    The fact that these concertos have been excluded from the present discussion should not be taken to imply a belittlement of the creative effort that led to their later versions for harpsichord (see Chapter 10 below). Their exclusion is simply intended to avoid distorting the statistics.

22    *BC* lists the movement under A 193; it is discussed at greater length by Ralph Leavis in his article 'Zur Authentizität von Bachs Violinkonzert d-moll', *BJb* 65 (1979), pp. 25–7.

23    The classification 'BWV 1059' represents the hypothetical oboe concerto that Bach must have had in front of him when he began his transcription, only to break off again after nine bars; this hypothetical model can be reconstructed from the first and fifth movements of Cantata 35 and the first movement of Cantata 156; see J. Rifkin, 'Ein langsamer Konzertsatz Johann Sebastian Bachs, *BJb* 64 (1978), pp. 140–7, and W. Breig, 'Bachs Cembalokonzert-Fragment in d-Moll (BWV 1059)', *BJb* 65 (1979), pp. 29–36.

24    K. Heller, *Antonio Vivaldi* (Leipzig, 1991), p. 358.

25    Exceptions to the basic three-movement type are the first and third Brandenburg Concertos; in its first version as the Sinfonia BWV 1046a, no. 1 was originally in three movements (ending with a multisectional dance movement); in its Brandenburg version, a further movement was inserted after the second movement. In no. 3, the middle movement has been reduced to a mere cadence. For a recent study of ritornello form, see M. Boyd, *Bach: the Brandenburg Concertos* (Cambridge, 1993), pp. 45–58.

26   Doubts have recently been thrown on the oft-repeated assertion that the Sinfonia BWV 1046 belongs with the hunting cantata BWV 208; see M. Marissen, 'On linking Bach's F-Major Sinfonia and his Hunt Cantata', *BACH* 23/2 (1992), pp. 31–46.

27   BWV 1041/1, 1043/3, 1046/1+3, 1047/1, 1048/1, 1050/1, 1051/1+3, 1055/1+3, 1056/1+3, 1059/1, 1060/1+3, 1063/1, 1064/1.

28   BWV 1050/2.

29   BWV 1042/1, 1049/1, 1051/3 and 1053/1+3.

30   BWV 1041/3, 1043/1, 1047/3, 1049/3, 1050/3, 1063/3 and 1064/5.

31   BWV 1046/4, 1048/3 and 1059/3.

32   BWV 1042/3.

33   See W. Breig, 'Das Ostinato-Prinzip in Johann Sebastian Bachs langsamen Konzertsätzen', *Von Isaac bis Bach. Studien zur älteren deutschen Musikgeschichte (Festschrift Martin Just zum 60. Geburtstag)*, ed. F. Heidlberger, W. Osthoff and R. Wiesend (Kassel, 1991), pp. 287–300.

34   BWV 1041/2, 1042/2, 1052/2, 1055/2 and 1064/2.

35   BWV 1049/2, 1053/3, 1056/3, 1059/2 and 1063/2.

36   BWV 1043/2, 1046/2, 1047/2, 1051/2 and 1060/2.

37   The middle movement of BWV 1050 has already been mentioned as an exception.

38   See M. Marissen, 'J. S. Bach's Brandenburg Concertos as a meaningful set', *MQ* 77 (1993), pp. 193–235, and *The social and religious designs of J. S. Bach's Brandenburg Concertos* (Princeton, 1995).

39   See W. Breig, 'Zum Kompositionsprozeß in Bachs Cembalokonzerten', *Johann Sebastian Bachs Spätwerk und dessen Umfeld. 61. Bachfest der Neuen Bachgesellschaft Duisburg 1986*, ed. C. Wolff (Kassel, 1988), pp. 32–47.

40   Johann Adolph Scheibe, *Der critische Musikus*, no. 73 (19 January 1740), (Leipzig, 1745; reprinted Wiesbaden, 1970), pp. 669–70.

41   On the fanfare theme and related figures in Bach's works, see K. Hofmann, '"Großer Herr, o starker König": Ein Fanfarenthema bei Bach' (in preparation). I am grateful to Klaus Hofmann for allowing me to see a copy of this article in typescript.

42   For an interesting hypothesis concerning the genesis of this piece, see I. Godt, 'Politics, patriotism, and a Polonaise: a possible revision in Bach's *Suite in B Minor*', *MQ* 74 (1990), pp. 610–22.

43   See my earlier remarks on the Flute Sonata BWV 1030.


## 9 *The keyboard works: Bach as teacher and virtuoso*

1   *Dok* II, p. 231; *BR*, p. 46.

2   H.-J. Schulze gives biographical details in *BJb* 71 (1985), pp. 55–81.

3   Letter of 13 January 1775, *Dok* III, p. 288; *BR*, p. 278.

4   In his letter of 13 January 1775 to Forkel, C. P. E. Bach initially wrote of his father's 'teacher Böhm', then crossed out these words and substituted 'the Lüneburg organist Böhm' (see *BR*, p. 278); this might suggest that the son distorted the record somewhat, in order to portray his father as a self-taught

genius. See C. Wolff, 'Bach and Johann Adam Reinken: a context for the early works', *Bach: essays on his life and music* (Cambridge, Mass., 1991), pp. 56–7.

5  Quoted from the Bach Obituary, *Dok* III, p. 81; *BR*, p. 216.

6  *Dok* III, p. 82; *BR*, p. 217.

7  J. N. Forkel, *Über J. S. Bachs Leben, Kunst und Kunstwerke* (Leipzig, 1802); quotation from the English trans. (London, 1820), reprinted in *BR*, pp. 293–356; see p. 317.

8  Forkel (*ibid.*) links this search for order with the influence of Vivaldi, but it surely dates from long before the Vivaldi transcriptions of 1713–14.

9  Told in the Bach Obituary, *Dok* III, pp. 81–2; *BR*, pp. 216–17.

10  Some idea of its contents can be gained from the 1692 tablature book of the Pachelbel pupil J. V. Eckelt; see, *inter alia*, R. S. Hill, '"Der Himmel weiss, wo diese Sachen hingekommen sind": reconstructing the lost keyboard notebooks of the young Bach and Handel', *Bach, Handel, Scarlatti: tercentenary essays*, ed. P. Williams (Cambridge, 1985), pp. 161–72.

11  *Dok* III, p. 82; *BR*, p. 217.

12  See H.-J. Schulze, *Studien zur Bach-Überlieferung im 18. Jahrhundert* (Leipzig and Dresden, 1984), pp. 30–56, and R. S. Hill, 'The Möller Manuscript and the Andreas Bach Book', 2 vols. (Ph.D. dissertation, Harvard University, 1987).

13  Letter to Forkel of 13 January 1775, *Dok* III, p. 288; *BR*, p. 278.

14  *Ibid.*, *Dok* III, p. 289; *BR*, p. 278.

15  However, like other German organists of his time, Bach improvised fugues as well as free fantasias. The fugue attached to the Chromatic Fantasia BWV 903/2 and the Ricercar a 3 from *The Musical Offering* BWV 1079 are probably examples of fugues based upon improvisation.

16  In particular, BWV 535a, BWV Anh. 205/Anh. II 45 and the last three bars of BWV 921.

17  See R. S. Hill, '*Echtheit angezweifelt*: style and authenticity in two suites attributed to Bach', *EM* 13 (1985), pp. 248–55.

18  BWV 967 has long been regarded as a keyboard transcription, but a different view is taken by R. S. Hill, 'The Möller Manuscript', pp. 448–58.

19  See C. P. E. Bach's letter to Forkel of 20 September 1775, *Dok* III, p. 292.

20  Letter to Forkel of 13 January 1775, *Dok* III, p. 288; *BR*, p. 278.

21  See I. Sumikura, 'Johann Sebastian Bach und Johann Kaspar Ferdinand Fischer', *Bericht über die Wissenschaftliche Konferenz zum III. Internationalen Bach-Fest der DDR Leipzig, 18./19. September 1975*, ed. W. Felix, W. Hoffmann and A. Schneiderheinze (Leipzig, 1977), pp. 233–8.

22  See H.-J. Schulze, 'The French influence in Bach's instrumental music', *EM* 13 (1985), pp. 180–4, and C. Wolff, 'Bach und die italienische Musik', *Bachtage Berlin. Vorträge 1970 bis 1981*, ed. G. Wagner (Neuhausen-Stuttgart, 1985), pp. 225–33.

23  *Dok* III, p. 82; *BR*, p. 217.

24  Letter to Forkel of 13 January 1775, *Dok* III, p. 288; *BR*, p. 278.

25  See J.-C. Zehnder, 'Georg Böhm und Johann Sebastian Bach. Zur Chronologie der Bachschen Stilentwicklung', *BJb* 74 (1988), pp. 73–110.

26   See R. S. Hill's study of BWV 832–3 in *EM* 13 (1985), pp. 248–55. R. Stinson
     makes out a good case for the authenticity of BWV 821 in *The Bach
     manuscripts of Johann Peter Kellner and his circle: a case study in reception
     history* (Durham, N.C. and London, 1990), pp. 123–4.

27   According to H. Eichberg (*NBA* V/10 *KB*, pp. 78–85), BWV 822 may be an
     arrangement by Bach of an overture-suite by a German contemporary.

28   See *Dok* III, p. 288; *BR*, p. 278.

29   See K. Beisswenger, *Johann Sebastian Bachs Notenbibliothek*, Catalogus
     musicus, vol. XIII (Kassel, 1992), VBN I/F/2 [catalogue], pp. 284–5. See also
     J. Ladewig, 'Bach and the *prima prattica*: the influence of Frescobaldi on a
     fugue from the *Well-tempered Clavier*', *JM* 9 (1991), pp. 358–75.

30   Beisswenger, *Johann Sebastian Bachs Notenbibliothek*, pp. 56–7 and VBN
     II/P/2, p. 367.

31   See Zehnder, 'Georg Böhm und J. S. Bach', pp. 76–9, and C. Wolff, 'Johann
     Adam Reinken und J. S. Bach', *BJb* 71 (1985), pp. 99–118; English trans., 'Bach
     and Johann Adam Reinken' (see note 4 above).

32   Wolff, 'Bach and Johann Adam Reinken', section III.

33   See G. Pestelli, 'Un'altra rielaborazione Bachiana: la fuga della Toccata BWV
     914', *Rivista Italiana di Musicologia* 16 (1981), pp. 40–4.

34   See Eichberg, *NBA* V/10 *KB*, pp. 47–9.

35   In the Frankfurt manuscript Mus. Hs. 1531; see Beisswenger, *Johann Sebastian
     Bachs Notenbibliothek*, pp. 190–202; see also G. B. Stauffer, 'Boyvin, Grigny,
     D'Anglebert, and Bach's assimilation of French classical organ music', *EM* 21
     (1993), pp. 83–96; V. Horn, 'French influence in Bach's organ works', *J. S. Bach
     as organist*, ed. G. B. Stauffer and E. May (Bloomington, 1986), pp. 256–73.

36   Beisswenger, *Johann Sebastian Bachs Notenbibliothek*, VBN I/A/1 and I/T/5,
     pp. 226 and 320.

37   *Ibid.*, VBN II/T/9–10, pp. 378–9.

38   *Dok* III, p. 189.

39   See J.-C. Zehnder, 'Giuseppe Torelli und Johann Sebastian Bach. Zu Bachs
     Weimarer Konzertform', *BJb* 77 (1991), pp. 33–95.

40   See H.-J. Schulze, *Studien zur Bach-Überlieferung*, pp. 146–73.

41   *Ibid.*, p. 156; quoted from J. Mattheson, *Das beschützte Orchestre* (Hamburg,
     1717), p. 129.

42   See Zehnder, 'Giuseppe Torelli und J. S. Bach', pp. 36–66.

43   It is entitled 'Concerto seu Toccata pour le Clavecin' in a lost copy of
     H. N. Gerber's; see *BG* 36, p. xxxviii.

44   See Zehnder, 'Giuseppe Torelli und J. S. Bach', pp. 92–3; a thematic link with
     the Torelli concerto that Bach transcribed as BWV 979 was noted by H. Keller,
     *Die Klavierwerke Bachs* (Leipzig, 1950), p. 82.

45   Forkel, *Über Johann Sebastian Bachs Leben*; see *BR*, p. 317.

46   The possible implications of this remark are explored by C. Wolff in 'Vivaldi's
     compositional art and the process of "musical thinking"', *Nuovi studi
     vivaldiani*, ed. A. Fanna and G. Morelli (Florence, 1988), reprinted as 'Vivaldi's
     compositional art, Bach and the process of "musical thinking"' in Wolff, *Bach:
     essays on his life and music*, pp. 72–83.

47    *Ibid.*, p. 74, and Wolff's comment in *The new Grove Bach family* (London and Basingstoke, 1983), p. 122.

48    See Stinson, *The Bach manuscripts of J. P. Kellner*, pp. 102–10; a table outlining the structure is given on p. 108.

49    See A. Dürr, 'Zur Form der Präludien in Bachs Englischen Suiten', *Bach-Studien* 6 (Leipzig, 1981), pp. 101ff.; reprinted in A. Dürr, *Im Mittelpunkt Bach* (Kassel, 1988), pp. 232–8.

50    *Dok* II, p. 65; *BR*, pp. 228–9.

51    *Dok* II, pp. 73–4.

52    See G. B. Stauffer's study of BWV 903 in *Bach studies*, ed. D. O. Franklin (Cambridge, 1989), pp. 160–82, especially p. 176.

53    See *BR*, pp. 312 and 342.

54    The title of the Weimar *Orgelbüchlein* (c. 1713–16), in which it is accorded a didactic purpose, was not added until the Köthen period (1717–23).

55    *Dok* I, pp. 220–1; *BR*, p. 86.

56    For an interesting study of composition as variation, see D. Schulenberg, 'Composition as variation: inquiries into the compositional procedures of the Bach circle of composers', *CM* 33 (1982), pp. 57–87; and *The keyboard music of J. S. Bach* (New York, 1992), pp. 24–5.

57    In the letter to Forkel of 13 January 1775, *Dok* III, p. 289; *BR*, p. 279.

58    See M. Helms, 'Zur Chronologie der Handschrift des Anonymus 5', *NBA* V/7 *KB*, pp. 183–95.

59    See A. Dürr, 'Heinrich Nicolaus Gerber als Schüler Bachs', *BJb* 64 (1978), pp. 7–18.

60    *Dok* III, p. 476; *BR*, p. 264.

61    Letter to Forkel of 13 January 1775, *Dok* III, p. 289; *BR*, p. 279.

62    *Dok* I, p. 220; *BR*, p. 86.

63    *BR*, p. 341.

64    Quoted from the title-page of the autograph fair copy P 415; *Dok* I, p. 219; *BR*, p. 85.

65    See Wolff's observation in *The new Grove Bach family*, p. 149.

66    Cf. the earlier and later versions as published in *NBA* V/6.1, ed. A. Dürr.

67    *Dok* II, pp. 160–1.

68    See Zehnder, 'Giuseppe Torelli und J. S. Bach', p. 93.

69    See H. Eppstein's study of BWV 1019 in *AfMw* 21 (1964), pp. 217–42, especially pp. 227 and 240 (fourth music example).

70    *Dok* II, p. 231; *BR*, p. 46.

71    *BR*, p. 337.

72    *Dok* II, pp. 220–1, 223 and 331.

73    *Dok* II, pp. 373–4; *BR*, p. 234; for an excellent study of the vogue for the solo keyboard concerto, see J. R. Swack, 'On the origins of the *Sonate auf Concertenart*', *JAMS* 46 (1993), pp. 369–414.

74    See Beisswenger, *Johann Sebastian Bachs Notenbibliothek*, pp. 78–85.

75    Lorenz Mizler (1739) in a refutation of Scheibe's criticisms; *Dok* II, p. 336; *BR*, p. 249.

76  *Dok* I, p. 63; *BR*, p. 123. For recent studies of stylistic trends in the last two decades of Bach's life and his response to them, see C. Ahrens, 'J. S. Bach und der "neue Gusto" in der Musik um 1740', *BJb* 72 (1986), pp. 69–79, and J. Butt, 'Bach and G. F. Kauffmann: reflections on Bach's later style', *Bach studies* 2, ed. D. Melamed (Cambridge, 1995), pp. 47–61.

77  See C. Wolff, *Der stile antico in der Musik Johann Sebastian Bachs. Studien zu Bachs Spätwerk* (Wiesbaden, 1968) and his 'Bach and the tradition of the Palestrina style', *Bach: essays on his life and music*, pp. 84–104.

78  Concerning the date of publication, see G. C. Butler, 'Neues zur Datierung der Goldberg-Variationen', *BJb* 74 (1988), pp. 219–23.

79  Quoted from Scarlatti's preface to the *Essercizi*. See R. L. Marshall's essay 'Bach the progressive' (1976), reprinted in *The music of J. S. Bach* (New York, 1989), pp. 23–58, especially pp. 46–8.

80  *BR*, pp. 338–9.

81  See C. Wolff, commentary to facsimile edition of *Clavier-Übung* I-IV (Leipzig, 1984), p. 32; reprinted in *Bach: essays on his life and music*, pp. 189–213, especially pp. 212–13.

82  *Dok* II, p. 399.

83  See Y. Kobayashi, 'Zur Chronologie der Spätwerke J. S. Bachs', *BJb* 74 (1988), pp. 7–72, especially p. 51.

84  Wolff's theory of a *conceptual* change (see the preface to his Peters edition (Frankfurt, 1987)) is questioned by the present writer in *ML* 69 (1988), p. 300.

85  The authenticity of the title – a subsequent addition to the autograph P 200 in the hand of Bach's pupil J. C. Altnikol – is not beyond doubt.

86  Other contemporary works based on similar principles are the Variations on 'Vom Himmel hoch' BWV 769, and the 14 Canons on the bass-line of the 'Goldberg Variations' BWV 1087, both of which date from around 1747–8 (see Kobayashi, 'Zur Chronologie der Spätwerke', p. 60).

87  See Wolff's *Bach: essays on his life and music*, pp. 254–5. For studies of evidence for Bach's acquaintance with the fortepiano, see E. Badura-Skoda, 'Komponierte J. S. Bach "Hammerklavier-Konzerte"?', *BJb* 77 (1991), pp. 159–71 and P. Badura-Skoda, *Interpreting Bach at the keyboard* (Oxford, 1993), pp. 157–69.

88  Wolff, *Bach: essays on his life and music*, p. 330 (see also pp. 324–31); quoted from J. G. Walther's definition of 'ricercare' in his *Musicalisches Lexicon* (Leipzig, 1732).

## 10  *Composition as arrangement and adaptation*

1  This subject was first treated by Ulrich Siegele in his 1957 Tübingen dissertation, *Kompositionsweise und Bearbeitungstechnik in der Instrumentalmusik Johann Sebastian Bachs*, Tübinger Beiträge zur Musikwissenschaft, vol. III (Stuttgart, 1975). More recently it has been approached from the standpoint of the adapted works by Kirsten Beisswenger, *Johann Sebastian Bachs Notenbibliothek*, Catalogus musicus, vol. XIII (Kassel, 1992).

2   See the essay by Robin Leaver, Chapter 7 in the present volume.

3   The third section 'c' of each sonata is something of a special case.
Reincken divided each into two parts, in the first of which the first violin
is used as a melody instrument, while in the second part – an exact repetition
of the first – the first violin is replaced by the gamba. Bach omitted these
repeats.

4   D. Schulenberg, *The keyboard music of J. S. Bach* (New York, 1992),
p. 69.

5   See the entry on 'Permutation fugue' in *The new Harvard dictionary of music*,
ed. D. M. Randel (Cambridge, Mass., 1986), p. 628.

6   See P. Walker, 'Die Entstehung der Permutationsfuge', *BJb* 75 (1989),
pp. 21–41.

7   The B♭ major and C major fugues are examples of the four-part structure that
the present writer has shown to be a formal principle of a whole series of
Bach's organ fugues; see Werner Breig, 'Form problems in Bach's early organ
fugues', *A Bach tribute: essays in honor of William H. Scheide*, ed. P. Brainard
and R. Robinson (Kassel and Chapel Hill, N.C., 1993), pp. 45–56; published in
German as 'Formprobleme in Bachs frühen Orgelfugen', *BJb* 78 (1992),
pp. 7–21; see also 'Versuch einer Theorie der Bachschen Orgelfuge', *Mf* 48
(1995), pp. 14–52.

8   See U. Siegele, 'Die musiktheoretische Lehre einer Bachschen Gigue', *AfMw* 17
(1960), pp. 152–67.

9   Johann Kuhnau, Preface to *Neuer Clavier-Übung Anderer Theil* (Leipzig,
1692).

10  It was from this collection that Bach took the subjects of his fugues BWV 946,
950 and 951/951a.

11  See K. Beisswenger, 'Zur Chronologie der Notenhandschriften Johann
Gottfried Walthers', *Acht kleine Präludien und Studien über BACH. Georg von
Dadelsen zum 70. Geburtstag*, ed. Kollegium des Johann-Sebastian-Bach-
Instituts Göttingen (Wiesbaden, 1992), pp. 11–39, especially pp. 21–2 and 27.
Beisswenger dates the copy of sonatas BWV 965 and 966 to the third stage
of Walther's scribal activities, a period which lasted from 1714 (or possibly
earlier) to 1717. The copy may be later, therefore, than Christoph Wolff
assumes in his essay 'Johann Adam Reinken und Johann Sebastian Bach.
Zum Kontext des Bachschen Frühwerks', *BJb* 71 (1985), pp. 99–118,
especially p. 111; English trans., 'Bach and Johann Adam Reinken: a context
for the early works', *Bach: essays on his life and music* (Cambridge, Mass.,
1991), pp. 56–71.

12  C. Wolff et al., *Die Bach-Familie* (Stuttgart and Weimar, 1993); Wolff, 'Johann
Adam Reinken und Johann Sebastian Bach'.

13  On the manuscript tradition and biographical context, see H.-J. Schulze,
*Studien zur Bach-Überlieferung im 18. Jahrhundert* (Leipzig and Dresden,
1984), especially chapter 5, pp. 146–73.

14  Because of the rapidly worsening state of his health, the prince had to leave
for a rest-cure on 4 July 1714. He did not return to Weimar, but died in
Frankfurt am Main in 1715 at the age of nineteen.

15   For a recent account of the harpsichord transcriptions, see Schulenberg, *The keyboard music of J. S. Bach*, pp. 90–109.

16   In the version adapted by Bach, the concerto has survived only in manuscript form; a version with a different middle movement (RV 208a) was printed as the penultimate piece in Vivaldi's Op. 7 (no. 11, i.e. Part II, no. 5). On Bach's transcription, see L. F. Tagliavini, 'Bach's transcription of Vivaldi's "Grosso Mogul" concerto', *J. S. Bach as Organist*, ed. G. B. Stauffer and E. May (Bloomington, 1986), pp. 240–55.

17   See M. Talbot, 'Vivaldi in the sale catalogue of Nicolaas Selhof', *Informazioni e studi vivaldiani* 6 (1985), pp. 57–62; Talbot suggests with some plausibility that this title 'is to be understood ... not as the ruler of an empire in India but ... as the name of the territory itself' (p. 60).

18   The source is published in the *NBA* IV/8 *KB*, pp. 105–22.

19   J. N. Forkel, *Über Johann Sebastian Bachs Leben, Kunst und Kunstwerke*, ed. J. Müller-Blattau (Kassel and Basle, 1950), pp. 39–40; trans. by A. C. F. Kollmann in *BR*, p. 317.

20   On this point, see also the reflections of Christoph Wolff, 'Vivaldi's compositional art and the process of "musical thinking"', *Nuovi studi vivaldiani*, ed. A. Fanna and G. Morelli (Florence, 1988), pp. 1–17; reprinted as 'Vivaldi's compositional art, Bach, and the process of "musical thinking"' in Wolff, *Bach: essays on his life and music*, pp. 72–83 and 405 (notes).

21   See H.-J. Schulze, 'Johann Sebastian Bachs Konzerte – Fragen der Überlieferung und Chronologie', *Beiträge zum Konzertschaffen Johann Sebastian Bachs*, Bach-Studien 6, ed. P. Ahnsehl, K. Heller and H.-J. Schulze (Leipzig, 1981), pp. 9–26, especially pp. 11–13.

22   Only BWV 1060 has a different genesis: it was initially a concerto for two harpsichords, the string ripieno being added only at a later date; see K. Heller, 'Zur Stellung des Concerto C-Dur für zwei Cembali BWV 1061 in Bachs Konzert-Oeuvre', *Bericht über die wissenschaftliche Konferenz zum V. Internationalen Bachfest der DDR in Verbindung mit dem 60. Bachfest der Neuen Bachgesellschaft* (1985) ed. W. Hoffmann and A. Schneiderheinze (Leipzig, 1988), pp. 241–52.

23   See *NBA* VII/5–6 *KB*.

24   Y. Kobayashi, 'Zur Chronologie der Spätwerke Johann Sebastian Bachs', *BJb* 74 (1988), pp. 7–72, especially p. 41.

25   The present writer has discussed this point in greater detail in his essay 'Zum Kompositionsprozeß in Bachs Cembalokonzerten', *Johann Sebastian Bachs Spätwerk und dessen Umfeld. 61. Bachfest der Neuen Bachgesellschaft Duisburg 1986*, ed. C. Wolff (Kassel, 1988), pp. 32–47.

26   Bach had already adopted this procedure in several of his concertos for more than one harpsichord.

27   See W. Breig, 'Bachs Cembalokonzert-Fragment in d-moll (BWV 1059)', *BJb* 65 (1979), pp. 29–36.

28   On Bach's source, see W. Breig, 'Bachs Violinkonzert d-moll. Studien zu seiner Gestalt und seiner Entstehungsgeschichte', *BJb* 62 (1976), pp. 7–34. (I no longer hold the belief, expressed there, that the original form of this work was

not by Bach; the assumption that it is an early work should be sufficient to explain its unusual form.)

29   The fact that such claims can be advanced in spite of the loss of the source is due to the fact that Bach had already used the original concerto – evidently with less striking changes – in movements of two of his sacred cantatas, BWV 169 and 49.

30   A. Schweitzer, *Joh. Seb. Bach* (Leipzig, 1908), pp. 382–3; English trans. by E. Newman, 2 vols. (New York, 1966), vol. I, p. 412.

## 11   Bachian invention and its mechanisms

1   I have treated this issue further in 'Music analysis and the historical imperative', *Revista de Musicologia: Actas del XV Congreso de la SIM*, vol. XVI, no. 1 (1993), pp. 407–19. See also my *Bach and the patterns of invention* (Cambridge, Mass., 1996), which develops many of the arguments contained in the present essay in greater detail.

2   See Johann Sebastian Bach, *Drei Sonaten für Viola da Gamba und Cembalo, BWV 1027–1029*, ed. L. Dreyfus (Frankfurt and Leipzig: Peters, 1985). Other recent critical editions include that found in *NBA* VI/4, ed. H. Eppstein (1989), and another edition by Lucy Robinson issued by Faber, 1987. Cantata 78 can be found in *NBA* I/21.

3   For a summary of historical doubts that must be shed on most numerological analyses of Bach, see R. Tatlow, *Bach and the riddle of the number alphabet* (Cambridge, 1991).

4   See also R. L. Marshall, *The music of Johann Sebastian Bach: the sources, the style, the significance* (New York, 1989), pp. 76–9, for another reading of this movement. The rhythmic gesture that Marshall identifies as evoking the sarabande (p. 78) is actually a clear reference to the French chaconne, since the phrases of the sarabande – despite the important weight accorded to some second beats – do not begin on the second crotchet, nor do they permit successive bars with consistent second-beat accents.

5   For ease of numbering I ignore the resolution of the 'period' on each ninth bar, since chaconnes conventionally begin after an uncounted downbeat and are 'measured' from the second crotchet.

## 12   Bach as teacher and model

1   The register of the alumni was itself not always accurate, since, for example, dates of birth were sometimes declared later than was the truth, to give the impression of greater promise when candidates enrolled. In any event, inaccuracies were very common in such lists of the time. The author is very grateful to Hans-Joachim Schulze of the Leipzig Bach-Archiv for this insight.

2   For example, Johann Bernhard Bach of Ohrdruf (1700–43) reportedly lodged and studied with Johan Sebastian successively in Weimar and Köthen; in

Leipzig, it looks as though Bernhard's younger brother, Johann Heinrich Bach (1707–83), did the same, while serving as an alumnus of the Thomasschule (and possibly before and/or after, too). See C. Wolff, *The new Grove Bach family* (London and Basingstoke, 1983), pp. 9, 13.

3   See C. Wolff, *Bach: essays on his life and music* (Cambridge, Mass., 1991), p. 401.

4   *BR*, 264–5; *Dok* III, p. 476. Gerber made only one extensive journey later in life, his son tells us. This was to revisit 'his beloved Bach' in 1737.

5   *BR*, p. 264; *Dok* III, p. 476. Gerber therefore commenced his learning from Bach by studying his music in performance as a pattern (as C. G. Meissner and others are presumed to have done); but whereas Meissner is not reported to have received direct teaching from Bach, Gerber requested it, after some hesitation, and pursued his studies for some time.

6   By 'Inventions' the Lexicographer may have signified both the *Inventiones* in 2 parts and the *Sinfoniae* in 3. The habit of referring to both of these collections by the one title seems to have started around 1790; there is even a reference to 'Inventions' in three parts in Forkel's biography, twelve years later (1802).

7   *BR*, p. 86; *Dok* I, pp. 220–1 (author's translation).

8   *BR*, p. 279; *Dok* III, p. 289.

9   Gerber's copies are examined by Alfred Dürr in *BJb* 64 (1978), pp. 7–18 (English summary, p. 251). There is further invaluable information in the *NBA* commentaries to relevant keyboard works: to *The Well-tempered Clavier*, Book I (vol. V/6, 1, ed. A. Dürr, pp. 51–3, 147–9, 194–7); the English Suites (vol. V/7, ed. A. Dürr, pp. 21–4, 85–98); and the French Suites (*BJb* 64 (1978) and *NBA* V/8, ed. A. Dürr, pp. 38–41, 57, 72–84). The three distinct sets of copies which constitute Heinrich Nicolaus Gerber's text of *The Well-tempered Clavier* include one which is partly in a different, anonymous, hand, and is therefore of inexact date. Dürr has also shown that H. N. Gerber's study of continuo realisation started earlier than his son's *Lexicon* article implied (see *BJb* 64(1978)), which seems better to correspond with C. P. E. Bach's evidence in the *Versuch*. The commentary to *NBA* V/3 (music text ed. G. von Dadelsen) has not yet been issued.

10   Cf. *Dok* I, pp. 127–8; pp. 53–4, 57–8 and 129.

11   Cf. J. Lester, *Compositional theory in the eighteenth century* (Cambridge, Mass., 1992), especially chapters 6–9.

12   Cf. J. Butt, *Music education and the art of performance in the German Baroque* (Cambridge, 1994), especially chapter 5.

13   *Dok* III, pp. 649f.

14   *Dok* III, p. 123; see also S. Daw, 'Copies of J. S. Bach by Walther and Krebs: a study of the Mss. P801, P802, P803', *OY* 7 (1976), pp. 31–67.

15   H.-J. Schulze, *Studien zur Bach-Überlieferung im 18. Jahrhundert* (Leipzig, 1984), pp. 59–68.

16   See *BJb* 56 (1970), pp. 44–63, also Schulze, *Studien zur Bach-Überlieferung*,

pp. 128–52. References to the possibility that Carl Friedrich Abel studied with
Bach around 1740 lead to the interesting conjecture that Agricola's copies of
Bach's sonatas for viola da gamba and harpsichord BWV 1027–9 were made
so that the two might play them together. There is no direct report of
Agricola's having studied formally with Bach, however.

17  See Yo Tomita, *A textual companion to part 2 of J. S. Bach's Wohltemperiertes
Clavier*, vol. I (Leeds, 1993); also R. D. P. Jones's edition, *J. S. Bach: The Well-
tempered Clavier, Part 2* (London, 1994), editorial notes and preface.

18  See P. Wollny, 'Wilhelm Friedemann Bach's Halle performance of cantatas by
his father', *Bach studies* 2, ed. D. Melamed (Cambridge, 1995), pp. 202–28.

19  Regarding Kauffmann, see J. Butt, 'Bach and G. F. Kauffmann: reflections on
Bach's later style', in *Bach studies* 2, ed. Melamed, pp. 47–61; the contents of
Walther's cited manuscript are listed in *NBA IV/3 KB*, ed. H. Klotz, 1962,
pp. 19–28.

20  Schulze, *Studien zur Bach-Überlieferung.*

21  See the fascimile issued with *NBA VI/2*, R. Stinson, *The Bach manuscripts of
J. P. Kellner and his circle: a case study in reception history* (Durham, N.C. and
London, 1990), and '"Ein Sammelband aus Johann Peter Kellners Besitz".
Neue Forschungen zur Berliner Bach-Handschrift P804', *BJb* 78 (1992),
pp. 45–64; also S. Daw, 'Slurs on the copyist's book', *The Strad* (October 1992),
pp. 904–5.

22  Mozart first referred to this in a letter dated 10 April 1782. For a general and
perceptive study of Bach reception during the latter half of the eighteenth
century, see L. Finscher, 'Bach in the eighteenth century', *Bach studies*, ed.
D. O. Franklin (Cambridge, 1989), pp. 281–96.

23  See K. Beisswenger, 'An early version of the first movement of the *Italian
Concerto* BWV 971 from the Scholz collection?', *Bach studies* 2, ed. Melamed,
pp. 1–19.

24  *BR*, pp. 447–50; for further extensive information on compositional theory of
the eighteenth century see Lester, *Compositional theory.*

25  The author would like to acknowledge the help and advice of Hans-Joachim
Schulze (Leipzig) and Yo Tomita (The Queen's University, Belfast).

## 13  *Changing issues of performance practice*

1  See *NBA V/2 KB*, pp. 48–51, and D. Fuller, 'Dotting, the "French style" and
Frederick Neumann's counter-reformation', *EM* 5 (1977), pp. 517–43.

2  For a detailed discussion see G. Herz, 'Lombard rhythm in the *Domine Deus*
of Bach's *B Minor Mass*' and 'Lombard rhythm in Bach's vocal music', in
G. Herz, *Essays on J. S. Bach* (Ann Arbor, 1985), pp. 221–9 and 233–68,
respectively.

3  *Dok* I, p. 63; *BR*, p. 123. Unless otherwise noted, translations in this chapter
are by the author.

4  C. V. Palisca, *Baroque music* (3rd edn, Englewood Cliffs, N.J., 1991), p. 2.

5  Unfortunately, Emanuel's arrangement of the Credo has never been
published. The materials from the 1786 performance are preserved in the

Staatsbibliothek zu Berlin-Preussischer Kulturbesitz, under the shelf marks *Mus.ms.Bach P 22* (score) and *Mus.ms.Bach St. 118* (parts).

6   See the discussion in J. Rifkin, '. . ."wobey aber die Singstimmen hinlänglich besetzt seyn müssen . . ." Zum Credo der h-Moll-Messe in der Aufführung Carl Philipp Emanuel Bachs', *Basler Jahrbuch für historische Musikpraxis* 9 (1985), pp. 157–72.

7   The best summary of Cantata 80's complicated evolution can be found in C. Wolff, 'The Reformation cantata "Ein feste Burg"', in Wolff, *Bach: essays on his life and music* (Cambridge, Mass., 1991), pp. 152–61.

8   The preludes of the six preludes and fugues K. 404a are probably not by Mozart, though they seem to stem from the van Swieten circle. See W. Kirkendale, 'More slow introductions by Mozart to fugues of J. S. Bach?', *JAMS* 17 (1964), pp. 53–5.

9   J. N. Forkel, *Über Johann Sebastian Bachs Leben, Kunst und Kunstwerk* (Leipzig, 1802; reprinted Berlin, 1982), p. 122; translation from the English edition (London, 1820), given in *BR*, p. 352.

10   Spontini's programme is described by F. Smend in *NBA* II/1 *KB*, pp. 40 and 44–5.

11   To be convinced of this, one need only compare the equally Olympian renderings of Bach by Carl Seffner (statue for the Thomasplatz, Leipzig, 1908) and of Beethoven by Max Klinger (statue for the Klimt exhibit, Vienna, 1886–1902).

12   *NZM* 8 (1838), p. 22.

13   See Mendelssohn's letter of 4 September 1832, to Marie Kiéné. The letter, and Mendelssohn's approach to performing the *Orgelbüchlein*, are discussed in R. Stinson, *J. S. Bach: the Orgelbüchlein* (New York, 1996), pp. 156–9.

14   Schumann, *NZM* 13 (1841), p. 43.

15   P. Spitta, *Johann Sebastian Bach*, 2 vols. (Leipzig, 1873–80; reprinted Darmstadt, 1979), vol. II, p. 530.

16   A. Schering, 'Verschwundene Traditionen des Bachzeitalter', *BJb* 1 (1904), pp. 104–15.

17   A. Schweitzer, *J. S. Bach*, trans. E. Newman (Leipzig, 1911; reprinted 1966), pp. 417–18. Schweitzer's biography originally appeared as *Jean-Sébastian Bach, le musicien-poète* (Leipzig, 1905).

18   By H. Klotz, in *Über die Orgelkunst der Gotik, der Renaissance und des Barock* (Kassel, 1934), for instance.

19   The long and complicated history of the Organ Reform Movement is traced in H. Eggebrecht, *Die Orgelbewegung* (Stuttgart, 1967); L. I. Phelps, *A short history of the organ revival* (St Louis, 1967); and F. Brouwer, *Orgelbewegung und Orgelgegenbewegung* (Utrecht, 1981).

20   The history of the harpsichord revival is traced in H. Schott's 'The harpsichord revival', *EM* 2 (1974), pp. 85–95.

21   F. Smend, 'Bachs h-moll-Messe. Entstehung, Überlieferung, Bedeutung', *BJb* 34 (1937), pp. 30–1.

22   P. Hindemith, *Johann Sebastian Bach. Ein verpflichtendes Erbe* (private printing, 1950), p. 11.

23   A complete list of these studies can be found in the 'Aufführungspraxis' sections of *Bach-Bibliographie*, ed. C. Wolff (Kassel, 1985).

24   R. L. Marshall, 'Tempo and dynamic indications in the Bach sources: a review of the terminology', in *Bach, Handel, Scarlatti: tercentenary essays*, ed. P. Williams (Cambridge, 1985), pp. 259–76.

25   In the *Versuch über die wahre Art das Clavier zu spielen*, Part I (Berlin, 1753), C. P. E. Bach credits his father with developing a 'new kind of fingering' (i.e. turning the thumb under as in modern scale fingering), but he still gives the standard late seventeenth-century 12343434 as one possible right-hand fingering for C major.

26   J. Butt, *Bach interpretation: articulation marks in primary sources of J. S. Bach* (Cambridge, 1990), pp. 94–6.

27   A policy that has been questioned lately even by some of its editors. See R. L. Marshall's comments in *NBA* I/19 *KB*, pp. 44–6, for instance.

28   D. Barnett, 'Non-uniform slurring in 18th century music: accident or design?' *Haydn Yearbook*, 10 (1978), pp. 179–99.

29   G. von Dadelsen, 'Die Crux der Nebensache – Editorische und praktische Bemerkungen zu Bachs Artikulation', in Dadelsen, *Über Bach und Anderes* (Tübingen, 1983), pp. 144–58.

30   N. Harnoncourt, 'The oboe da caccia', Liner notes to *Das Kantatenwerk*, vol. 7 (Teldec Records, 1973), p. 13.

31   In a review published in *High Fidelity/Musical America* 19 (July 1969), p. 77.

32   For instance, see the final comments in the discussion of 'The Bach organ' in P. Williams, *The organ music of J. S. Bach*, 3 vols. (Cambridge, 1980–4), vol. III, pp. 117–38.

33   See G. B. Stauffer, 'J. S. Bach's harpsichords', *Festa musicologica: essays in honor of George J. Buelow*, ed. T. J. Mathiesen and B. V. Rivera (Stuyvesant, New York, 1995), pp. 289–318.

34   E. Badura-Skoda, 'Komponierte J. S. Bach "Hammerklavier-Konzerte"?', *BJb* 77 (1991), pp. 159–71.

35   J. Rifkin, 'Bachs Chor – Ein vorläufiger Bericht', *Basler Jahrbuch für historische Musikpraxis* 9 (1985), pp. 141–55.

36   N. Harnoncourt, liner notes, TELDEC recording *8.35716* (1986).

## 14  Bach reception: some concepts and parameters

1   F. Busoni, 'Selbst-Rezension', *Von der Einheit der Musik* (Berlin, 1922), p. 175.

2   The term 'horizon of expectation' comes from German phenomenology and hermeneutics and is particularly important in the German school of reception theory (led by such figures as Hans Robert Jauss). It refers to the cultural and personal conditions ('situatedness') of any historical object, meaning or mode of understanding. What one can expect (or even conceive of) is conditioned by one's situation and consequent perspective, just as a horizon is defined by the viewer's position.

3   In the sense of Liszt's 'Après une lecture', a poem that expresses in musical notes how Liszt understood Victor Hugo's readings of Dante in 'Les voix

intérieures', Liszt's Schubert and Bach transcriptions are also 'Tone-poems':
poetic readings which result in 'poetry' without words.

4   On the distinction between the history of influence and reception history,
see C. Dahlhaus, *Grundlagen der Musikgeschichte* (Cologne, 1977), p. 238;
trans. J. B. Robinson, *Foundations of music history* (Cambridge, 1983),
chapter 10, p. 150.

5   See M. Geck, *Die Wiederentdeckung der Matthäus-Passion im 19. Jahrhundert.*
*Die zeitgenössischen Dokumente und ihre ideengeschichtliche Deutung*
(Regensburg, 1967).

6   See M. Zenck, *Die Bach-Rezeption des späten Beethoven. Zum Verhältnis von*
*Musikhistoriographie und Rezeptionsgeschichtsschreibung der 'Klassik'*, BzAfMw
24 (Stuttgart, 1986); W. Dömling, 'Franz Liszt und B-A-C-H', *Alte Musik als*
*ästhetische Gegenwart. Bach. Händel. Schütz.* Report of the International
Music Symposium, Stuttgart 1985, vol. I (Kassel, 1987), pp. 159–61; A.
Riethmüller, *Ferruccio Busonis Poetik,* Neue Studien zur Musikwissenschaft 4
(Mainz, 1988), chapter 2; M. Zenck, 'Tradition as authority and provocation:
Anton Webern's confrontation with Johann Sebastian Bach', *Bach studies*, ed.
D. O. Franklin (Cambridge, 1989), pp. 297–322; 'Beyond Neoclassicism and
Dodecaphony: Stefan Wolpe's Third Way in the music of the 20th century'
(Paper presented at the International Stefan Wolpe conference, April 1993,
conference proceedings forthcoming); Erich Itor Kahn, 'Actus tragicus' (New
York, 1950); see also R. Leibowitz and K. Wolff, *Erich Itor Kahn – un grand*
*représentant de la musique contemporaine* (Paris, 1958); Karel Goeyvaerts, 'Ach
Golgatha!' (1975) for Harp, Organ, and Percussion (Brussels, Centre Belge de
Documentation Musicale).

7   See Dahlhaus, *Foundations*, chapter 9, p. 129.

8   F. Nietzsche, *Unzeitgemäße Betrachtungen*, part 2: 'Vom Nutzen und Nachteil
der Historie für das Leben'; Friedrich Nietzsche, *Werke*, 3 vols. (Darmstadt,
1966), vol. I, pp. 215ff.

9   *Ibid.*, p. 213.

10  F. Nietzsche, *Die Geburt der Tragödie [The birth of tragedy]*, *Werke*, vol. I, p. 109.

11  F. Nietzsche, *Menschliches, Allzumenschliches*, *Werke*, vol. I, p. 576. Translations
adapted from Nietzsche, *Human, all too human*, trans. R. J. Hollingdale
(Cambridge, 1986), p. 101.

12  See H. Besseler, 'Bach als Wegbereiter', *Aufsätze zur Musikästhetik und*
*Musikgeschichte* (Leipzig, 1978), pp. 367–419.

13  Nietzsche, *Menschliches, Allzumenschliches*, *Werke*, vol. I, Aphorism 149,
p. 934. Translation adapted from Hollingdale trans., pp. 344–5.

14  See E. Bloch, *Der Geist der Utopie*, 2nd edn of 1923 (Frankfurt am Main,
1973), pp. 105ff. See also M. Geck, 'Bach und Tristan – Musik aus dem Geist
der Utopie', *Bach-Interpretationen*, ed. M. Geck (Göttingen, 1969), pp. 190–6.

15  H. Blumenberg, *Matthäuspassion* (Frankfurt am Main, 1988), p. 8.

16  *Ibid.*, pp. 9 and 15.

17  See C. Dahlhaus, 'Bach und der Zerfall der musikalischen Figurenlehre',
*Jahrbuch des Staatlichen Instituts für Musikforschung Preußischer Kulturbesitz*
1985–6 (Kassel, 1989), pp. 169–74.

18  See Dahlhaus, 'Bach und der Zerfall', pp. 172f.

19  See Chapter 5, above.

20  See M. Zenck, '1740–1750 und das ästhetische Bewußtsein einer Epochenschwelle? Zum Text und Kontext von Bachs Spätwerk', *Johann Sebastian Bachs Spätwerk und dessen Umfeld. 61. Bachfest der Neuen Bachgesellschaft, Duisburg 1986*, ed. C. Wolff (Kassel, 1988), pp. 109–16.

21  See T. Kuhn, *Die Struktur wissenschaftlicher Revolutionen*, 2nd revised edn expanded to include the 1969 postscript (Frankfurt am Main, 1976).

22  See H. Blumenberg, *Die Legitimität der Neuzeit* (Frankfurt am Main, 1966), pp. 440f.

23  See C. Dahlhaus, 'Bach-Rezeption und ästhetische Autonomie', *Alte Musik als ästhetische Gegenwart. Bach. Händel. Schütz. Report of the International Music Symposium, Stuttgart 1985*, vol. I (Kassel 1987), pp. 18–26.

24  See M. Zenck, 'Stadien der Bach-Deutung in der Musikkritik, Musikästhetik und Musikgeschichtsschreibung zwischen 1750 und 1800', *BJb* 68 (1982), Part II, 'Die "klassische" Umdeutung Bachs', pp. 17–32.

25  See C. Dahlhaus, 'Zur Entstehung der romantischen Bach-Deutung', *BJb* 64 (1978), pp. 192–210.

## 15  Reinterpreting Bach in the nineteenth and twentieth centuries

1  See H. H. Eggebrecht, 'Über Bachs geschichtlichen Ort', *Johann Sebastian Bach*, ed. W. Blankenburg (Darmstadt, 1970), pp. 247–89; 'Bach – wer ist das', *AfMw* 42 (1985), pp. 215–28; L. Finscher, 'Bach and the Viennese Classics', *Miscellanea Musicologica. Adelaide Studies in Musicology* 10 (1979), pp. 47–58; 'Bach in the eighteenth century', *Bach studies*, ed. D. O. Franklin (Cambridge, 1989), pp. 281–96; M. Zenck, 'Bach in der Musikgeschichtsschreibung und in der Musik des 18. Jahrhunderts', *Jahrbuch des Staatlichen Instituts für Musikforschung Preußischer Kulturbesitz*, 1985–6 (Kassel, 1989), pp. 239–56.

2  See KV 404a, 404b (=443) and KV 405; See also, with reference to A. Hohlschneider and W. Kirkendale, M. Zenck, *Die Bach-Rezeption des späten Beethoven. Zum Verhältnis von Musikhistoriographie und Rezeptionsgeschichtsschreibung der 'Klassik'*, *BzAfMw* 24 (Stuttgart, 1986) pp. 86ff.

3  If one takes these Bach-like structures of 'general bass', melodic main voice and contrapuntal counter and middle voices as the basis, then there are also direct connections with the six string quartets dedicated to Joseph Haydn.

4  See R. Hammerstein, '"Der Gesang der Geharnischten", Eine Studie zu Mozarts Bach-Bild', *AfMw* 13 (1956), pp. 1–24.

5  See M. Zenck, 'Stadien der Bach-Deutung in der Musikkritik, Musikästhetik und Musikgeschichtsschreibung zwischen 1750 und 1800', *BJb* 68 (1982), pp. 7–32.

6  See C. Dahlhaus, 'Zur Entstehung der romantischen Bach-Deutung', *BJb* 64 (1978) p. 192.

7  See Zenck, 'Stadien der Bach-Deutung', p. 18.

8  *Ibid.*, p. 8.

9  See F. Nietzsche, *Menschliches, Allzumenschliches*, vol. II, 'Der Wanderer und sein Schatten', Aphorism 152, p. 935.

10  Liszt used this term in connection with his Symphonic Poems, 1860; quoted in W. Dömling, 'Franz Liszts Hommage an Bach', *Johann Sebastian Bach. Spätwerk und Umfeld. 61. Bachfest der Neuen Bachgesellschaft* (Duisburg, 1986), p. 224.

11  See C. Dahlhaus, *Zwischen Romantik und Moderne. Vier Studien zur Musikgeschichte des späteren 19. Jahrhunderts* (Munich, 1974).

12  See W. Dömling, 'Franz Liszt und B-A-C-H', *Alte Musik als ästhetische Gegenwart. Bach. Händel. Schütz. Report of the International Music Symposium, Stuttgart 1985*, vol. I (Kassel, 1987), p. 161.

13  See T. Kabisch, 'Zur Bach-Rezeption Franz Liszts', *Alte Musik als ästhetische Gegenwart*, pp. 478f.

14  Like his 'Après une lecture du Dante', Liszt's variation cycle on the chaconne is a rereading of the way Bach read the text 'Weinen, Klagen . . .' by Salomon Franck in the cantata. See, in particular, S. Döhring, 'Réminiscences. Liszts Konzeption der Klavierparaphrase', *Festschrift Heinz Becker* (Laaber, 1982), pp. 131–51.

15  It is not coincidental that R. Leibowitz, whom we have to thank for the first significant work on the 'dilution de la tonalité' in Liszt's late works, speaks of the 'structural dialectic in the work of J. S. Bach' (see *Johann Sebastian Bach*, ed. W. Blankenburg, pp. 85–99).

16  See A. Riethmüller, 'Zu den Transkriptionen Bachscher Orgelwerke durch Busoni und Reger', *Reger-Studien* 3. Analysen und Quellenstudien (Wiesbaden, 1988), pp. 137–46.

17  F. Busoni, *Von der Einheit der Musik. Von Dritteltönen und junger Klassizität. Von Bühnen und Bauten und anschließenden Bezirken* (Berlin, 1922).

18  *Ibid.*, pp. 275–9.

19  F. Busoni, foreword to the first edition of the organ toccatas in C BWV 564 and D minor BWV 565 (Leipzig, 1900).

20  *J. S. Bach. Klavierwerke unter Mitwirkung von Egon Petri und Bruno Mugellini*, ed. F. Busoni (Leipzig, 1894–), 25 vols.

21  See F. Busoni, 'Zum Entwurf einer szenischen Aufführung von J. S. Bachs Matthäuspassion', in F. Busoni, *Von der Einheit*, p. 341 and sketch 4 in the appendix.

22  *Von der Einheit*, p. 130.

23  See M. Zenck, '"Die Lust am Text" versus Werktreue. Zur musikalischen Interpretation des 1. Satzes von Schuberts Klaviersonate B-Dur (D 960)', *Das Wissen vom Menschen*, ed. W. Faber (Bamberg, 1993), pp. 142–7.

24  *Von der Einheit*, p. 150.

25  J. Kindermann, *Thematisch-chronologisches Verzeichnis der Werke von Ferruccio Busoni* (Regensburg, 1980); G. D. Madge, *The Piano Works. Ferruccio Busoni*: 6 CDs on Philips 420 740 and Madge's text in the booklet, which also contains excellent contributions by P. Op de Coul and U. Prinz.

26  F. Busoni, 'Die Ausgabe der Liszt'schen Klavierwerke', *Von der Einheit*, p. 54.

27   See J. S. Bach. *Klavierwerke*, vol. XV. *Aria mit 30 Veränderungen (Goldberg-Variationen)*, ed. E. Petri with a forward entitled 'Begründung dieser Ausgabe'; Busoni is also cited as the editor in the music text (Leipzig, 1915).

28   See M. Zenck, '"Bach, der Progressive". Die Goldberg-Variationen in der Perspektive von Beethovens Diabelli-Variationen', *Johann Sebastian Bach. Goldberg-Variationen. Musik-Konzepte* 42 (Munich, 1985), pp. 29–92.

29   See E. Kurth, *Grundlagen des linearen Kontrapunkts. Einführung in Stil und Technik von Bachs melodische Polyphonie* (Berne, 1917).

30   The original title, referring to Beethoven's op. 133, runs thus: 'Große Fuge. Kontrapunktische Fantasie über die Kunst der Fuge von Johann Sebastian Bach (BWV 1080) für Pianoforte' (K 255).

31   F. Busoni, 'Gedanken über den Ausdruck in der Architektur', *Von der Einheit*, p. 230.

32   F. Busoni, 'Selbst-Rezension', *Von der Einheit*, p. 175.

33   On Busoni's critique of Schoenberg's 'all too great conciseness', see K. Kropfinger, 'Busonis Utopie der Musik und das Berlin der zwanziger Jahre', *Musica* 41 (1987), p. 23.

34   'Sketch of a new esthetic of music', trans. by T. Baker in *Three classics in the aesthetic of music* (New York, 1962).

35   For an extensive discussion of the relationship between Busoni's Toccata and his revision of Bach's Toccata (BWV 564) see M. Zenck, 'Beyond Neoclassicism and Dodecaphony': Stefan Wolpe's Third Way in the Music of the 20th century' (paper presented at the International Stefan Wolpe conference, April 1993, conference proceedings forthcoming).

36   See R. Stephan, 'Zum Thema "Schoenberg und Bach"', *BJb* 64 (1978), pp. 232–44; see also H. Danuser, 'Bach und die zeitgenössische Musik', *Musik im 20. Jahrhundert. 59. Bachfest der Neuen Bachgesellschaft* (Leipzig and Kassel, 1984), pp. 96–101 and introduction, pp. 76f.

37   On Anton Webern's and Alban Berg's studies with Schoenberg, see M. Zenck, 'Tradition as authority and provocation: Anton Webern's confrontation with Johann Sebastian Bach', *Bach studies*, ed. D. O. Franklin (Cambridge, 1989), pp. 297–322.

38   'Kunst der Fuge' (K 255 and K 256) and 'Musikalisches Opfer' (K; B 40 from 1916).

39   See A. Clarkson, 'Stefan Wolpe's Berlin years', *Music and civilisation: essays in honor of Paul Henry Lang*, ed. E. Strainchamps and M. R. Maniatis (New York, n.d.), p. 375, note 15; see also T. Levita, 'The would-be master student? Stefan Wolpe and Ferruccio Busoni' (Paper presented at the International Stefan Wolpe conference, April 1993, conference proceedings forthcoming).

40   See Clarkson, 'Stefan Wolpe's Berlin years', pp. 382 and 385.

41   See Zenck, 'Tradition as authority', p. 309.

42   E. Budde, 'Webern und Bach', *Alte Musik als ästhetische Gegenwart*, pp. 201f., and Zenck, 'Tradition as Authority', pp. 314f.

43   On the relationship between Wolpe and Webern, see M. Zenck, 'Das revolutionäre Klavierwerk des Komponisten Stefan Wolpe – Mit kritischen Anmerkungen zur Musikgeschichtsschreibung der dreißiger und vierziger

Jahre', *Künste im Exil. Exilforschung. Ein Internationales Jahrbuch* 10 (Munich, 1992), pp. 134–42.

44  See Zenck, 'Beyond Neoclassicism and Dodecaphony', note 98, pp. 11–16.

45  See A. Clarkson, 'The works of Stefan Wolpe: a brief catalog', *Notes* 41 (1985), pp. 667–82.

46  All of these manuscripts are the property of the International Wolpe Society, New York and Toronto. Recently Wolpe's estate was taken over by the Paul-Sacher-Stiftung in Basel.

47  Consider also the meaning of 'constellation' for Boulez in reference to Mallarmé.

48  See Zenck, '"Bach, der Progressive"', pp. 29–92.

49  For a thorough discussion of 'stationary music', see Zenck, 'Beyond Neoclassicism and Dodecaphony', pp. 4–9.

50  S. Wolpe, 'Über Dance in the form of a Chaconne' (MS, 1938), p. 11.

51  On the relationship between Wolpe's Chaconne, Busoni and Bach, see Zenck, 'Beyond Neoclassicism and Dodecaphony', pp. 11–15.

# Select bibliography

Ahrens, C., 'J. S. Bach und der "neue Gusto" in der Musik um 1740', *BJb* 72 (1986), pp. 69–79

Arnold, D., *Bach* (Oxford, 1984)

Axmacher, E., 'Eine Quellenfund zum Text der Matthäus-Passion', *BJb* 64 (1978), pp. 181–191

   *'Aus Liebe will mein Heyland sterben'. Untersuchungen zum Wandel des Passionsverständnisses im frühen 18. Jahrhundert* (Neuhausen-Stuttgart, 1984)

   'Die Deutung der Passion Jesu im Text der Matthäus-Passion von J. S. Bach', *Luther: Zeitschrift der Luther-Gesellschaft* 56 (1985), pp. 49–69

Badura-Skoda, E., 'Komponierte J. S. Bach "Hammerklavier-Konzerte"?', *BJb* 77 (1991), pp. 159–71

Badura-Skoda, P., *Interpreting Bach at the keyboard* (Oxford, 1993)

Basso, A., *Frau Musika: la vita e le opere di J. S. Bach*, 2 vols. (Turin, 1979–83)

Beisswenger, K., *Johann Sebastian Bachs Notenbibliothek*, Catalogus musicus, vol. XIII (Kassel, 1992)

   'Zur Chronologie der Notenhandschriften Johann Gottfried Walthers', *Acht kleine Präludien und Studien über BACH. Georg von Dadelsen zum 70. Geburtstag*, ed. Kollegium des Johann-Sebastian-Bach-Instituts Göttingen (Wiesbaden, 1992), pp. 11–39

Besseler, H., 'Bach als Wegbereiter', *Johann Sebastian Bach*, Wege der Forschung, vol. CLXX, ed. W. Blankenburg (Darmstadt, 1970), pp. 196–246; reprinted in *Aufsätze zur Musikästhetik und Musikgeschichte* (Leipzig, 1978) pp. 367–419

Blankenburg, W., 'J. S. Bach und die Aufklärung', *Bach Gedenkschrift* 1950, ed. K. Matthaei (Zurich, 1950), pp. 25–34

   *Das Weihnachts-Oratorium von Johann Sebastian Bach* (Kassel, 1982)

   *Einführung in Bachs h-Moll-Messe BWV 232* (Kassel, 1974; reprinted 1986)

Blume, F., 'Outlines of a new picture of Bach', *ML* 44 (1963), pp. 214–27; reprinted in W. Hays, ed., *Twentieth-century views of music history* (New York, 1972), pp. 225–38

   *Protestant church music: a history* (London, 1974)

Blumenberg, H., *Matthäuspassion* (Frankfurt am Main, 1988)

Boyd, M., *Bach* (London, 1983)

   *Bach: the Brandenburg Concertos* (Cambridge, 1993)

Brainard, P., 'Bach's parody procedure and the St. Matthew Passion', *JAMS* 22 (1969), pp. 241–60

Breig, W., 'Bachs Violinkonzert d-moll. Studien zu seiner Gestalt und seiner Entstehungsgeschichte', *BJb* 62 (1976), pp. 7–34

   'Der norddeutsche Orgelchoral und Johann Sebastian Bach. Gattung, Typus, Werk', *Gattung und Werk in der Musikgeschichte Norddeutschlands und*

*Skandinaviens*, ed. F. Krummacher and H. W. Schwab (Kassel, 1982)
  pp. 79–94

'Bemerkungen zur zyklischen Symmetrie in Bachs Leipziger Kirchenmusik',
  *MuK* 53 (1983), pp. 173–9

'Zum Kompositionsprozeß in Bachs Cembalokonzerten', *Johann Sebastian*
  *Bachs Spätwerk und dessen Umfeld. 61. Bachfest der Neuen Bachgesellschaft,*
  *Duisburg 1986*, ed. C. Wolff (Kassel, 1988), pp. 32–47

'Textbezug und Werkidee in Johann Sebastian Bachs frühen Orgelchorälen',
  *Musikkulturgeschichte. Festschrift für Constantin Floros zum 60. Geburtstag,*
  ed. P. Petersen (Wiesbaden, 1990), pp. 167–82

'Das Ostinato-Prinzip in Johann Sebastian Bachs langsamen Konzertsätzen',
  *Von Isaac zu Bach. Studien zur älteren deutschen Musikgeschichte (Festschrift*
  *Martin Just zum 60. Geburtstag)*, ed. F. Heidlberger, W. Osthoff and
  R. Wiesend (Kassel, 1991), pp. 287–300

'Formprobleme in Bachs frühen Orgelfugen', *BJb* 78 (1992), pp. 7–21; English
  trans., 'Form problems in Bach's early organ fugues', *A Bach tribute: essays in*
  *honor of William H. Scheide*, ed. P. Brainard and R. Robinson (Kassel and
  Chapel Hill, N.C., 1993), pp. 45–56

'Zur Gestalt von Johann Sebastian Bachs Konzert für Oboe d'amore', *Tibia* 18
  (1993), pp. 431–48

'Versuch einer Theorie der Bachschen Orgelfuge', *Mf* 48 (1995), pp. 14–52

Buelow, G. J., 'In defence of J. A. Scheibe against J. S. Bach', *PRMA* 101 (1974–5),
  pp. 85–100

Butler, G. G., 'Neues zur Datierung der Goldberg-Variationen', *BJb* 74 (1988),
  pp. 219–23

'Johann Sebastian Bachs Gloria in excelsis Deo BWV 191. Musik für ein
  Leipziger Dankfest', *BJb* 78 (1992), pp. 65–71

Butt, J., *Bach interpretation: articulation marks in primary sources of J. S. Bach*
  (Cambridge, 1990)

*Bach: Mass in B Minor* (Cambridge, 1991)

'Bach's *Mass in B Minor*: considerations of its early performance and use', *JM*
  (1991), pp. 109–23

*Music and the art of performance in the German Baroque* (Cambridge, 1994)

'Bach and G. F. Kauffmann: reflections on Bach's later style', *Bach studies* 2, ed.
  D. Melamed (Cambridge, 1995), pp. 47–61

Cammarota, R. M., 'The sources of the Christmas interpolations in J. S. Bach's
  Magnificat in E-flat major (BWV 243a)', *CM* 36 (1983), pp. 79–99

'The repertoire of Magnificats in Leipzig at the time of J. S. Bach: a study of the
  manuscript sources' (Ph.D. dissertation, New York University, 1986)

Chafe, E., 'J. S. Bach's St. Matthew Passion: aspects of planning, structure, and
  chronology', *JAMS* 35 (1982), pp. 49–114

'The St. John Passion: theology and musical structure', *Bach studies*, ed.
  D. O. Franklin (Cambridge, 1989), pp. 75–112

*Tonal allegory in the vocal music of J. S. Bach* (Berkeley, 1991)

Cox, H. H. (ed.), *The Calov Bible of J. S. Bach* (Ann Arbor, 1985)

Crist, S. A., 'Beyond "Bach-centrism": historiographic perspectives on Johann
    Sebastian Bach and seventeenth-century music', *CMS* 33/34 (1993–4),
    pp. 56–69
Dadelsen, G. von, *Beiträge zur Chronologie der Werke Johann Sebastian Bachs*
    (Trossingen, 1958)
  *Über Bach und Anderes* (Tübingen, 1983)
Dahlhaus, C., 'Zur Entstehung der romantischen Bach-Deutung', *BJb* 64 (1978),
    pp. 192–210
  'Bach-Rezeption und ästhetische Autonomie', *Alte Musik als ästhetische
    Gegenwart. Bach. Händel. Schütz. Report of the International Music
    Symposium, Stuttgart 1985*, vol. I (Kassel 1987), pp. 18–26
  'Bach und der Zerfall der musikalischen Figurenlehre', *Jahrbuch des Staatlichen
    Instituts für Musikforschung Preußischer Kulturbesitz 1985–6* (Kassel, 1989),
    pp. 169–74
Dammann, R., *Der Musikbegriff im deutschen Barock* (Cologne, 1967; revised
    1984)
Danuser, H., 'Bach und die zeitgenössische Musik', *Musik im 20. Jahrhundert. 59.
    Bachfest der Neuen Bachgesellschaft* (Leipzig and Kassel, 1984),
    pp. 96–101
Dömling, W., 'Franz Liszt und B-A-C-H', *Alte Musik als ästhetische Gegenwart.
    Bach. Händel. Schütz. Report of the International Music Symposium, Stuttgart
    1985*, vol. I (Kassel 1987), pp. 159–61
  'Franz Liszts Hommage an Bach', *Johann Sebastian Bach. Spätwerk und Umfeld.
    61. Bachfest der Neuen Bachgesellschaft* (Duisburg, 1986), pp. 224–36
Donington, R., *The interpretation of early music* (London, 1963; rev. edn, London,
    1974)
Dreyfus, L. D., *Bach's continuo group* (Cambridge, Mass., 1987)
  'Music analysis and the historical imperative', *Revista de Musicologia: Actas del
    XV Congreso de la SIM*, vol. XVI, no. 1 (1993), pp. 407–19
  *Bach and the patterns of invention* (Cambridge, Mass., 1996)
Dürr, A., 'Bachs Trauer-Ode und Markus-Passion', *NZM* 124 (1963), pp. 459–66
  *Zur Chronologie der Leipziger Vokalwerke J. S. Bachs*, 2nd edn (Kassel, 1976)
  *Studien über die frühen Kantaten Johann Sebastian Bachs* (Leipzig, 1951; rev.
    edn, Wiesbaden, 1977)
  *Johann Sebastian Bach. Seine Handschrift. Abbild seines Schaffens* (Wiesbaden,
    1984)
  *Die Kantaten von Johann Sebastian Bach*, 5th edn (Kassel, 1985)
  'Kein Meister fällt vom Himmel. Zu Johann Sebastian Bachs Orgelchorälen der
    Neumeister-Sammlung', *Musica* 40 (1986), pp. 309–12
  *Die Johannes-Passion von Johann Sebastian Bach. Entstehung, Überlieferung,
    Werkeinführung* (Munich and Kassel, 1988)
  *Im Mittelpunkt Bach. Ausgewählte Aufsätze und Vorträge* (Kassel, 1988)
  'Schriftcharakter und Werkchronologie bei Johann Sebastian Bach', *Bericht über
    die Wissenschaftliche Konferenz zum V. Internationalen Bachfest der DDR in
    Verbindung mit dem 60. Bachfest der Neuen Bachgesellschaft* (1985), ed.
    W. Hoffmann and A. Scheiderheinze (Leipzig, 1988), pp. 283–9

Eggebrecht, H. H., 'Über Bachs geschichtlichen Ort', *Johann Sebastian Bach*, Wege
    der Forschung, vol. CLXX, ed. W. Blankenburg (Darmstadt, 1970),
    pp. 247–89
    'Bach – wer ist das', *AfMw* 42 (1985), pp. 215–28
Eppstein, H., 'Zur Problematik von J. S. Bachs Sonate für Violine und Cembalo
    G-dur (BWV 1019)', *AfMw* 21 (1964), pp. 217–42
    *Studien über J.S. Bachs Sonaten für ein Melodieinstrument und obligates
    Cembalo*, Studia musicologica Upsaliensia (new series), vol. II (Uppsala,
    1966)
Finscher, L., 'Bach and the Viennese Classics', *Miscellanea Musicologica*, Adelaide
    Studies in Musicology, vol. X (1979), pp. 47–58
    'Bach in the eighteenth century', *Bach studies*, ed. D. O. Franklin (Cambridge,
    1989), pp. 281–96
Fock, G., *Der junge Bach in Lüneburg. 1700 bis 1702* (Hamburg, 1950)
Forchert, A., 'Johann Sebastian Bachs Verhältnis zur Tradition', *51. Bachfest der
    Neuen Bachgesellschaft in Berlin (West) vom 25. bis 30. August 1976* (Berlin,
    1976), pp. 5–16
Forkel, J. N., *Über Johann Sebastian Bachs Leben, Kunst und Kunstwerke* (Leipzig,
    1802; reprinted Berlin, 1982; English trans., London, 1820)
Franklin, D. O. (ed.), *Bach studies* (Cambridge, 1989)
    'The Carnegie Manuscript and J. S. Bach', *BACH* 22/1 (1991), pp. 5–15
Fröde, C., 'Zu einer Kritik des Thomanerchores von 1749', *BJb* 70 (1984),
    pp. 53–8
Fuller, D., 'Dotting, the "French style" and Frederick Neumann's
    counter-reformation', *EM* 5 (1977), pp. 517–43
Geck, M., *Die Wiederentdeckung der Matthäus-Passion im 19. Jahrhundert. Die
    zeitgenössischen Dokumente und ihre ideengeschichtliche Deutung*
    (Regensburg, 1967)
Glöckner, A., 'Bach and the Passion music of his contemporaries', *MT* 116 (1975),
    pp. 613–16
    'Johann Sebastian Bachs Aufführungen zeitgenössischer Passionsmusiken', *BJb*
    63 (1977), pp. 75–119
    'Zur Echtheit und Datierung der Kantate BWV 150 "Nach dir, Herr, verlanget
    mich"', *BJb* 74 (1988), pp. 195–203
Godt, I., 'Politics, patriotism, and a Polonaise: a possible revision in Bach's *Suite in
    B Minor*', *MQ* 74 (1990), pp. 610–22
Gojowy, D., 'Zur Frage der Köthener Trauermusik und der Matthäuspassion', *BJb*
    51 (1965), pp. 86–134
Häfner, K., *Aspekte des Parodieverfahrens bei Johann Sebastian Bachs. Beiträge zur
    Wiederentdeckung verschollener Vokalwerke* (Laaber, 1987)
Hartmann, G., 'Authentischer Bach-Elbel. Marginalie zu einem der angeblichen
    Bach-Choräle der Neumeister-Sammlung', *NZM* 147 (1986), no. 4, pp. 4–6
Heller, K., 'Norddeutsche Musikkultur als Traditionsraum des jungen Bach', *BJb* 75
    (1989), pp. 7–19
    'Die freien Allegrosätze in der frühen Tastenmusik Johann Sebastian Bachs',
    *BzBF* 9/10 (1991), pp. 173–85

Herz, G., 'BWV 131: Bach's first cantata', *Studies in eighteenth-century music: a tribute to Karl Geiringer on his seventieth birthday*, ed. H. C. Robbins Landon and R. E. Chapman (London and New York, 1970), pp. 272–91; reprinted in *Essays on J. S. Bach*, pp. 127–45

*Essays on J. S. Bach* (Ann Arbor, 1985)

Hill, R. S., '*Echtheit angezweifelt*: style and authenticity in two suites attributed to Bach', *EM* 13 (1985), pp. 248–55

'"Der Himmel weiss, wo diese Sachen hingekommen sind": reconstructing the lost keyboard notebooks of the young Bach and Handel', *Bach, Handel, Scarlatti: tercentenary essays*, ed. P. Williams (Cambridge, 1985), pp. 161–72

'The Möller manuscript and the Andreas Bach Book: two keyboard anthologies from the circle of the young Johann Sebastian Bach', 2 vols. (Ph.D. dissertation, Harvard University, 1987)

'Stilanalyse und Überlieferungsproblematik. Das Variationssuiten-Repertoire J. A. Reinckens', *Dietrich Buxtehude und die europäische Musik seiner Zeit. Bericht über das Lübecker Symposion 1987*, ed. A. Edler and F. Krummacher (Kassel, 1990), pp. 204–14

'Tablature versus staff notation: or, why did the young J. S. Bach compose in tablature?', *Church, stage, and studio: music and its contexts in seventeenth-century Germany*, ed. P. Walker (Ann Arbor, 1990), pp. 349–59

Hofmann, K., 'Neue Überlegungen zu Bachs Weimarer Kantaten-Kalender', *BJb* 79 (1993), pp. 9–29

Humphreys, D., 'A Bach polyglot: the A major prelude & fugue BWV 536', *OY* 20 (1989), pp. 72–87

Irwin, J. L., *Neither voice nor heart alone: German Lutheran theology of music in the age of the Baroque* (New York, 1993)

Kilian, D., 'Zu einem Bachschen Tabulaturautograph', *Bachiana et alia musicologica. Festschrift Alfred Dürr zum 65. Geburtstag*, ed. W. Rehm (Kassel, 1983), pp. 161–7

Kobayashi, Y., 'Die Universalität in Bachs h-moll-Messe. Ein Beitrag zum Bach-Bild der letzten Lebensjahre', *MuK* 57 (1987), pp. 9–24; English trans. by J. W. Baxter, 'Universality in Bach's B Minor Mass: a portrait of Bach in his final years', *BACH* 24/2 (1993), pp. 3–25

'Zur Chronologie der Spätwerke Johann Sebastian Bachs. Kompositions- und Aufführungstätigkeit von 1736 bis 1750', *BJb* 74 (1988), pp. 7–72; summary and partial trans. by G. Herz, in *BACH* 21/1 (1990), pp. 3–25

*Die Notenschrift Johann Sebastian Bachs. Dokumentation ihrer Entwicklung* (Kassel, 1989) (*NBA*, IX/2)

Koch, E., 'Tröstendes Echo. Zur theologischen Deutung der Echo-Arie im IV. Teil des Weihnachts-Oratoriums von Johann Sebastian Bach', *BJb* 75 (1989), pp. 203–11

Kraft, G., 'Neue Beiträge zur Bach-Genealogie', *Beiträge zur Musikwissenschaft* 1 (1959), pp. 29–61

Kreutzer, H. J., 'Johann Sebastian Bach und das literarische Leipzig der Aufklärung,' *BJb* 77 (1991), pp. 7–31

Krumbach, W., 'Sechzig unbekannte Orgelwerke von Johann Sebastian Bach? Ein vorläufiger Fundbericht', *NZM* 146 (1985), no. 3, pp. 4–12, and no. 5, pp. 6–18

Krummacher, F., 'Bach und die norddeutsche Orgeltoccata. Fragen und Überlegungen', *BJb* 71 (1985), pp. 119–34

'Dietrich Buxtehude. Musik zwischen Geschichte und Gegenwart', *Dietrich Buxtehude und die europäische Musik seiner Zeit. Bericht über das Lübecker Symposion 1987*, ed. A. Edler and F. Krummacher (Kassel, 1990), pp. 9–30

'Bachs frühe Kantaten im Kontext der Tradition', *Mf* 44 (1991), pp. 9–32

Ladewig, J., 'Bach and the *prima prattica*: the influence of Frescobaldi on a fugue from the *Well-tempered Clavier*', *JM* 9 (1991), 358–75

Leaver, R. A., 'Bach's "Clavierübung III": some historical and theological considerations', *OY* 6 (1975), pp. 17–32

*Bachs theologische Bibliothek; eine kritische Bibliographie/Bach's theological library; a critical bibliography* (Neuhausen-Stuttgart, 1983)

*J. S. Bach as preacher: his Passions and music in worship* (St Louis, 1984)

'Bach and hymnody: the evidence of the Orgelbüchlein', *EM* 13 (1985), pp. 227–36

*J. S. Bach and Scripture: glosses from the Calov Bible Commentary* (St Louis, 1985)

'The Lutheran Reformation', *The Renaissance: from the 1470s to the end of the 16th century*, ed. I. Fenlon (Englewood Cliffs, N.J., 1989), pp. 263–85

'Parody and theological consistency: notes on Bach's A-Major Mass', *BACH* 21/3 (1990), pp. 30–43

'Bach and the German Agnus Dei', *A Bach tribute: essays in honor of William H. Scheide*, ed. P. Brainard and R. Robinson (Kassel, 1993), pp. 163–171

'Theological consistency, liturgical integrity, and musical hermeneutic in Luther's liturgical reforms', *The Lutheran Quarterly* 9 (1994), pp. 117–38

Linton, M., 'Bach, Luther, and the Magnificat', *BACH* 17/2 (1986), pp. 2–15

Mann, A., '"Missa Brevis" and "Historia": Bach's A Major Mass', *BACH* 16/1 (1985), pp. 6–11

Marissen, M., 'On linking Bach's F-Major Sinfonia and his Hunt Cantata, BWV 208', *BACH* 23/2 (1992), pp. 31–46

'J. S. Bach's Brandenburg Concertos as a meaningful set', *MQ* 77 (1993), pp. 193–235

*The social and religious designs of J. S. Bach's Brandenburg Concertos* (Princeton, 1995)

Marshall, R. L., *The compositional process of J. S. Bach*, 2 vols. (Princeton, 1972)

'Bach the progressive. Observations on his later works', *MQ* 62 (1976), pp. 313–57; reprinted in *The music of Johann Sebastian Bach: the sources, the style, the significance* (New York, 1989), pp. 23–58

'Beobachtungen am Autograph der h-moll-Messe. Zum Kompositionsprozess', *MuK* 50 (1980), pp. 230–9; English trans.,'The Mass in B Minor: the autograph scores and the compositional process', *The music of Johann Sebastian Bach*, pp. 175–89

'Organ or "Klavier"? Instrumental prescriptions in the sources of the
keyboard works', *J. S. Bach as organist: his instruments, music,
and performance practices*, ed. G. Stauffer and E. May (Bloomington,
1986), pp. 193–211; also in *The music of Johann Sebastian Bach*,
pp. 271–93

'On the origin of Bach's Magnificat: a Lutheran composer's challenge', *Bach
studies*, ed. D. Franklin (Cambridge, 1989), pp. 3–17; also in R. L. Marshall,
*The Music of Johann Sebastian Bach*, pp. 161–73

*The music of Johann Sebastian Bach: the sources, the style, the significance* (New
York, 1989)

'Johann Sebastian Bach', *Eighteenth-century keyboard music*, ed. R. L. Marshall
(New York, 1994), pp. 68–123

Mathiesen, T. J., and Rivera, B. V. (eds.), *Festa musicologica: essays in honor of
George J. Buelow* (New York, 1995)

May, E., 'The types, uses, and historical position of Bach's organ chorales', *J. S. Bach
as organist: his instruments, music, and performance practices*, ed. G. Stauffer
and E. May (Bloomington, 1986), pp. 81–101

Melamed, D. R., *J. S. Bach and the German motet* (Cambridge, 1995)

Melamed, D. R. (ed.), *Bach studies* 2 (Cambridge, 1995)

Mendel, A., 'Traces of the pre-history of Bach's St John and St Matthew Passions',
*Festschrift Otto Erich Deutsch zum 80. Geburtstag*, ed. W. Gerstenberg et al.
(Kassel, 1963), pp. 31–48

Neumann, W., 'Über Ausmaß und Wesen des Bachschen Parodieverfahrens', *BJb* 51
(1965), pp. 63–85

*Sämtliche von Johann Sebastian Bach vertonte Texte* (Leipzig, 1974)

*Handbuch der Kantaten Joh. Seb. Bachs*, 5th edn (Wiesbaden, 1984)

Oefner, C., 'Eisenach zur Zeit des jungen Bach', *BJb* 71 (1985), pp. 43–54

Palisca, C. V., 'The genesis of Mattheson's style classification', *New Mattheson
Studies*, ed. G. Buelow (Cambridge, 1983), pp. 409–23

*Baroque music*, 3rd edn (Englewood Cliffs, N.J., 1991)

Pelikan, J., *Bach among the theologians* (Philadelphia, 1986)

Petzoldt, M., 'Die theologische Bedeutung der Choräle in Bachs Matthäus-Passion',
*MuK* 53 (1983), pp. 53–63

'"Ut probus & doctus reddar". Zum Anteil der Theologie bei der
Schulausbildung Johann Sebastian Bachs in Eisenach, Ohrdruf und
Lüneburg', *BJb* 71 (1985), pp. 7–42

Petzoldt, M., and Petri, J., *Johann Sebastian Bach Ehre sei dir Gott gesungen. Bilder
und Texte zu Bachs Leben als Christ und seinem Wirken für die Kirche*
(Göttingen, 1988)

Poulin, P. L., trans. and commentary, with a preface by C. Wolff, *J. S. Bach –
Precepts and principles for playing the thorough-bass or accompanying in four
parts* (Oxford, 1994)

Riethmüller, A., *Ferruccio Busonis Poetik*, Neue Studien zur Musikwissenschaft,
vol. IV (Mainz 1988)

Rifkin, J., 'The Chronology of Bach's Saint Matthew Passion', *MQ* 61 (1975),
pp. 360–87

'Bachs Chor – Ein vorläufiger Bericht', *Basler Jahrbuch für historische Musikpraxis* 9 (1985), pp. 141–155

'..."wobey aber die Singstimmen hinlänglich besetzt seyn müssen . . ." Zum Credo der h-Moll-Messe in der Aufführung Carl Philipp Emanuel Bachs', *Basler Jahrbuch für historische Musikpraxis* 9 (1985), pp. 157–72

'More (and less) on Bach's orchestra', *Performance Practice Review* 4 (1991), pp. 5–13

Rilling, H., *Johann Sebastian Bach's B-minor Mass* (Princeton, 1984), a translation of the German edition (1979); revised and expanded German edition (Stuttgart, 1986)

Robertson, A., *The church cantatas of J. S. Bach* (London and New York, 1972)

Sackmann, D., 'Der "Yaler" Bach. Beobachtungen zur Handschrift US-NH (Yale) LM 4708 und deren Umfeld', *BzBF* 9/10 (1991), pp. 165–72

Scheide, W. H., 'Johann Sebastian Bachs Sammlung von Kantaten seines Vetters Johann Ludwig Bach', *BJb* 46 (1959), pp. 52–94

'Bach vs. Bach – Mühlhausen dismissal request vs. Erdmann letter', *Bachiana et alia musicologica – Festschrift Alfred Dürr zum 65. Geburtstag*, ed. W. Rehm (Kassel, 1983), pp. 234–42

Schering, A., *Johann Sebastian Bachs Leipziger Kirchenmusik. Studien und Wege zu ihrer Erkenntnis* (Leipzig, 1936)

*Johann Sebastian Bach und das Musikleben in Leipzig im 18. Jahrhundert* (Leipzig, 1941)

Schiffner, M., 'Johann Sebastian Bach in Arnstadt', *BzBF* 4 (1985), pp. 5–22

Schrade, L., 'Bach: the conflict between the sacred and the secular', *Journal of the History of Ideas* 7 (1946), pp. 151–94

Schulenberg, D., 'Composition as variation: inquires into the compositional procedures of the Bach circle of composers', *CM* 33 (1982), pp. 57–87

*The keyboard music of J. S. Bach* (New York, 1992)

Schulze, H.-J., 'Johann Sebastian Bachs Konzerte – Fragen der Überlieferung und Chronologie', *Beiträge zum Konzertschaffen Johann Sebastian Bachs, Bach-Studien* 6, ed. P. Ahnsehl, K. Heller and H.-J. Schulze (Leipzig, 1981), pp. 9–26.

*Studien zur Bach-Überlieferung im 18. Jahrhundert* (Leipzig and Dresden, 1984)

'Johann Christoph Bach (1671–1721), "Organist und Schul Collega in Ohrdruf", Johann Sebastian Bachs erster Lehrer', *BJb* 71 (1985), pp. 55–81

'Johann Sebastian Bach und die Tradition', *Bach-Händel-Schütz-Ehrung der DDR 1985. V. Internationales Bachfest in Verbindung mit dem 60. Bachfest der Neuen Bachgesellschaft, Leipzig, 19. bis 27. März 1985*, ed. W. Felix et al. (Leipzig, 1985), pp. 33–7

'The French influence in Bach's instrumental music', *EM* 13 (1985), pp. 180–4

'"Die Bachen stammen aus Ungarn her". Ein unbekannter Brief Johann Nikolaus Bachs aus dem Jahre 1728', *BJb* 75 (1989), pp. 213–20

'Johann Sebastian Bach's orchestra: some unanswered questions', *EM* 17 (1989), pp. 3–15

'The parody process in Bach's music: an old problem reconsidered', *BACH* 20 (1989), pp. 7–21

'Bach und Buxtehude. Eine wenig beachtete Quelle in der Carnegie Library zu
   Pittsburgh/PA', *BJb* 77 (1991), pp. 177–81
Schulze, H.-J. (ed.), *Die Thomasschule Leipzig zur Zeit Johann Sebastian Bachs.*
   *Ordnungen und Gesetze 1634, 1723, 1733* (Leipzig, 1987)
Schweitzer, A., *Jean-Sébastian Bach, le musicien-poète* (Leipzig, 1905); German
   trans., *Joh. Seb. Bach* (Leipzig, 1908); trans. Ernest Newman, as *J. S. Bach*, 2
   vols. (Leipzig, 1911; reprinted 1966)
Siegele, U., *Kompositionsweise und Bearbeitungstechnik in der Instrumentalmusik*
   *Johann Sebastian Bachs* (dissertation, University of Tübingen, 1957);
   published as Tübinger Beiträge zur Musikwissenschaft, vol. III (Stuttgart,
   1975).
'Bachs Endzweck einer regulierten und Entwurf einer wohlbestallten
   Kirchenmusik', *Festschrift Georg von Dadelsen zum 60. Geburtstag*, ed.
   T. Kohlhase und V. Scherliess (Neuhausen-Stuttgart, 1978), pp. 313–51
   (reprinted in *The Garland Library of the history of western music*, 6:
   *Baroque music II: eighteenth century* (New York and London 1985),
   pp. 195–233)
'Bachs Stellung in der Leipziger Kulturpolitik seiner Zeit', *BJb* 69 (1983),
   pp. 7–50; 70 (1984), pp. 7–43; 72 (1986), pp. 33–67
'Johann Sebastian Bach – "Deutschlands größter Kirchenkomponist".
   Zur Entstehung und Kritik einer Identifikationsfigur', *Gattungen der*
   *Musik und ihre Klassiker*, Publikationen der Hochschule für Musik
   und Theater Hannover, vol. I, ed. H. Danuser (Laaber, 1988), pp. 59–85
'"Ich habe fleißig sein müssen . . ." Zur Vermittlung von Bachs sozialem und
   musikalischem Charakter', *MuK* 61 (1991), pp. 73–78, also in *BzBF* 9/10
   (1991), pp. 13–19 (trans. G. Herz as '"I had to be industrious . . .": thoughts
   about the relationship between Bach's social and musical character', *BACH*
   22/2 (1991), pp. 5–12).
Smend, F., 'Die Johannes-Passion von Bach. Auf ihren Bau untersucht', *BJb* 23
   (1926), pp. 105–28; reprinted in F. Smend, *Bach-Studien. Gesammelte Reden*
   *und Aufsätze*, ed. C. Wolff (Kassel, 1969), pp. 11–23
'Bachs Matthäus-Passion. Untersuchungen zur Geschichte des Werkes bis 1750',
   *BJb* 25 (1928), pp. 1–95; reprinted in Smend, *Bach-Studien*, pp. 24–83
'Bachs Markus-Passion', *BJb* 37 (1940–8), pp. 1–35, reprinted in Smend, *Bach-*
   *Studien*, pp. 110–36
*Bach in Köthen* (Berlin, 1951); trans. J. Page, ed. S. Daw (St Louis, 1985)
Spitta, P., *Johann Sebastian Bach: his work and influence on the music of Germany,*
   *1685–1750*, trans. C. Bell and J. A. Fuller-Maitland, 3 vols. (London, 1889;
   reprinted New York, 1951)
Stauffer, G. B., *The organ preludes of Johann Sebastian Bach* (Ann Arbor, 1980)
'Bach's Pastorale in F: a closer look at a maligned work', *OY* 14 (1983),
   pp. 44–60
'Fugue types in Bach's free organ works', *J. S. Bach as organist*, ed. Stauffer and
   May, pp. 133–56
'Boyvin, Grigny, D'Anglebert, and Bach's assimilation of French classical organ
   music', *EM* 21 (1993), pp. 83–96

'J. S. Bach's harpsichords', *Festa musicologica: essays in honor of George J. Buelow*, ed. T. J. Mathiesen and B. V. Rivera (Stuyvesant, New York, 1995), pp. 289–318

Stauffer, G. B., and E. May (eds.), *J. S. Bach as organist: his instruments, music, and performance practices* (Bloomington, 1986)

Steiger, R., 'Die Einheit des Weihnachtsoratorium von J. S. Bach', *MuK* 51 (1981), pp. 273–80 and 52 (1982), pp. 9–15

'"Fallt mit Danken, fallt mit Loben Vor des Höchsten Gnaden-Thron". Zum IV. Teil des Weihnachts-Oratoriums von Johann Sebastian Bach', *Ars et musica in liturgia: celebratory volume presented to Casper Honders on the occasion of his seventieth birthday*, ed. F. Brouwer and R. A. Leaver (Utrecht, 1993), pp. 198–211

Steiger, R., and L. Steiger, *Sehet! Wir gehn hinauf gen Jerusalem. Johann Sebastian Bachs Kantaten auf den Sonntag Estomihi* (Göttingen, 1992)

Stiller, G., *Johann Sebastian Bach and liturgical life in Leipzig* (Kassel, 1970); trans. H. J. A. Bouman, D. F. Poellot and H. C. Oswald, ed. R. A. Leaver (St Louis, 1984)

Stinson, R., 'Bach's earliest autograph', *MQ* 71 (1985), pp. 235–63

*The Bach manuscripts of Johann Peter Kellner and his circle: a case study in reception history* (Durham, N.C. and London, 1990)

'"Ein Sammelband aus Johann Peter Kellners Besitz": Neue Forschungen zur Berliner Bach-Handschrift *P 804*', *BJb* 78 (1992), pp. 45–64

'Some thoughts on Bach's Neumeister chorales', *JM* 11 (1993), pp. 455–77

'The compositional history of Bach's *Orgelbüchlein* reconsidered', *Bach perspectives* 1, ed. R. Stinson (Lincoln, Nebr. and London, 1995), pp. 43–78

*J. S. Bach: the Orgelbüchlein* (New York, forthcoming)

Streck, H., *Die Verskunst in den poetischen Texten zu den Kantaten J. S. Bachs* (Hamburg, 1971)

Sumikura, I., 'Johann Sebastian Bach und Johann Kaspar Ferdinand Fischer', *Bericht über die Wissenschaftliche Konferenz zum III. Internationalen Bach-Fest der DDR: Leipzig, 18./19. September 1975*, ed. W. Felix, W. Hoffmann and A. Schneiderheinze (Leipzig, 1977), pp. 233–8

Swack, J. R., 'On the origins of the *Sonate auf Concertenart*', *JAMS* 46 (1993), pp. 369–414

Tatlow, R., *Bach and the riddle of the number alphabet* (Cambridge, 1991)

Terry, C. S., *Bach's orchestra* (London, 1932)

*Joh. Seb. Bach: cantata texts, sacred and secular with a reconstruction of the Leipzig liturgy of his period* (London, 1926; reprinted 1964)

Wagner, G., 'J. A. Scheibe – J. S. Bach: Versuch einer Bewertung', *BJb* 68 (1982), pp. 33–49

Walker, P., 'Die Entstehung der Permutationsfuge', *BJb* 75 (1989), pp. 21–41; English trans., 'The origin of the permutation fugue', *Studies in the history of music*, vol. III, *The creative process* (New York, 1993), pp. 57–91

Walker, P. (ed.), *Church, stage, and studio: music and its contexts in seventeenth-century Germany* (Ann Arbor, 1990)

Whaples, M. K., 'Bach's earliest arias', *BACH* 20/1 (1989), pp. 31–54

Williams, P., *The organ music of J. S. Bach*, 3 vols. (Cambridge, 1980–4)
  'BWV 565: a Toccata in D Minor for organ by J. S. Bach?' *EM* 9 (1981),
    pp. 330–7
Williams, P. (ed.), *Bach, Handel, Scarlatti: tercentenary essays* (Cambridge, 1985)
Wolff, C., *Der stile antico in der Musik Johann Sebastian Bachs. Studien zu Bachs
    Spätwerk* (Wiesbaden, 1968)
  'Zur musikalischen Vorgeschichte des Kyrie aus Johann Sebastian Bachs Messe
    in h-Moll', *Festschrift Bruno Stäblein zum 70. Geburtstag*, ed. M. Ruhnke
    (Kassel, 1967), pp. 316–26; English translation by A. Mann, 'Origins of the
    Kyrie of the B Minor Mass', in C. Wolff, *Bach: essays on his life and music*
    (Cambridge, Mass., 1991), pp. 141–51
  '"Die sonderbaren Vollkommenheiten des Herrn Hofcompositeurs".
    Versuch über die Eigenart der Bachschen Musik', *Bachiana et alia
    musicologica – Festschrift Alfred Dürr zum 65. Geburtstag*, ed. W. Rehm
    (Kassel, 1983), pp. 356–62; trans. in C. Wolff, *Bach: essays on his life and
    music*, pp. 391–7
  *The new Grove Bach family* (London and Basingstoke, 1983)
  'Bach's Leipzig chamber music', *EM* 13 (1985), pp. 165–75
  'Bach's organ music: studies and discoveries', *MT* 126 (1985), pp. 149–52
  'Bach und die italienische Musik', *Bachtage Berlin. Vorträge 1970 bis 1981*, ed.
    G. Wagner (Neuhausen-Stuttgart, 1985), pp. 225–33
  'Johann Adam Reinken und Johann Sebastian Bach. Zum Kontext des
    Bachschen Frühwerks', *BJb* 71 (1985), pp. 99–118; English trans., 'Bach and
    Johann Adam Reinken: a context for the early works', in C. Wolff, *Bach:
    essays on his life and music* (Cambridge, Mass., 1991), pp. 56–71
  'Vivaldi's compositional art and the process of "musical thinking"', *Nuovi studi
    vivaldiani*, ed. A. Fanna and G. Morelli (Florence, 1988), pp. 1–17; English
    trans: 'Vivaldi's compositional art, Bach, and the process of "musical
    thinking"', in C. Wolff, *Bach: essays on his life and music* (Cambridge, Mass.,
    1991), pp. 72–83
  *Bach: essays on his life and music* (Cambridge, Mass., 1991)
  'The identity of the "Fratro Dilettissimo" in the Capriccio in B-Flat Major and
    other problems of Bach's early harpsichord works', *The harpsichord and its
    repertoire*, Proceedings of the International Harpsichord Symposium,
    Utrecht 1990, ed. P. Dirksen (Utrecht, 1992), pp. 145–56
Wolff, C. (ed.), *Bach-Bibliographie* (Kassel, 1985)
Zehnder, J. -C., 'Georg Böhm und Johann Sebastian Bach. Zur Chronologie der
    Bachschen Stilentwicklung', *BJb* 74 (1988), pp. 73–110
  'Giuseppe Torelli und Johann Sebastian Bach. Zu Bachs Weimarer
    Konzertform', *BJb* 77 (1991), pp. 33–95
Zenck, M., 'Stadien der Bach-Deutung in der Musikkritik, Musikästhetik und
    Musikgeschichtsschreibung zwischen 1750 und 1800', *BJb* 68 (1982),
    pp. 7–32
  '"Bach, der Progressive". Die Goldberg-Variationen in der Perspektive von
    Beethovens Diabelli-Variationen', *Johann Sebastian Bach. Goldberg-
    Variationen*, Musik-Konzepte vol. XLII (Munich, 1985), pp. 29–92

*Die Bach-Rezeption des späten Beethoven. Zum Verhältnis von
  Musikhistoriographie und Rezeptionsgeschichtsschreibung der 'Klassik',*
  BzAfMw 24 (Stuttgart, 1986)
'1740–1750 und das ästhetische Bewußtsein einer Epochenschwelle? Zum Text
  und Kontext von Bachs Spätwerk', *Johann Sebastian Bachs Spätwerk und
  dessen Umfeld. 61. Bachfest der Neuen Bachgesellschaft, Duisburg 1986*, ed. C.
  Wolff (Kassel, 1988), pp. 109–16
'Bach in der Musikgeschichtsschreibung und in der Musik des 18.
  Jahrhunderts', *Jahrbuch des Staatlichen Instituts für Musikforschung
  Preußischer Kulturbesitz*, 1985–6 (Kassel, 1989), pp. 239–56
'Tradition as authority and provocation: Anton Webern's confrontation with
  Johann Sebastian Bach', *Bach studies*, ed. D. O. Franklin (Cambridge, 1989),
  pp. 297–322

# General index

# Index of works by J. S. Bach